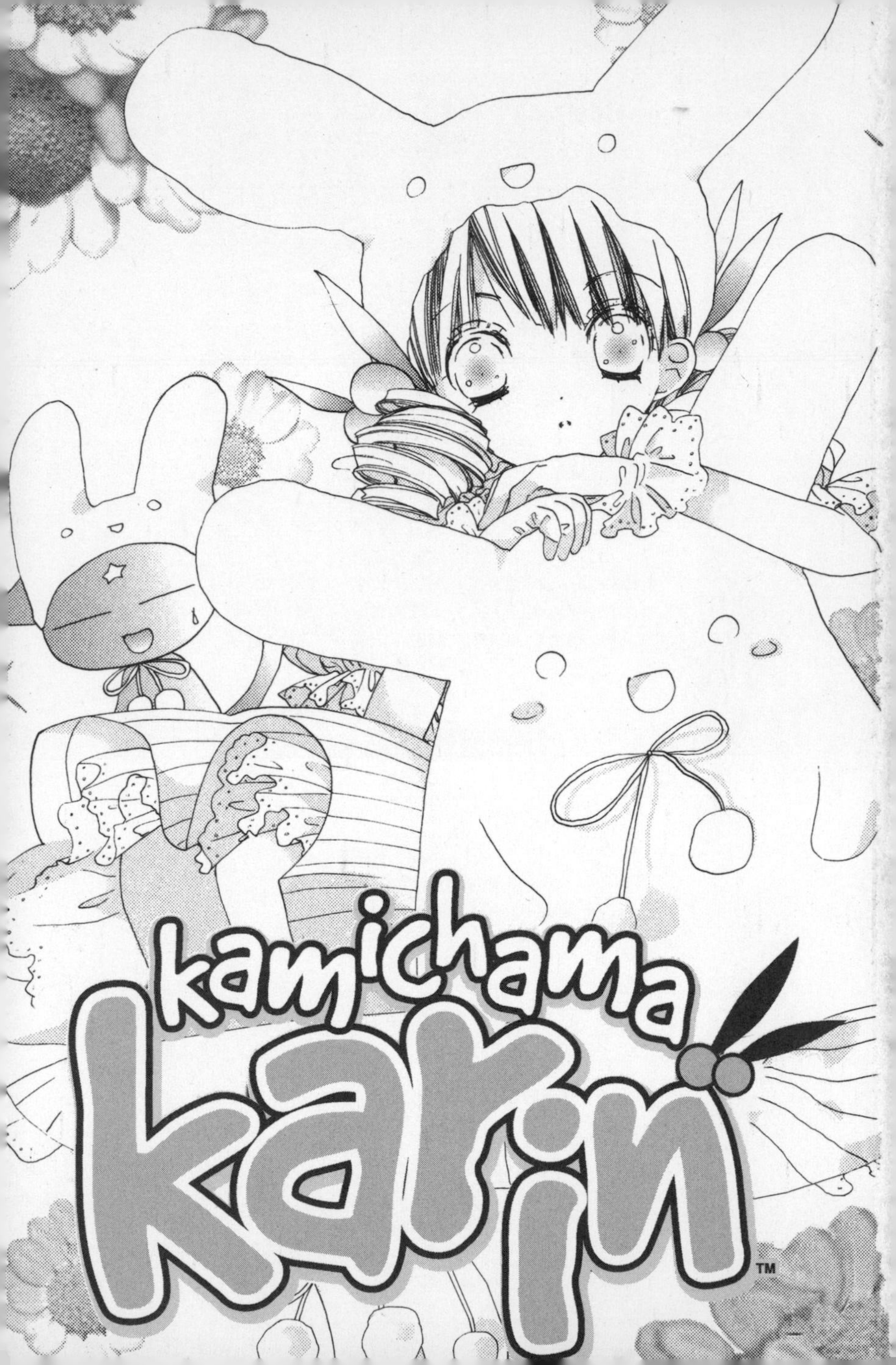
kamichama
karin™

Kamichama Karin Vol. 3
created by Koge-Donbo

Translation - Nan Rymer
English Adaptation - Lianne Sentar
Retouch and Lettering - Erika "Skooter" Terriquez
Production Artist - Jose Macasocol, Jr.
Cover Design - Thea Willis

Editor - Carol Fox
Digital Imaging Manager - Chris Buford
Production Manager - Jennifer Miller
Managing Editor - Lindsey Johnston
VP of Production - Ron Klamert
Publisher and E.I.C. - Mike Kiley
President and C.O.O. - John Parker
C.E.O. and Chief Creative Officer - Stuart Levy

A  Manga

TOKYOPOP Inc.
5900 Wilshire Blvd. Suite 2000
Los Angeles, CA 90036

E-mail: info@TOKYOPOP.com
Come visit us online at www.TOKYOPOP.com

© 2004 Koge-Donbo. All Rights Reserved. All rights reserved. No portion of this book may be
First published in Japan in 2004 by Kodansha Ltd., Tokyo reproduced or transmitted in any form or by any means
English publication rights arranged without written permission from the copyright holders.
through Kodansha Ltd. This manga is a work of fiction. Any resemblance to
actual events or locales or persons, living or dead, is
English text copyright © 2006 TOKYOPOP Inc. entirely coincidental.

ISBN: 1-59532-849-1

First TOKYOPOP printing: March 2006
10 9 8 7 6 5 4 3 2 1
Printed in Canada

kamichama karin™

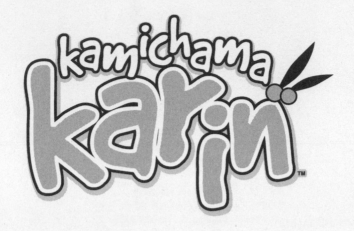

Volume 3

Created by
Koge-Donbo

TOKYOPOP®

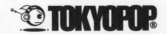

HAMBURG // LONDON // LOS ANGELES // TOKYO

Story So Far

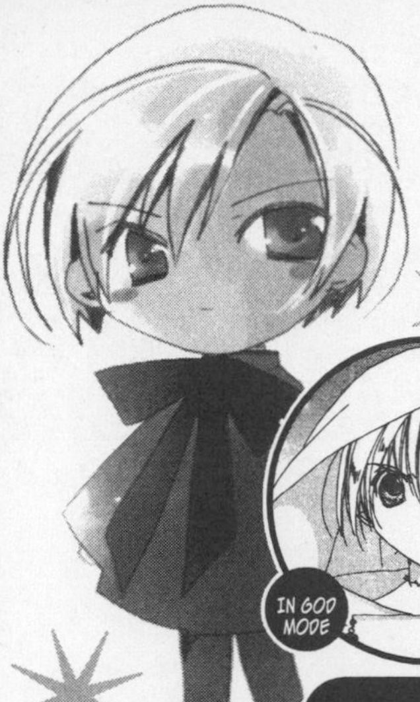

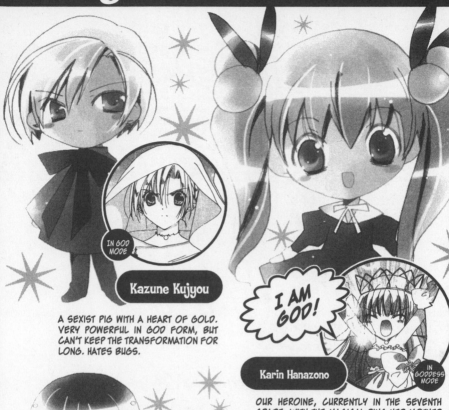

IN GOD MODE

Kazune Kujyou

A SEXIST PIG WITH A HEART OF GOLD. VERY POWERFUL IN GOD FORM, BUT CAN'T KEEP THE TRANSFORMATION FOR LONG. HATES BUGS.

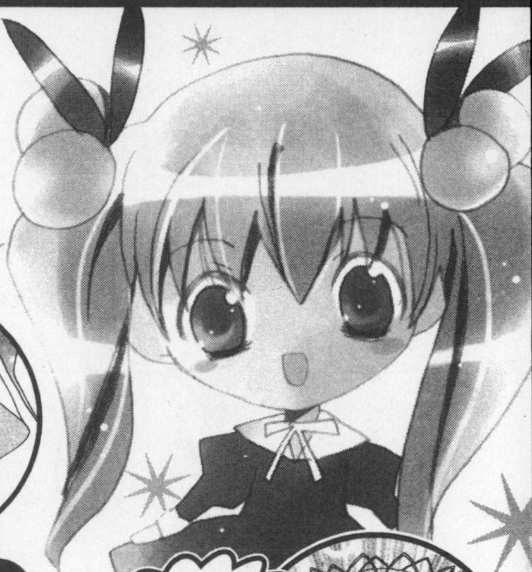

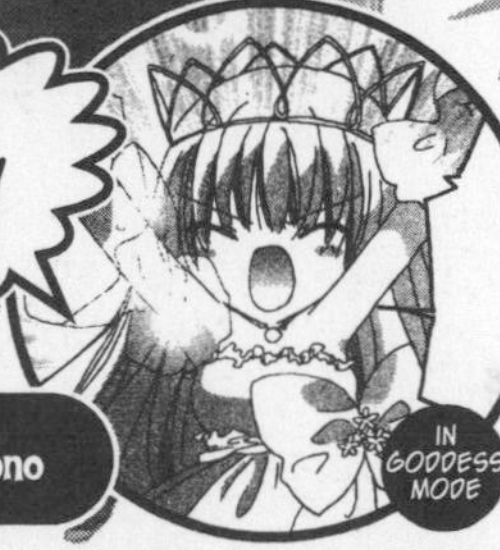

I AM GOD!
IN GODDESS MODE

Karin Hanazono

OUR HEROINE, CURRENTLY IN THE SEVENTH GRADE. WITH THE MAGICAL RING HER MOTHER LEFT HER, SHE CAN CHANGE FROM A BELOW-AVERAGE SCHOOLGIRL INTO A POWERFUL GODDESS!

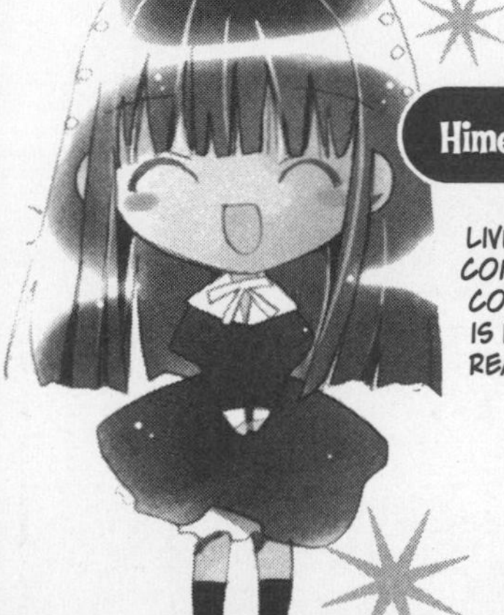

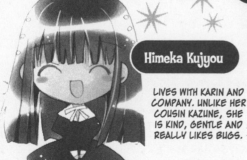

Himeka Kujyou

LIVES WITH KARIN AND COMPANY. UNLIKE HER COUSIN KAZUNE, SHE IS KIND, GENTLE AND REALLY LIKES BUGS.

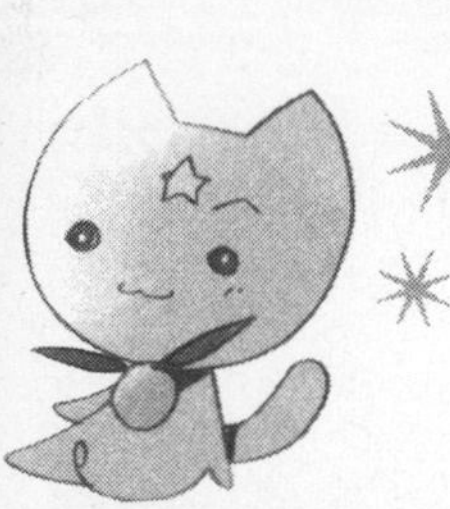

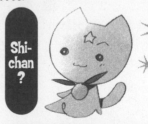

Shi-chan?

A CAT THAT KARIN FOUND AT KAZUNE'S HOUSE...WHO LOOKS JUST LIKE KARIN'S DEAD PET, SHI-CHAN. COULD IT BE THEY'RE ONE AND THE SAME?!

Characters and

Kirio Karasuma

STUDENT COUNCIL PRESIDENT AND VILLAIN EXTRAORDINAIRE. SPENDS ALL HIS FREE TIME TRACKING AND ATTACKING KARIN.

Kirika

KARIN'S CRUSH. ALMOST ALWAYS WITH KIRIO. IS HE MOVING IN ON KARIN WITH THAT HEART-MELTING SMILE?!

IN GOD MODE

Mystery Goddess

ATTACKED KARIN IN THE LAST VOLUME. IS SHE HERE TO TEST KARIN'S POWERS?

Miyon

HIMEKA'S FRIEND FROM ELEMENTARY SCHOOL. THEY'RE STILL VERY CLOSE.

Yuuki Sakurai

MIYON'S FRIEND SINCE ELEMENTARY SCHOOL. HE THINKS KARIN TESTED INTO THEIR VERY DIFFICULT PRIVATE ACADEMY, SO HE GREATLY RESPECTS HER.

The Story Thus Far:

THANKS TO THE RING HER MOTHER LEFT HER, KARIN HANAZONO IS THE PROUD NEW RECIPIENT OF THE POWER OF ATHENA! SHE MOVED IN WITH KAZUNE AND HIMEKA BECAUSE OF HER MYSTERIOUS ABILITY, AND EVEN TRANSFERRED (WITH SOME HELP) TO THEIR PRESTIGIOUS SCHOOL. ONE DAY, KARIN FOUND OUT ABOUT A DUEL BETWEEN KAZUNE AND KIRIO. KARIN RACED TO KAZUNE'S SIDE AND HELPED HIM REPEL KIRIO, BUT KAZUNE STILL FELL UNCONSCIOUS AT THE END OF THE BATTLE. AND NOW, 'TIS THE SEASON OF THE SCHOOL FESTIVAL...WHAT WILL HAPPEN BETWEEN KARIN AND HER CRUSH, KIRIKA-SENPAI?

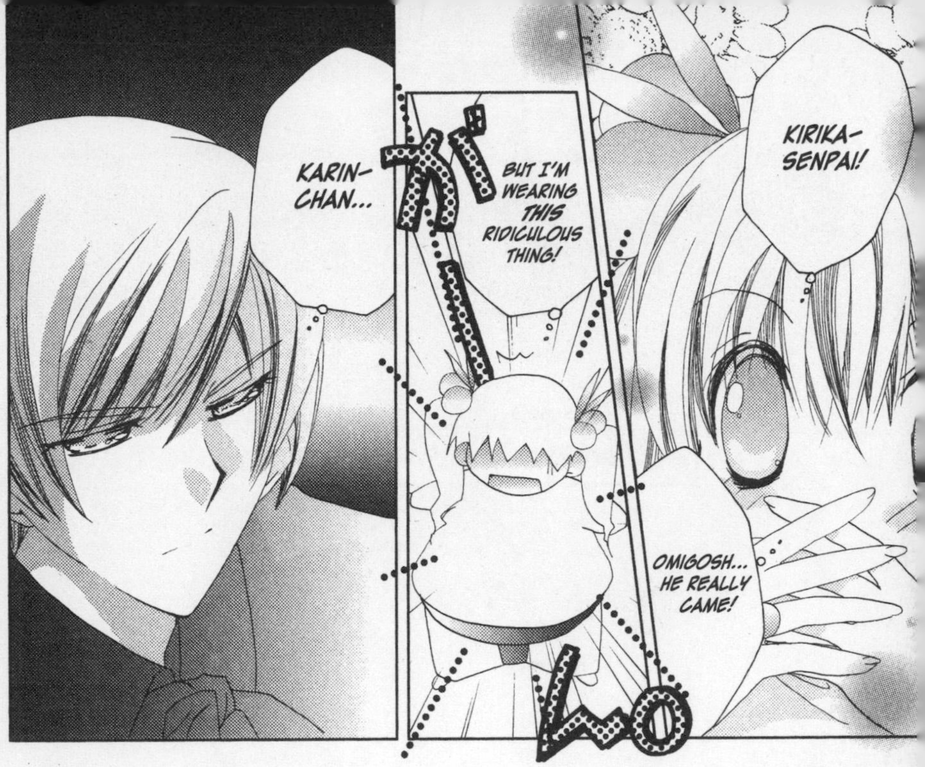
KIRIKA-SENPAI!
OMIGOSH... HE REALLY CAME!
BUT I'M WEARING THIS RIDICULOUS THING!
ガーン
KARIN-CHAN...

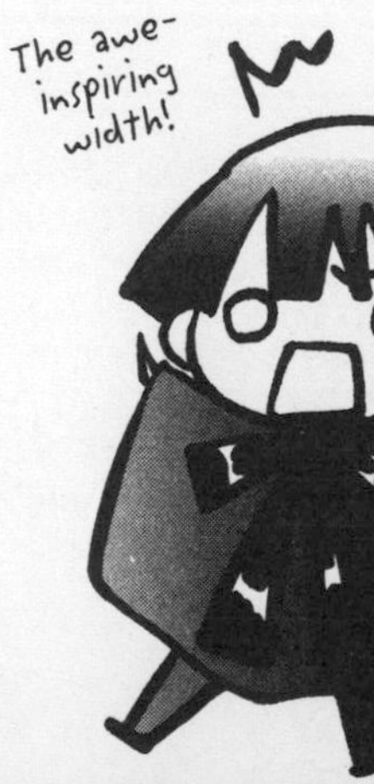
The awe-inspiring width!

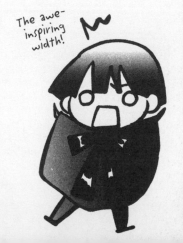

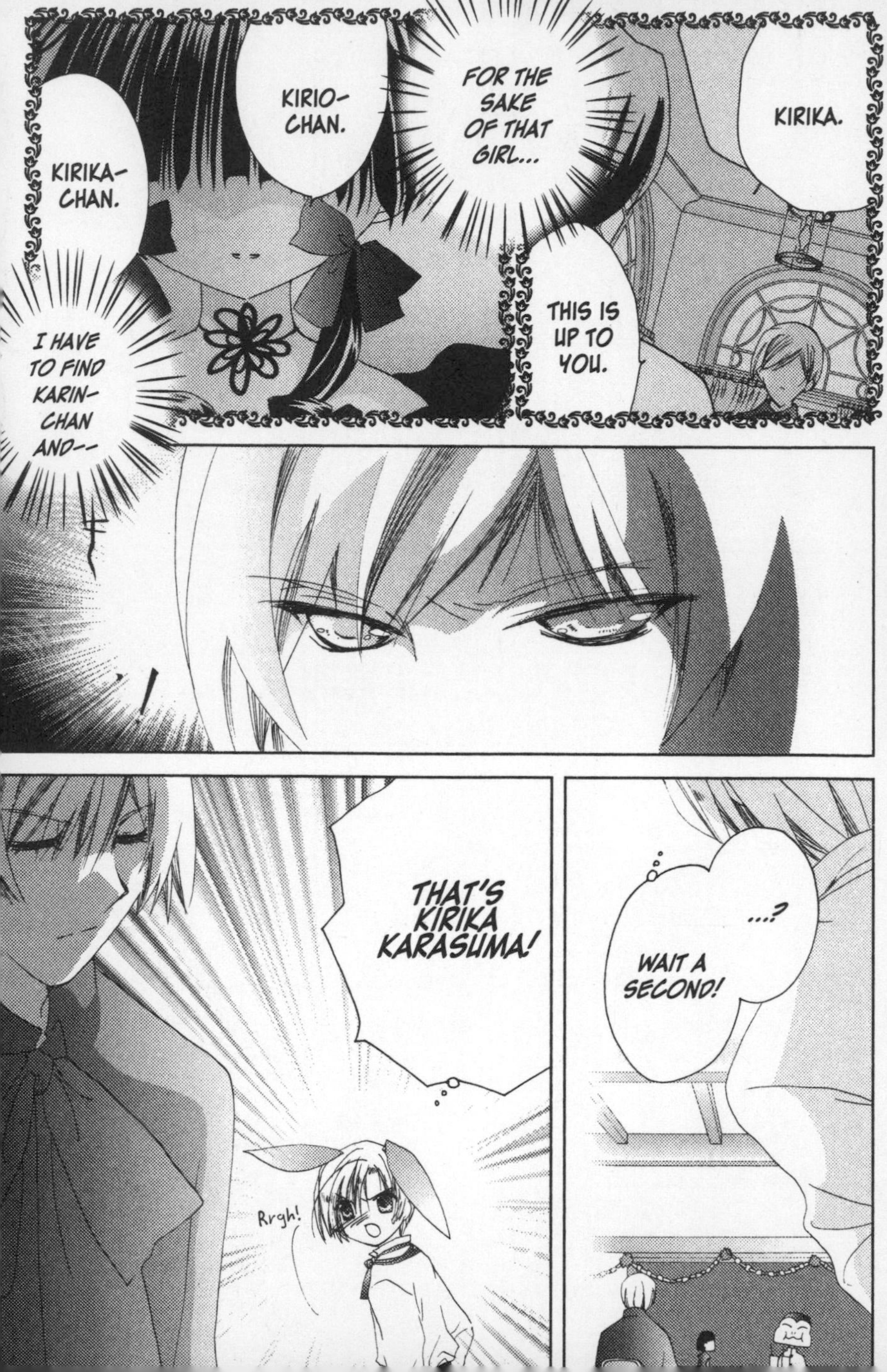
KIRIKA.
THIS IS UP TO YOU.
FOR THE SAKE OF THAT GIRL...
KIRIO-CHAN.
KIRIKA-CHAN.
I HAVE TO FIND KARIN-CHAN AND--
...?
WAIT A SECOND!
THAT'S KIRIKA KARASUMA!
Rrgh!

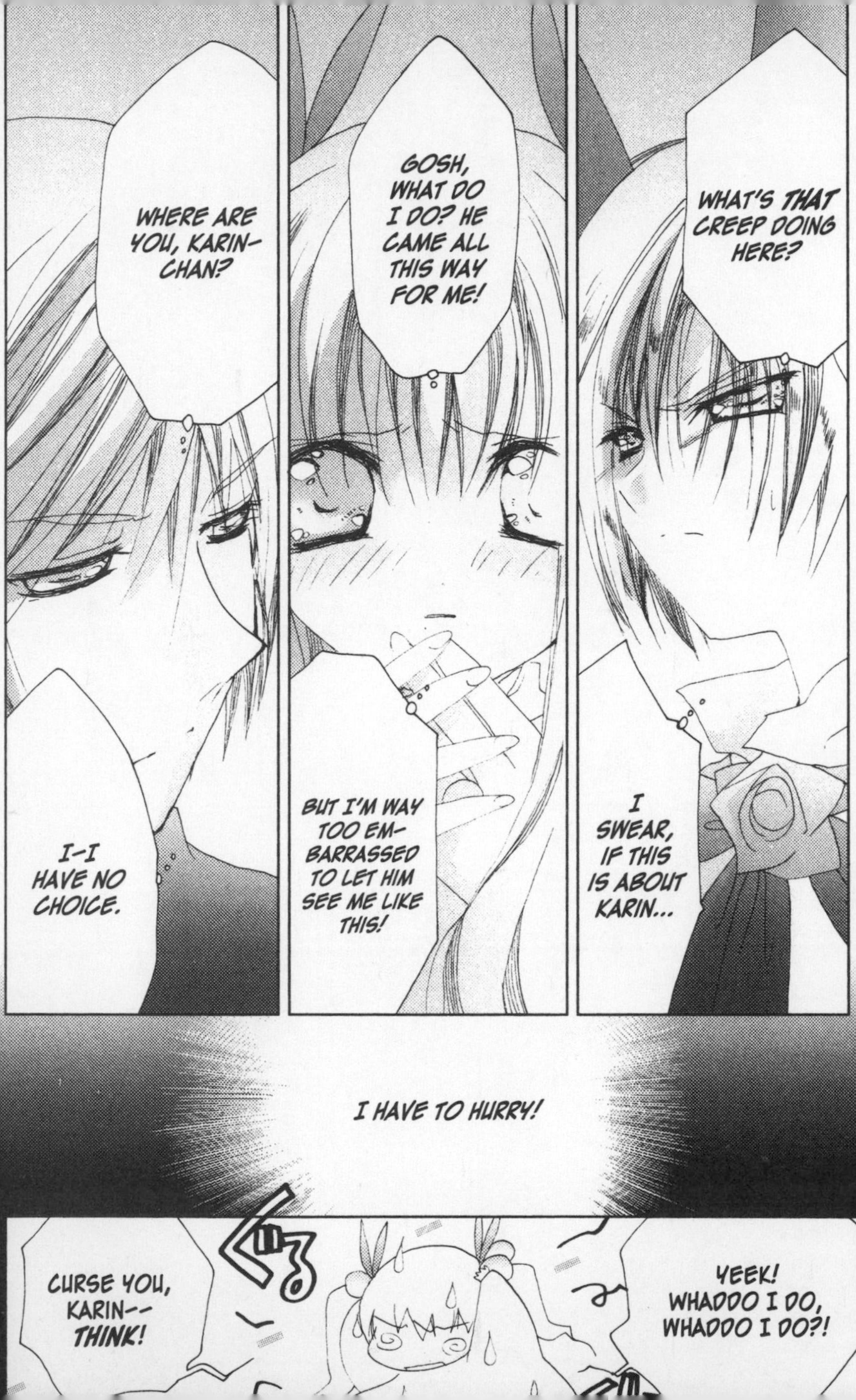
WHAT'S *THAT* CREEP DOING HERE?
I SWEAR, IF THIS IS ABOUT KARIN...
GOSH, WHAT DO I DO? HE CAME ALL THIS WAY FOR ME!
BUT I'M WAY TOO EM-BARRASSED TO LET HIM SEE ME LIKE THIS!
WHERE ARE YOU, KARIN-CHAN?
I-I HAVE NO CHOICE.
I HAVE TO HURRY!
YEEK! WHADDO I DO, WHADDO I DO?!
CURSE YOU, KARIN-- **THINK!**

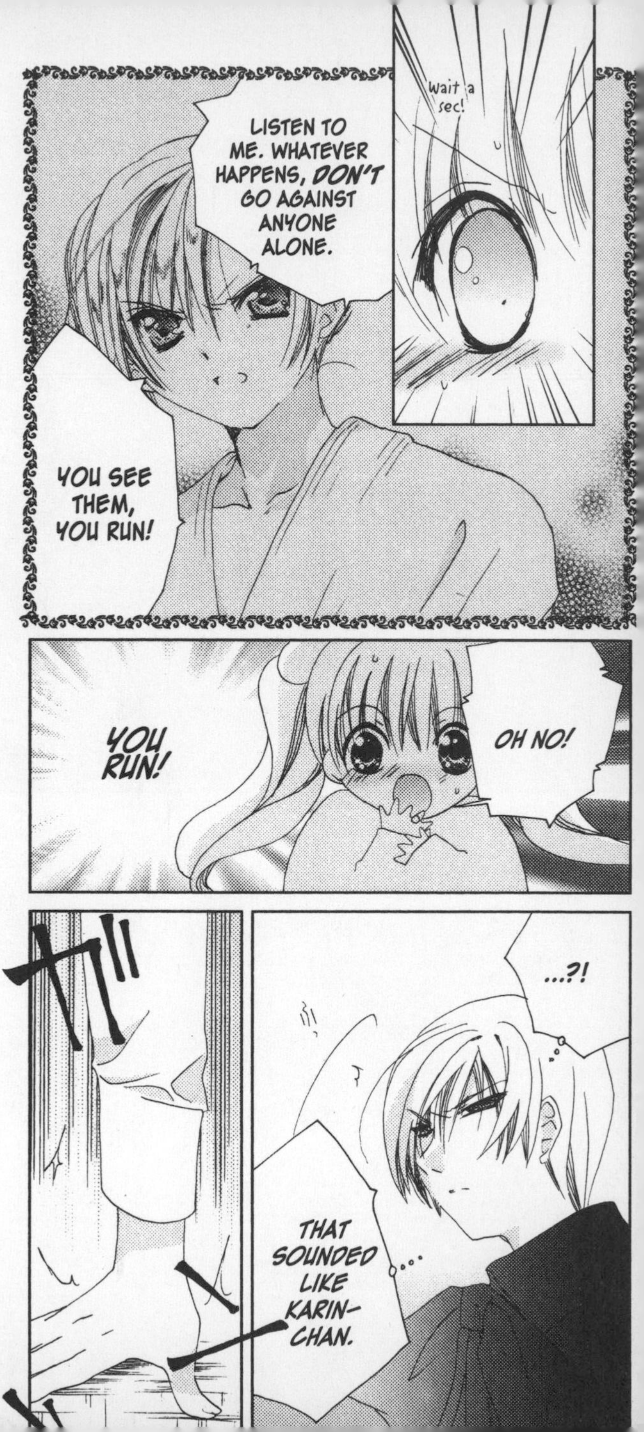
Wait a sec!
LISTEN TO ME. WHATEVER HAPPENS, DON'T GO AGAINST ANYONE ALONE.
YOU SEE THEM, YOU RUN!
OH NO!
YOU RUN!
...?!
THAT SOUNDED LIKE KARIN-CHAN.
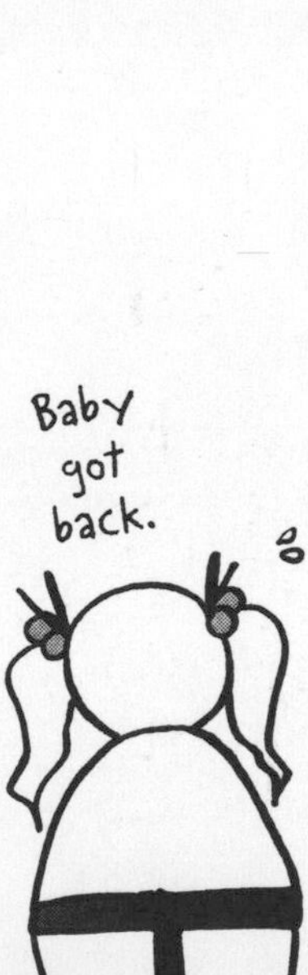
Baby got back.

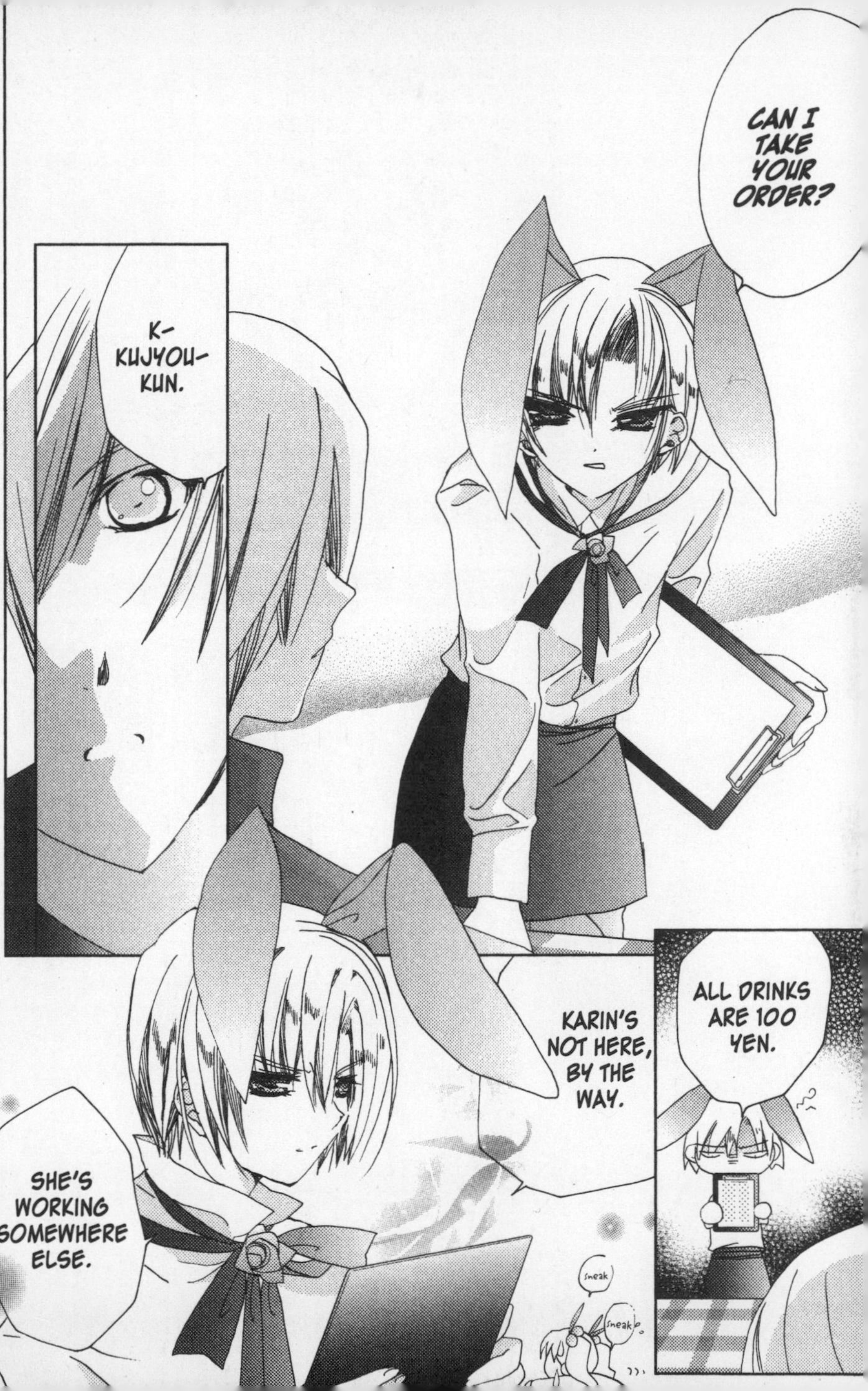
CAN I TAKE YOUR ORDER?
K-KUJYOU-KUN.
ALL DRINKS ARE 100 YEN.
KARIN'S NOT HERE, BY THE WAY.
SHE'S WORKING SOMEWHERE ELSE.
sneak
sneak

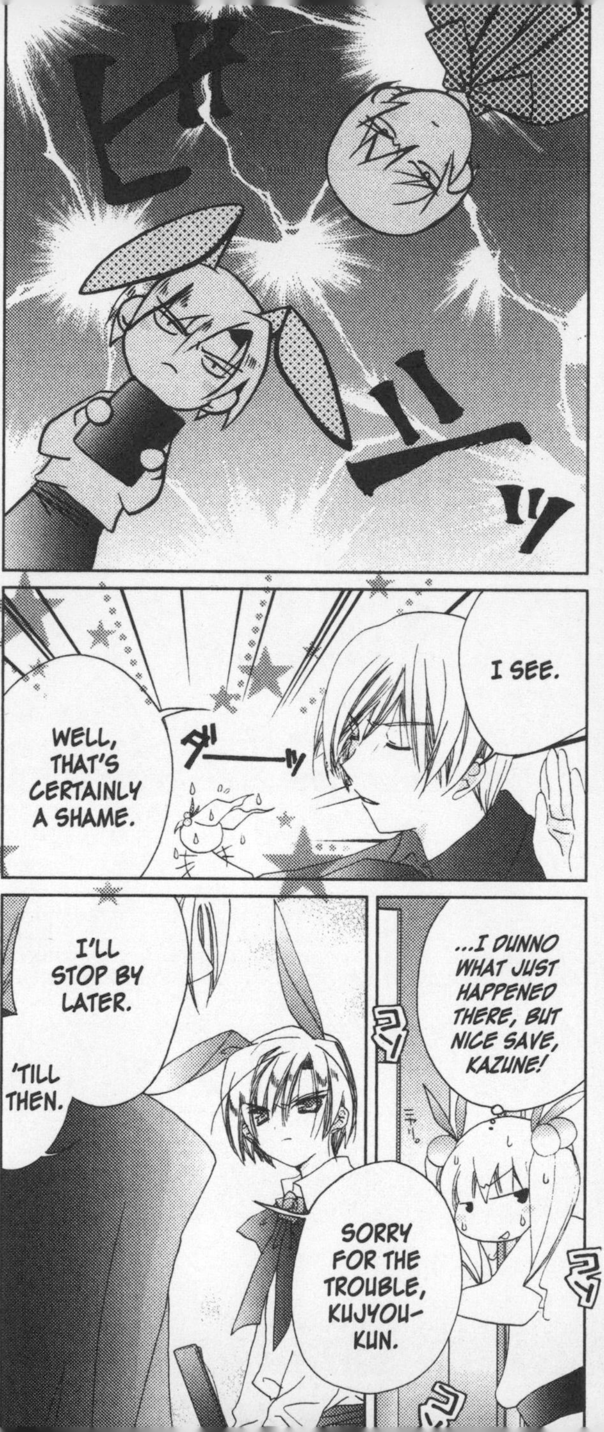
I SEE.
WELL, THAT'S CERTAINLY A SHAME.
...I DUNNO WHAT JUST HAPPENED THERE, BUT NICE SAVE, KAZUNE!
SORRY FOR THE TROUBLE, KUJYOU-KUN.
I'LL STOP BY LATER.
'TILL THEN.

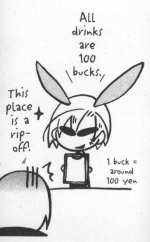

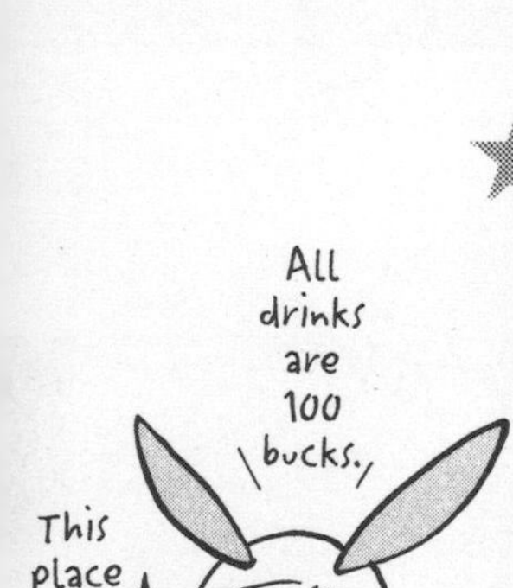
All drinks are 100 bucks.
This place is a rip-off!
1 buck = around 100 yen

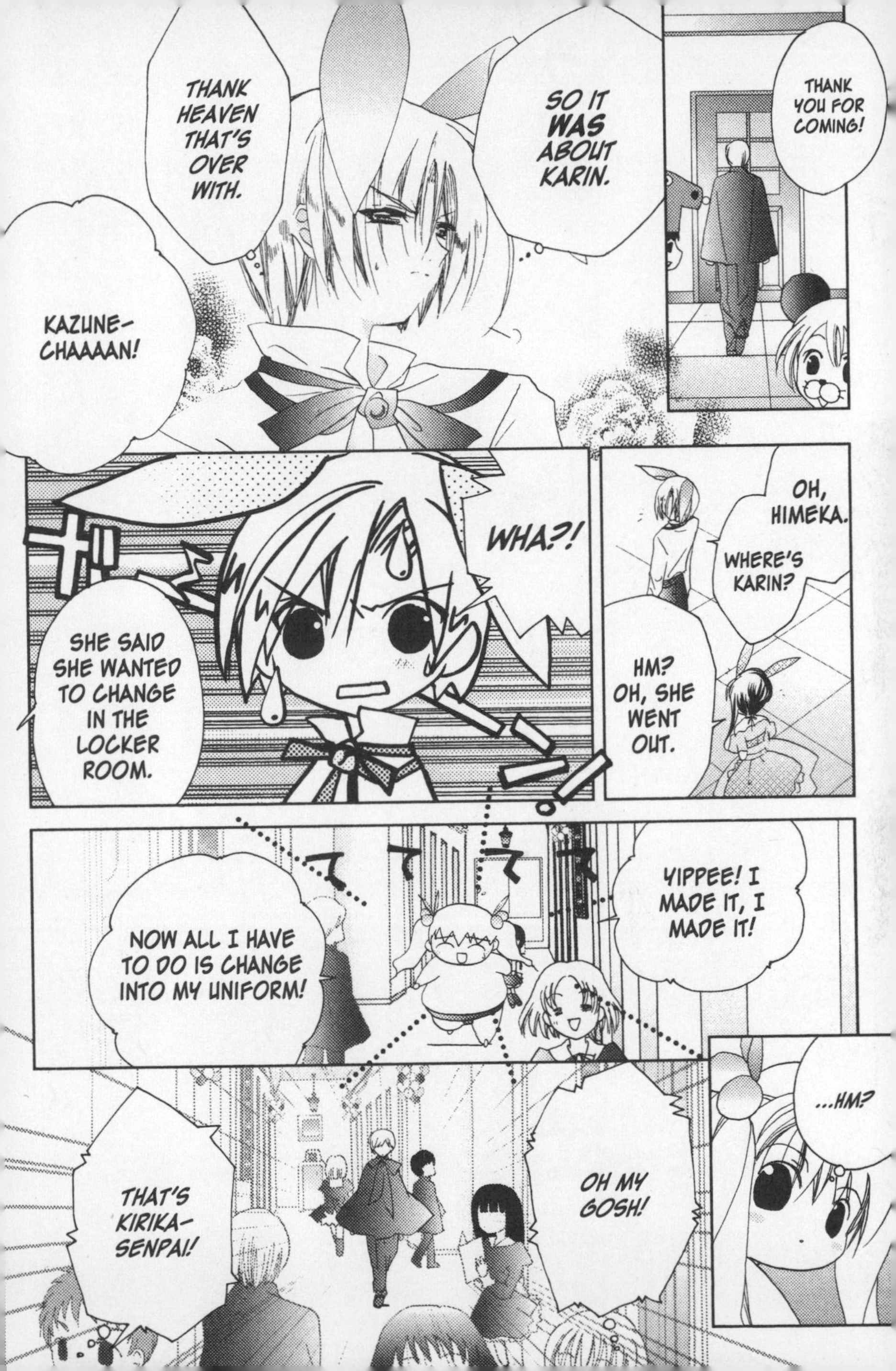
THANK YOU FOR COMING!
SO IT WAS ABOUT KARIN.
THANK HEAVEN THAT'S OVER WITH.
KAZUNE-CHAAAAN!
OH, HIMEKA.
WHERE'S KARIN?
HM? OH, SHE WENT OUT.
WHA?!
SHE SAID SHE WANTED TO CHANGE IN THE LOCKER ROOM.
YIPPEE! I MADE IT, I MADE IT!
NOW ALL I HAVE TO DO IS CHANGE INTO MY UNIFORM!
...HM?
OH MY GOSH!
THAT'S KIRIKA-SENPAI!

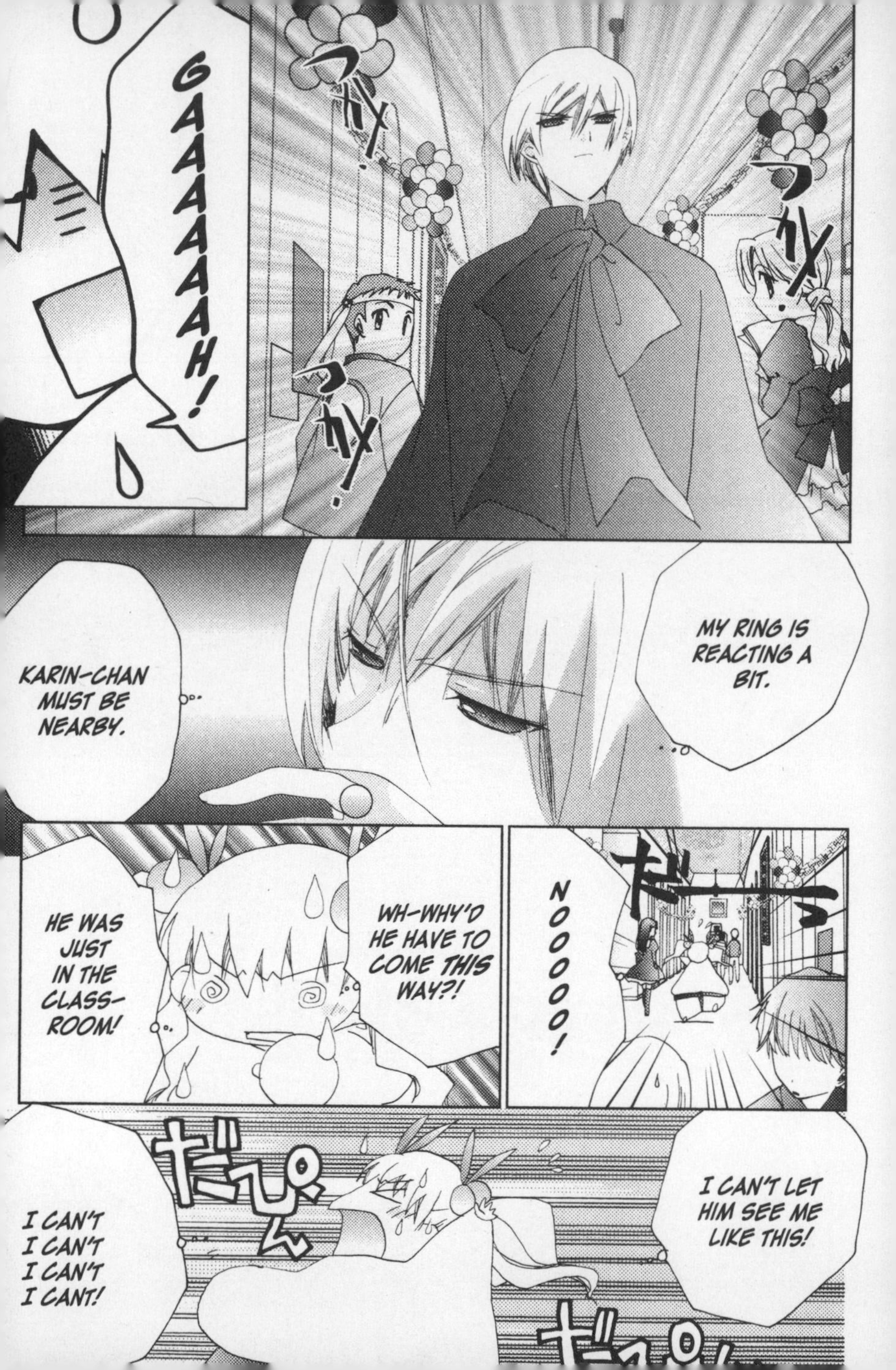
GAAAAAAAH!
MY RING IS REACTING A BIT.
KARIN-CHAN MUST BE NEARBY.
NOOOOOO!
WH-WHY'D HE HAVE TO COME THIS WAY?!
HE WAS JUST IN THE CLASS-ROOM!
I CAN'T LET HIM SEE ME LIKE THIS!
I CAN'T I CAN'T I CAN'T I CANT!

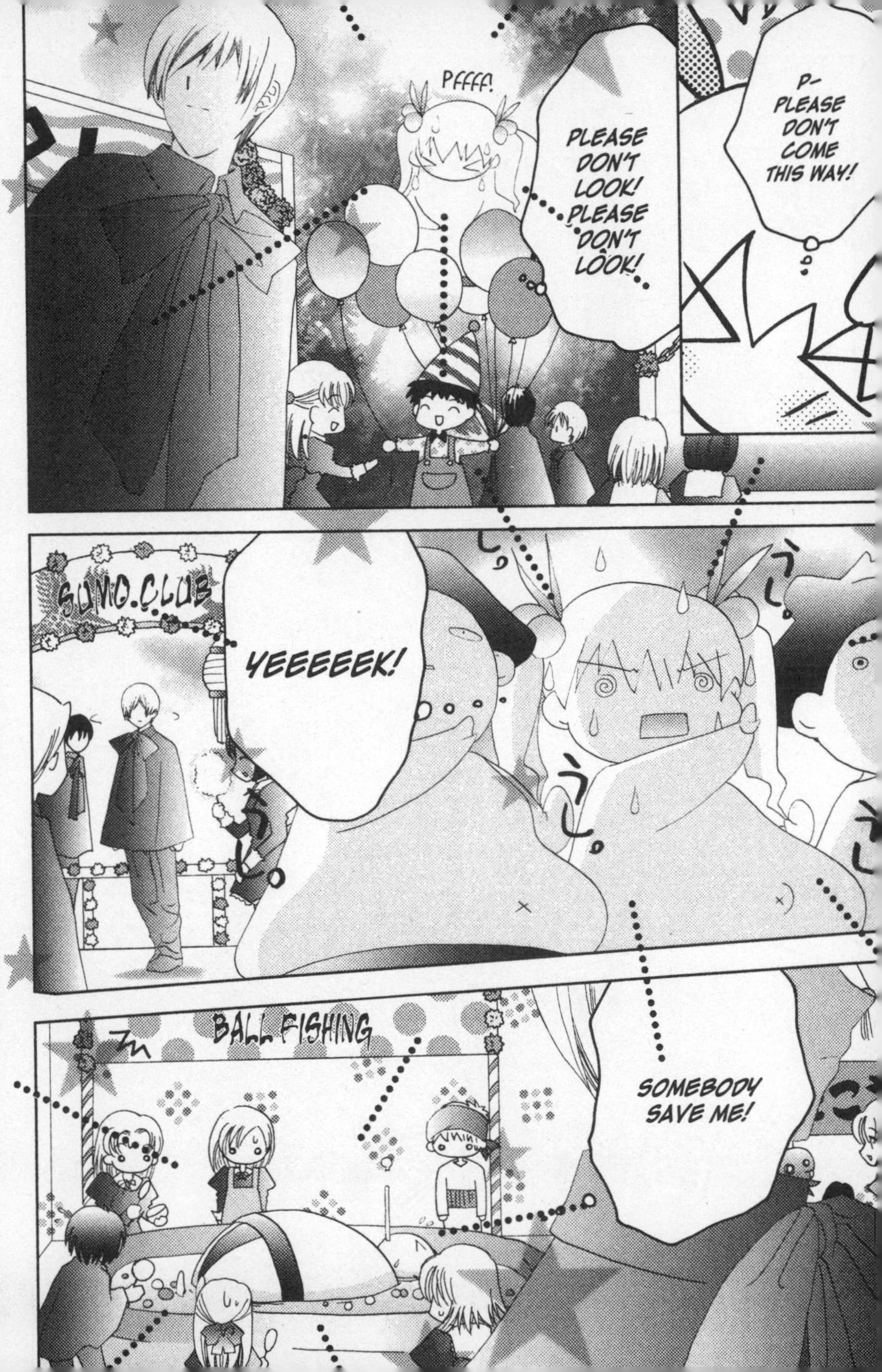

P-PLEASE DON'T COME THIS WAY!
PLEASE DON'T LOOK! PLEASE DON'T LOOK!
PFFFF!
YEEEEEK!
SUMO CLUB
SOMEBODY SAVE ME!
BALL FISHING

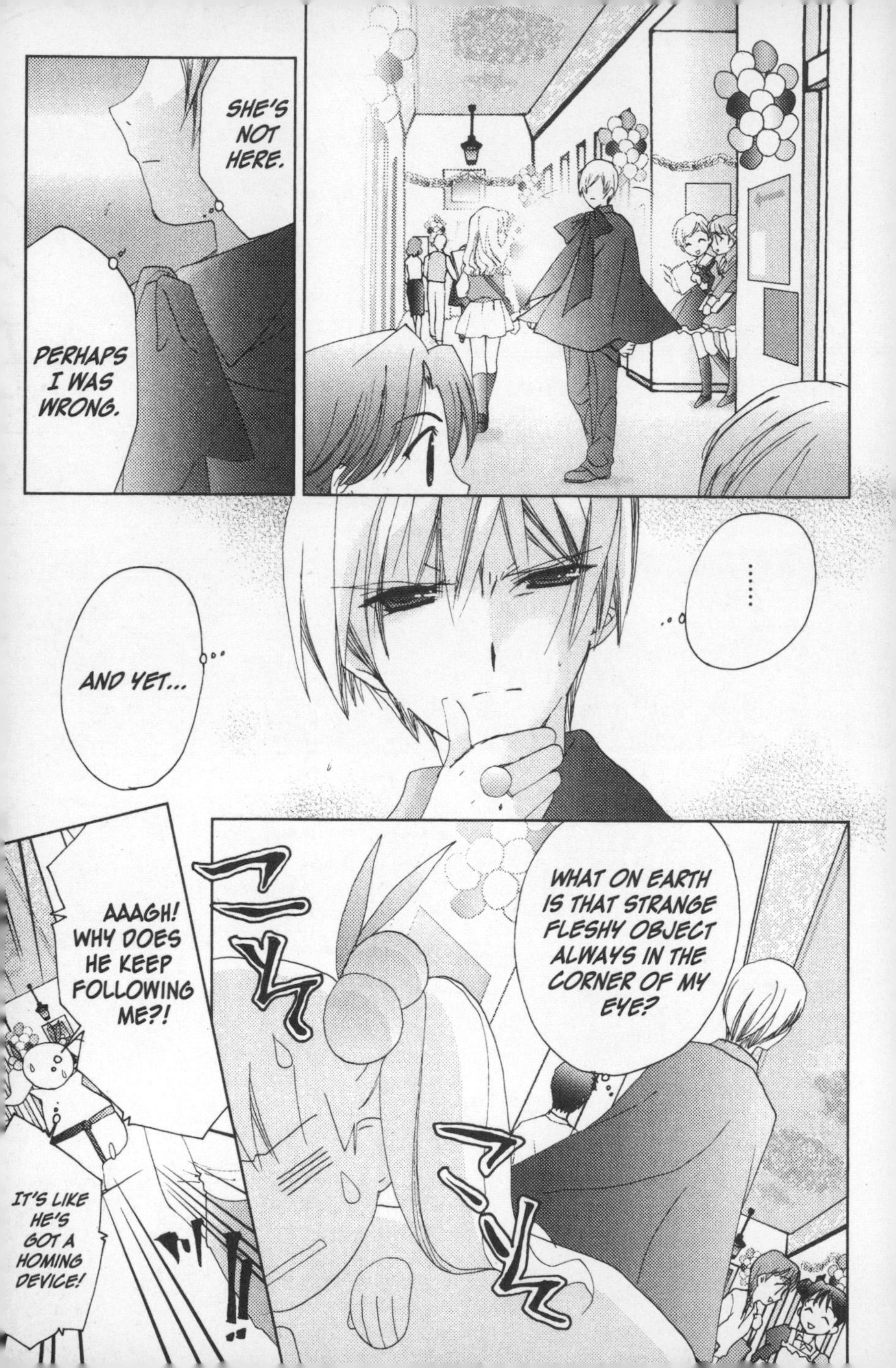
SHE'S NOT HERE.
PERHAPS I WAS WRONG.
......
AND YET...
WHAT ON EARTH IS THAT STRANGE FLESHY OBJECT ALWAYS IN THE CORNER OF MY EYE?
AAAGH! WHY DOES HE KEEP FOLLOWING ME?!
IT'S LIKE HE'S GOT A HOMING DEVICE!

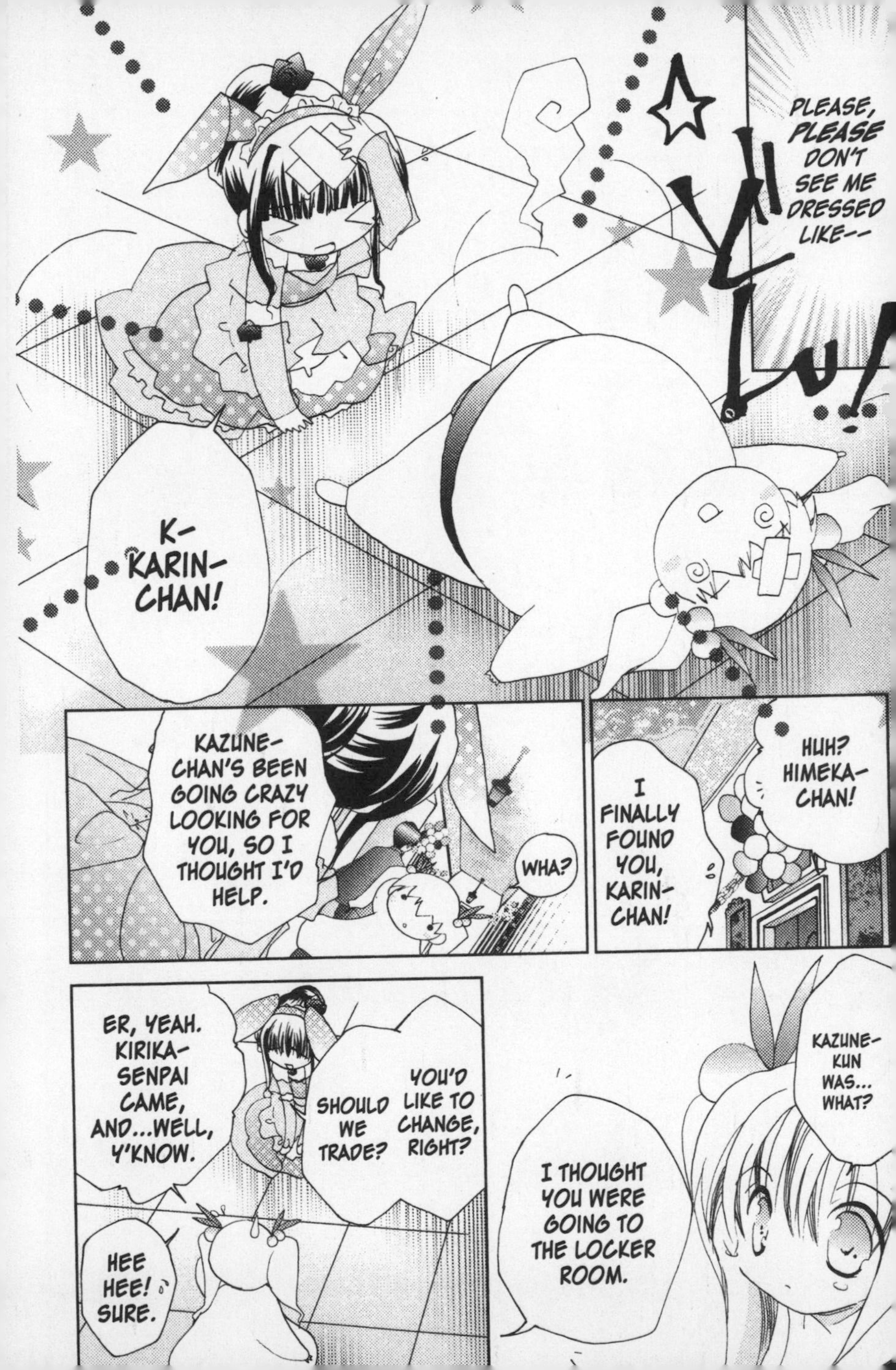
PLEASE, PLEASE DON'T SEE ME DRESSED LIKE--
K-KARIN-CHAN!
HUH? HIMEKA-CHAN!
I FINALLY FOUND YOU, KARIN-CHAN!
WHA?
KAZUNE-CHAN'S BEEN GOING CRAZY LOOKING FOR YOU, SO I THOUGHT I'D HELP.
KAZUNE-KUN WAS... WHAT?
I THOUGHT YOU WERE GOING TO THE LOCKER ROOM.
ER, YEAH. KIRIKA-SENPAI CAME, AND...WELL, Y'KNOW.
YOU'D LIKE TO CHANGE, RIGHT?
SHOULD WE TRADE?
HEE HEE! SURE.

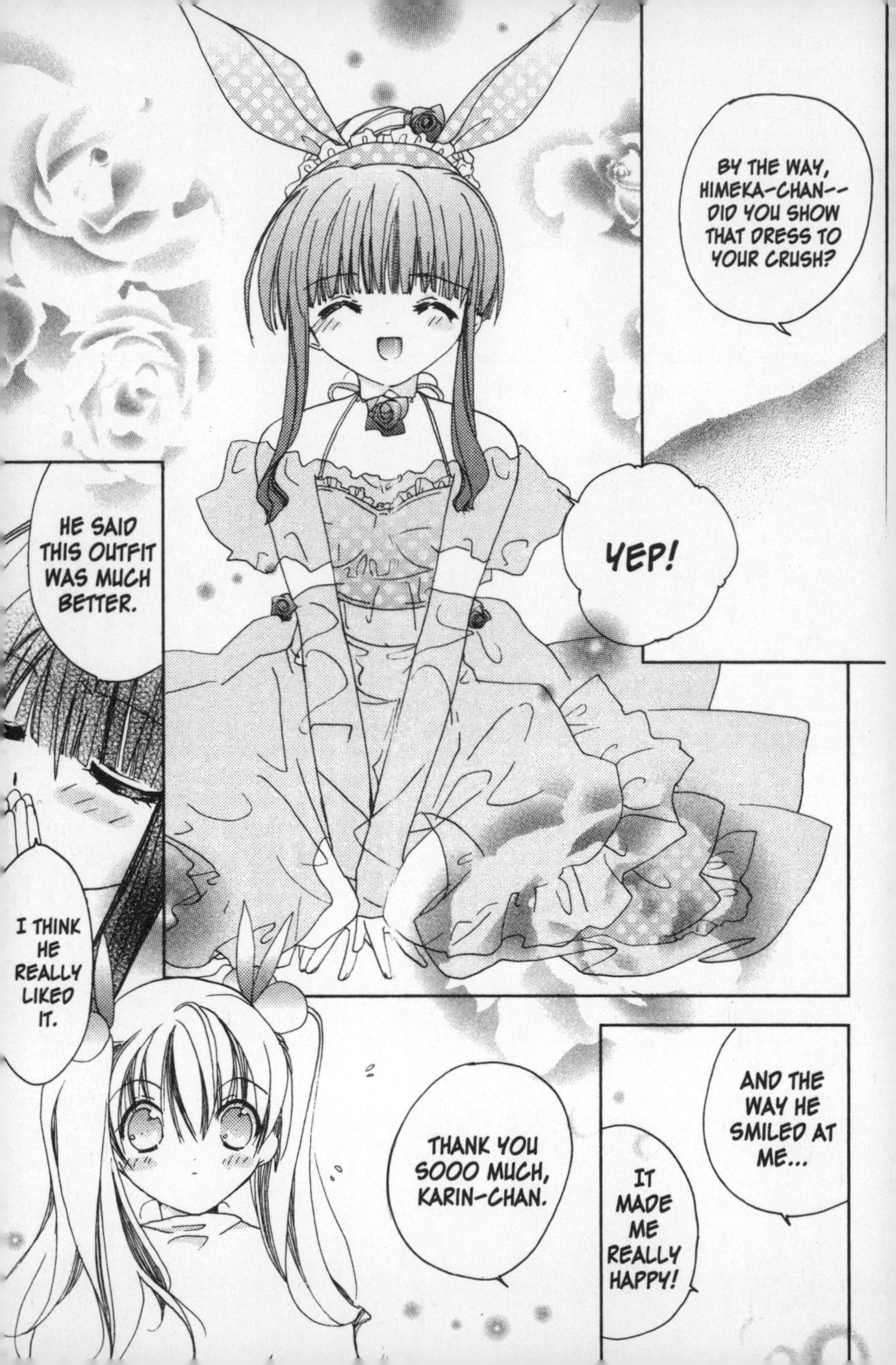
BY THE WAY, HIMEKA-CHAN-- DID YOU SHOW THAT DRESS TO YOUR CRUSH?
YEP!
HE SAID THIS OUTFIT WAS MUCH BETTER.
I THINK HE REALLY LIKED IT.
AND THE WAY HE SMILED AT ME...
IT MADE ME REALLY HAPPY!
THANK YOU SOOO MUCH, KARIN-CHAN.

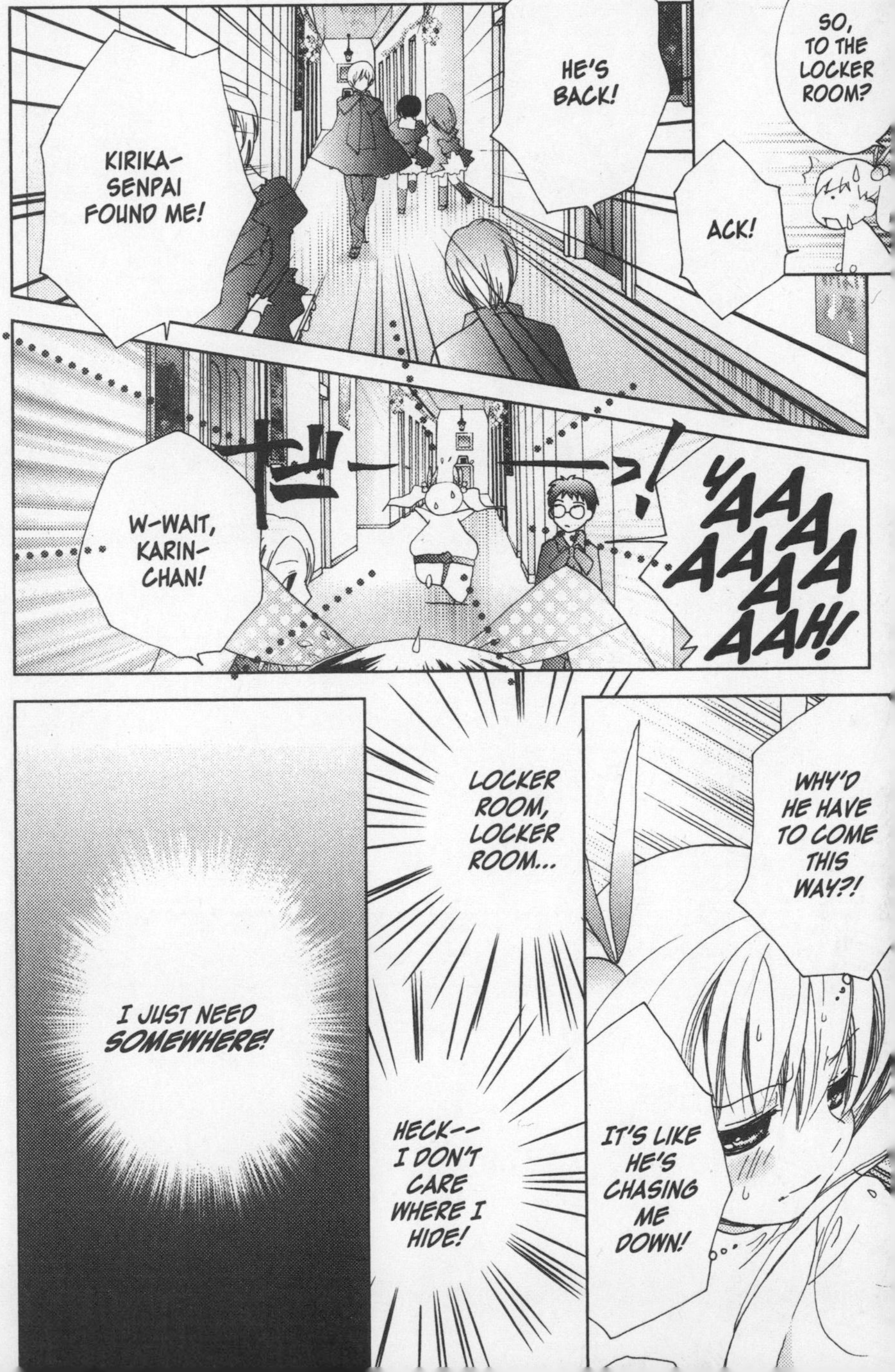
SO, TO THE LOCKER ROOM?
ACK!
HE'S BACK!
KIRIKA-SENPAI FOUND ME!
YAAAAAAAAAAH!
W-WAIT, KARIN-CHAN!
WHY'D HE HAVE TO COME THIS WAY?!
IT'S LIKE HE'S CHASING ME DOWN!
LOCKER ROOM, LOCKER ROOM...
HECK-- I DON'T CARE WHERE I HIDE!
I JUST NEED SOMEWHERE!

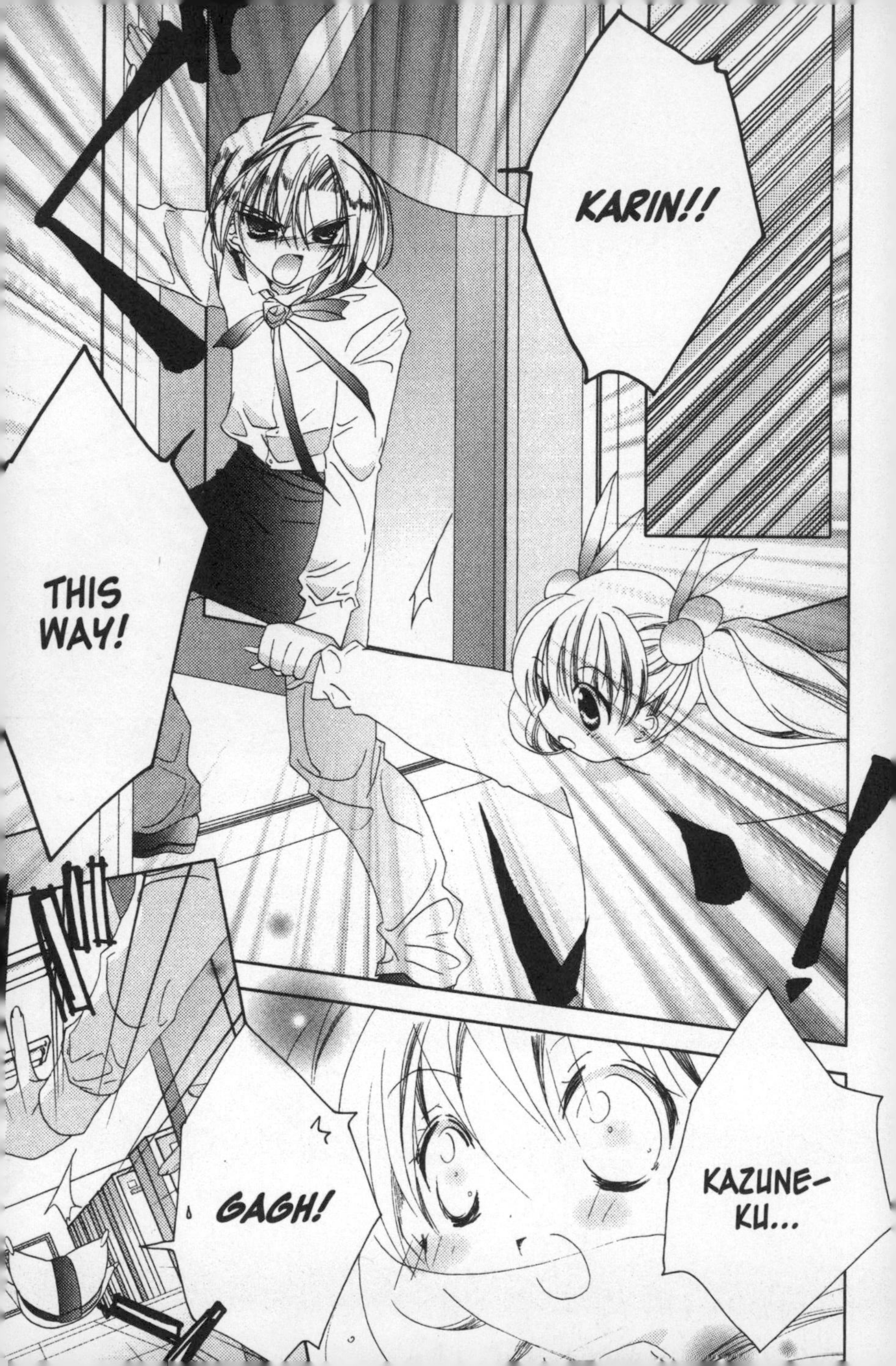
KARIN!!
THIS WAY!
KAZUNE-KU...
GAGH!

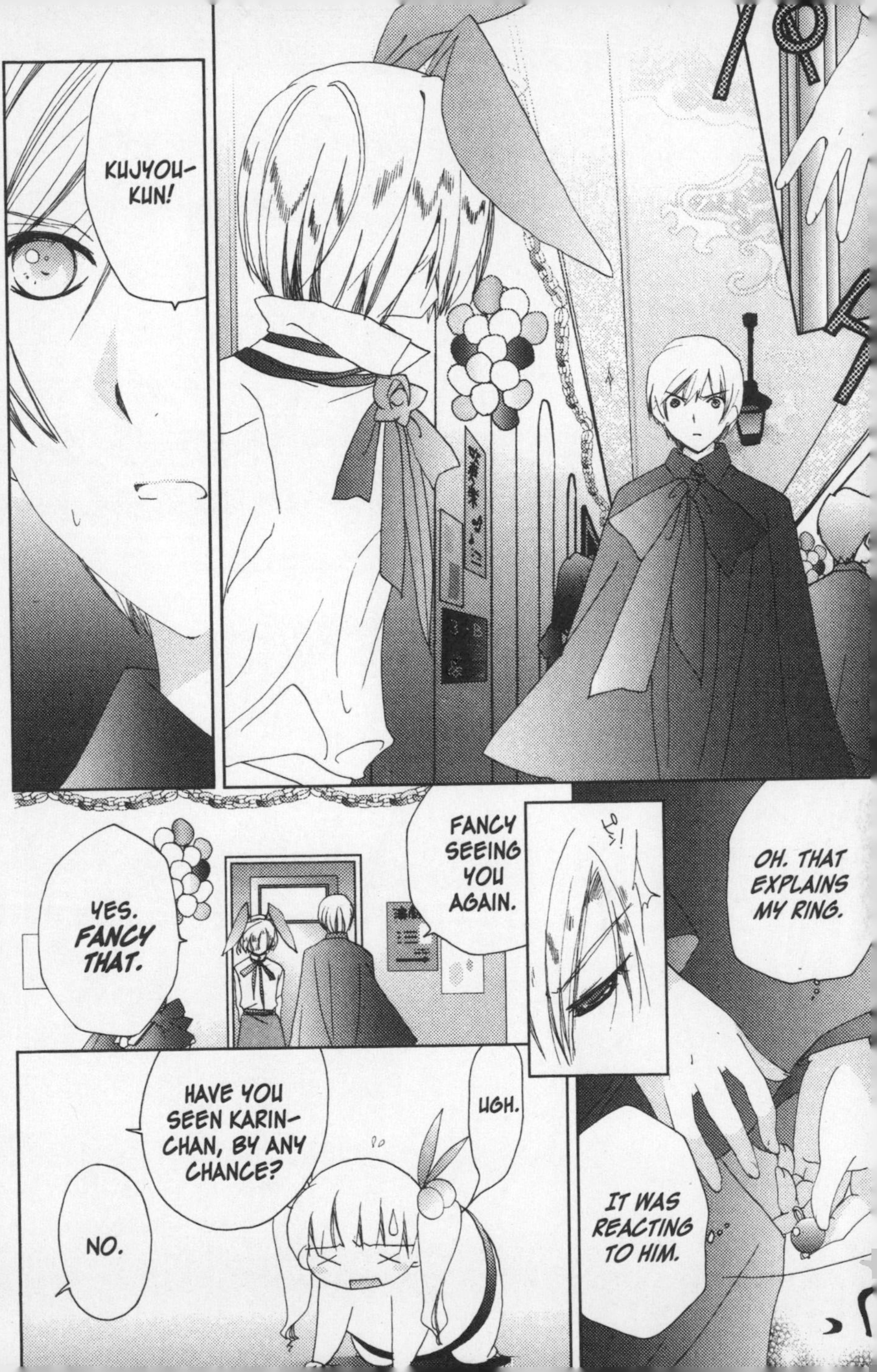
KUJYOU-KUN!
OH. THAT EXPLAINS MY RING.
IT WAS REACTING TO HIM.
FANCY SEEING YOU AGAIN.
YES. FANCY THAT.
UGH.
HAVE YOU SEEN KARIN-CHAN, BY ANY CHANCE?
NO.

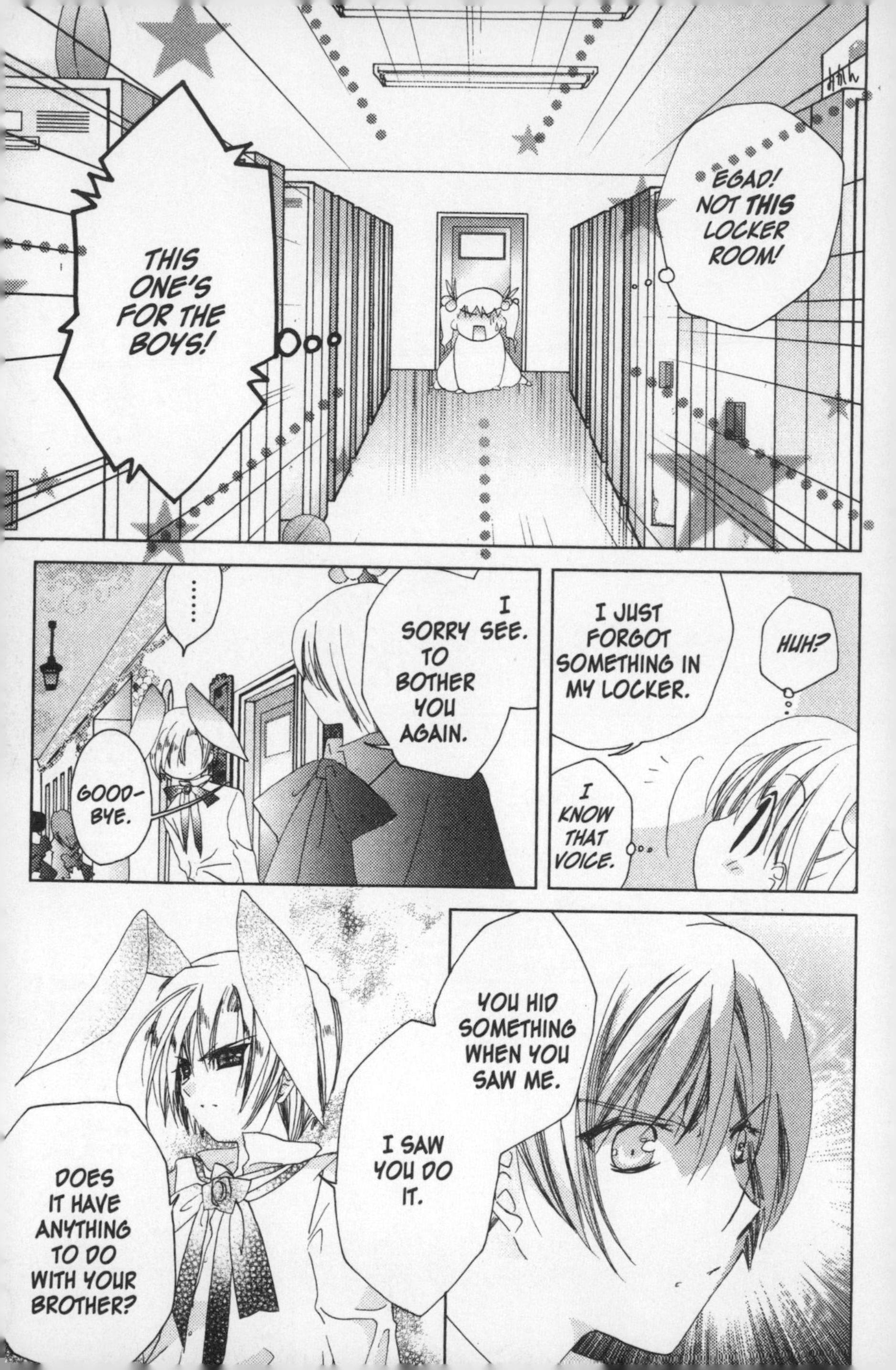
EGAD! NOT THIS LOCKER ROOM!
THIS ONE'S FOR THE BOYS!
HUH?
I JUST FORGOT SOMETHING IN MY LOCKER.
I KNOW THAT VOICE.
I SEE.
SORRY TO BOTHER YOU AGAIN.
......
GOOD-BYE.
YOU HID SOMETHING WHEN YOU SAW ME.
I SAW YOU DO IT.
DOES IT HAVE ANYTHING TO DO WITH YOUR BROTHER?

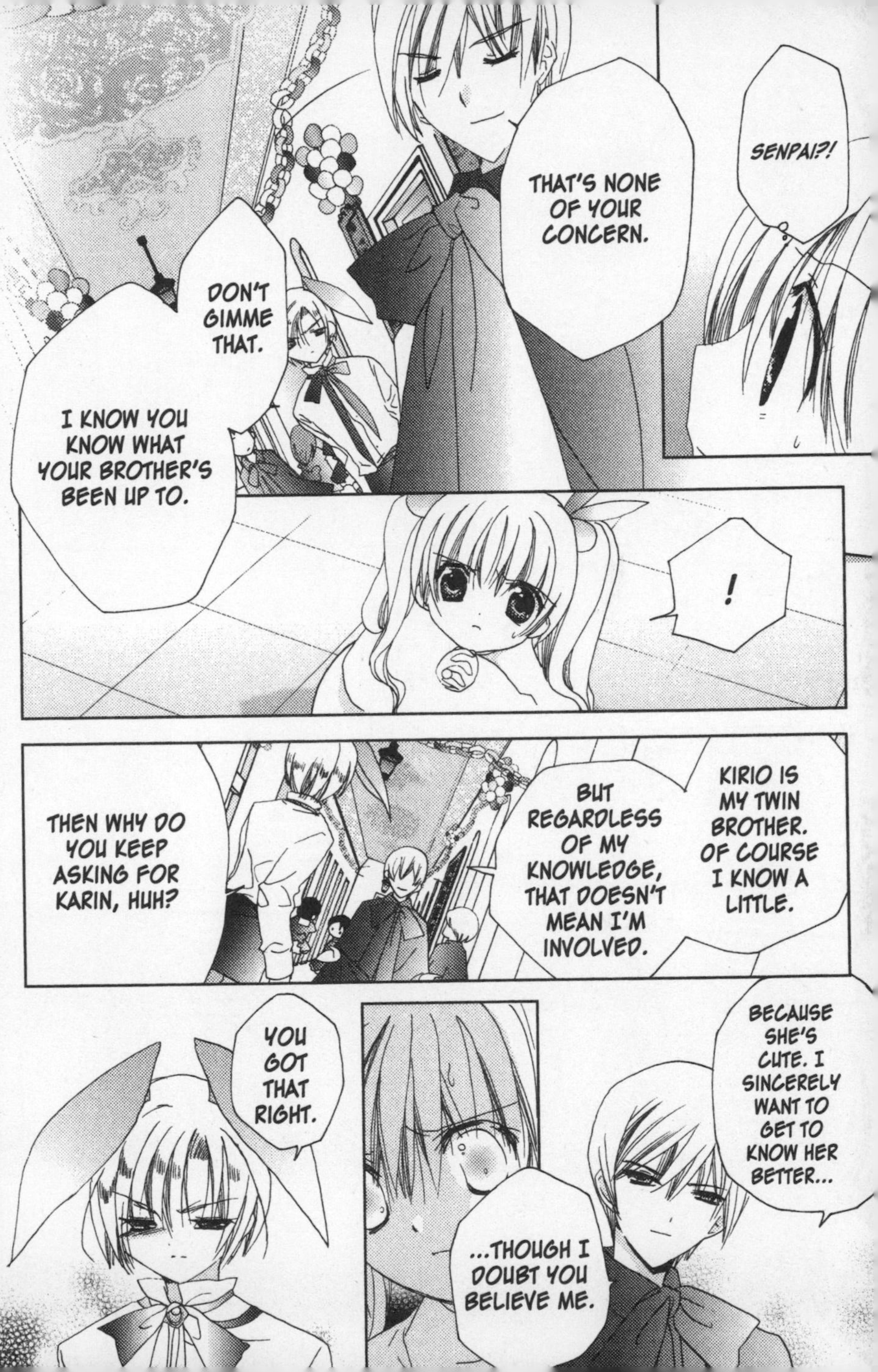
SENPAI?!
THAT'S NONE OF YOUR CONCERN.
DON'T GIMME THAT.
I KNOW YOU KNOW WHAT YOUR BROTHER'S BEEN UP TO.
!
KIRIO IS MY TWIN BROTHER. OF COURSE I KNOW A LITTLE.
BUT REGARDLESS OF MY KNOWLEDGE, THAT DOESN'T MEAN I'M INVOLVED.
THEN WHY DO YOU KEEP ASKING FOR KARIN, HUH?
BECAUSE SHE'S CUTE. I SINCERELY WANT TO GET TO KNOW HER BETTER...
...THOUGH I DOUBT YOU BELIEVE ME.
YOU GOT THAT RIGHT.

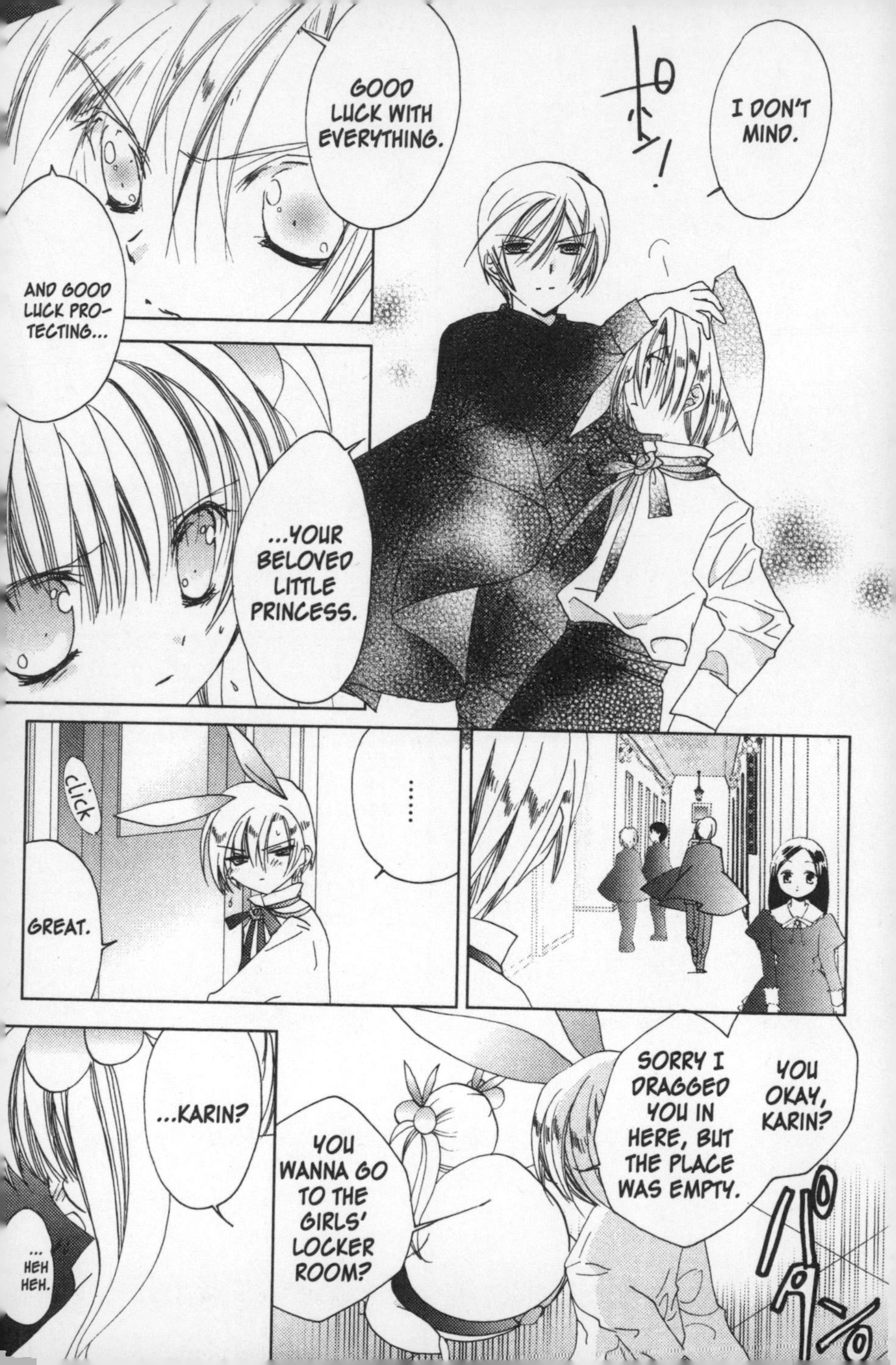
GOOD LUCK WITH EVERYTHING.
AND GOOD LUCK PRO-TECTING...
...YOUR BELOVED LITTLE PRINCESS.
I DON'T MIND.
......
click
GREAT.
YOU OKAY, KARIN?
SORRY I DRAGGED YOU IN HERE, BUT THE PLACE WAS EMPTY.
YOU WANNA GO TO THE GIRLS' LOCKER ROOM?
...KARIN?
... HEH HEH.

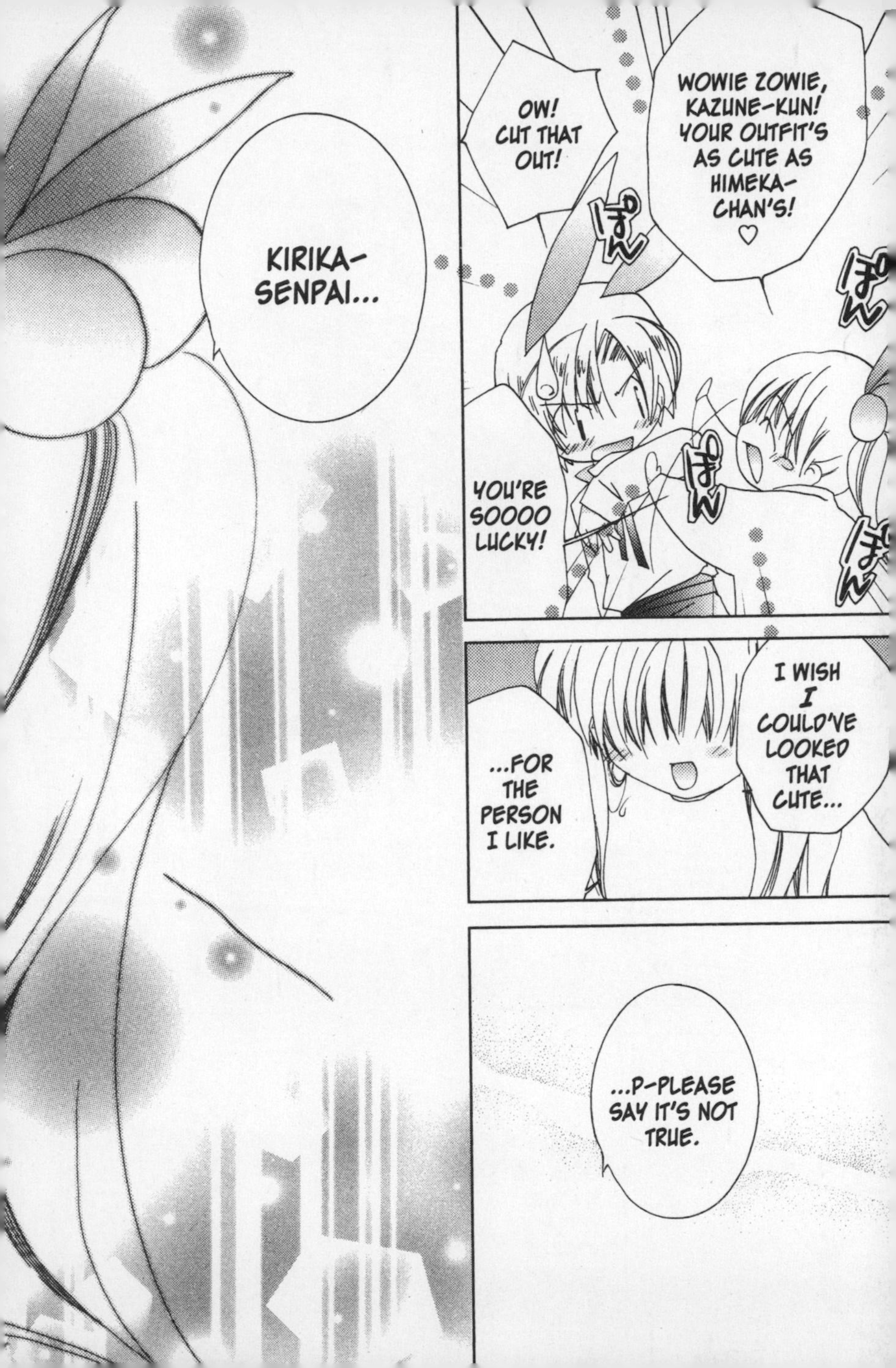
WOWIE ZOWIE, KAZUNE-KUN! YOUR OUTFIT'S AS CUTE AS HIMEKA-CHAN'S! ♡
ぽん
OW! CUT THAT OUT!
ぽん
ぽん
ぽん
YOU'RE SOOOO LUCKY!
I WISH I COULD'VE LOOKED THAT CUTE...
...FOR THE PERSON I LIKE.
...P-PLEASE SAY IT'S NOT TRUE.
KIRIKA-SENPAI...

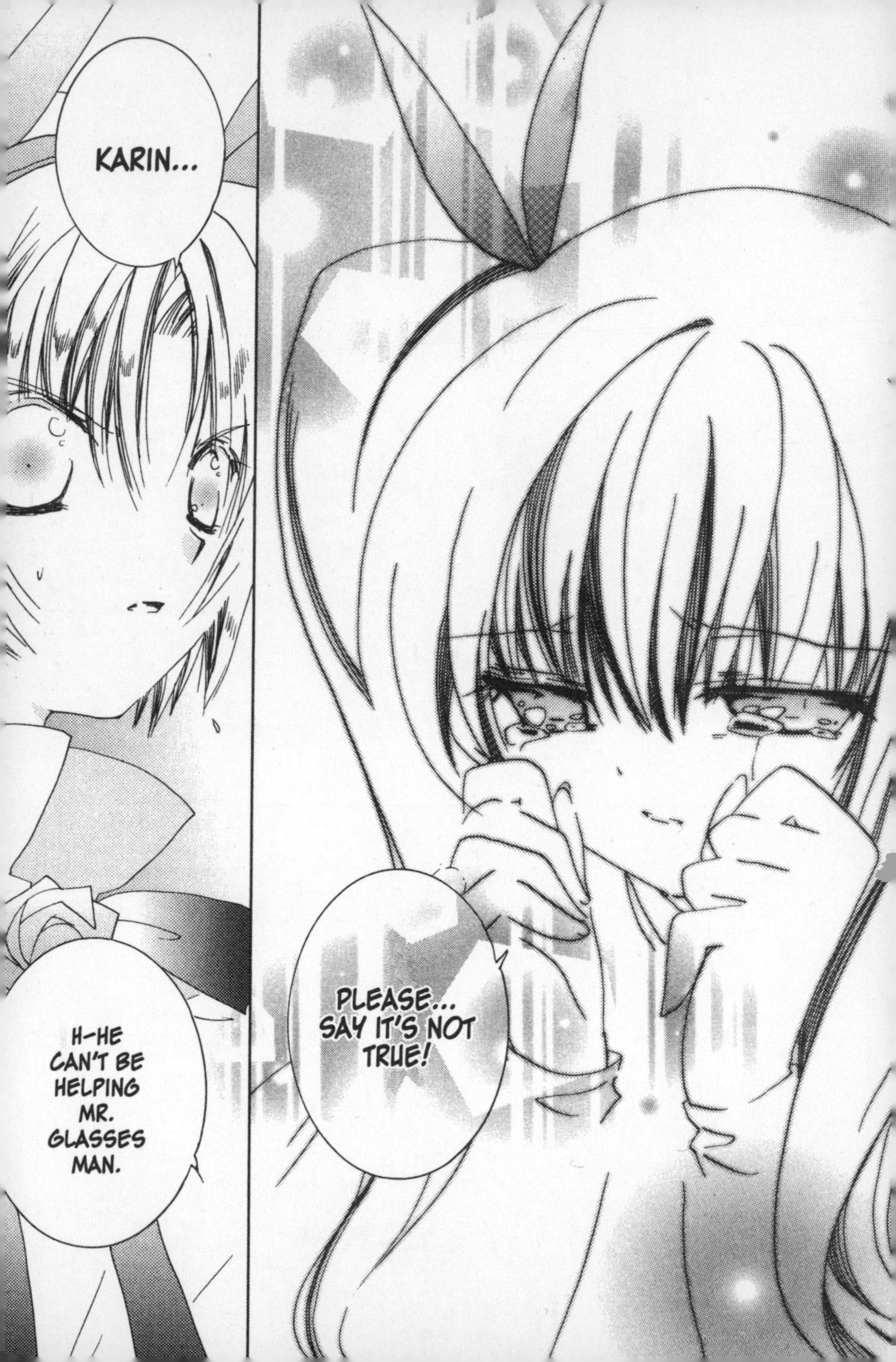
PLEASE... SAY IT'S NOT TRUE!
KARIN...
H-HE CAN'T BE HELPING MR. GLASSES MAN.

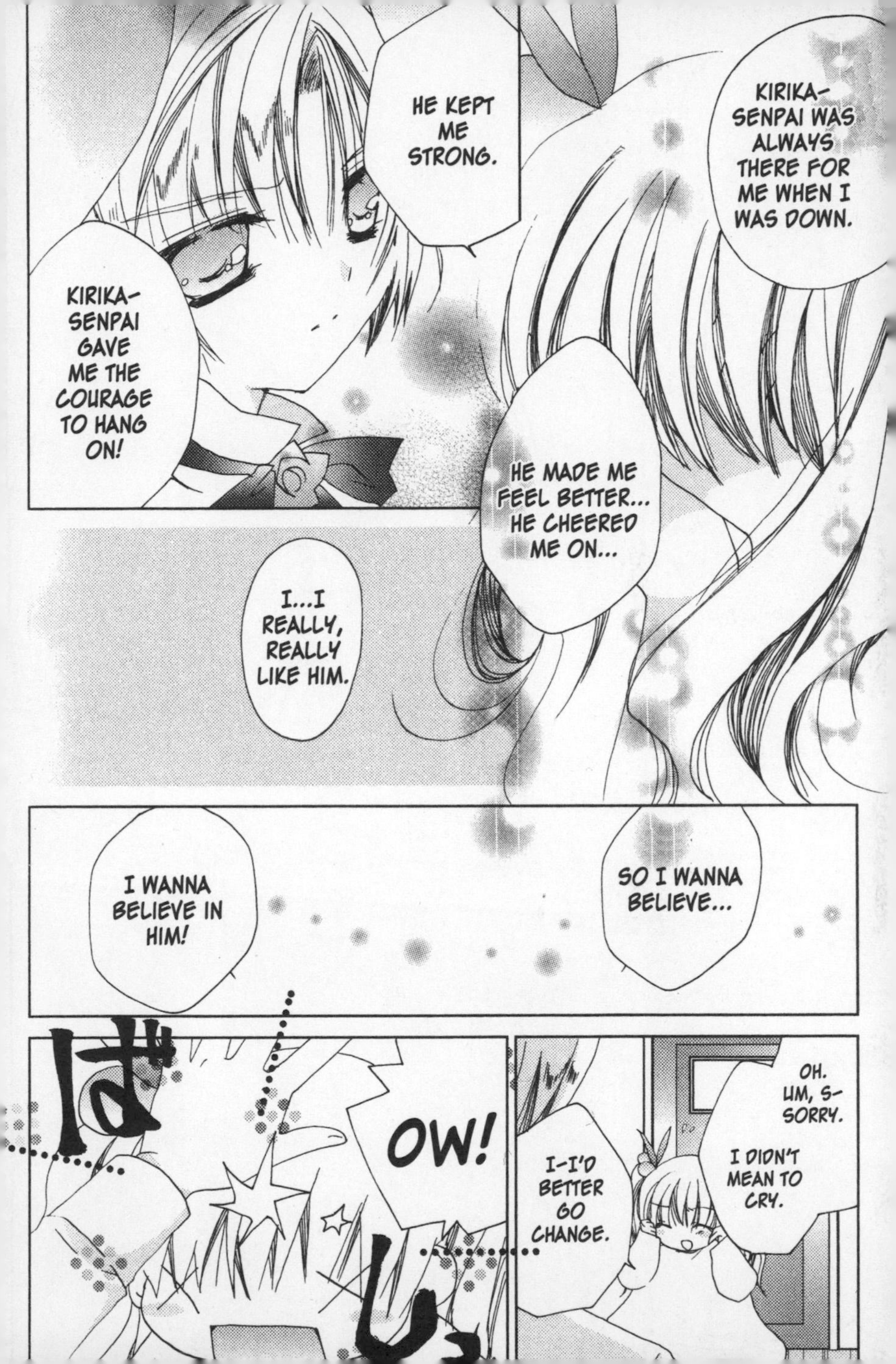
KIRIKA-SENPAI WAS ALWAYS THERE FOR ME WHEN I WAS DOWN.
HE KEPT ME STRONG.
KIRIKA-SENPAI GAVE ME THE COURAGE TO HANG ON!
HE MADE ME FEEL BETTER... HE CHEERED ME ON...
I...I REALLY, REALLY LIKE HIM.
SO I WANNA BELIEVE...
I WANNA BELIEVE IN HIM!
OH. UM, S-SORRY.
I DIDN'T MEAN TO CRY.
I-I'D BETTER GO CHANGE.
OW!
ばしっ

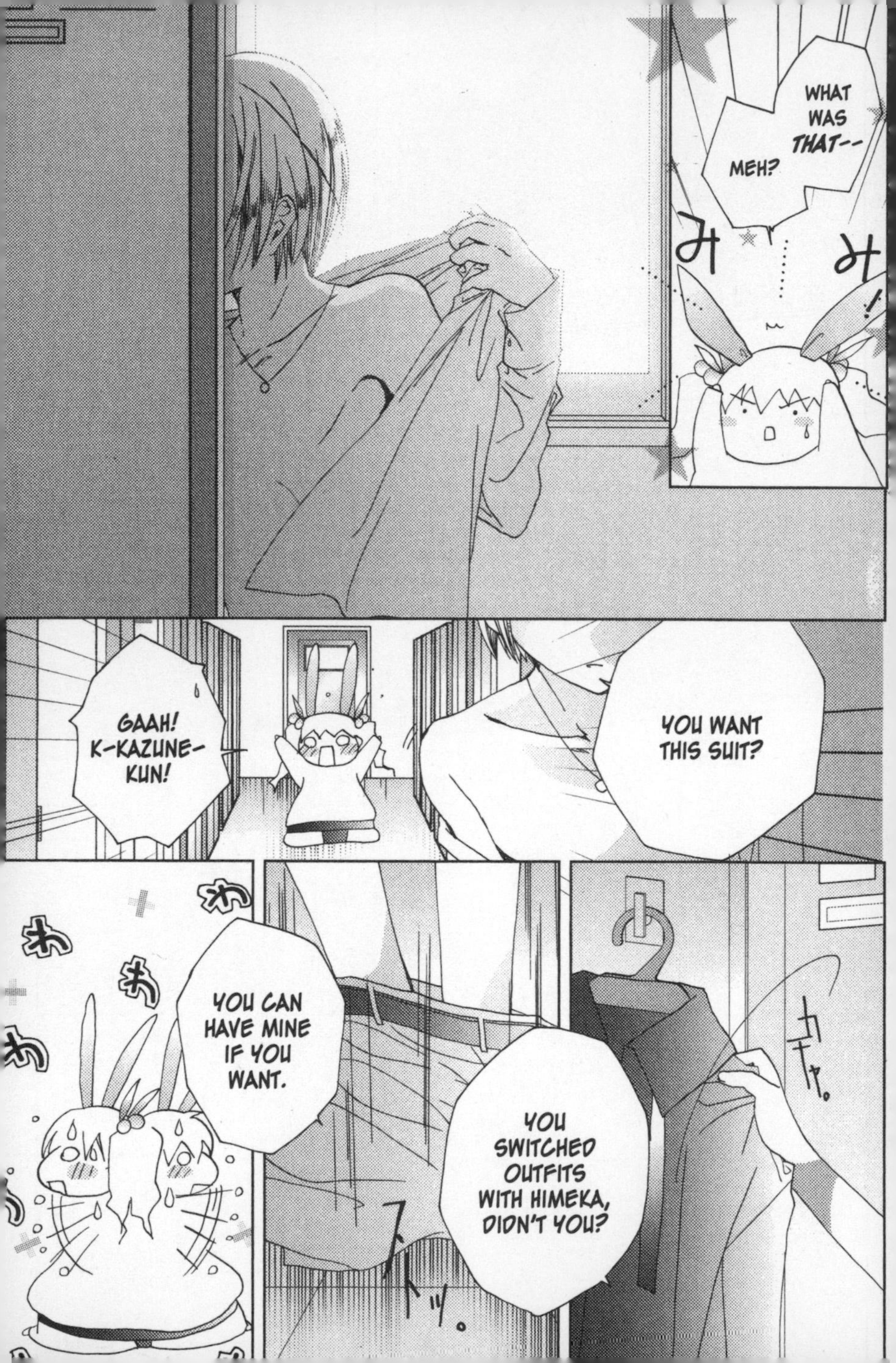
WHAT WAS THAT-- MEH?
み み
YOU WANT THIS SUIT?
GAAH! K-KAZUNE-KUN!
カチャ。
YOU SWITCHED OUTFITS WITH HIMEKA, DIDN'T YOU?
YOU CAN HAVE MINE IF YOU WANT.

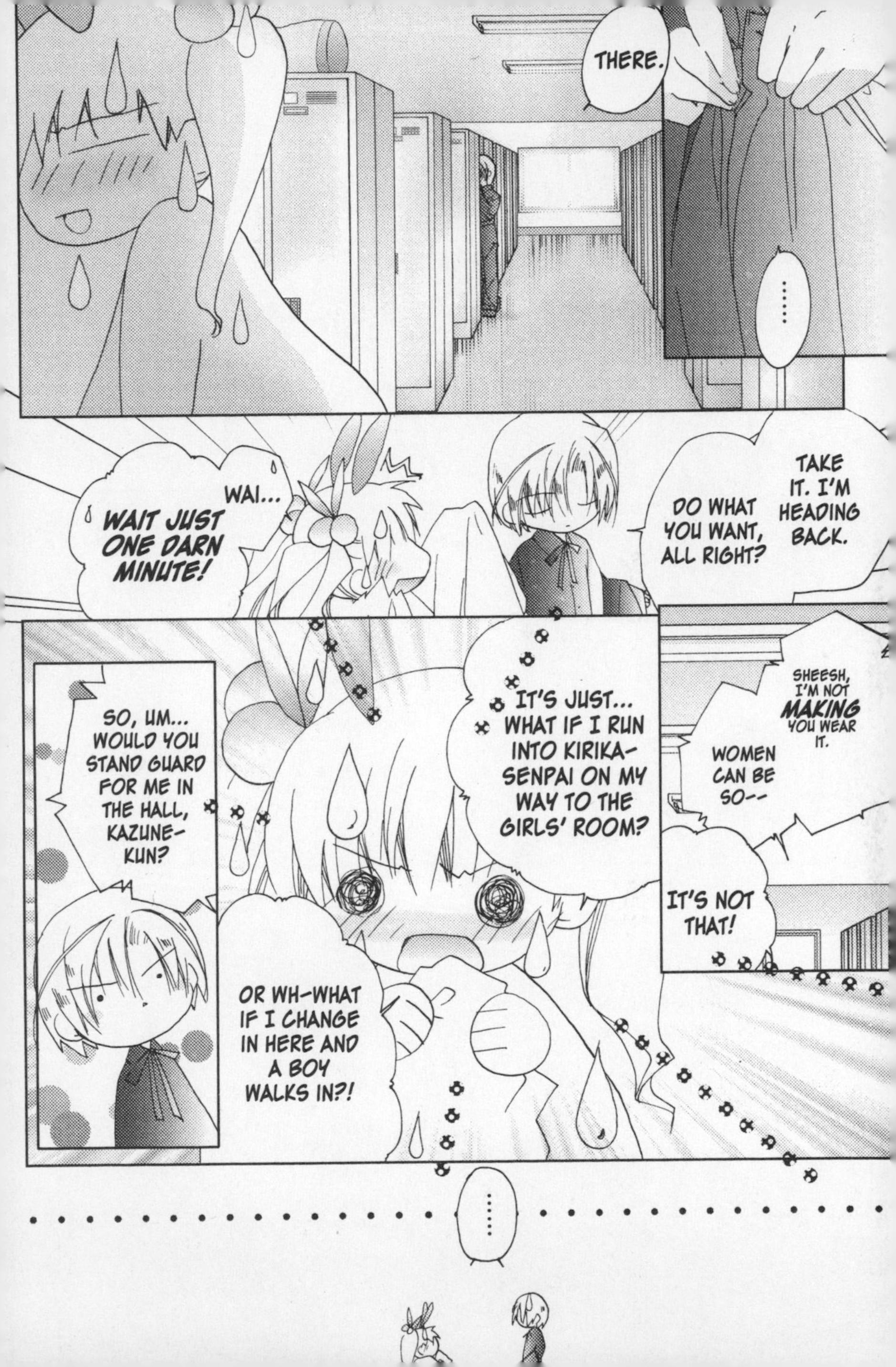
THERE.
......
TAKE IT. I'M HEADING BACK.
DO WHAT YOU WANT, ALL RIGHT?
WAI...
WAIT JUST ONE DARN MINUTE!
SHEESH, I'M NOT MAKING YOU WEAR IT.
WOMEN CAN BE SO--
IT'S NOT THAT!
IT'S JUST... WHAT IF I RUN INTO KIRIKA-SENPAI ON MY WAY TO THE GIRLS' ROOM?
OR WH-WHAT IF I CHANGE IN HERE AND A BOY WALKS IN?!
SO, UM... WOULD YOU STAND GUARD FOR ME IN THE HALL, KAZUNE-KUN?
......

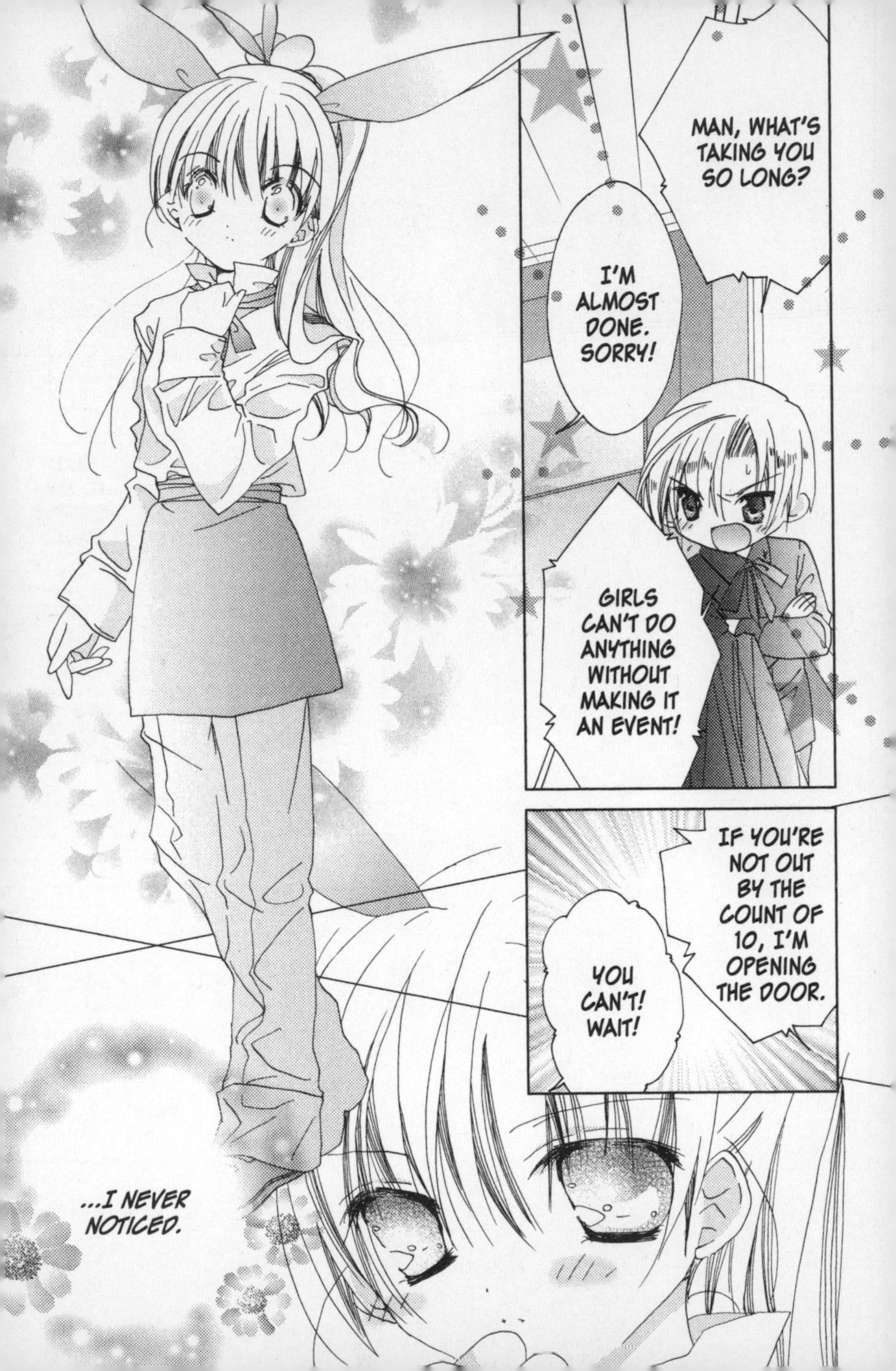
MAN, WHAT'S TAKING YOU SO LONG?
I'M ALMOST DONE. SORRY!
GIRLS CAN'T DO ANYTHING WITHOUT MAKING IT AN EVENT!
IF YOU'RE NOT OUT BY THE COUNT OF 10, I'M OPENING THE DOOR.
YOU CAN'T! WAIT!
...I NEVER NOTICED.

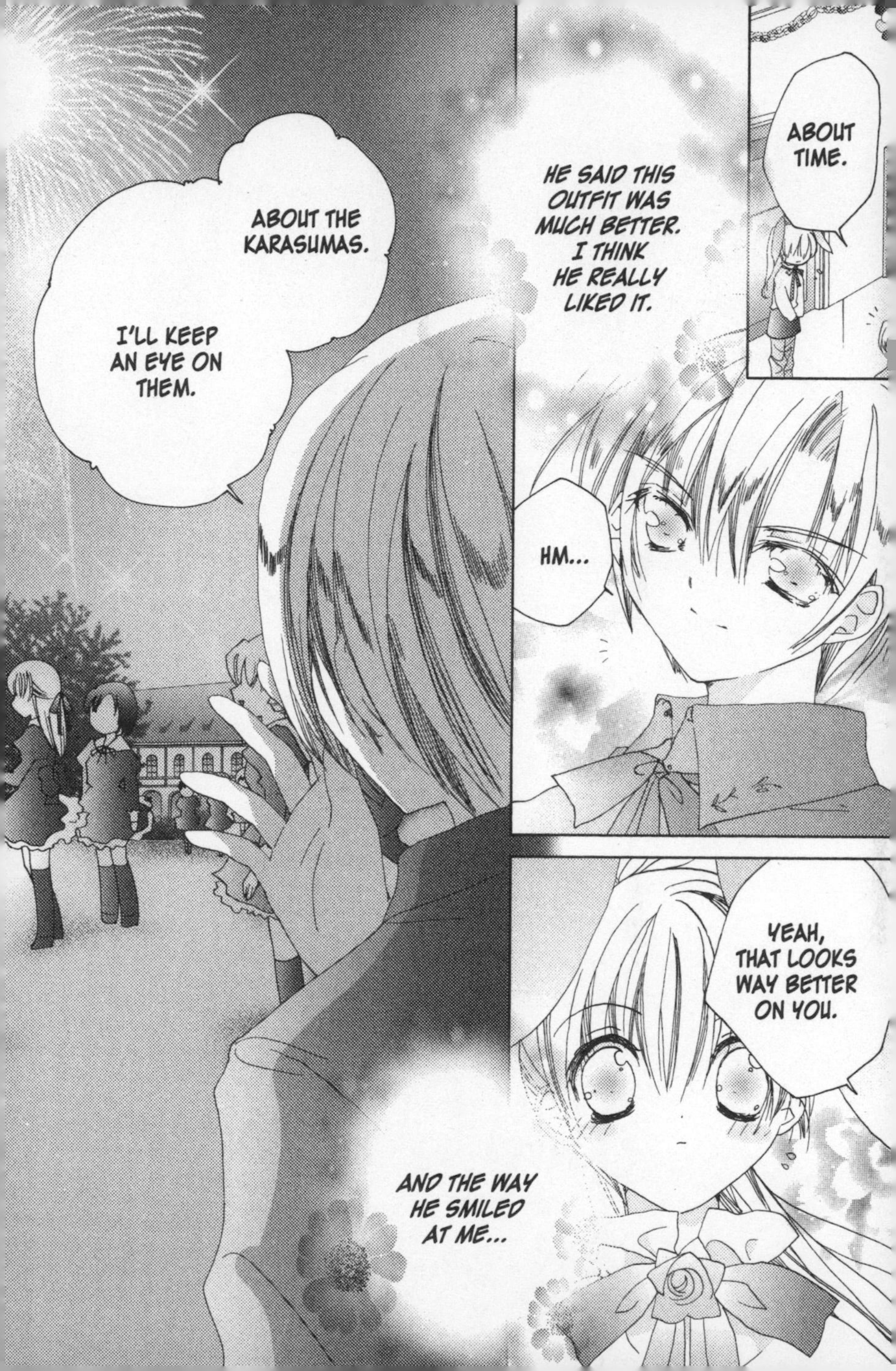
ABOUT TIME.
HE SAID THIS OUTFIT WAS MUCH BETTER. I THINK HE REALLY LIKED IT.
HM...
YEAH, THAT LOOKS WAY BETTER ON YOU.
AND THE WAY HE SMILED AT ME...
ABOUT THE KARASUMAS.
I'LL KEEP AN EYE ON THEM.

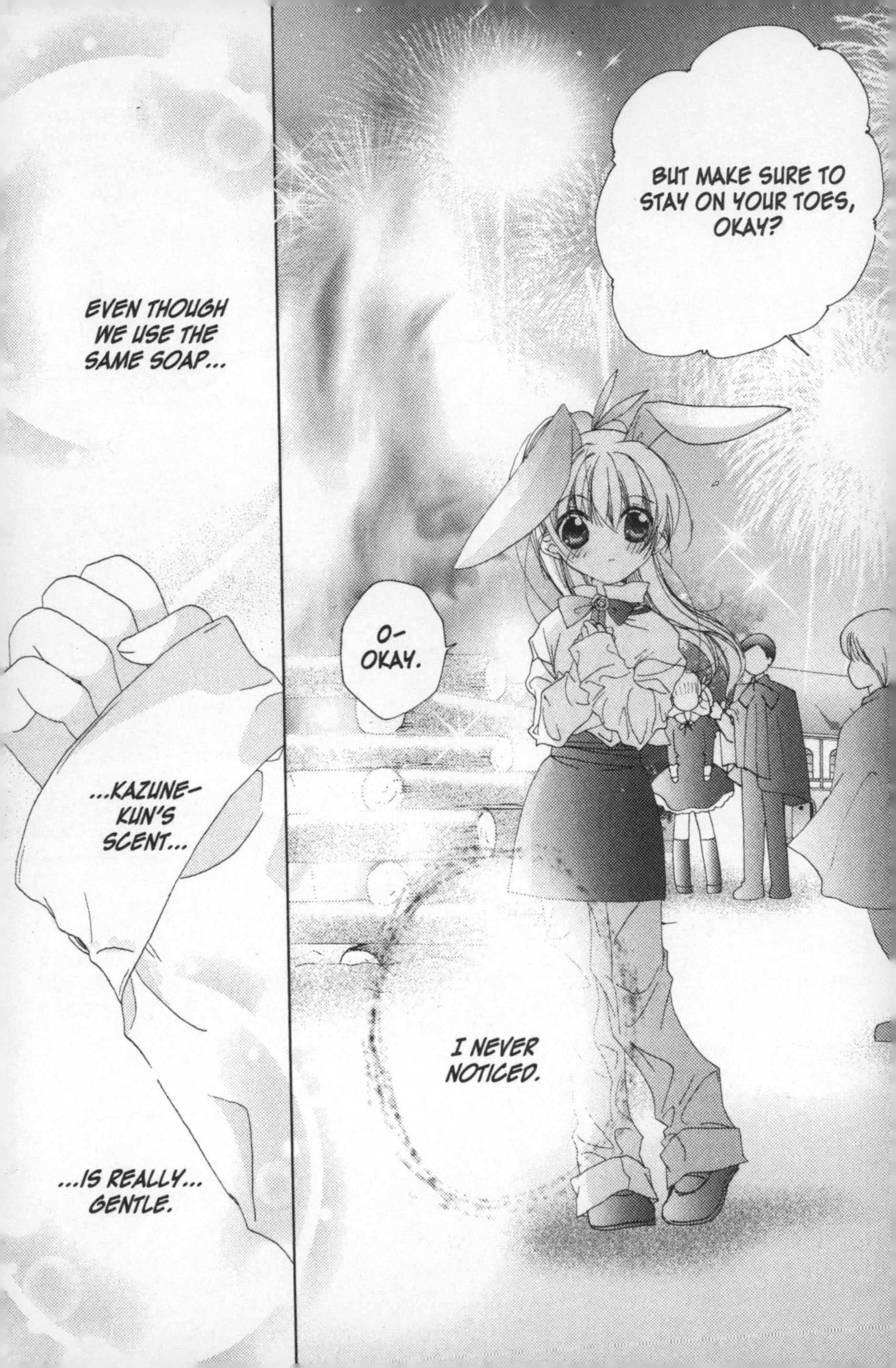
BUT MAKE SURE TO STAY ON YOUR TOES, OKAY?
O-OKAY.
I NEVER NOTICED.
EVEN THOUGH WE USE THE SAME SOAP...
...KAZUNE-KUN'S SCENT...
...IS REALLY... GENTLE.

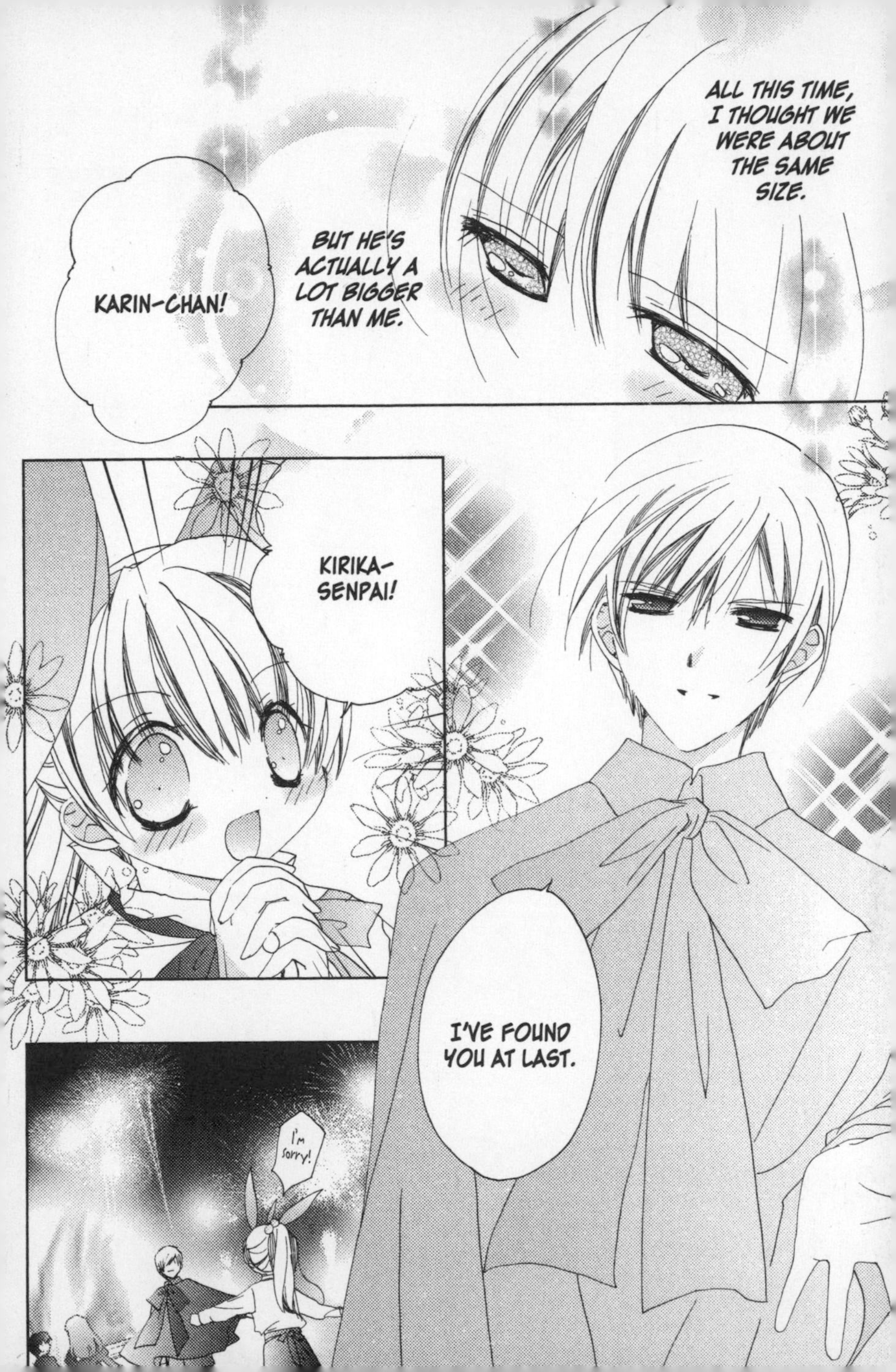
ALL THIS TIME, I THOUGHT WE WERE ABOUT THE SAME SIZE.
BUT HE'S ACTUALLY A LOT BIGGER THAN ME.
KARIN-CHAN!
I'VE FOUND YOU AT LAST.
KIRIKA-SENPAI!
I'm sorry!

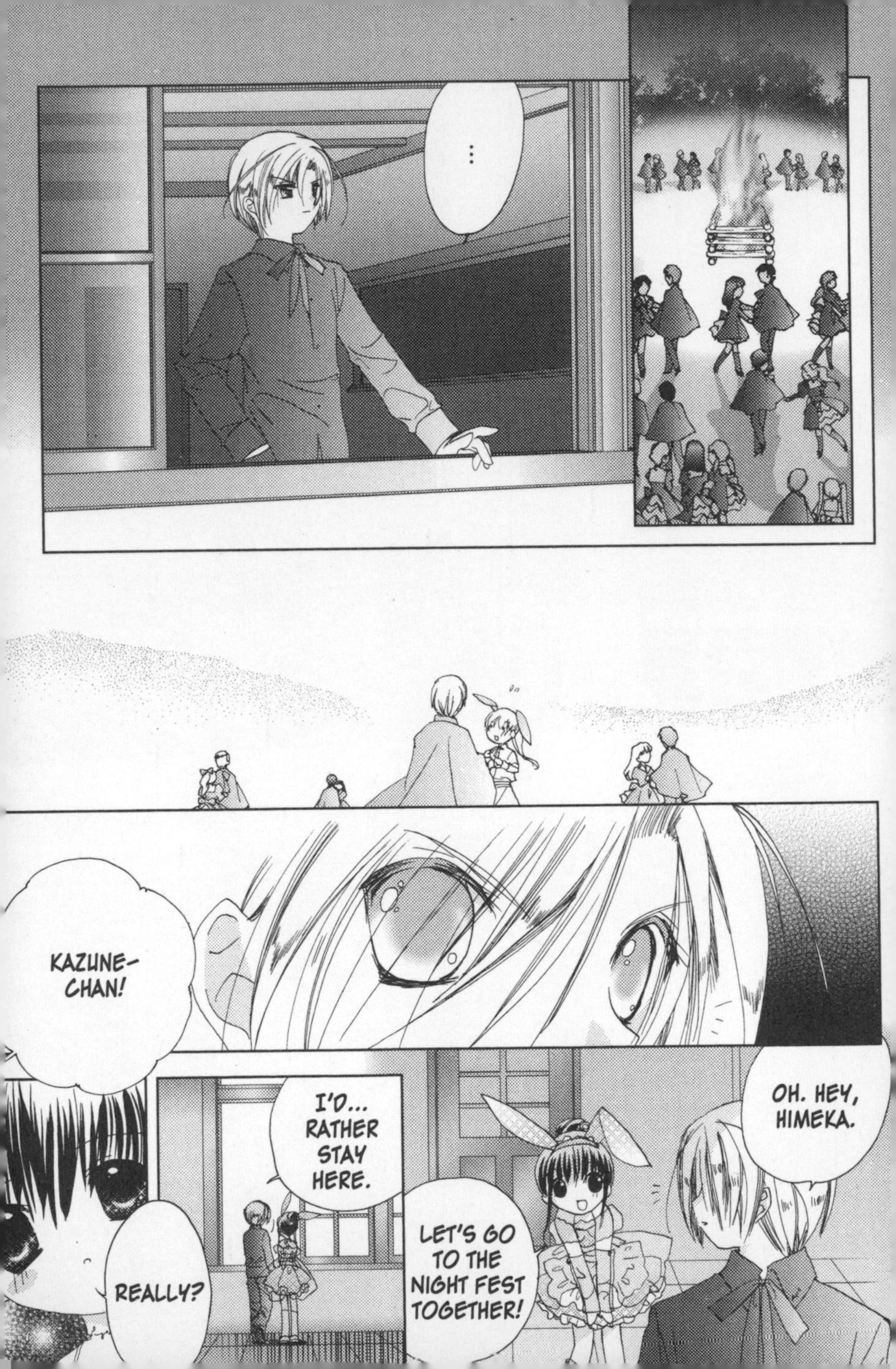
...
KAZUNE-CHAN!
OH. HEY, HIMEKA.
LET'S GO TO THE NIGHT FEST TOGETHER!
I'D... RATHER STAY HERE.
REALLY?

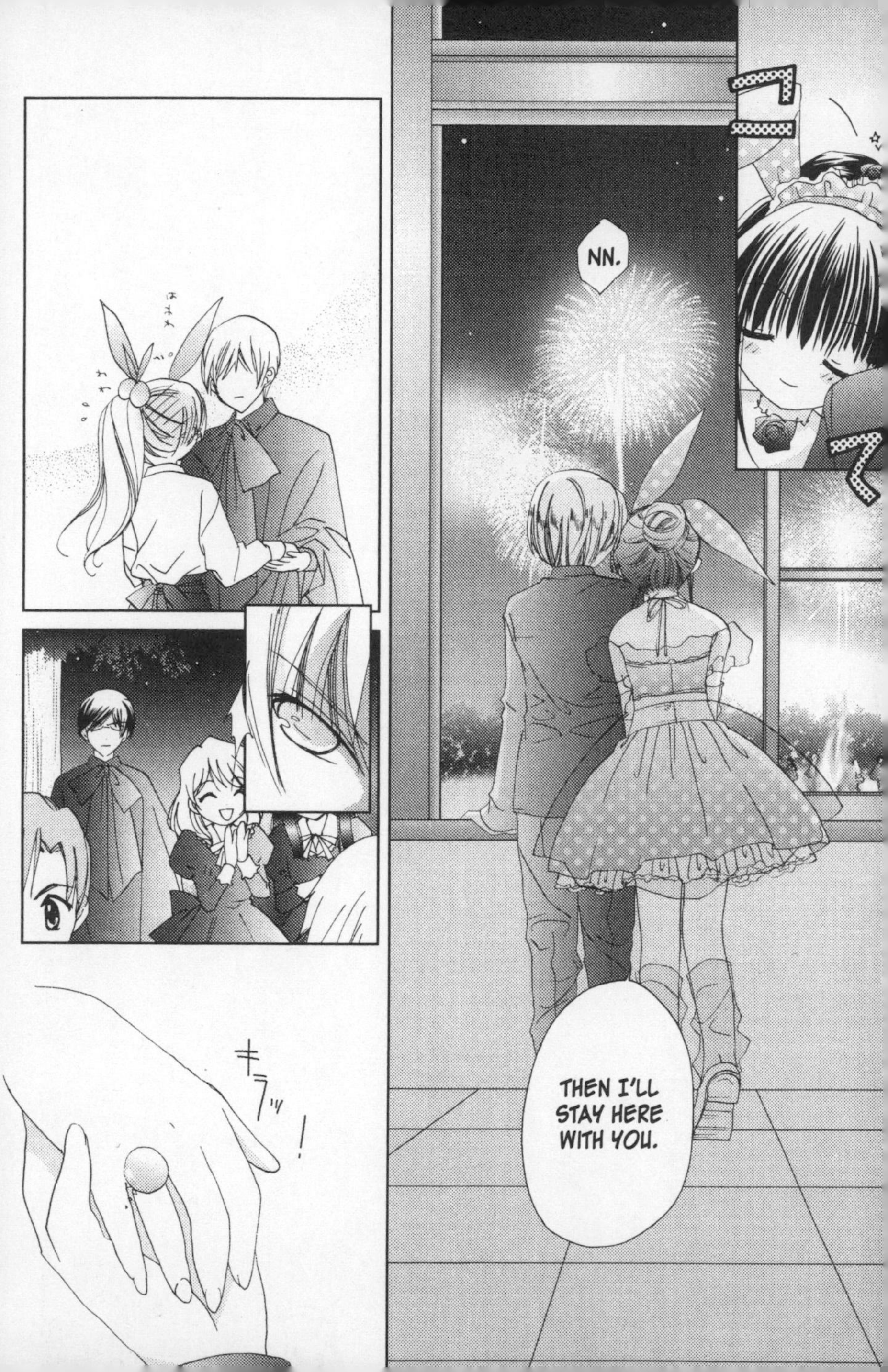
NN.
THEN I'LL STAY HERE WITH YOU.
キラッ!

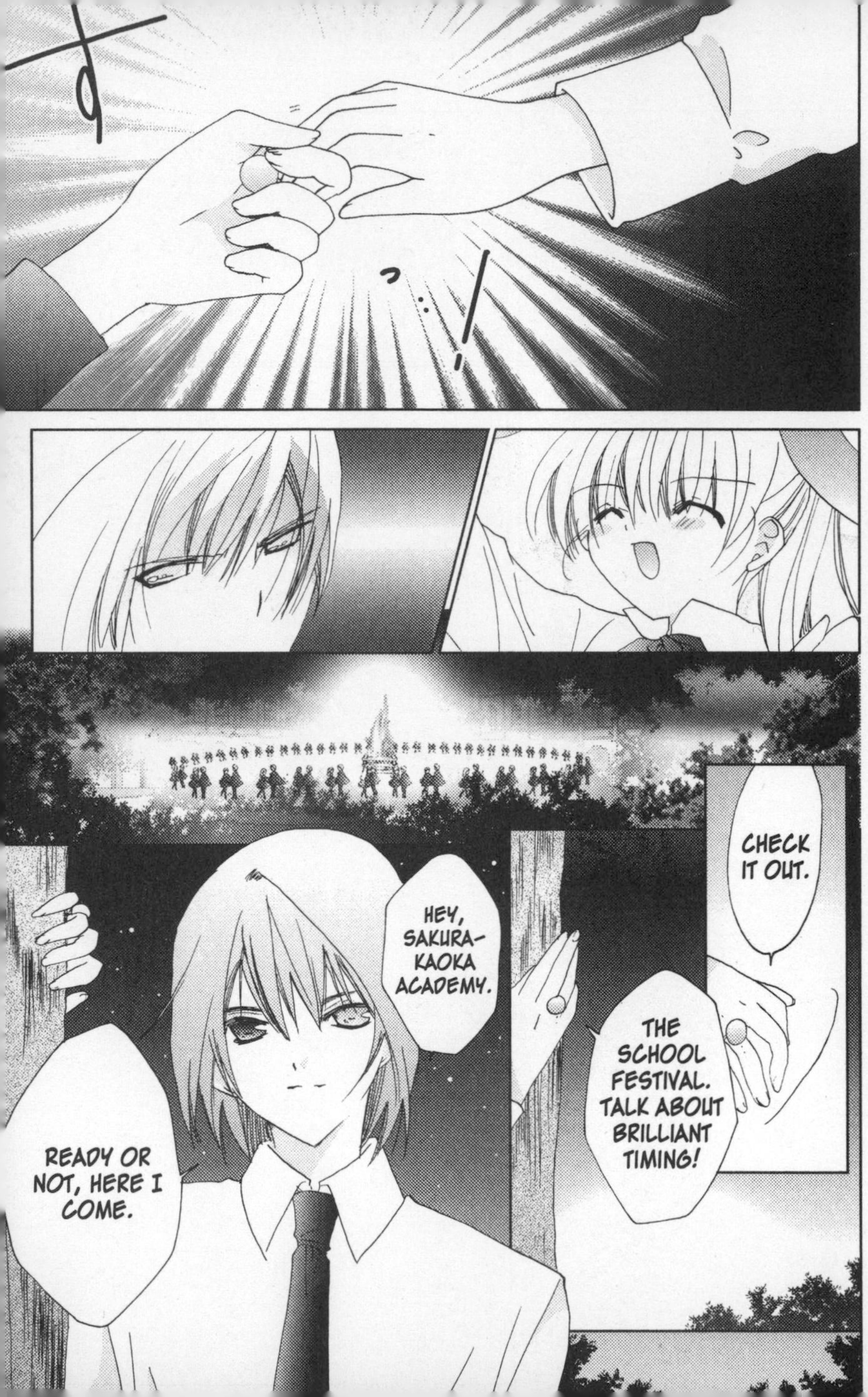
CHECK IT OUT.
THE SCHOOL FESTIVAL. TALK ABOUT BRILLIANT TIMING!
HEY, SAKURA-KAOKA ACADEMY.
READY OR NOT, HERE I COME.

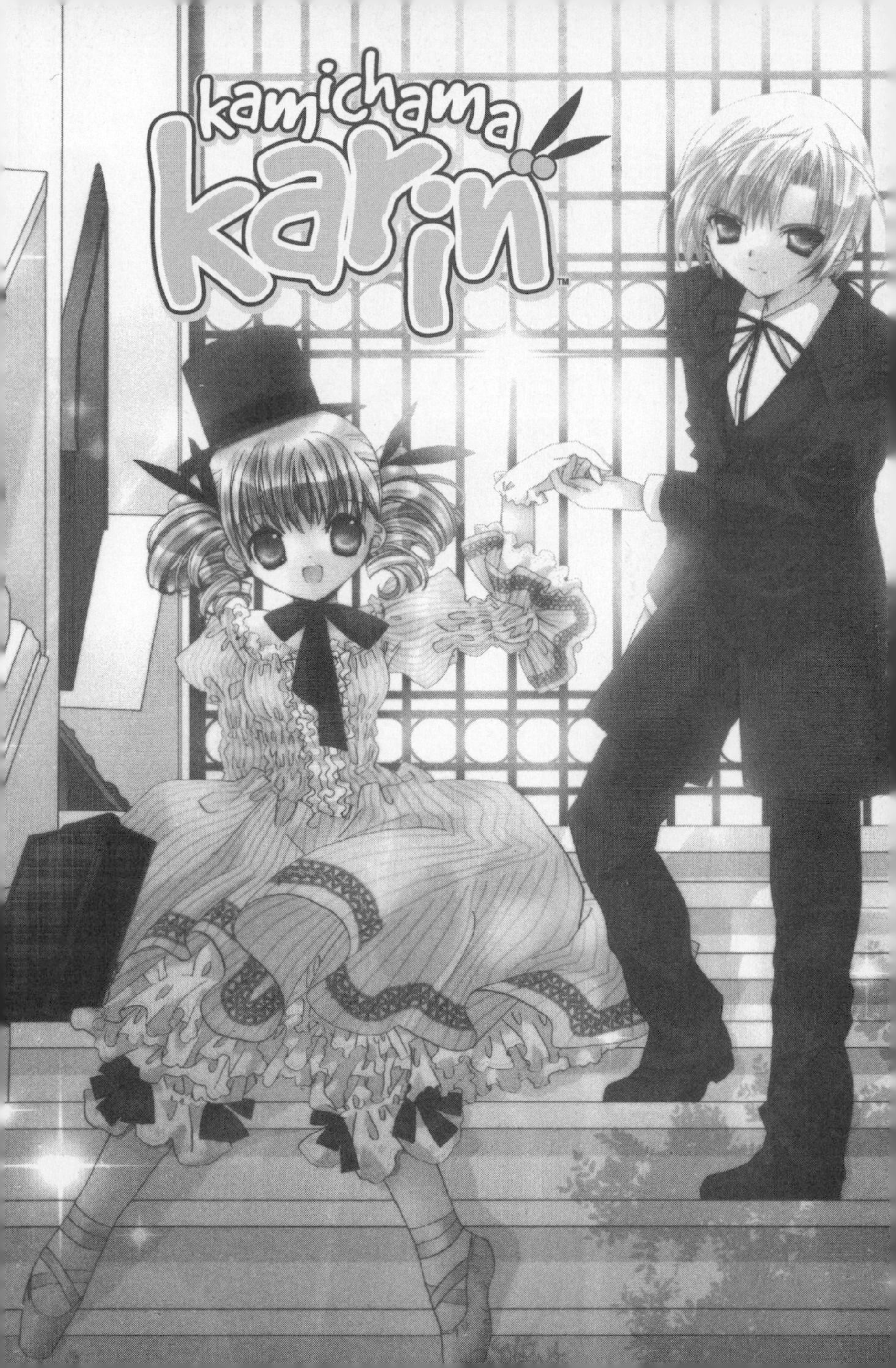
kamichama karin™

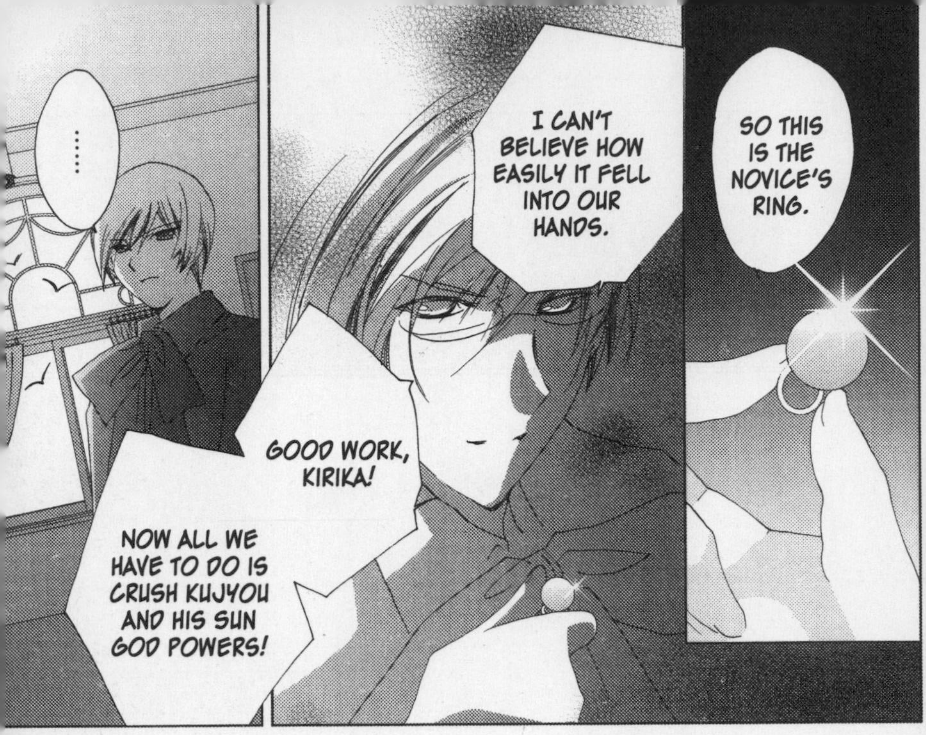
SO THIS IS THE NOVICE'S RING.
I CAN'T BELIEVE HOW EASILY IT FELL INTO OUR HANDS.
GOOD WORK, KIRIKA!
NOW ALL WE HAVE TO DO IS CRUSH KUJYOU AND HIS SUN GOD POWERS!
......
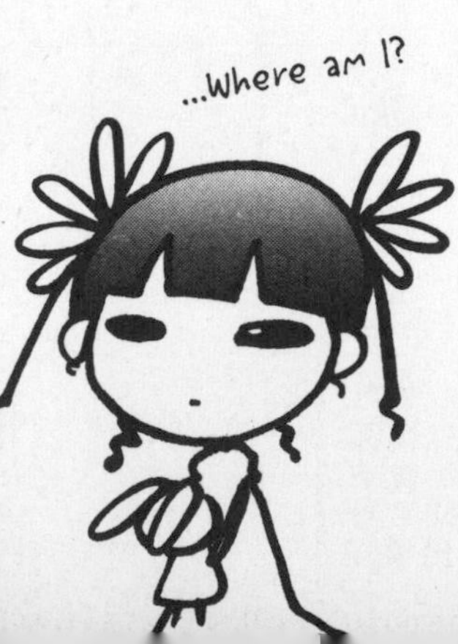
...Where am I?

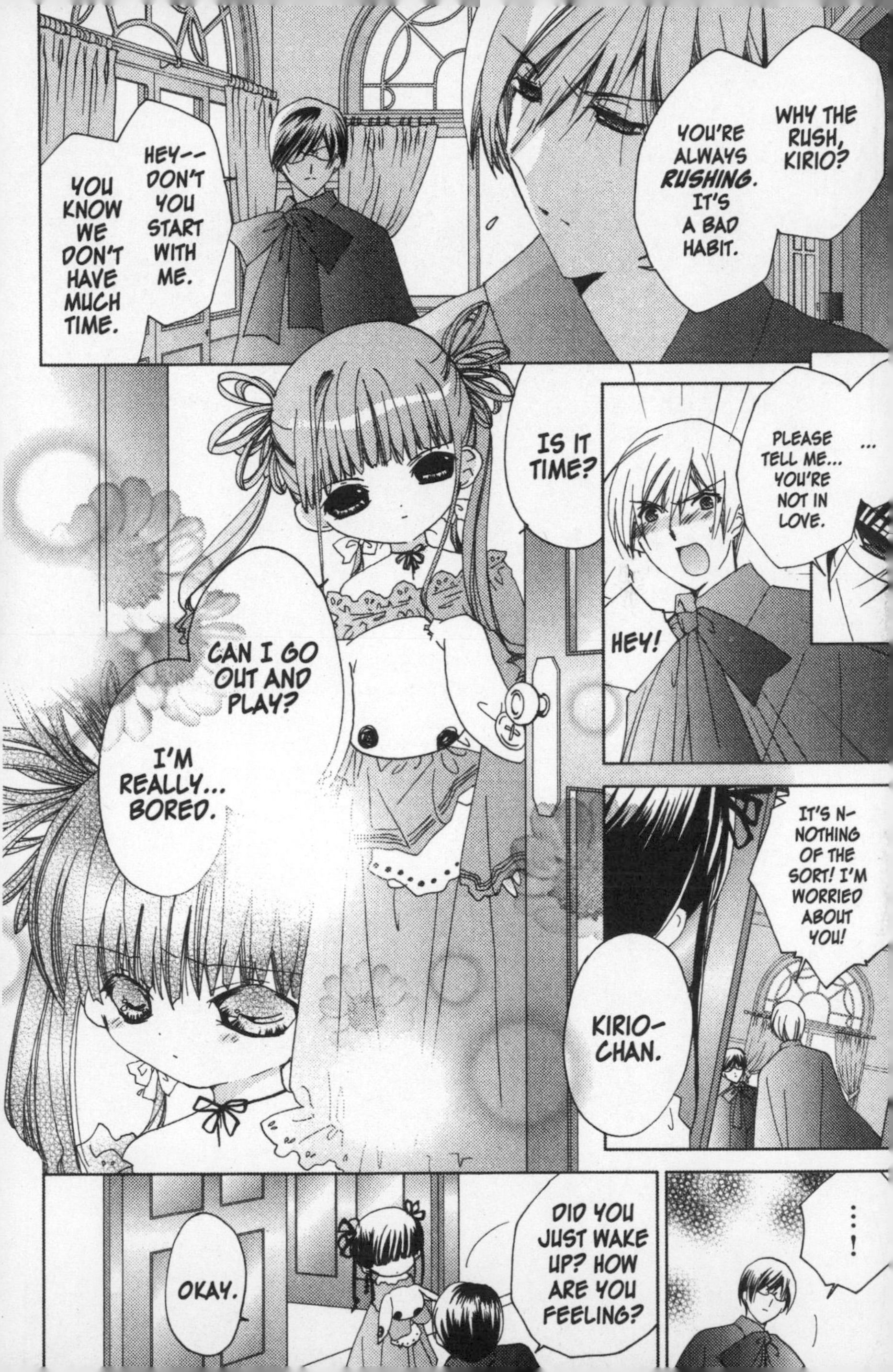
WHY THE RUSH, KIRIO?
YOU'RE ALWAYS *RUSHING*. IT'S A BAD HABIT.
HEY-- DON'T YOU START WITH ME.
YOU KNOW WE DON'T HAVE MUCH TIME.
...
PLEASE TELL ME... YOU'RE NOT IN LOVE.
HEY!
IT'S N-NOTHING OF THE SORT! I'M WORRIED ABOUT YOU!
KIRIO-CHAN.
IS IT TIME?
CAN I GO OUT AND PLAY?
I'M REALLY... BORED.
...!
DID YOU JUST WAKE UP? HOW ARE YOU FEELING?
OKAY.

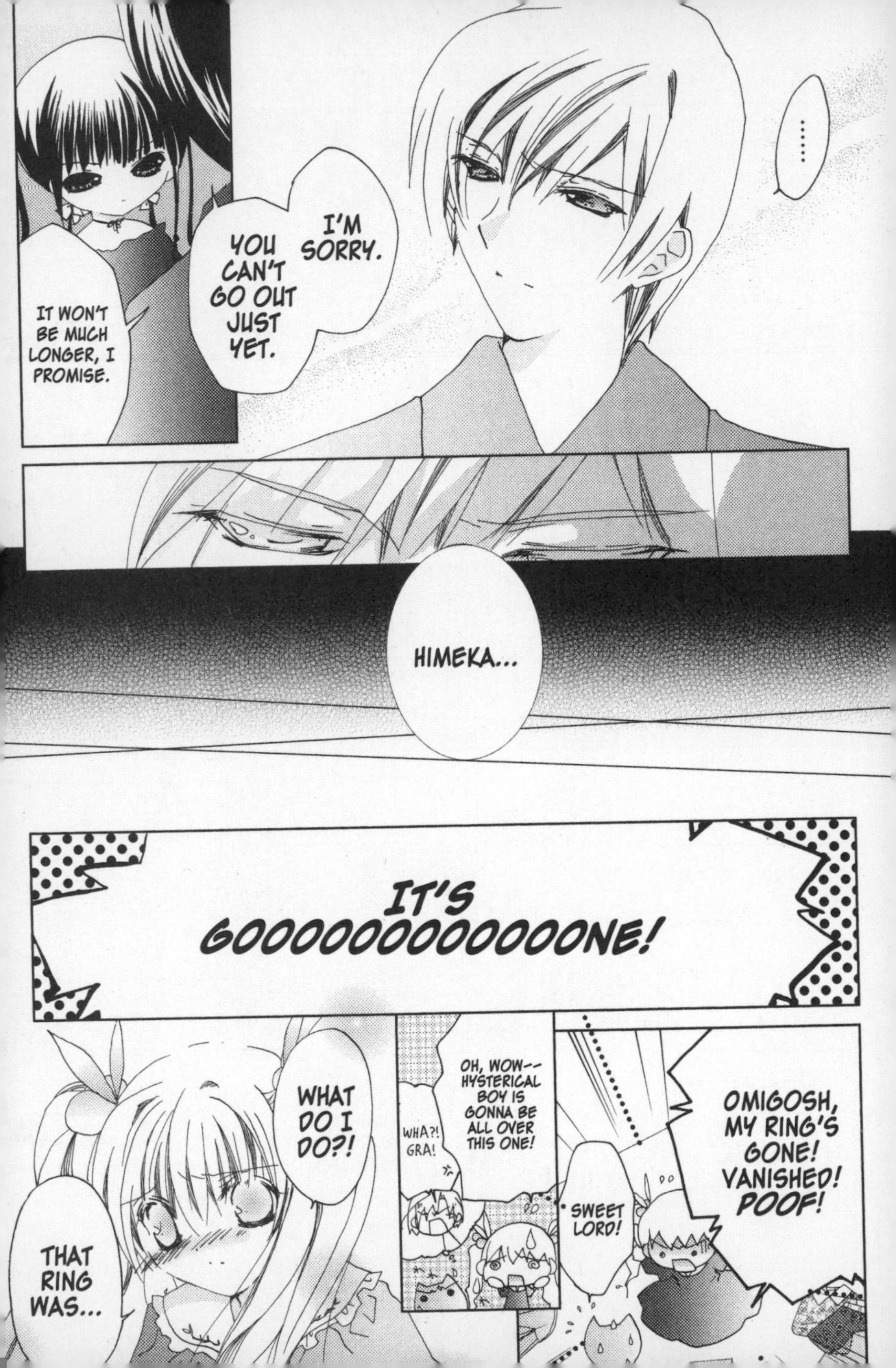
......
I'M SORRY.
YOU CAN'T GO OUT JUST YET.
IT WON'T BE MUCH LONGER, I PROMISE.
HIMEKA...
IT'S GOOOOOOOOOOONE!
OMIGOSH, MY RING'S GONE! VANISHED! POOF!
SWEET LORD!
OH, WOW-- HYSTERICAL BOY IS GONNA BE ALL OVER THIS ONE!
WHA?! GRA!
WHAT DO I DO?!
THAT RING WAS...

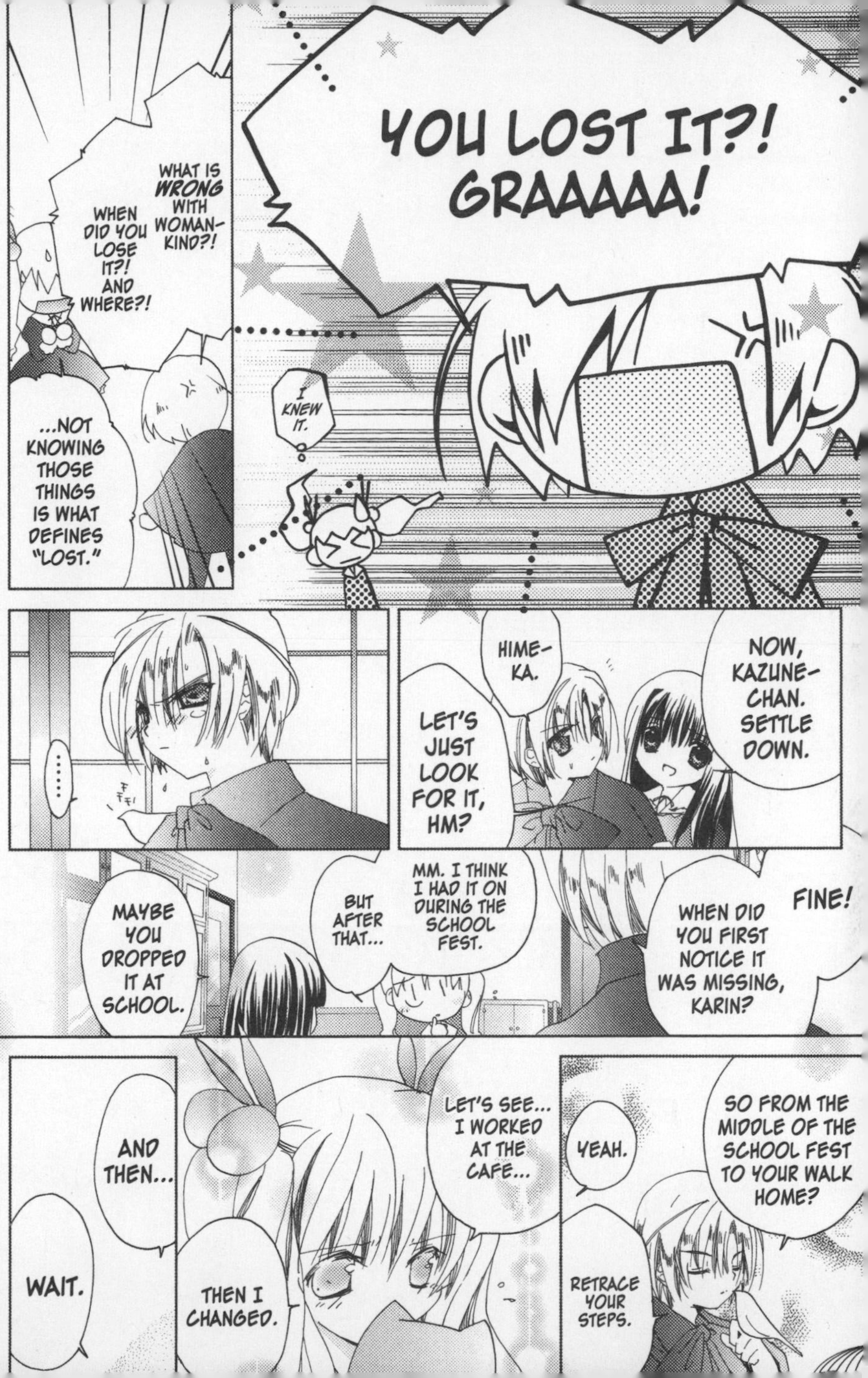
YOU LOST IT?! GRAAAAA!
I KNEW IT.
WHAT IS WRONG WITH WOMAN-KIND?!
WHEN DID YOU LOSE IT?! AND WHERE?!
...NOT KNOWING THOSE THINGS IS WHAT DEFINES "LOST."
NOW, KAZUNE-CHAN. SETTLE DOWN.
HIME-KA.
LET'S JUST LOOK FOR IT, HM?
......
FINE!
WHEN DID YOU FIRST NOTICE IT WAS MISSING, KARIN?
MM. I THINK I HAD IT ON DURING THE SCHOOL FEST.
BUT AFTER THAT...
MAYBE YOU DROPPED IT AT SCHOOL.
SO FROM THE MIDDLE OF THE SCHOOL FEST TO YOUR WALK HOME?
YEAH.
RETRACE YOUR STEPS.
LET'S SEE... I WORKED AT THE CAFE...
THEN I CHANGED.
AND THEN...
WAIT.

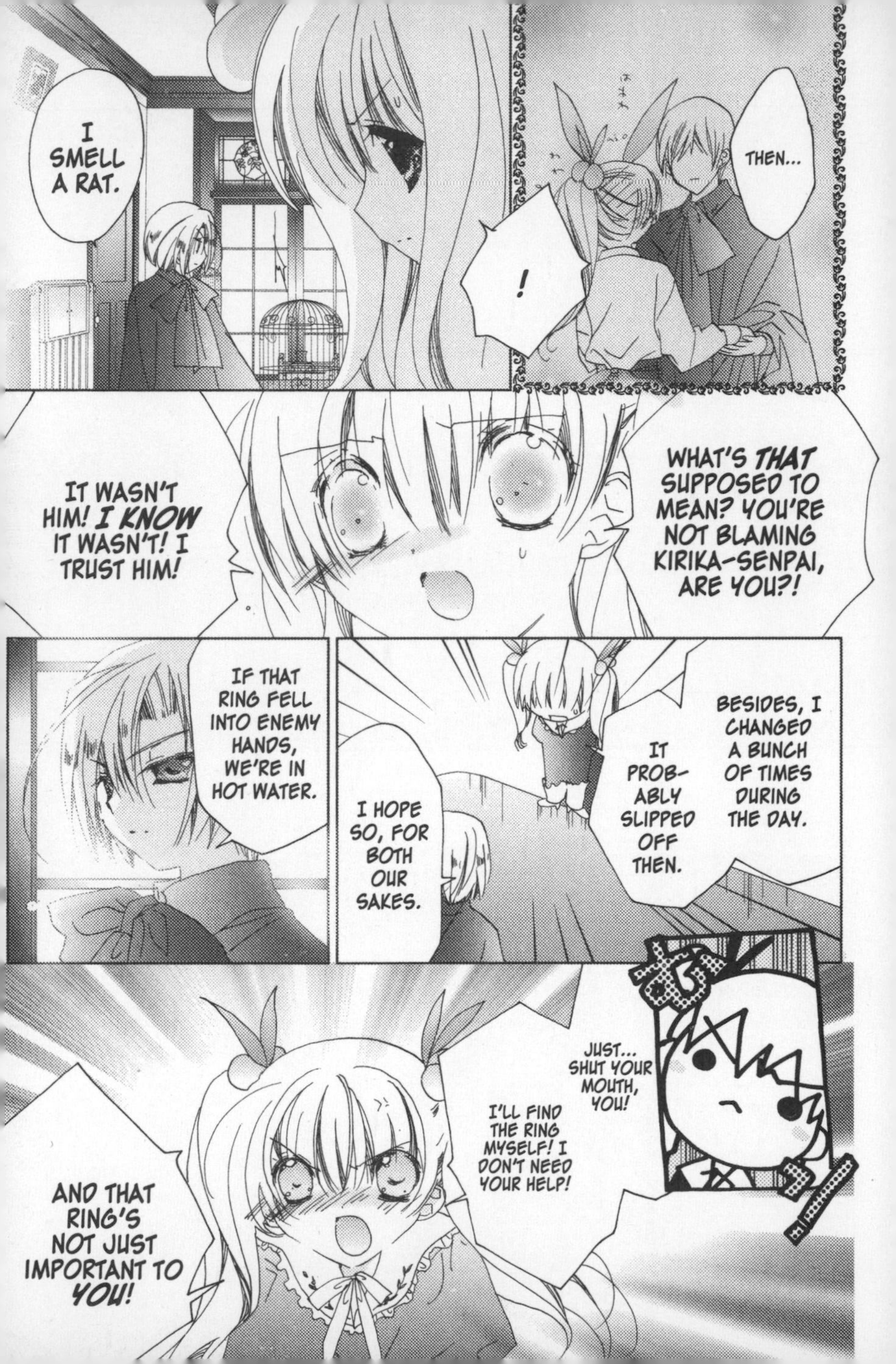
THEN...
!
I SMELL A RAT.
WHAT'S THAT SUPPOSED TO MEAN? YOU'RE NOT BLAMING KIRIKA-SENPAI, ARE YOU?!
IT WASN'T HIM! I KNOW IT WASN'T! I TRUST HIM!
BESIDES, I CHANGED A BUNCH OF TIMES DURING THE DAY.
IT PROBABLY SLIPPED OFF THEN.
I HOPE SO, FOR BOTH OUR SAKES.
IF THAT RING FELL INTO ENEMY HANDS, WE'RE IN HOT WATER.
JUST... SHUT YOUR MOUTH, YOU!
I'LL FIND THE RING MYSELF! I DON'T NEED YOUR HELP!
AND THAT RING'S NOT JUST IMPORTANT TO YOU!

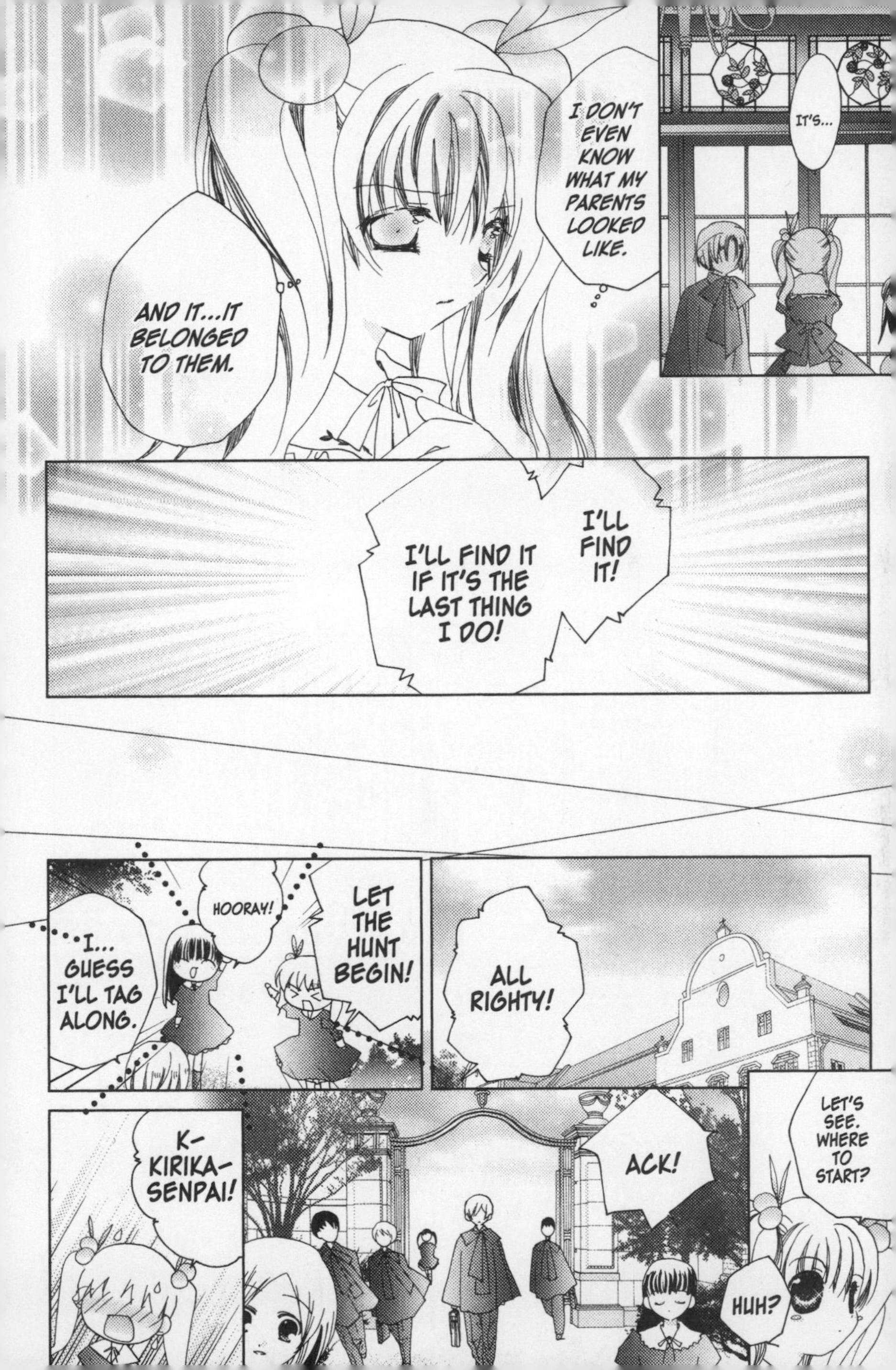
IT'S...
I DON'T EVEN KNOW WHAT MY PARENTS LOOKED LIKE.
AND IT...IT BELONGED TO THEM.
I'LL FIND IT!
I'LL FIND IT IF IT'S THE LAST THING I DO!
ALL RIGHTY!
LET THE HUNT BEGIN!
HOORAY!
I... GUESS I'LL TAG ALONG.
LET'S SEE. WHERE TO START?
HUH?
ACK!
K-KIRIKA-SENPAI!

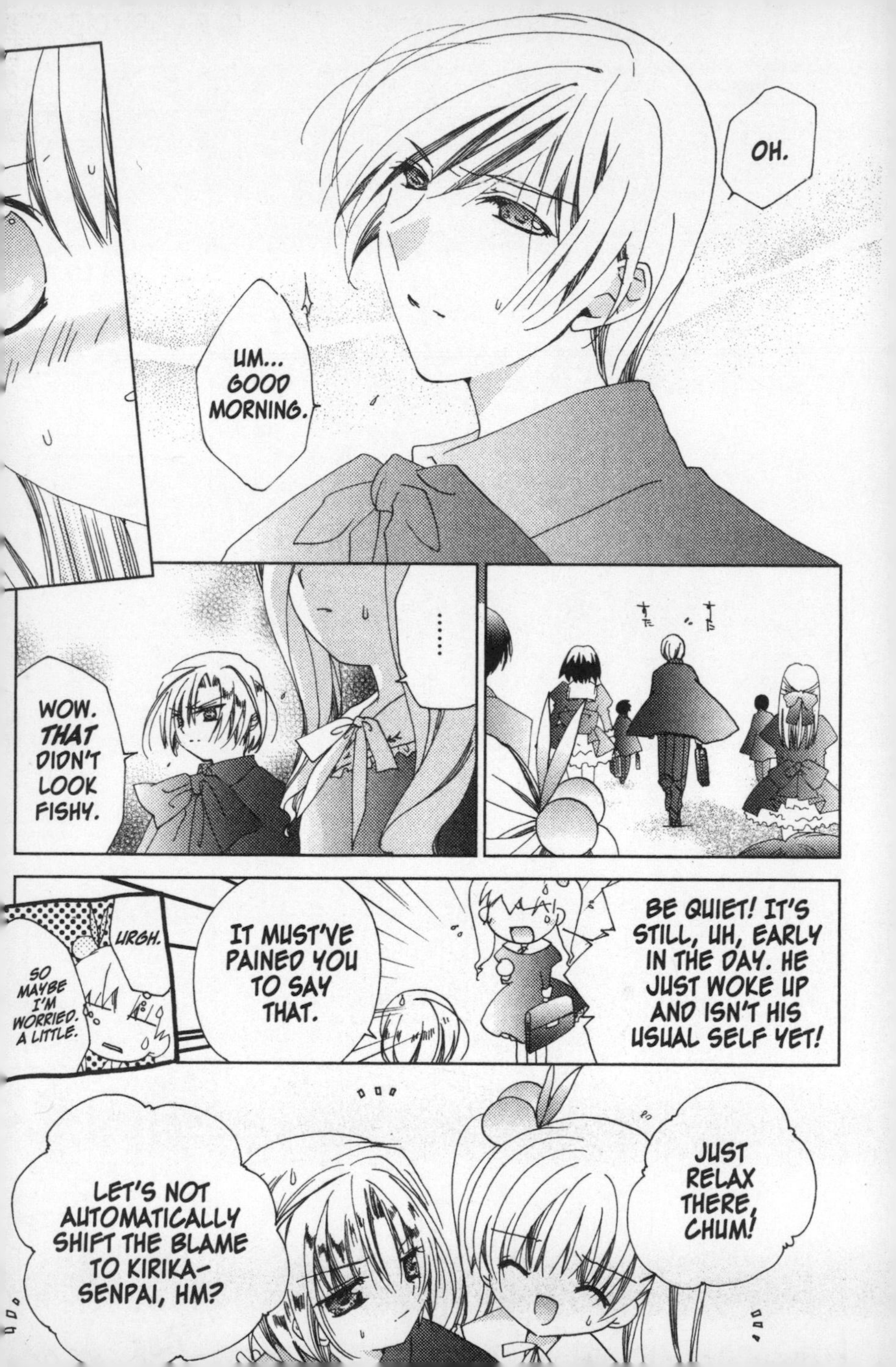
OH.
UM... GOOD MORNING.
......
WOW. *THAT* DIDN'T LOOK FISHY.
BE QUIET! IT'S STILL, UH, EARLY IN THE DAY. HE JUST WOKE UP AND ISN'T HIS USUAL SELF YET!
IT MUST'VE PAINED YOU TO SAY THAT.
URGH.
SO MAYBE I'M WORRIED. A LITTLE.
JUST RELAX THERE, CHUM!
LET'S NOT AUTOMATICALLY SHIFT THE BLAME TO KIRIKA-SENPAI, HM?

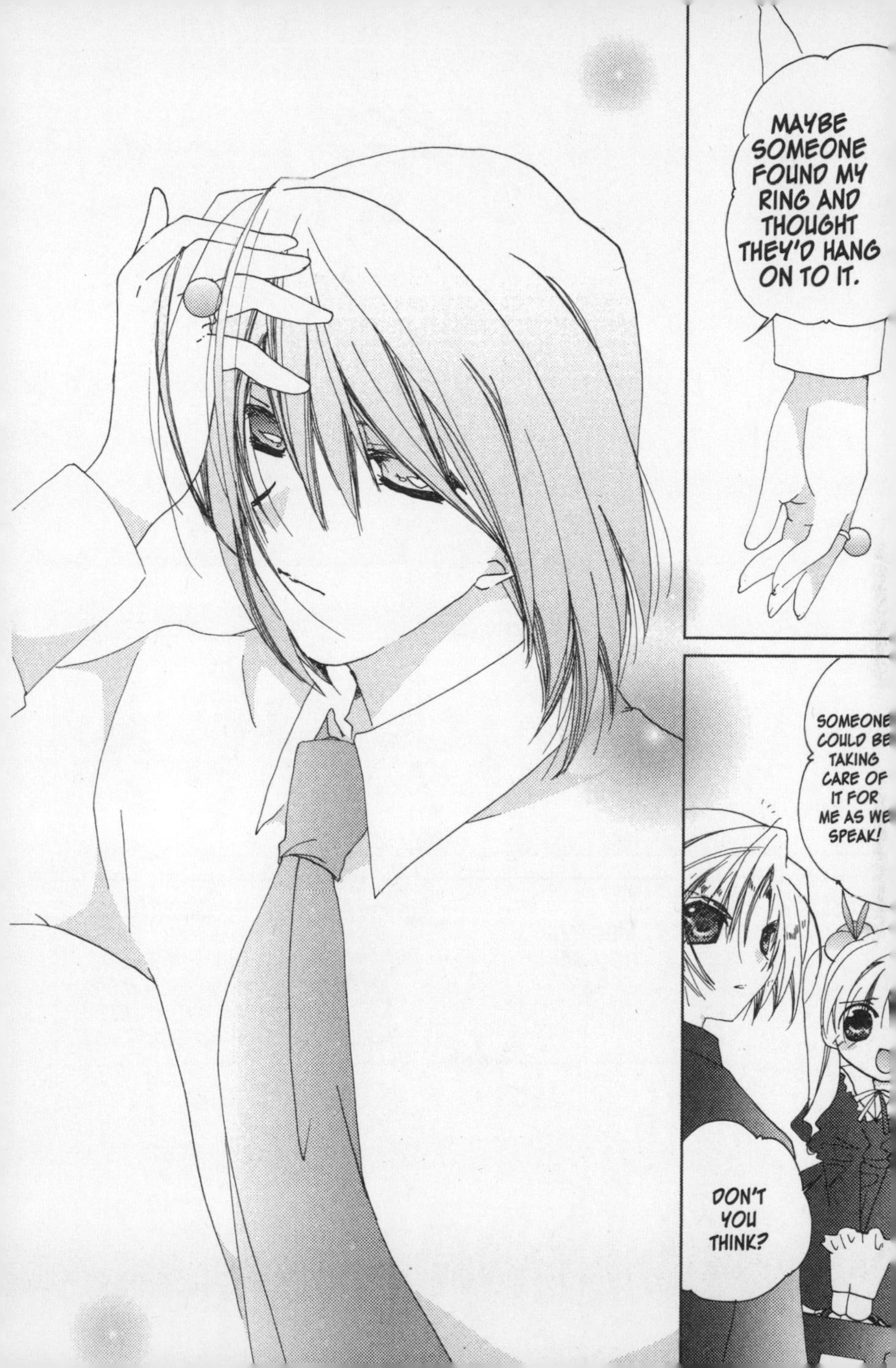
MAYBE SOMEONE FOUND MY RING AND THOUGHT THEY'D HANG ON TO IT.
SOMEONE COULD BE TAKING CARE OF IT FOR ME AS WE SPEAK!
DON'T YOU THINK?

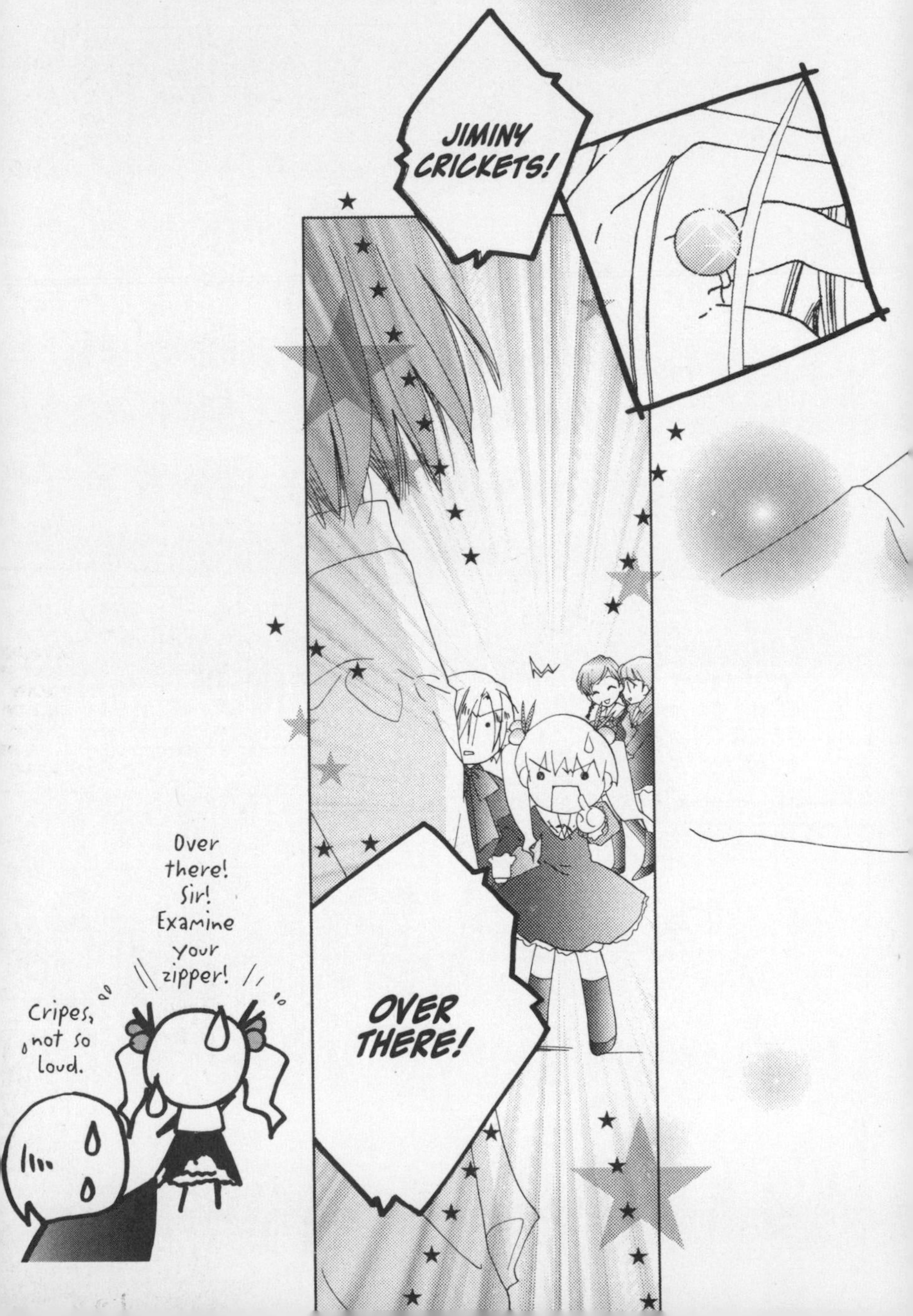
JIMINY CRICKETS!
OVER THERE!
Over there! Sir! Examine your zipper!
Cripes, not so loud.

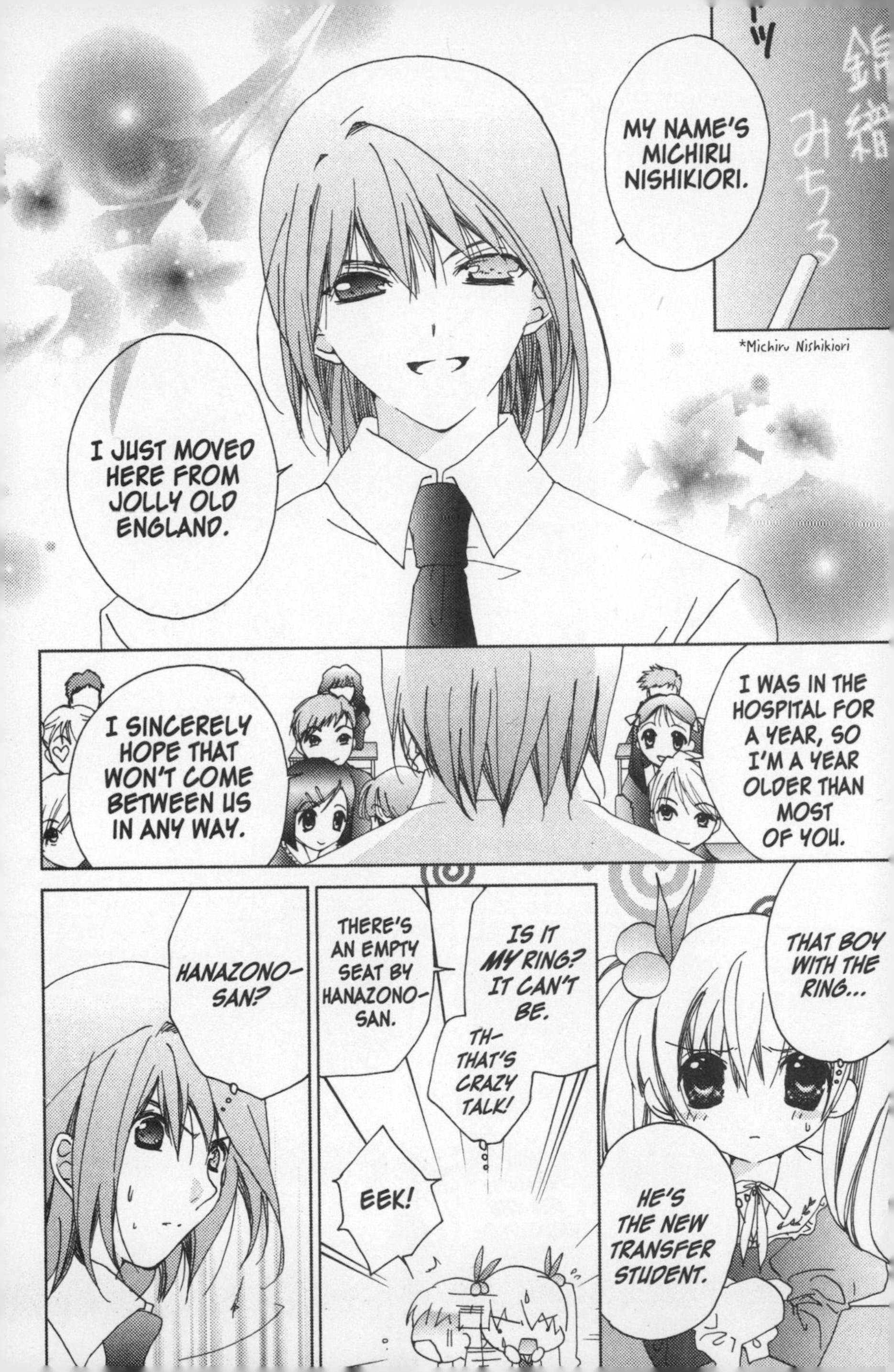
錦織みちる
MY NAME'S MICHIRU NISHIKIORI.
*Michiru Nishikiori
I JUST MOVED HERE FROM JOLLY OLD ENGLAND.
I WAS IN THE HOSPITAL FOR A YEAR, SO I'M A YEAR OLDER THAN MOST OF YOU.
I SINCERELY HOPE THAT WON'T COME BETWEEN US IN ANY WAY.
THAT BOY WITH THE RING...
HE'S THE NEW TRANSFER STUDENT.
IS IT MY RING? IT CAN'T BE.
THERE'S AN EMPTY SEAT BY HANAZONO-SAN.
TH-THAT'S CRAZY TALK!
EEK!
HANAZONO-SAN?

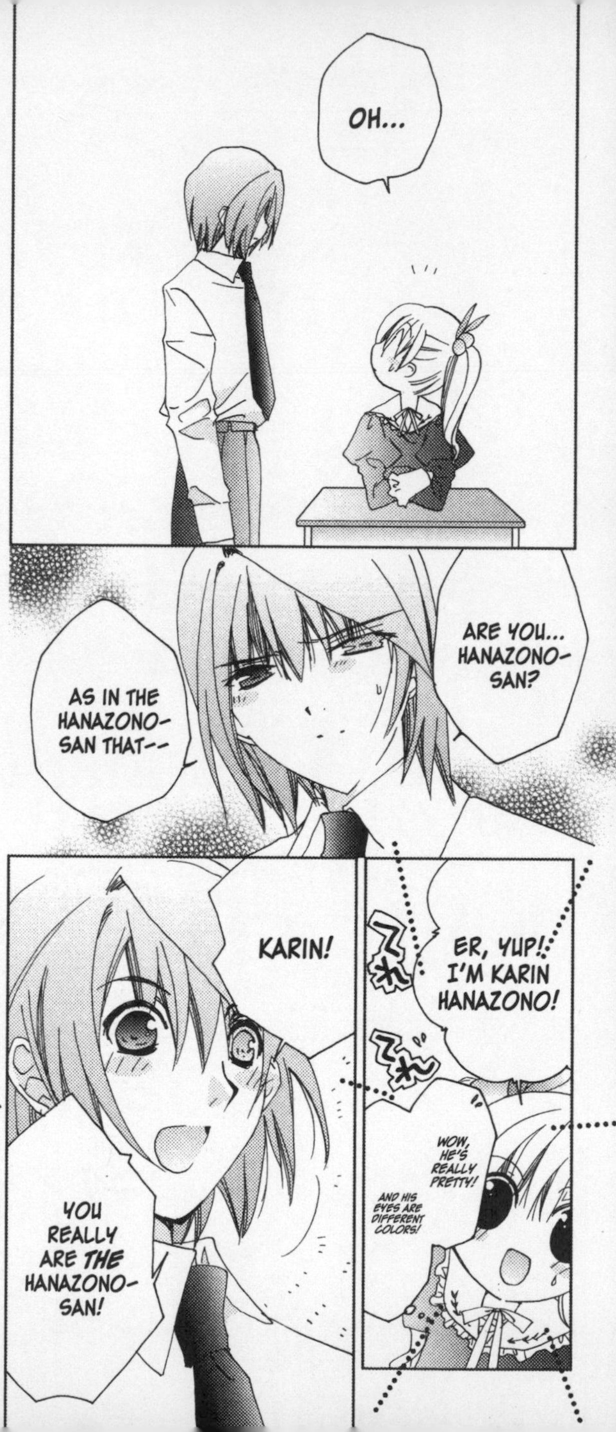
OH...
ARE YOU... HANAZONO-SAN?
AS IN THE HANAZONO-SAN THAT--
ER, YUP!! I'M KARIN HANAZONO!
WOW, HE'S REALLY PRETTY!
AND HIS EYES ARE DIFFERENT COLORS!
KARIN!
YOU REALLY ARE *THE* HANAZONO-SAN!

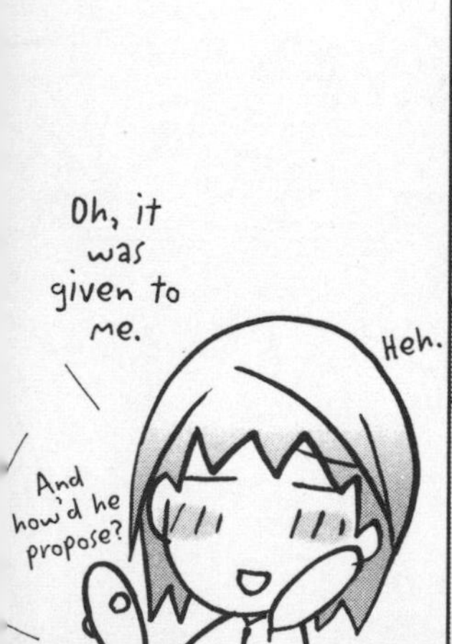
Oh, it was given to me.
Heh.
And how'd he propose?

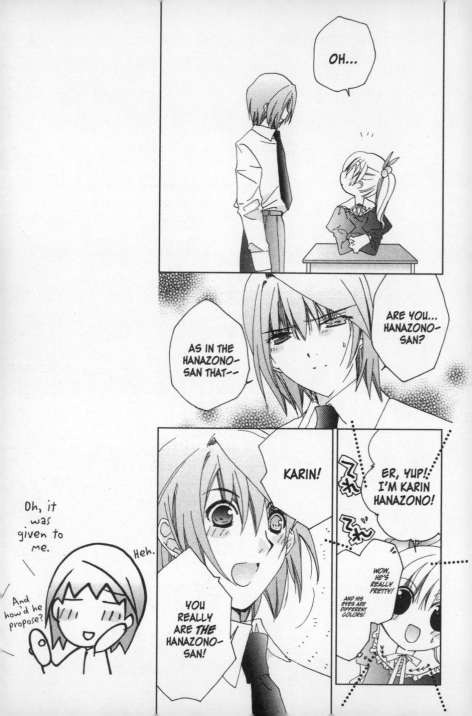

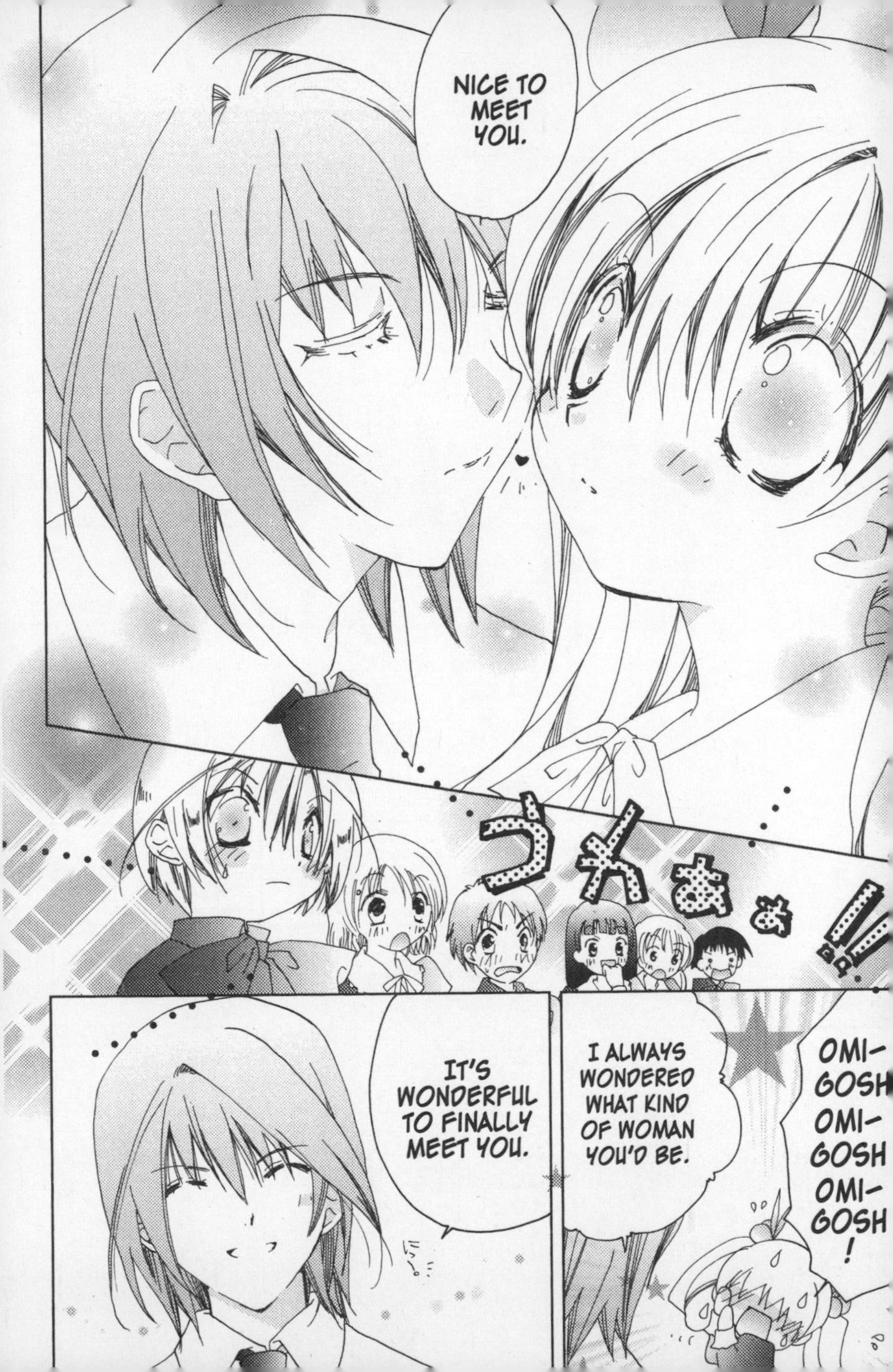
NICE TO MEET YOU.
うわぁぁ!!
OMI-GOSH OMI-GOSH OMI-GOSH!
I ALWAYS WONDERED WHAT KIND OF WOMAN YOU'D BE.
IT'S WONDERFUL TO FINALLY MEET YOU.

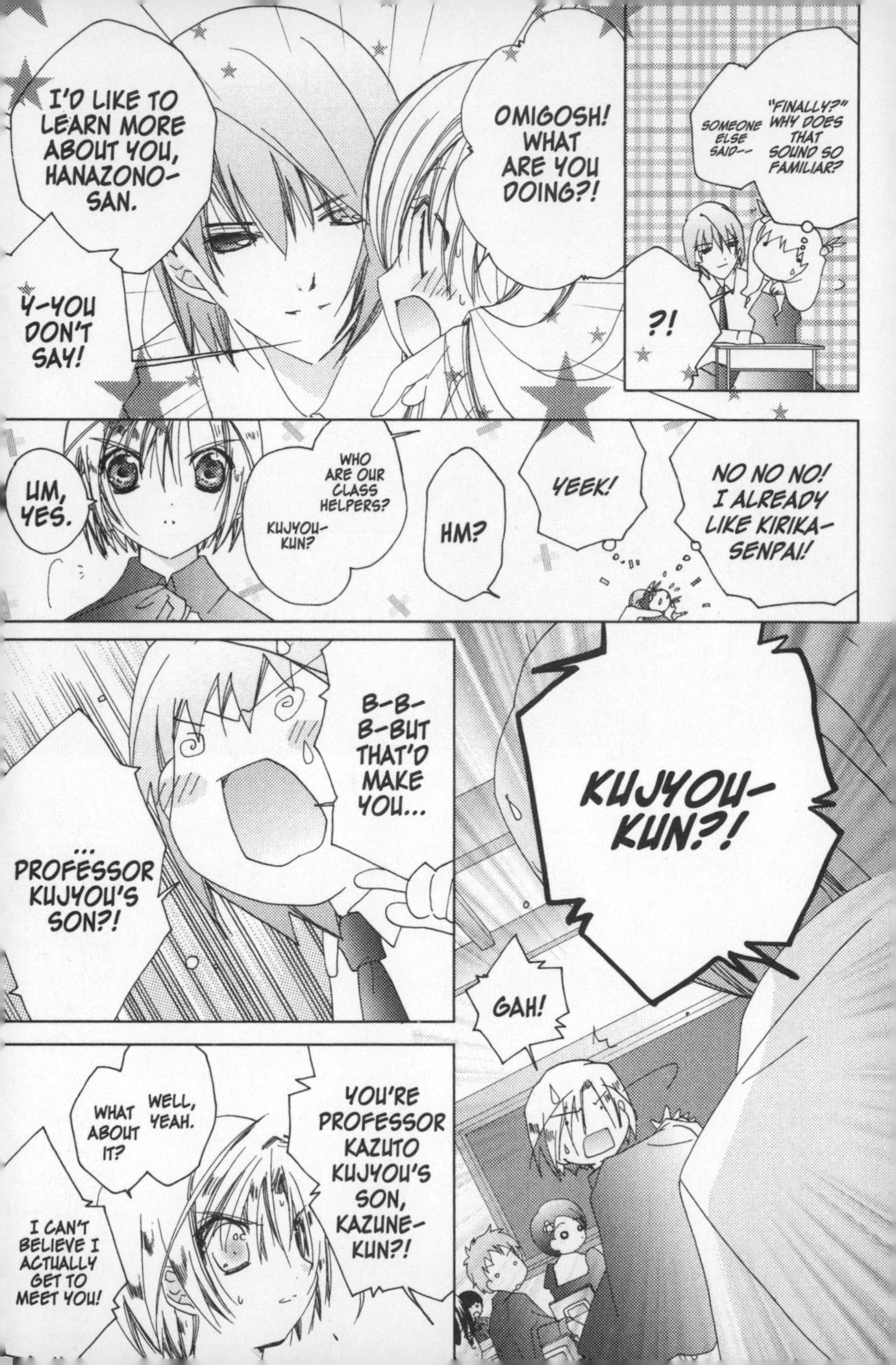
"FINALLY?" WHY DOES THAT SOUND SO FAMILIAR?
SOMEONE ELSE SAID--
?!
OMIGOSH! WHAT ARE YOU DOING?!
I'D LIKE TO LEARN MORE ABOUT YOU, HANAZONO-SAN.
Y-YOU DON'T SAY!
NO NO NO! I ALREADY LIKE KIRIKA-SENPAI!
YEEK!
HM?
WHO ARE OUR CLASS HELPERS?
KUJYOU-KUN?
UM, YES.
KUJYOU-KUN?!
GAH!
B-B-B-BUT THAT'D MAKE YOU...
...PROFESSOR KUJYOU'S SON?!
YOU'RE PROFESSOR KAZUTO KUJYOU'S SON, KAZUNE-KUN?!
WELL, YEAH.
WHAT ABOUT IT?
I CAN'T BELIEVE I ACTUALLY GET TO MEET YOU!

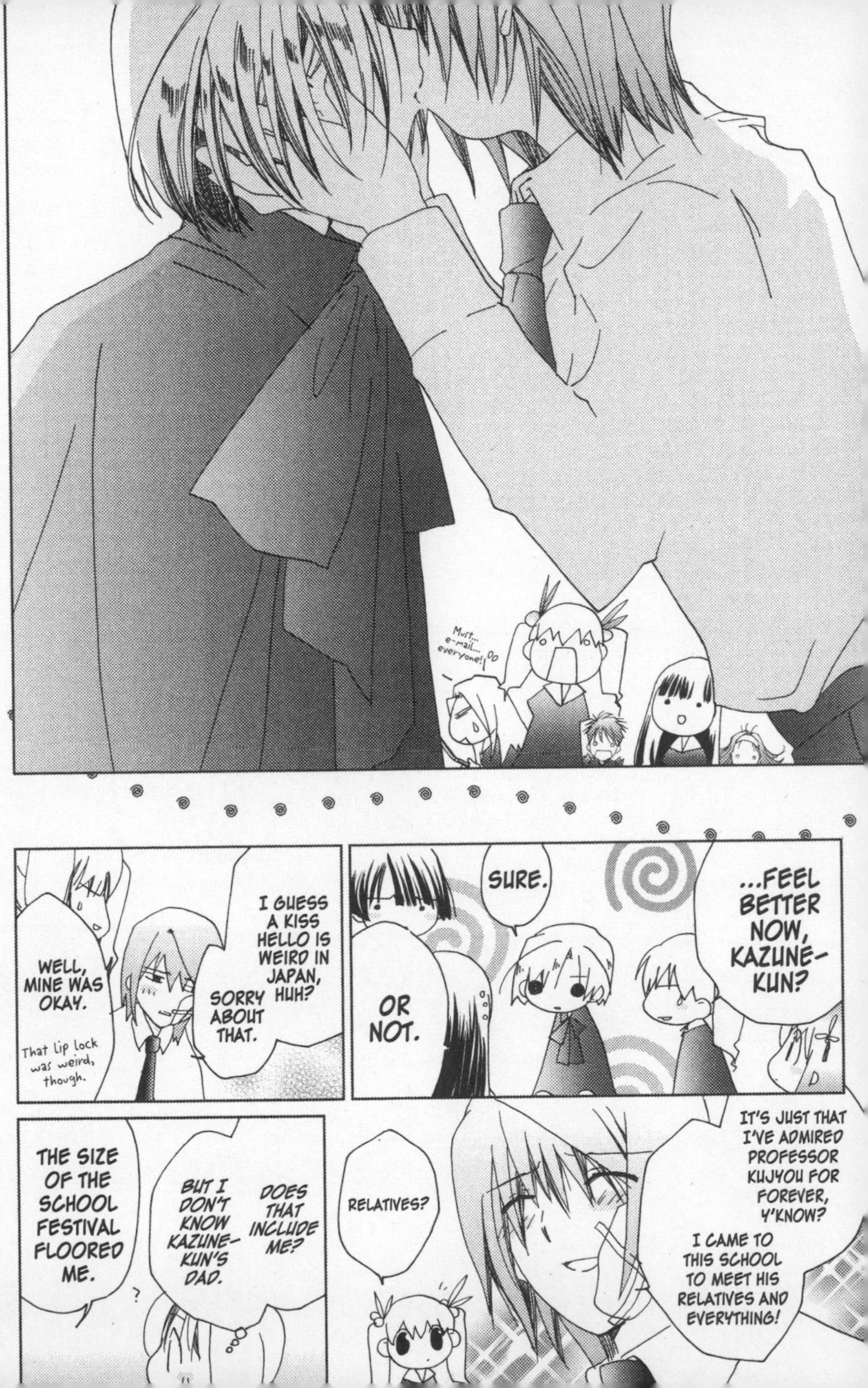
Must... e-mail... everyone!
...FEEL BETTER NOW, KAZUNE-KUN?
SURE.
OR NOT.
I GUESS A KISS HELLO IS WEIRD IN JAPAN, HUH?
SORRY ABOUT THAT.
WELL, MINE WAS OKAY.
That lip lock was weird, though.
IT'S JUST THAT I'VE ADMIRED PROFESSOR KUJYOU FOR FOREVER, Y'KNOW?
I CAME TO THIS SCHOOL TO MEET HIS RELATIVES AND EVERYTHING!
RELATIVES?
DOES THAT INCLUDE ME?
BUT I DON'T KNOW KAZUNE-KUN'S DAD.
THE SIZE OF THE SCHOOL FESTIVAL FLOORED ME.

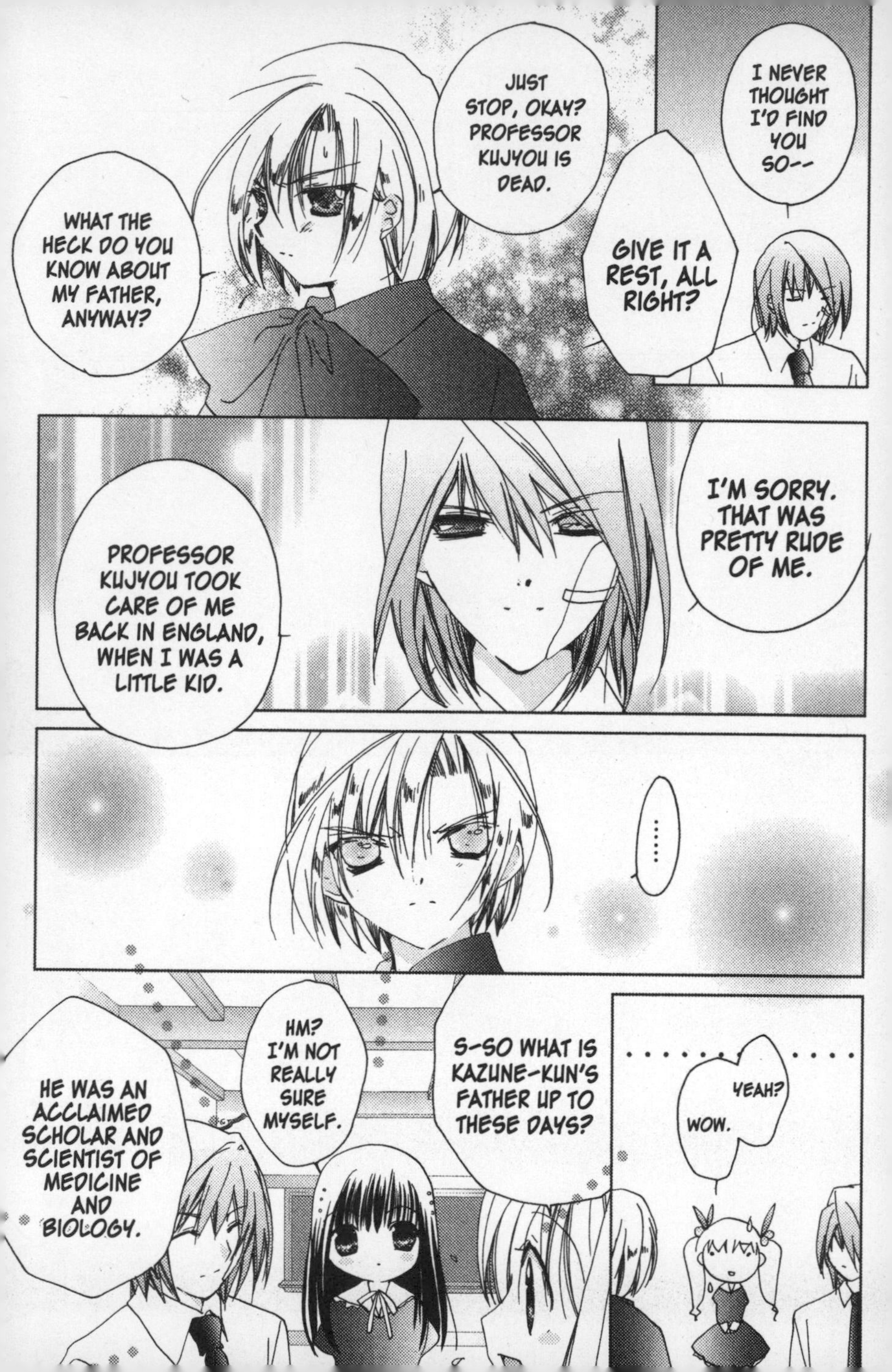
I NEVER THOUGHT I'D FIND YOU SO--
GIVE IT A REST, ALL RIGHT?
JUST STOP, OKAY? PROFESSOR KUJYOU IS DEAD.
WHAT THE HECK DO YOU KNOW ABOUT MY FATHER, ANYWAY?
I'M SORRY. THAT WAS PRETTY RUDE OF ME.
PROFESSOR KUJYOU TOOK CARE OF ME BACK IN ENGLAND, WHEN I WAS A LITTLE KID.
......
....
YEAH?
WOW.
S-SO WHAT IS KAZUNE-KUN'S FATHER UP TO THESE DAYS?
HM? I'M NOT REALLY SURE MYSELF.
HE WAS AN ACCLAIMED SCHOLAR AND SCIENTIST OF MEDICINE AND BIOLOGY.

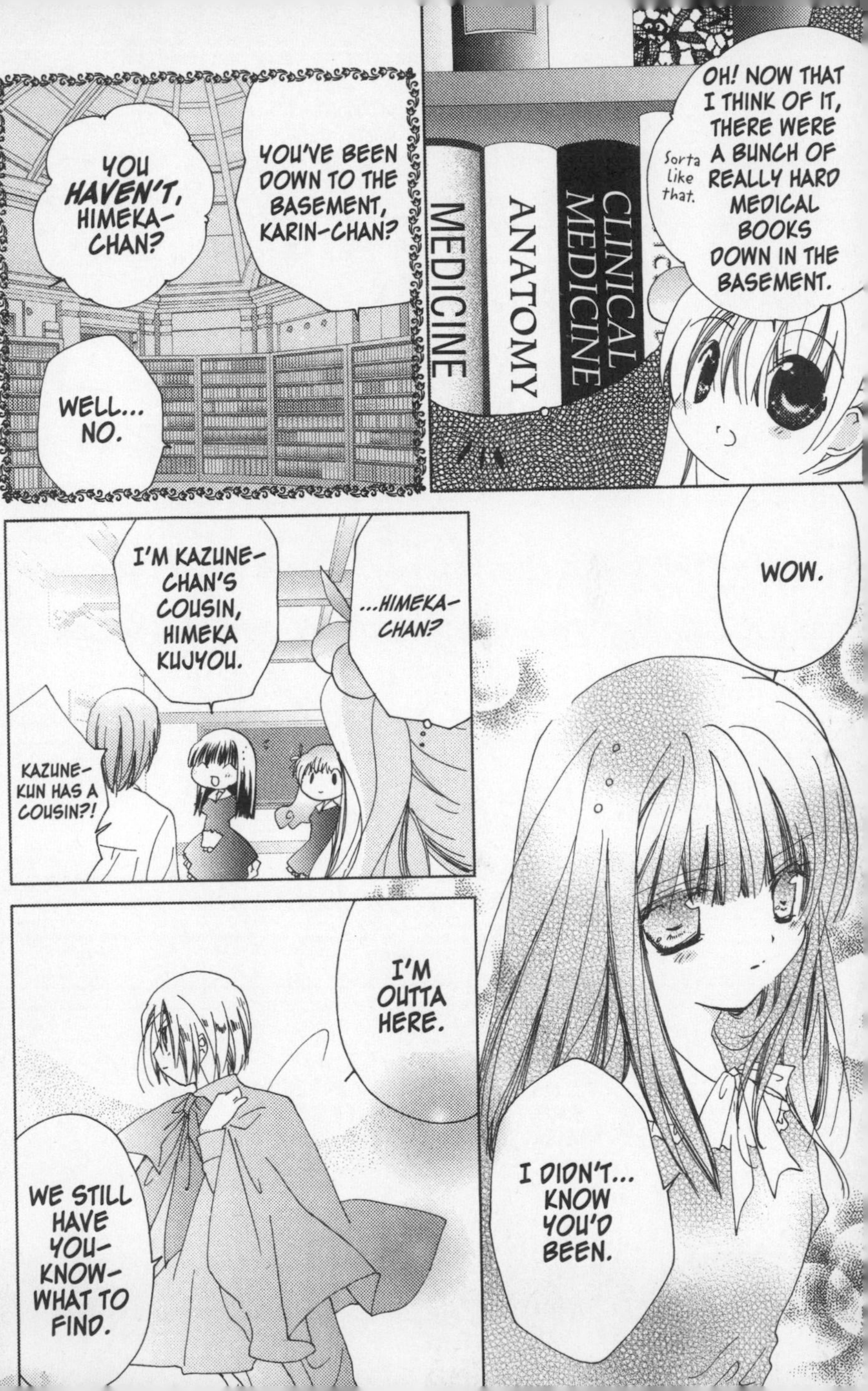
OH! NOW THAT I THINK OF IT, THERE WERE A BUNCH OF REALLY HARD MEDICAL BOOKS DOWN IN THE BASEMENT.
Sorta like that.
CLINICAL MEDICINE
ANATOMY
MEDICINE
YOU'VE BEEN DOWN TO THE BASEMENT, KARIN-CHAN?
YOU *HAVEN'T*, HIMEKA-CHAN?
WELL... NO.
WOW.
I DIDN'T... KNOW YOU'D BEEN.
...HIMEKA-CHAN?
I'M KAZUNE-CHAN'S COUSIN, HIMEKA KUJYOU.
KAZUNE-KUN HAS A COUSIN?!
I'M OUTTA HERE.
WE STILL HAVE YOU-KNOW-WHAT TO FIND.

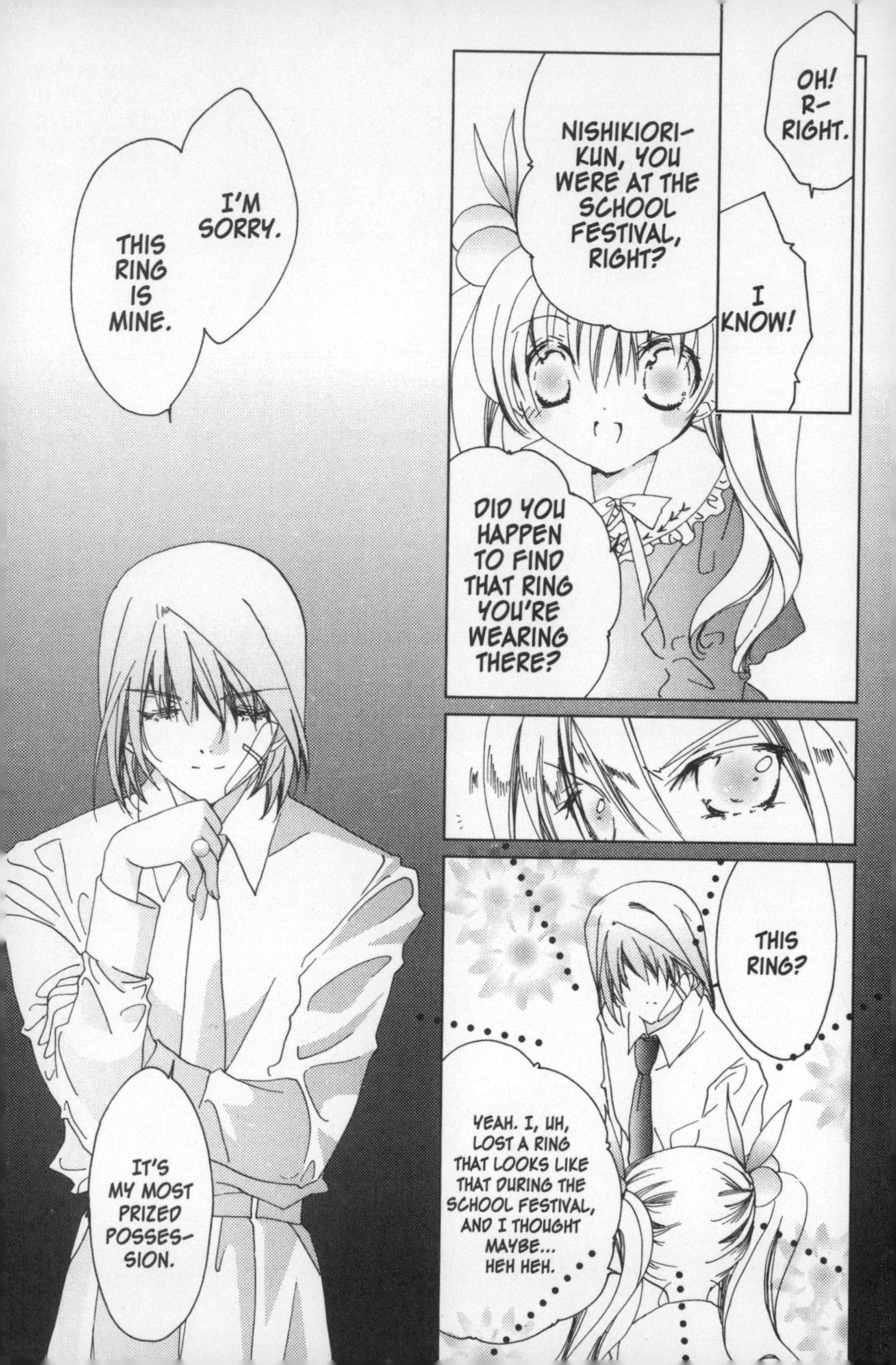
OH! R-RIGHT.
I KNOW!
NISHIKIORI-KUN, YOU WERE AT THE SCHOOL FESTIVAL, RIGHT?
DID YOU HAPPEN TO FIND THAT RING YOU'RE WEARING THERE?
THIS RING?
YEAH. I, UH, LOST A RING THAT LOOKS LIKE THAT DURING THE SCHOOL FESTIVAL, AND I THOUGHT MAYBE... HEH HEH.
I'M SORRY.
THIS RING IS MINE.
IT'S MY MOST PRIZED POSSESSION.

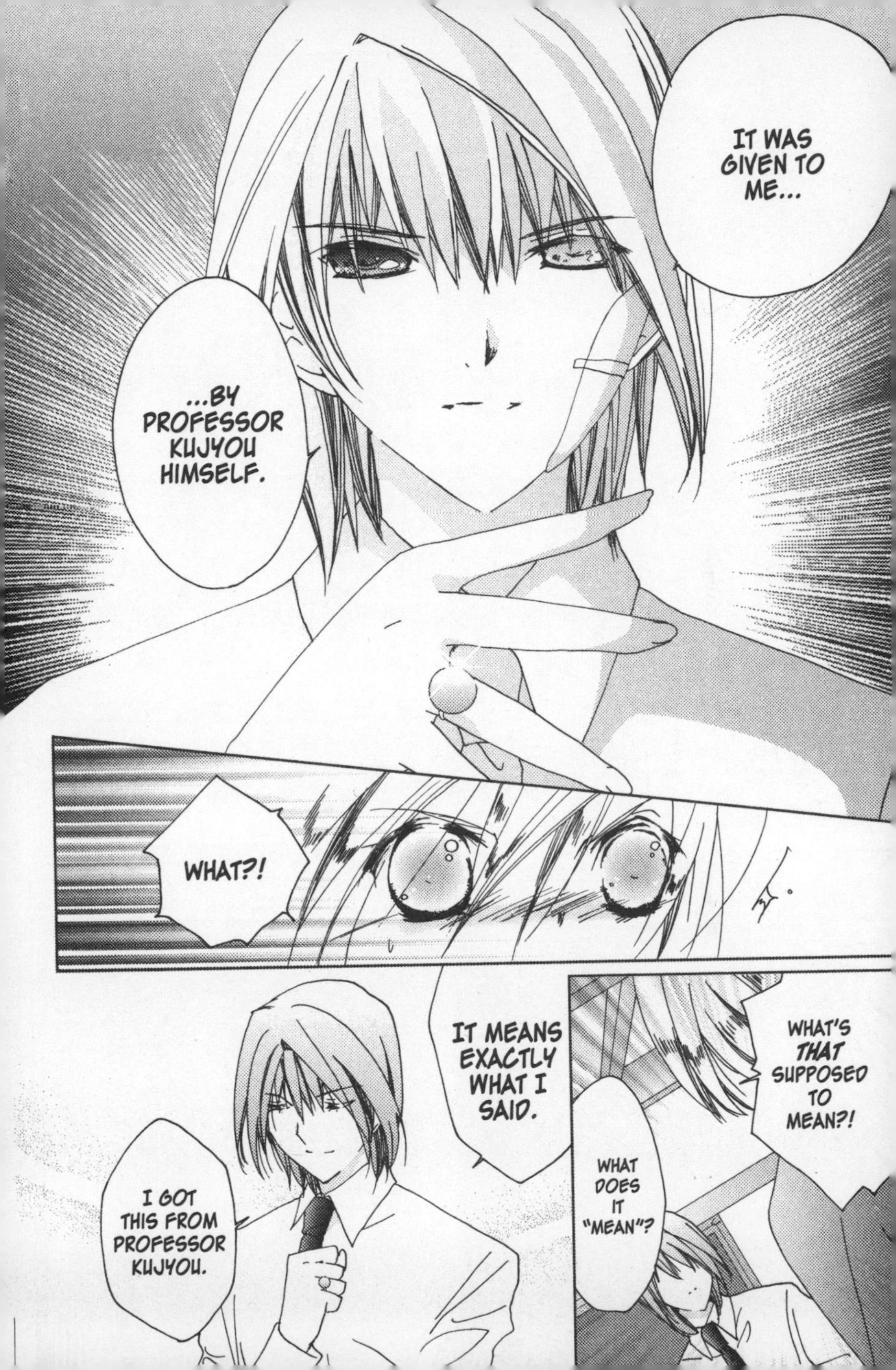
IT WAS GIVEN TO ME...
...BY PROFESSOR KUJYOU HIMSELF.
WHAT?!
WHAT'S *THAT* SUPPOSED TO MEAN?!
WHAT DOES IT "MEAN"?
IT MEANS EXACTLY WHAT I SAID.
I GOT THIS FROM PROFESSOR KUJYOU.

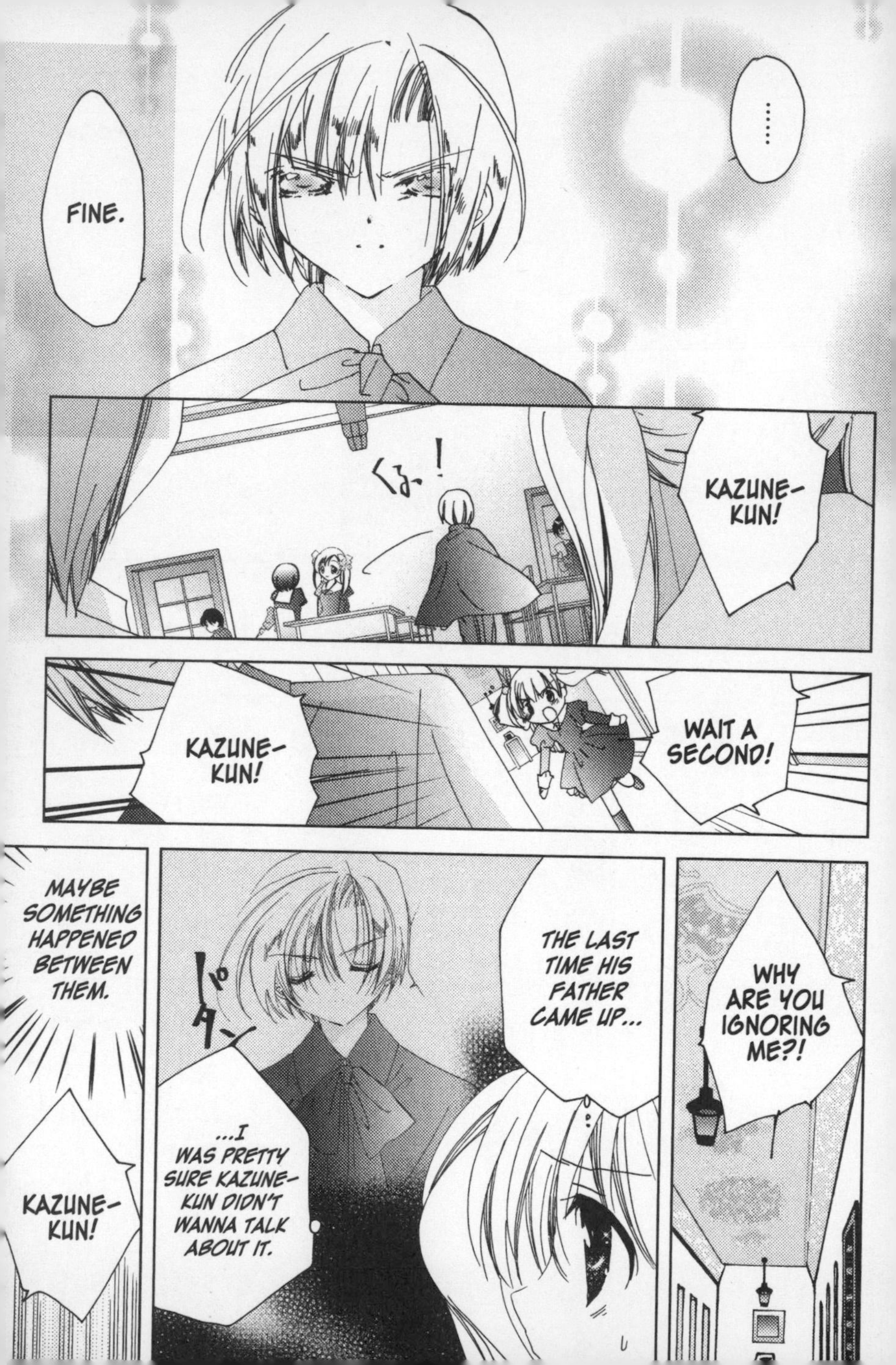
……
FINE.
KAZUNE-KUN!
WAIT A SECOND!
KAZUNE-KUN!
WHY ARE YOU IGNORING ME?!
THE LAST TIME HIS FATHER CAME UP...
...I WAS PRETTY SURE KAZUNE-KUN DIDN'T WANNA TALK ABOUT IT.
MAYBE SOMETHING HAPPENED BETWEEN THEM.
KAZUNE-KUN!

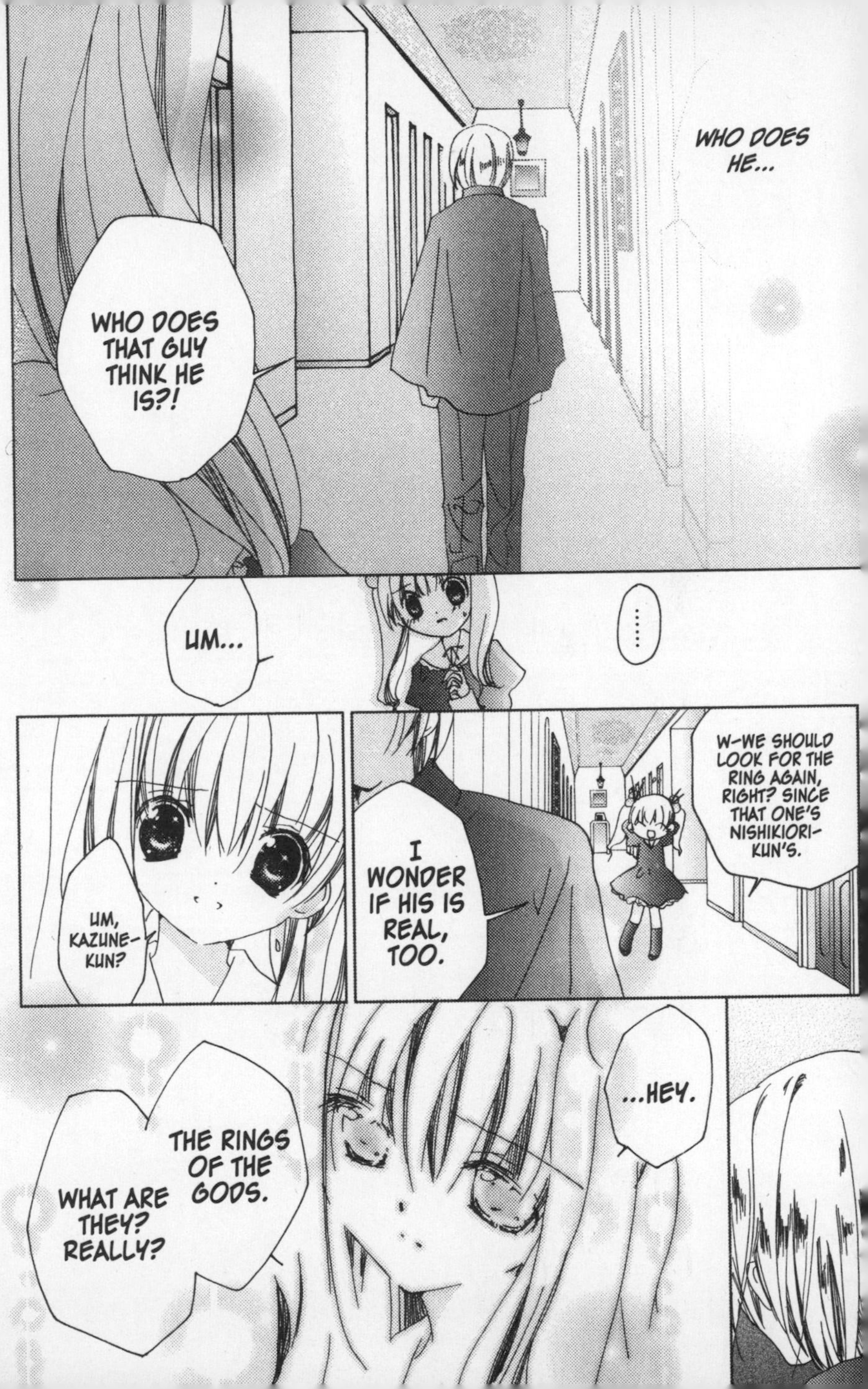
WHO DOES HE...
WHO DOES THAT GUY THINK HE IS?!
......
UM...
W-WE SHOULD LOOK FOR THE RING AGAIN, RIGHT? SINCE THAT ONE'S NISHIKIORI-KUN'S.
I WONDER IF HIS IS REAL, TOO.
UM, KAZUNE-KUN?
...HEY.
THE RINGS OF THE GODS.
WHAT ARE THEY? REALLY?

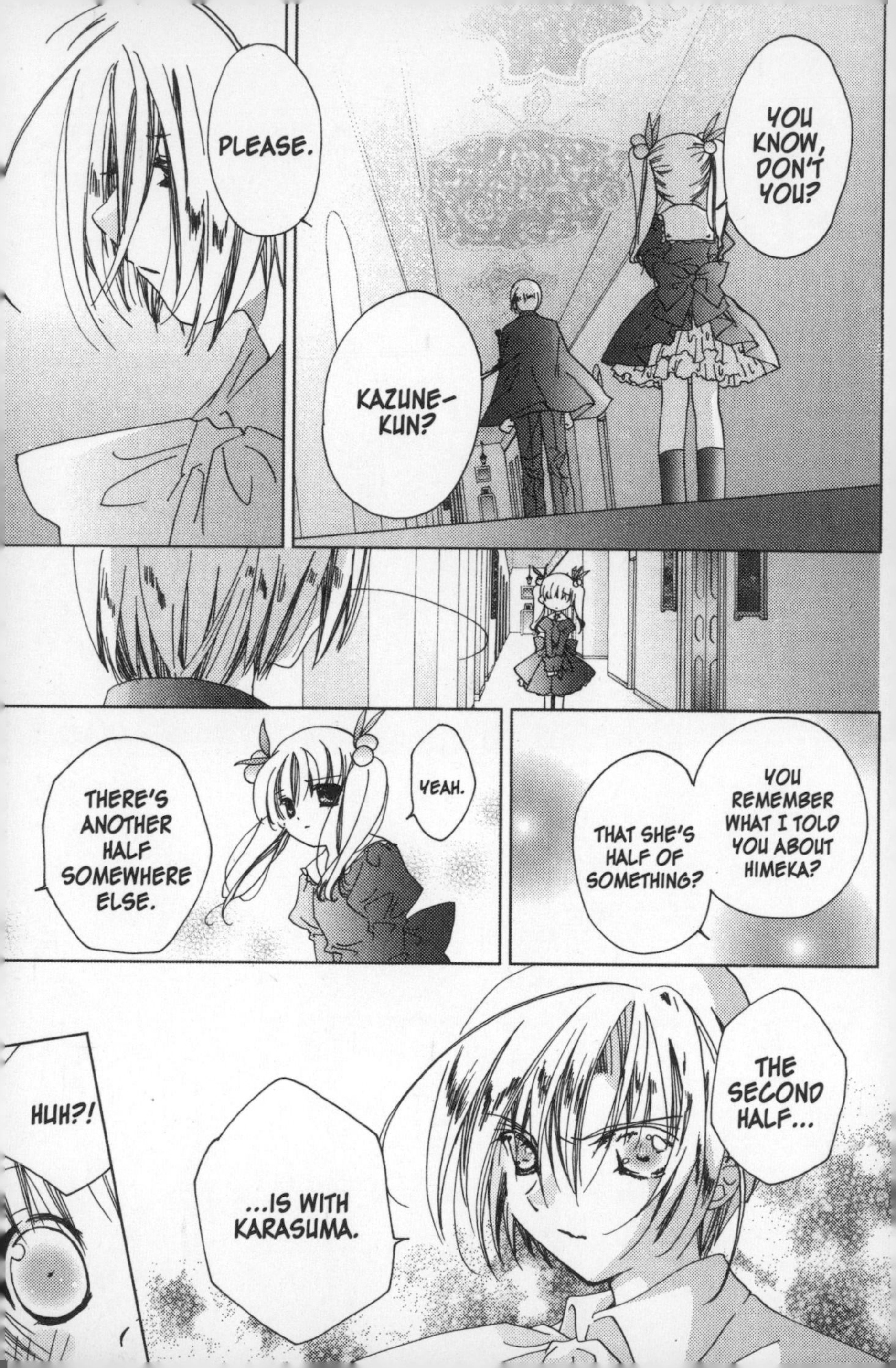
YOU KNOW, DON'T YOU?
KAZUNE-KUN?
PLEASE.
YOU REMEMBER WHAT I TOLD YOU ABOUT HIMEKA?
THAT SHE'S HALF OF SOMETHING?
YEAH.
THERE'S ANOTHER HALF SOMEWHERE ELSE.
THE SECOND HALF...
...IS WITH KARASUMA.
HUH?!

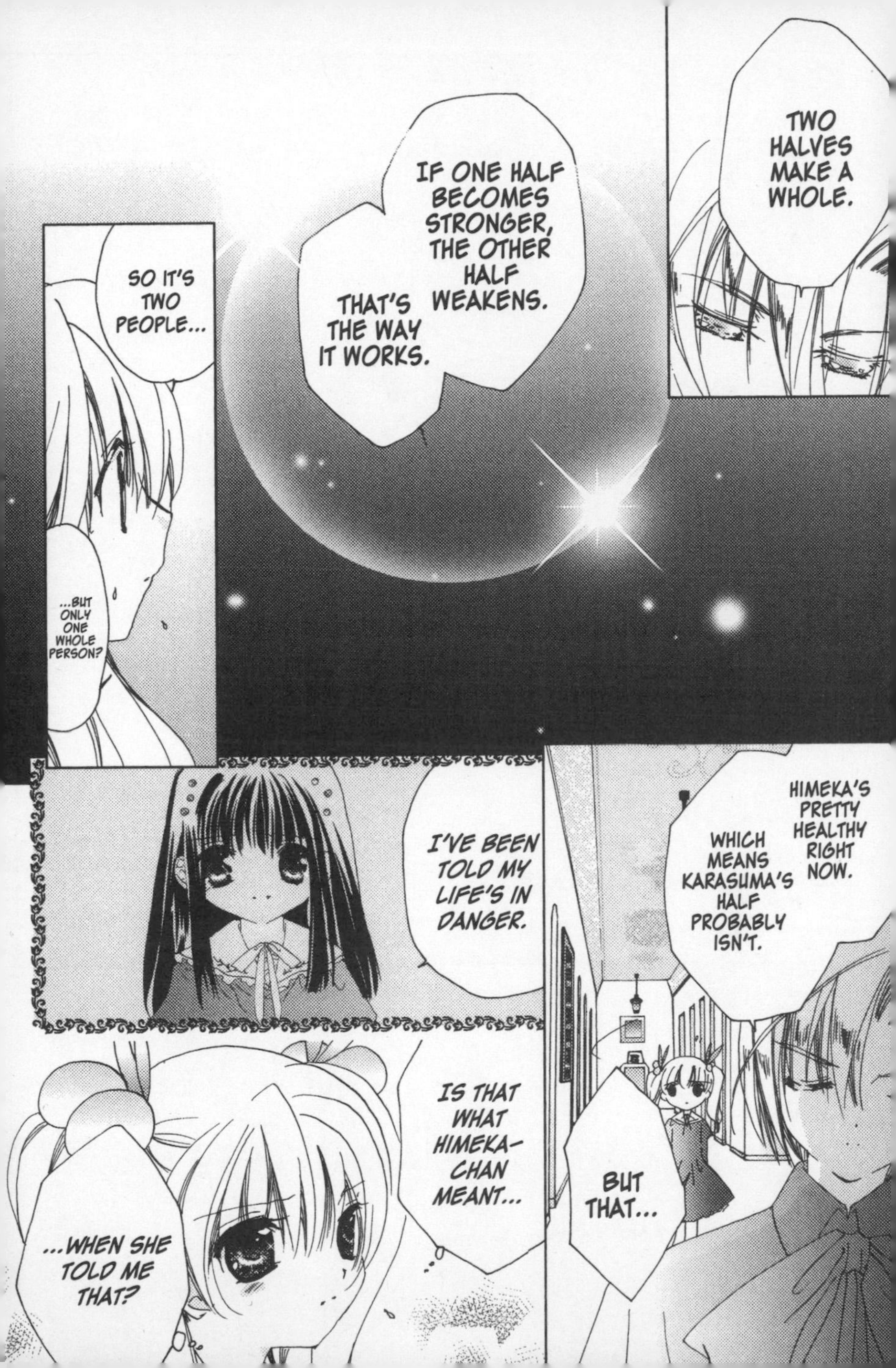
TWO HALVES MAKE A WHOLE.
IF ONE HALF BECOMES STRONGER, THE OTHER HALF WEAKENS.
THAT'S THE WAY IT WORKS.
SO IT'S TWO PEOPLE...
...BUT ONLY ONE WHOLE PERSON?
HIMEKA'S PRETTY HEALTHY RIGHT NOW.
WHICH MEANS KARASUMA'S HALF PROBABLY ISN'T.
BUT THAT...
I'VE BEEN TOLD MY LIFE'S IN DANGER.
IS THAT WHAT HIMEKA-CHAN MEANT...
...WHEN SHE TOLD ME THAT?

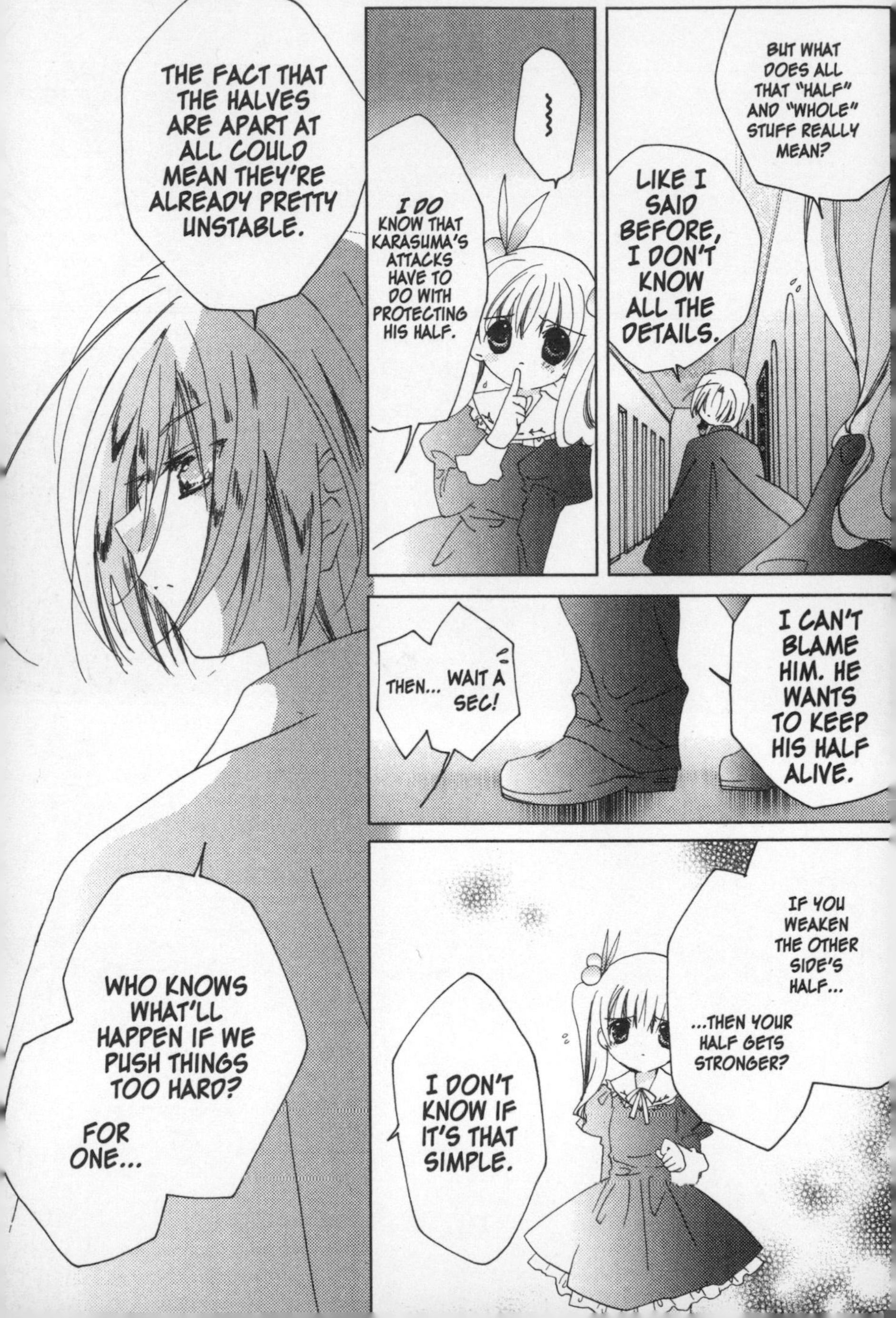

BUT WHAT DOES ALL THAT "HALF" AND "WHOLE" STUFF REALLY MEAN?
LIKE I SAID BEFORE, I DON'T KNOW ALL THE DETAILS.
...
I DO KNOW THAT KARASUMA'S ATTACKS HAVE TO DO WITH PROTECTING HIS HALF.
I CAN'T BLAME HIM. HE WANTS TO KEEP HIS HALF ALIVE.
THEN... WAIT A SEC!
IF YOU WEAKEN THE OTHER SIDE'S HALF...
...THEN YOUR HALF GETS STRONGER?
I DON'T KNOW IF IT'S THAT SIMPLE.
THE FACT THAT THE HALVES ARE APART AT ALL COULD MEAN THEY'RE ALREADY PRETTY UNSTABLE.
WHO KNOWS WHAT'LL HAPPEN IF WE PUSH THINGS TOO HARD?
FOR ONE...

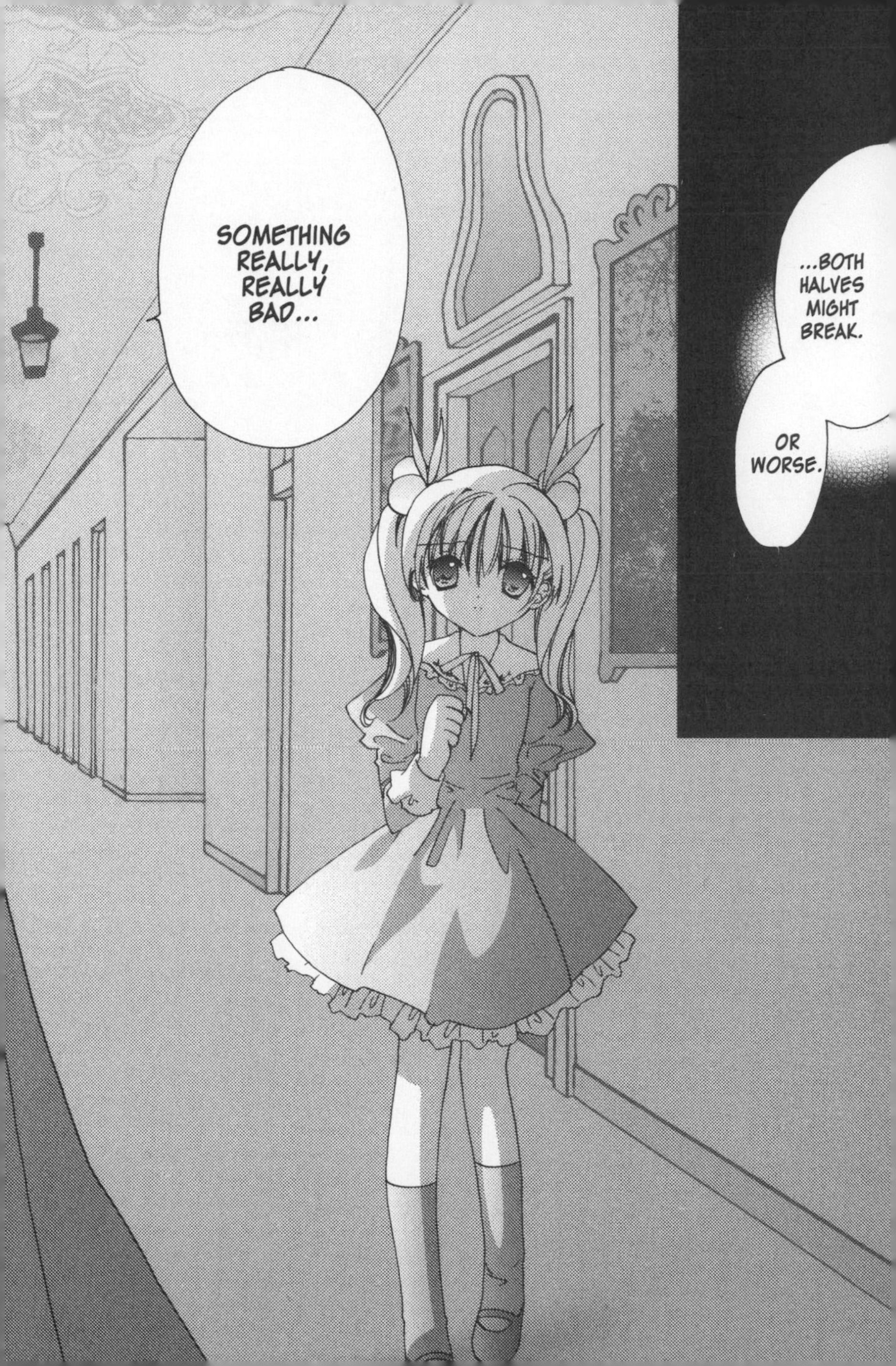
...BOTH HALVES MIGHT BREAK.
OR WORSE.
SOMETHING REALLY, REALLY BAD...

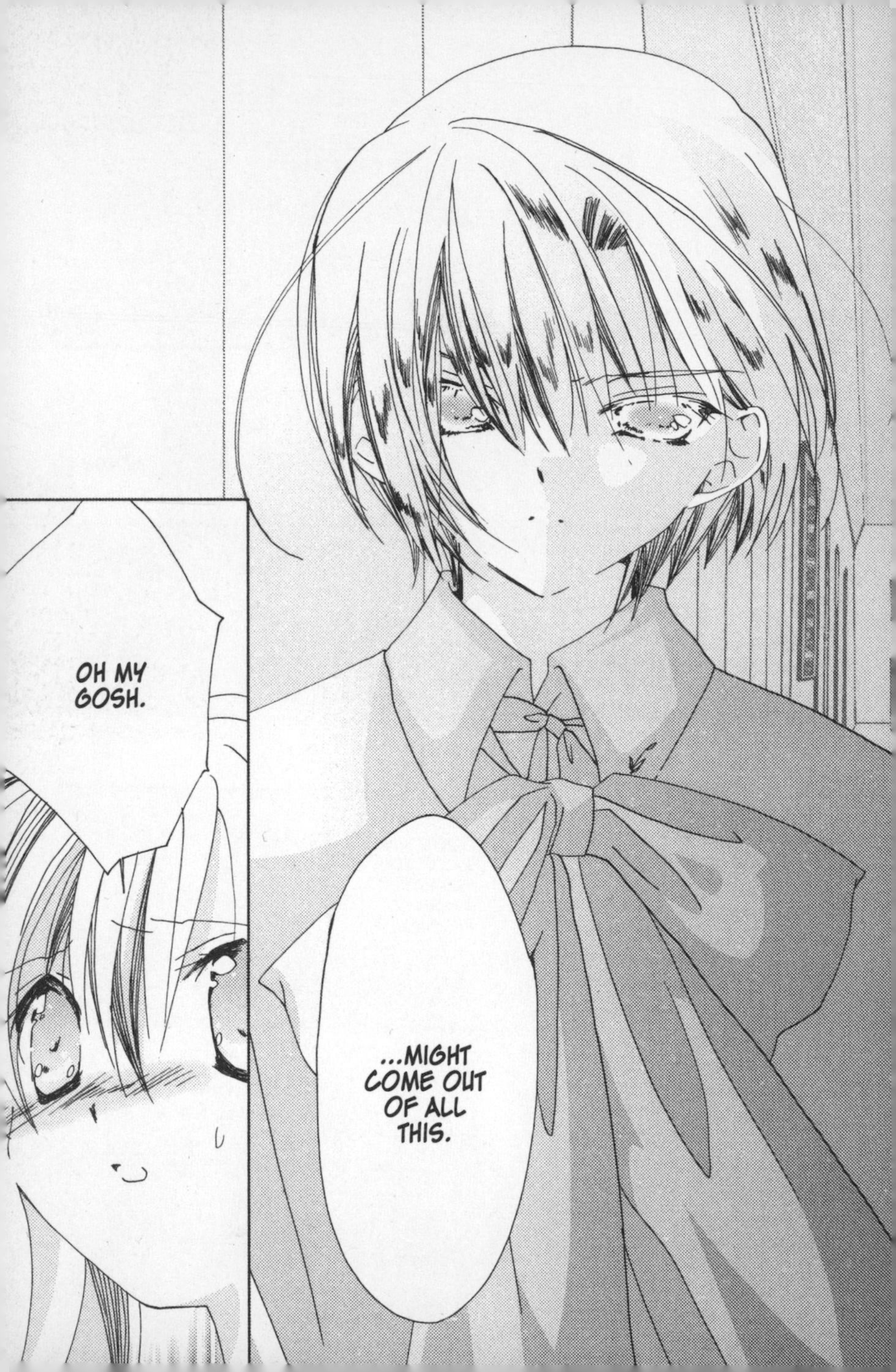
...MIGHT COME OUT OF ALL THIS.
OH MY GOSH.

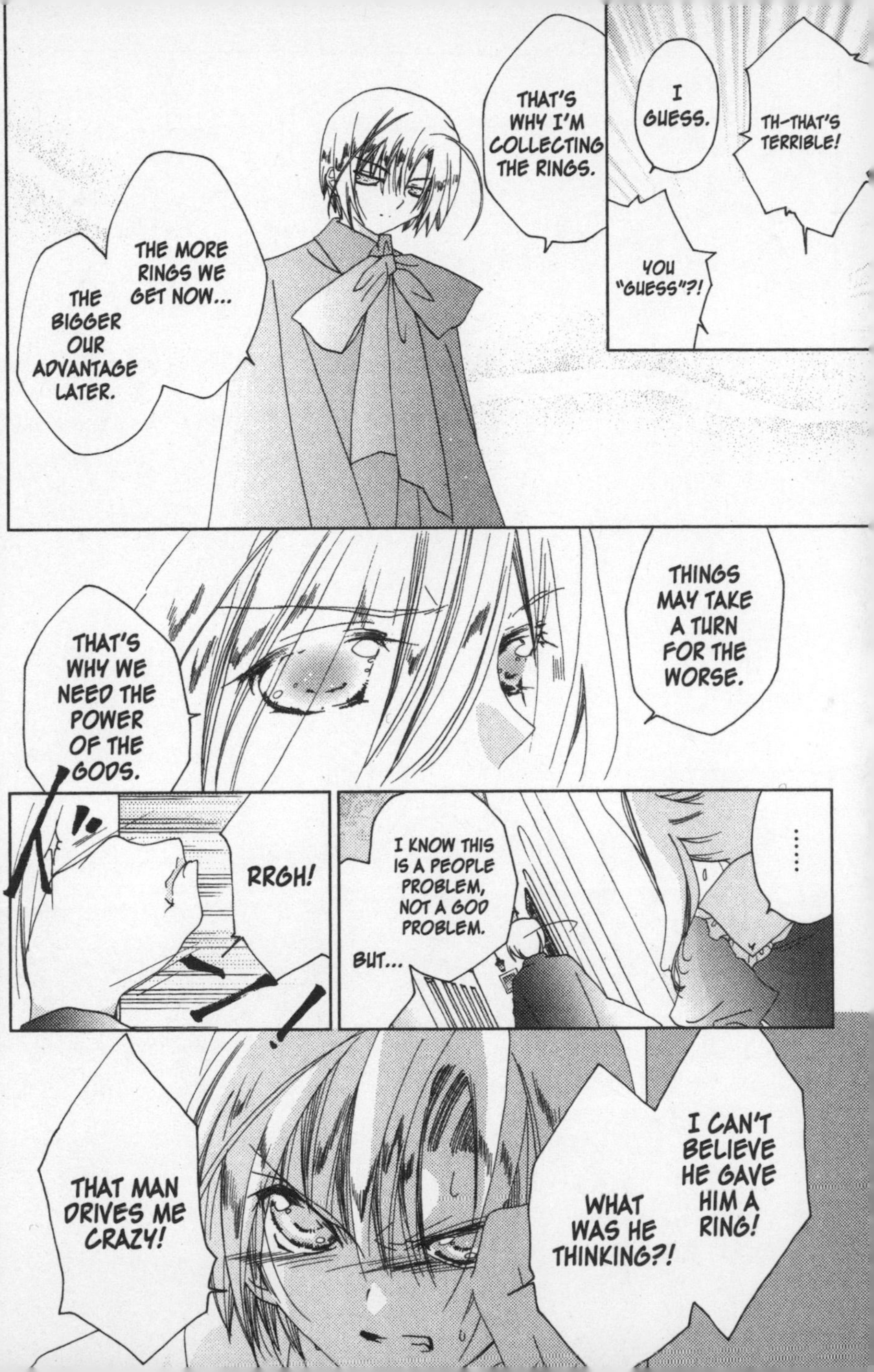
TH-THAT'S TERRIBLE!
I GUESS.
YOU "GUESS"?!
THAT'S WHY I'M COLLECTING THE RINGS.
THE MORE RINGS WE GET NOW...
THE BIGGER OUR ADVANTAGE LATER.
THINGS MAY TAKE A TURN FOR THE WORSE.
THAT'S WHY WE NEED THE POWER OF THE GODS.
......
I KNOW THIS IS A PEOPLE PROBLEM, NOT A GOD PROBLEM.
BUT...
RRGH!
I CAN'T BELIEVE HE GAVE HIM A RING!
WHAT WAS HE THINKING?!
THAT MAN DRIVES ME CRAZY!

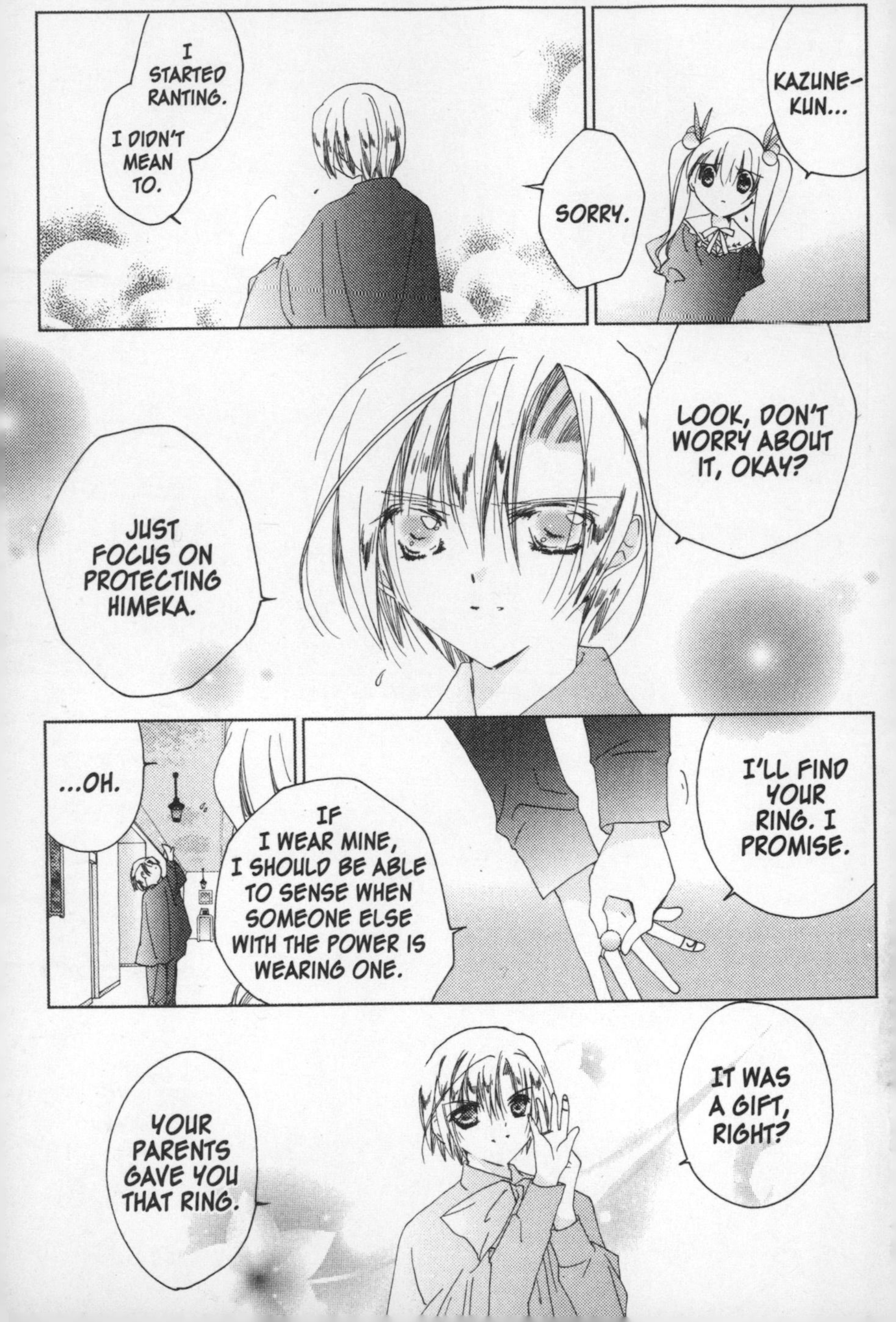
KAZUNE-KUN...
SORRY.
I STARTED RANTING.
I DIDN'T MEAN TO.
LOOK, DON'T WORRY ABOUT IT, OKAY?
JUST FOCUS ON PROTECTING HIMEKA.
I'LL FIND YOUR RING. I PROMISE.
IF I WEAR MINE, I SHOULD BE ABLE TO SENSE WHEN SOMEONE ELSE WITH THE POWER IS WEARING ONE.
...OH.
IT WAS A GIFT, RIGHT?
YOUR PARENTS GAVE YOU THAT RING.

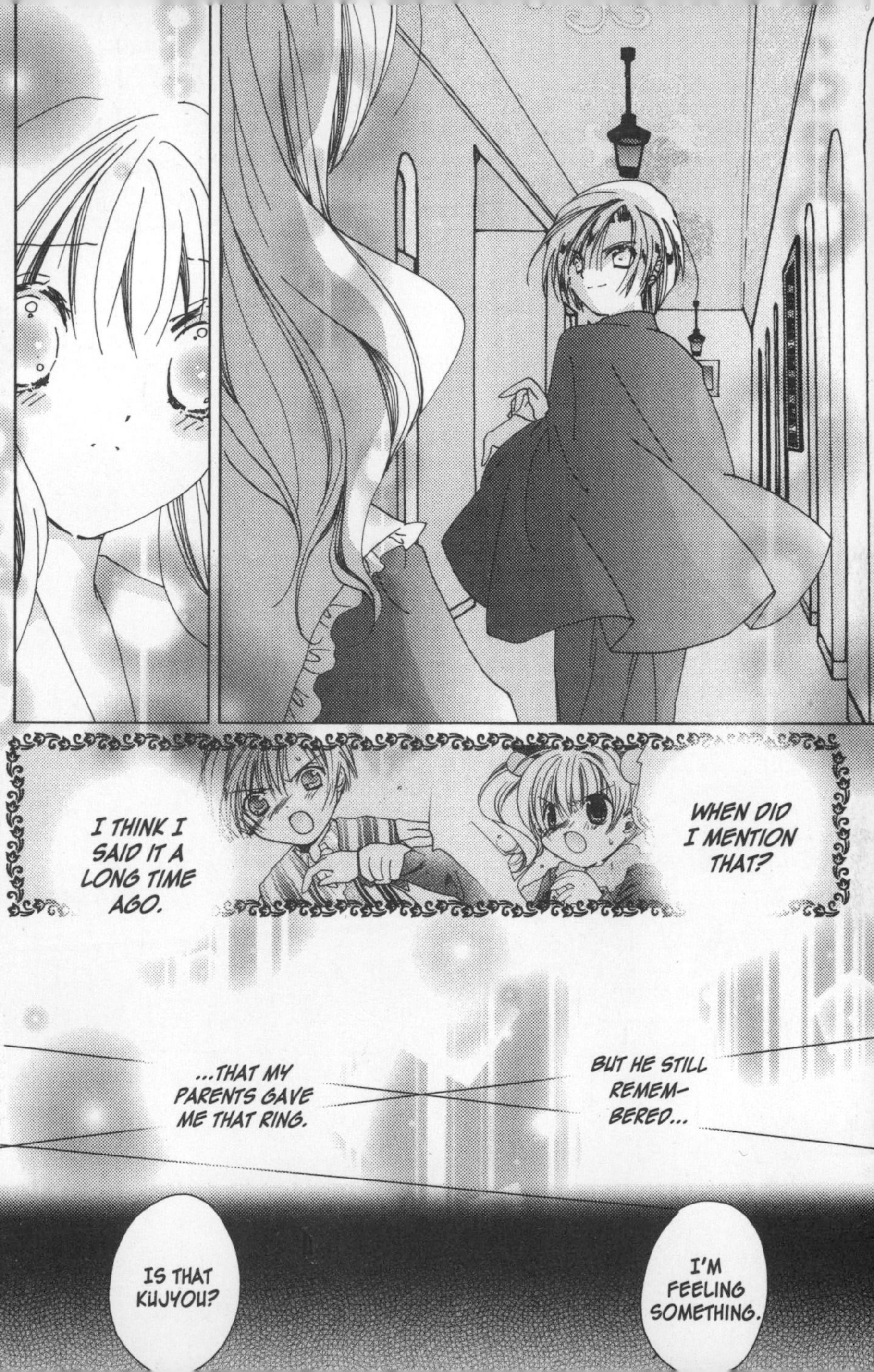
WHEN DID I MENTION THAT?
I THINK I SAID IT A LONG TIME AGO.
BUT HE STILL REMEM-BERED...
...THAT MY PARENTS GAVE ME THAT RING.
I'M FEELING SOMETHING.
IS THAT KUJYOU?

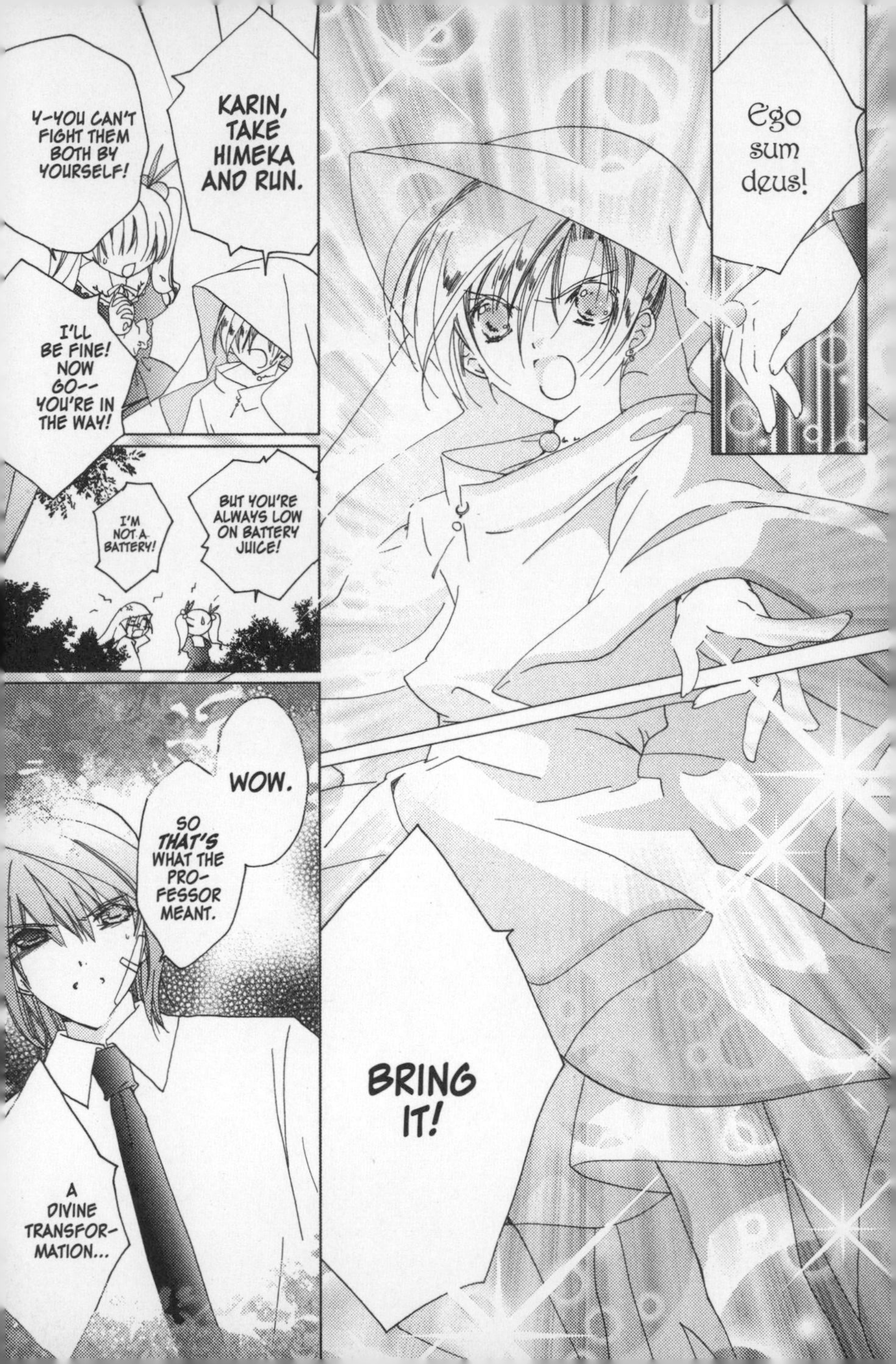
Ego sum deus!
BRING IT!
KARIN, TAKE HIMEKA AND RUN.
Y-YOU CAN'T FIGHT THEM BOTH BY YOURSELF!
I'LL BE FINE! NOW GO-- YOU'RE IN THE WAY!
BUT YOU'RE ALWAYS LOW ON BATTERY JUICE!
I'M NOT A BATTERY!
WOW.
SO THAT'S WHAT THE PRO-FESSOR MEANT.
A DIVINE TRANSFOR-MATION...

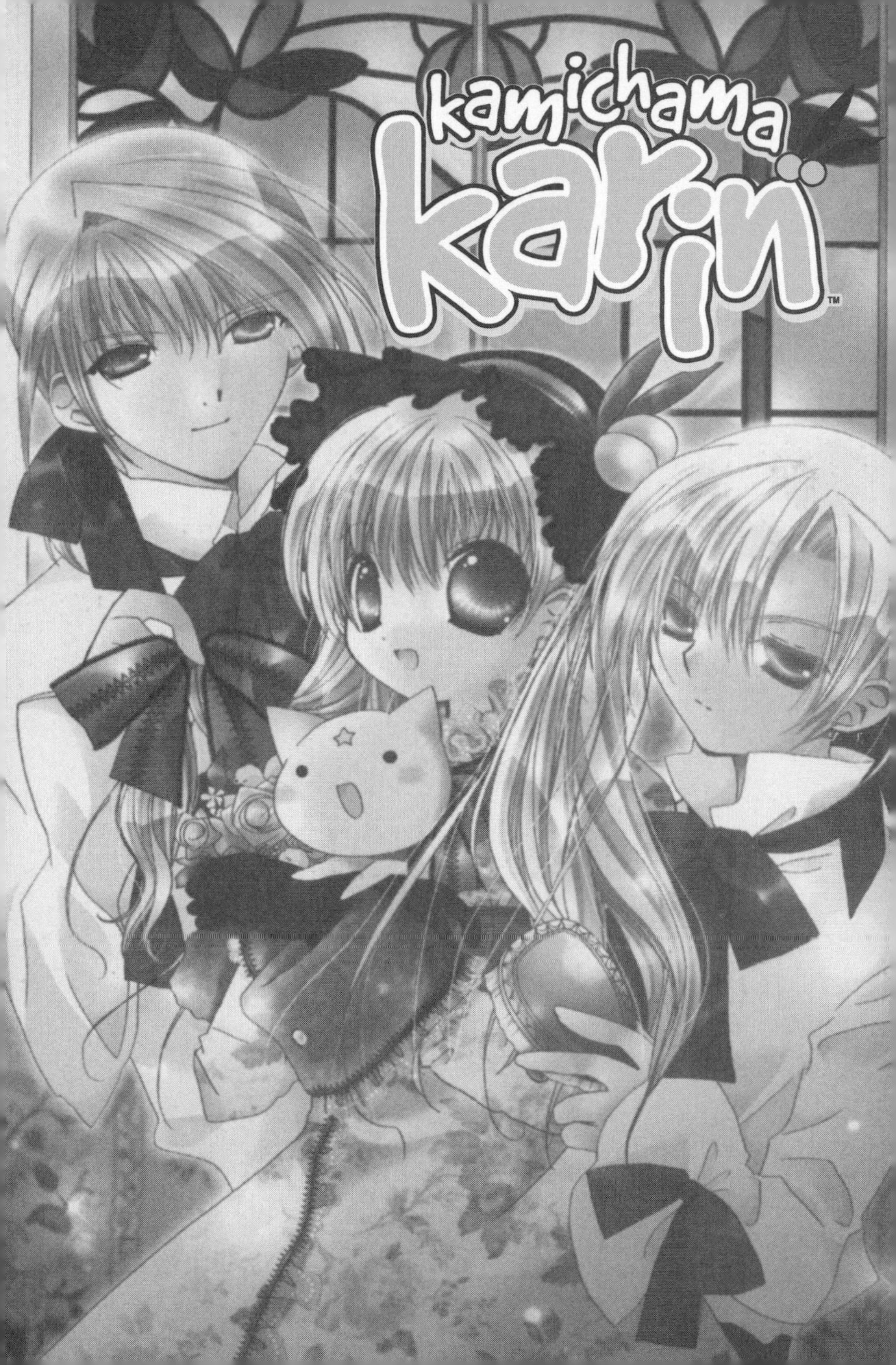
kamichama karin™

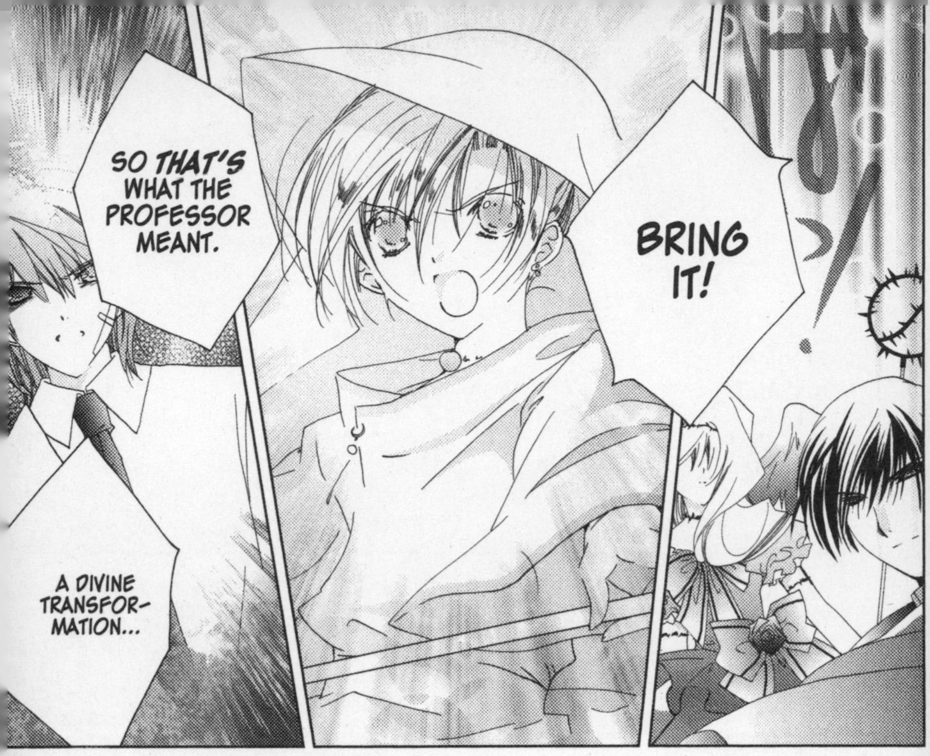
BRING IT!
SO THAT'S WHAT THE PROFESSOR MEANT.
A DIVINE TRANSFORMATION...

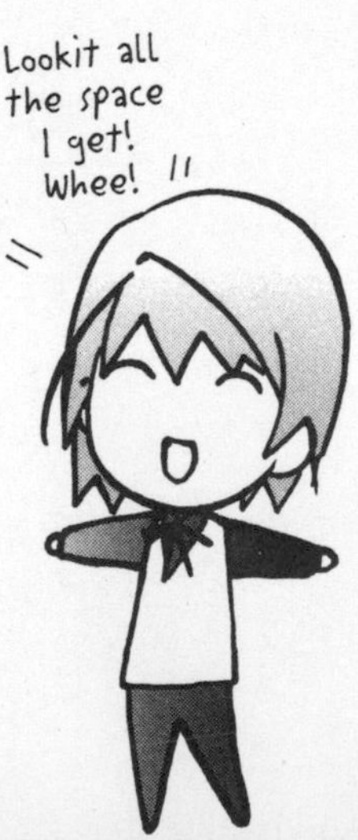
Lookit all the space I get! Whee!

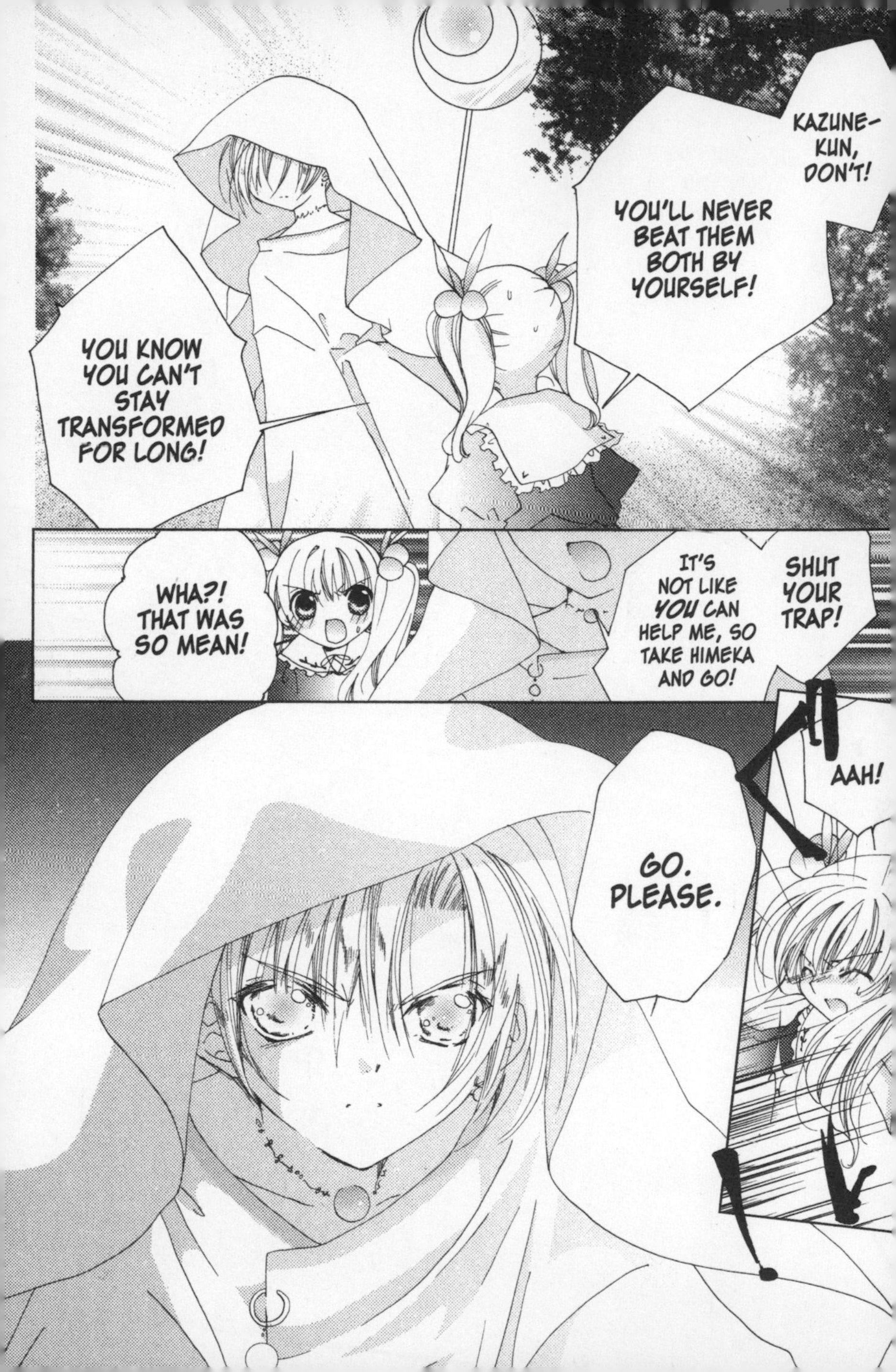
KAZUNE-KUN, DON'T!
YOU'LL NEVER BEAT THEM BOTH BY YOURSELF!
YOU KNOW YOU CAN'T STAY TRANSFORMED FOR LONG!
SHUT YOUR TRAP!
IT'S NOT LIKE YOU CAN HELP ME, SO TAKE HIMEKA AND GO!
WHA?! THAT WAS SO MEAN!
AAH!
GO. PLEASE.

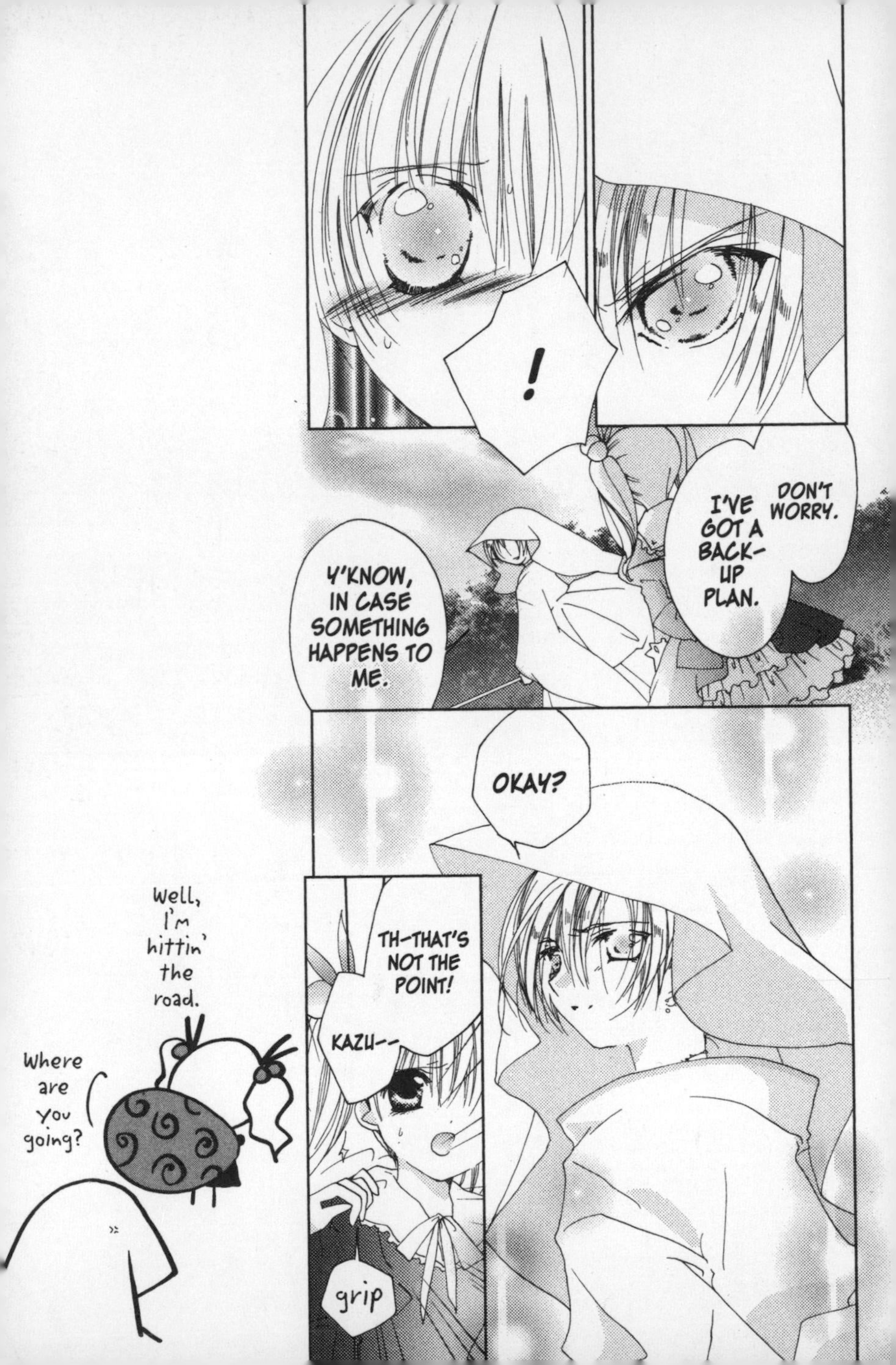
!
DON'T WORRY.
I'VE GOT A BACK-UP PLAN.
Y'KNOW, IN CASE SOMETHING HAPPENS TO ME.
OKAY?
TH-THAT'S NOT THE POINT!
KAZU--
grip
Well, I'm hittin' the road.
Where are you going?

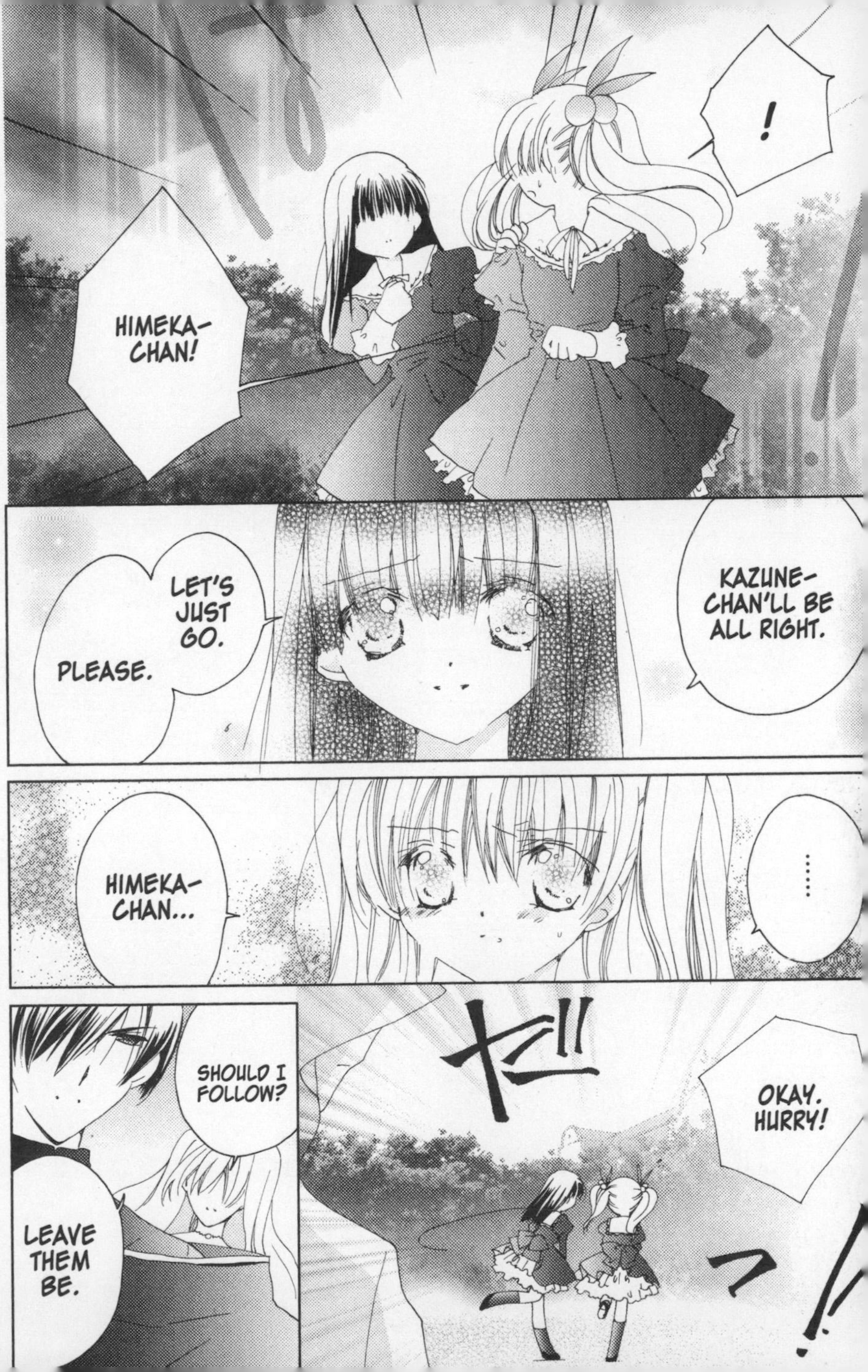
!
HIMEKA-CHAN!
KAZUNE-CHAN'LL BE ALL RIGHT.
LET'S JUST GO.
PLEASE.
......
HIMEKA-CHAN...
OKAY. HURRY!
SHOULD I FOLLOW?
LEAVE THEM BE.

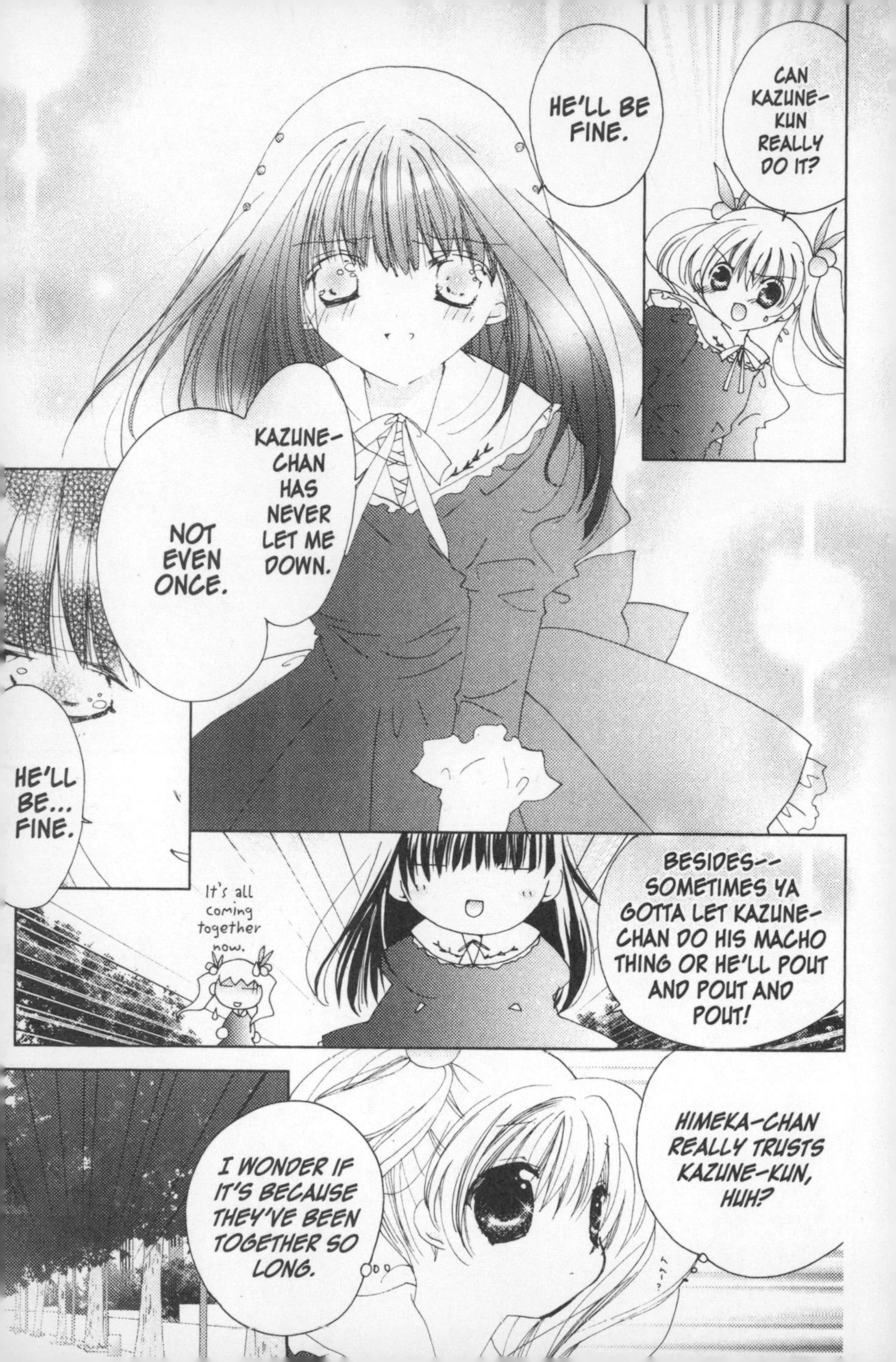
CAN KAZUNE-KUN REALLY DO IT?
HE'LL BE FINE.
KAZUNE-CHAN HAS NEVER LET ME DOWN.
NOT EVEN ONCE.
HE'LL BE... FINE.
BESIDES-- SOMETIMES YA GOTTA LET KAZUNE-CHAN DO HIS MACHO THING OR HE'LL POUT AND POUT AND POUT!
It's all coming together now.
HIMEKA-CHAN REALLY TRUSTS KAZUNE-KUN, HUH?
I WONDER IF IT'S BECAUSE THEY'VE BEEN TOGETHER SO LONG.

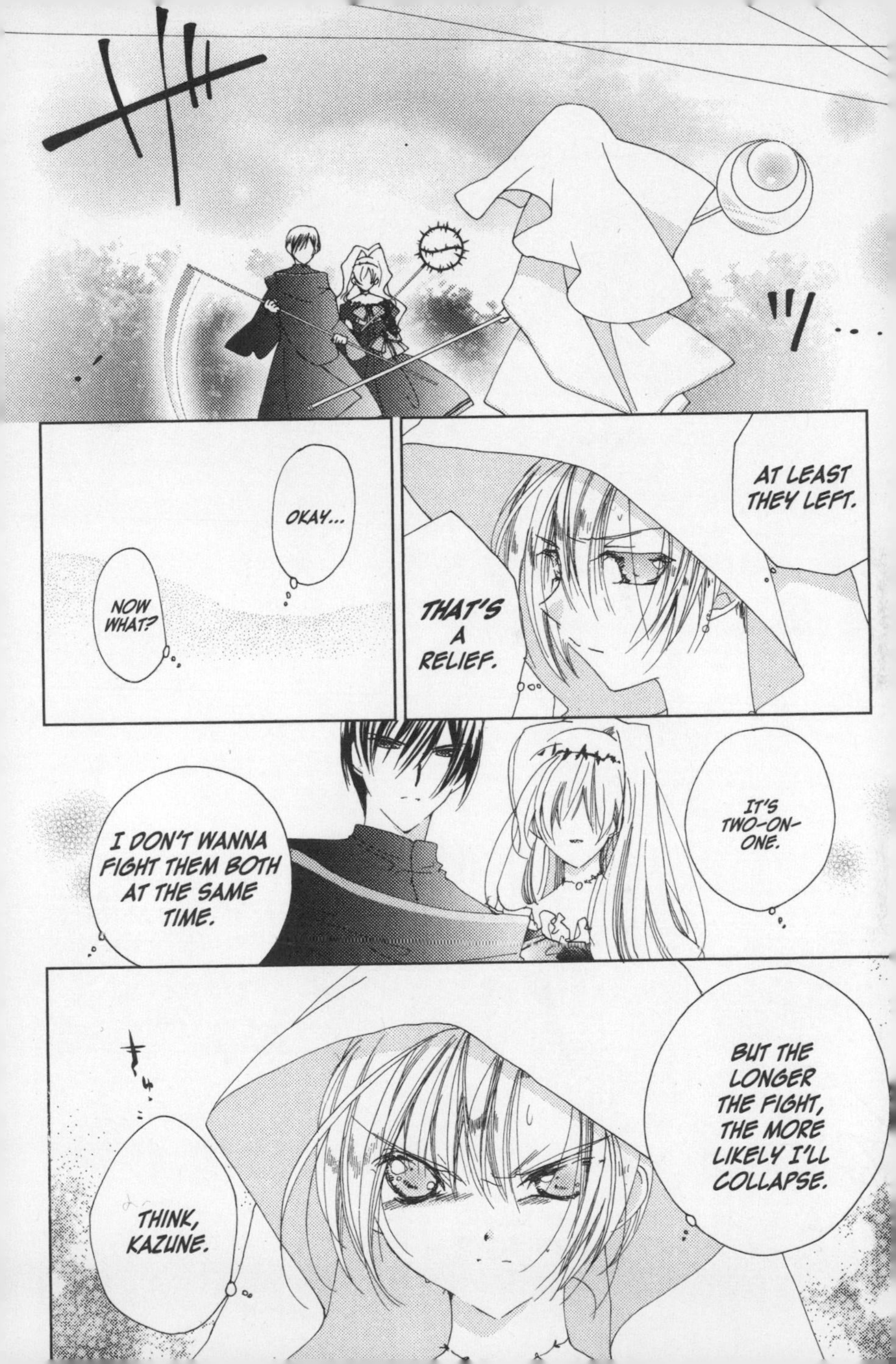
AT LEAST THEY LEFT.
THAT'S A RELIEF.
OKAY...
NOW WHAT?
IT'S TWO-ON-ONE.
I DON'T WANNA FIGHT THEM BOTH AT THE SAME TIME.
BUT THE LONGER THE FIGHT, THE MORE LIKELY I'LL COLLAPSE.
THINK, KAZUNE.

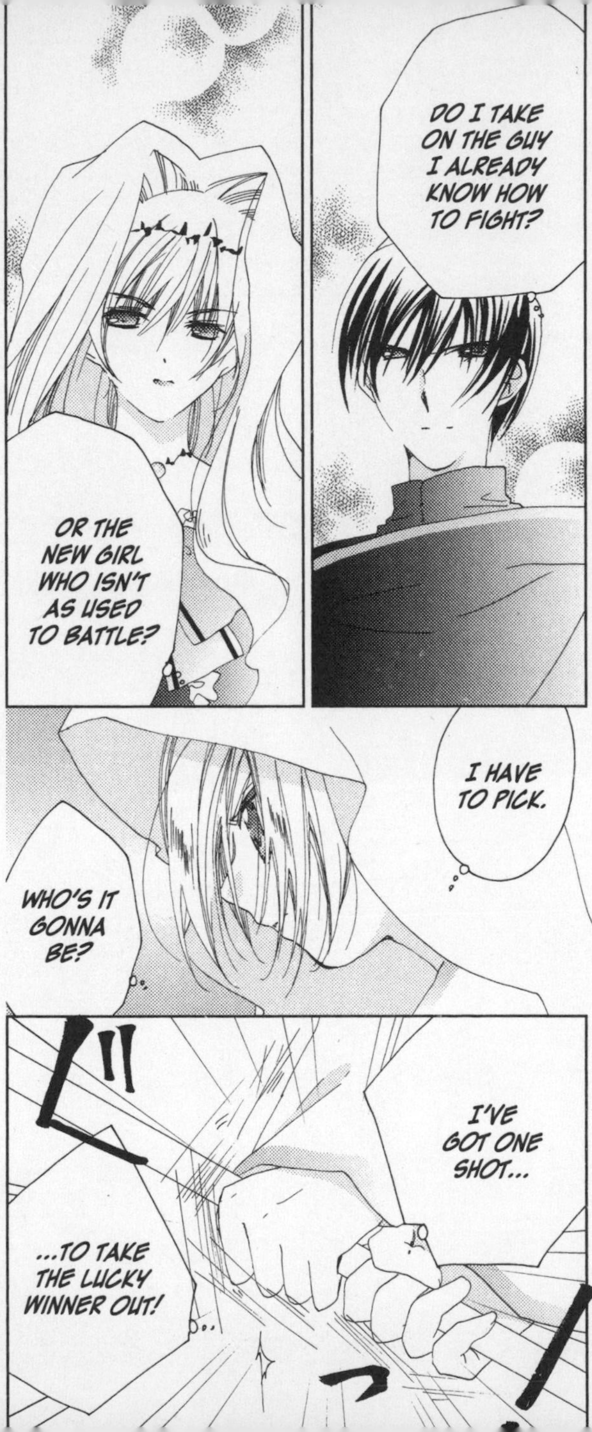
DO I TAKE ON THE GUY I ALREADY KNOW HOW TO FIGHT?
OR THE NEW GIRL WHO ISN'T AS USED TO BATTLE?
I HAVE TO PICK.
WHO'S IT GONNA BE?
I'VE GOT ONE SHOT...
...TO TAKE THE LUCKY WINNER OUT!
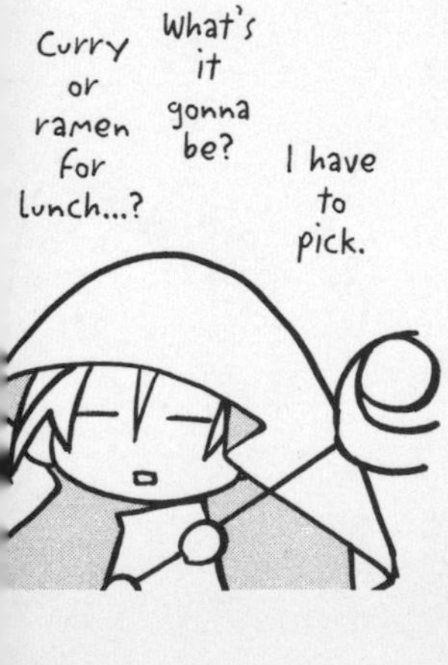
I have to pick.
What's it gonna be?
Curry or ramen for lunch...?

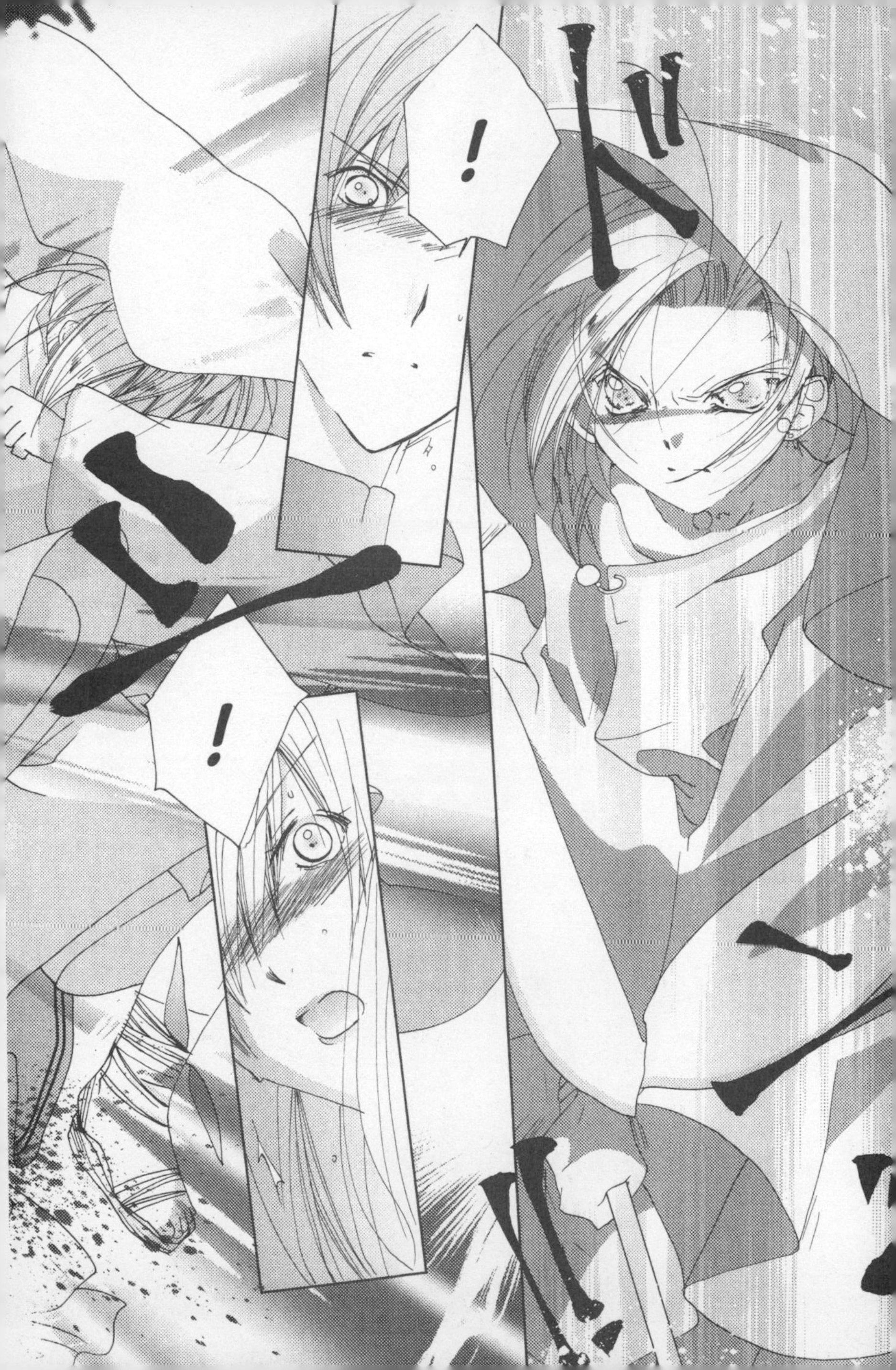
!
!

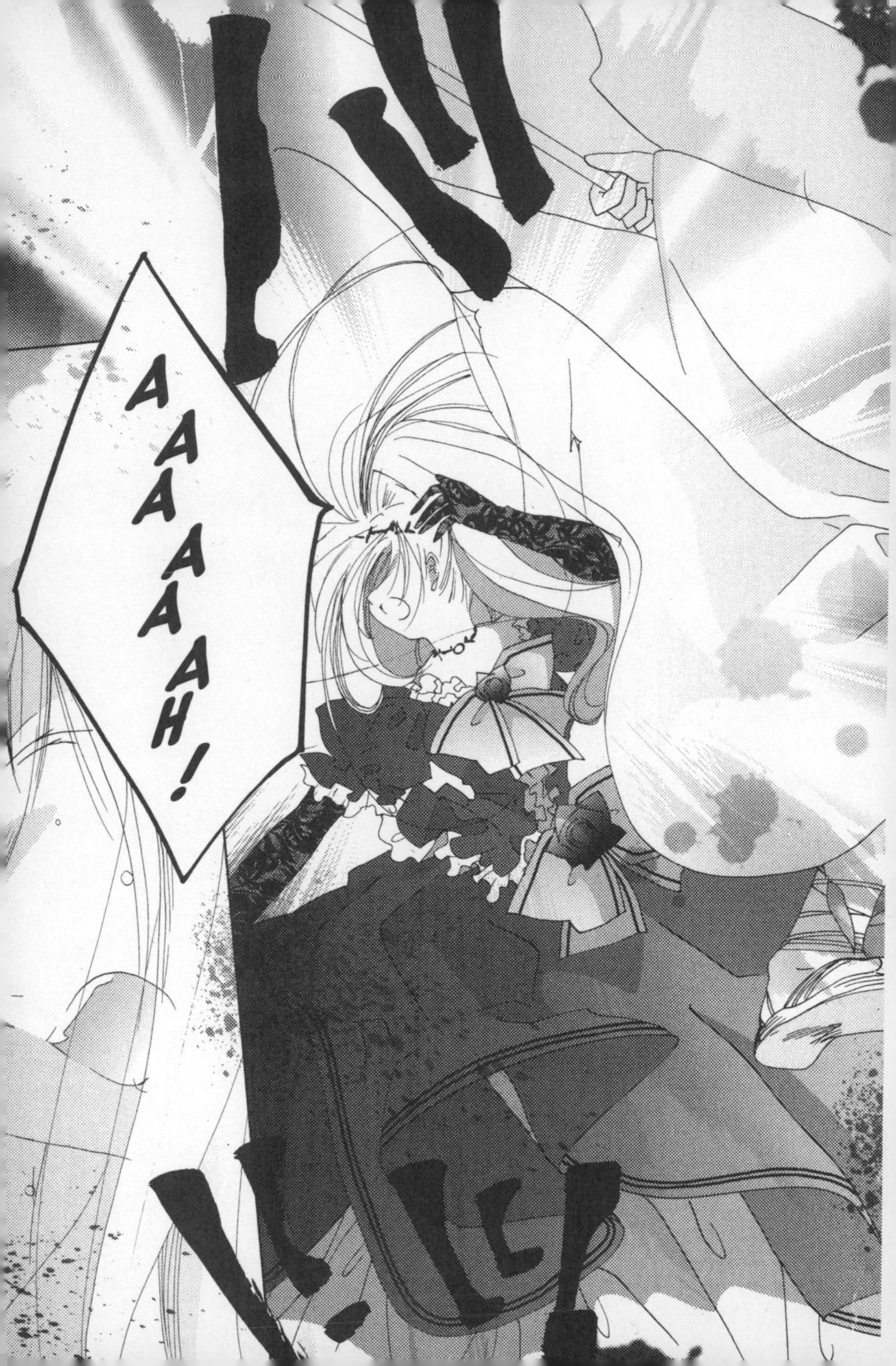
AAAAAAH!

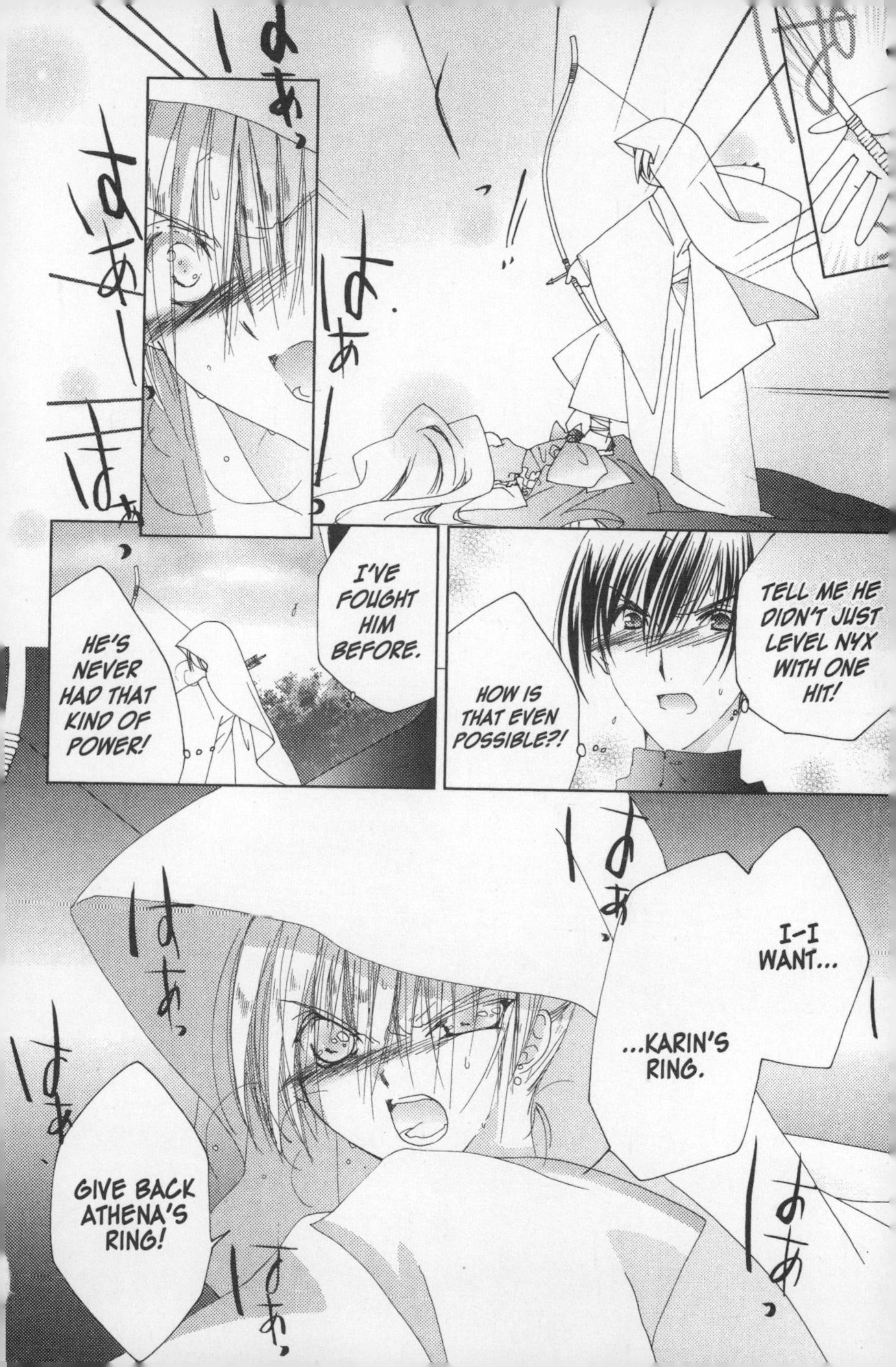
TELL ME HE DIDN'T JUST LEVEL NYX WITH ONE HIT!
HOW IS THAT EVEN POSSIBLE?!
I'VE FOUGHT HIM BEFORE.
HE'S NEVER HAD THAT KIND OF POWER!
I-I WANT...
...KARIN'S RING.
GIVE BACK ATHENA'S RING!

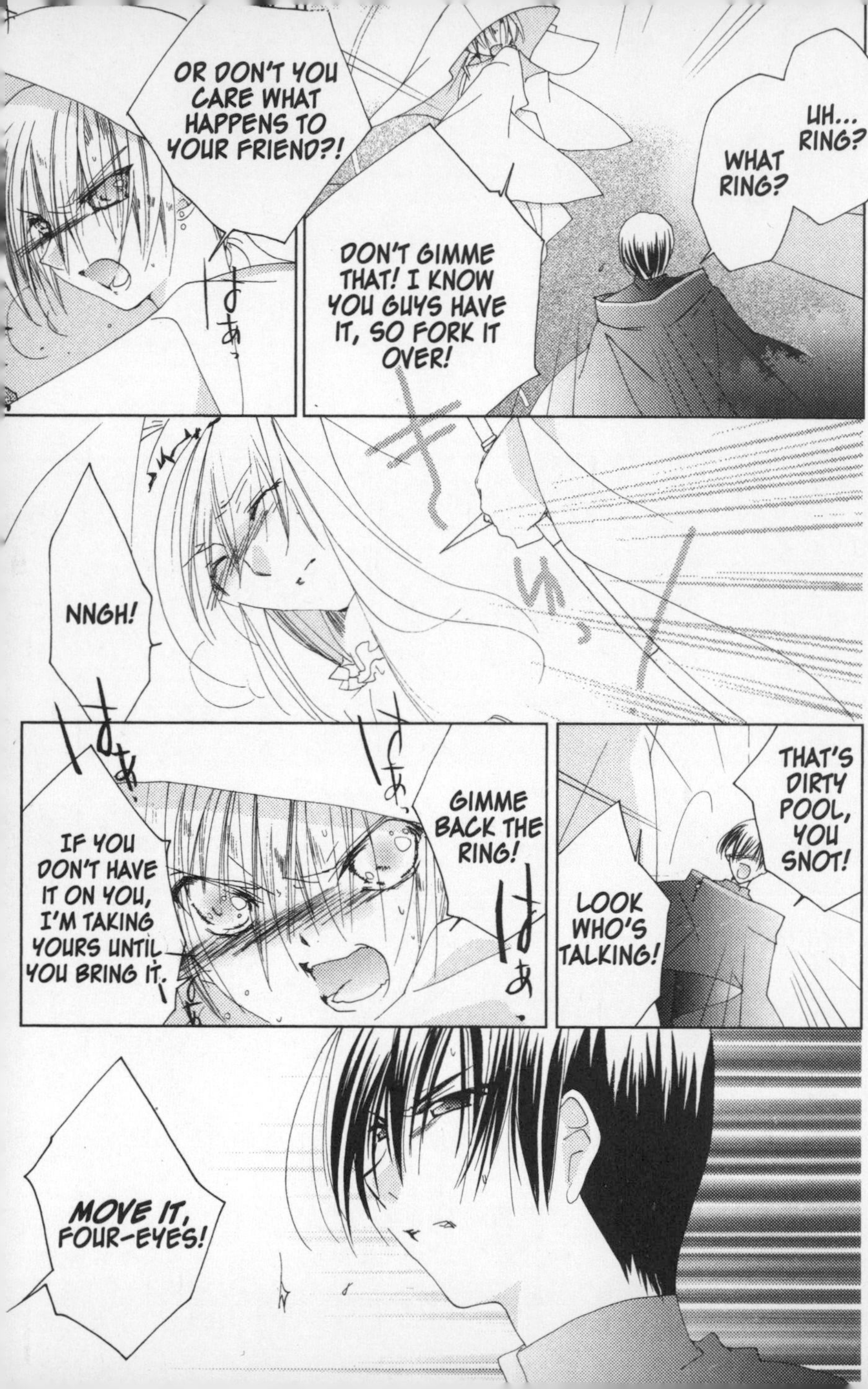
UH... RING? WHAT RING?
DON'T GIMME THAT! I KNOW YOU GUYS HAVE IT, SO FORK IT OVER!
OR DON'T YOU CARE WHAT HAPPENS TO YOUR FRIEND?!
NNGH!
THAT'S DIRTY POOL, YOU SNOT!
LOOK WHO'S TALKING!
GIMME BACK THE RING!
IF YOU DON'T HAVE IT ON YOU, I'M TAKING YOURS UNTIL YOU BRING IT.
MOVE IT, FOUR-EYES!

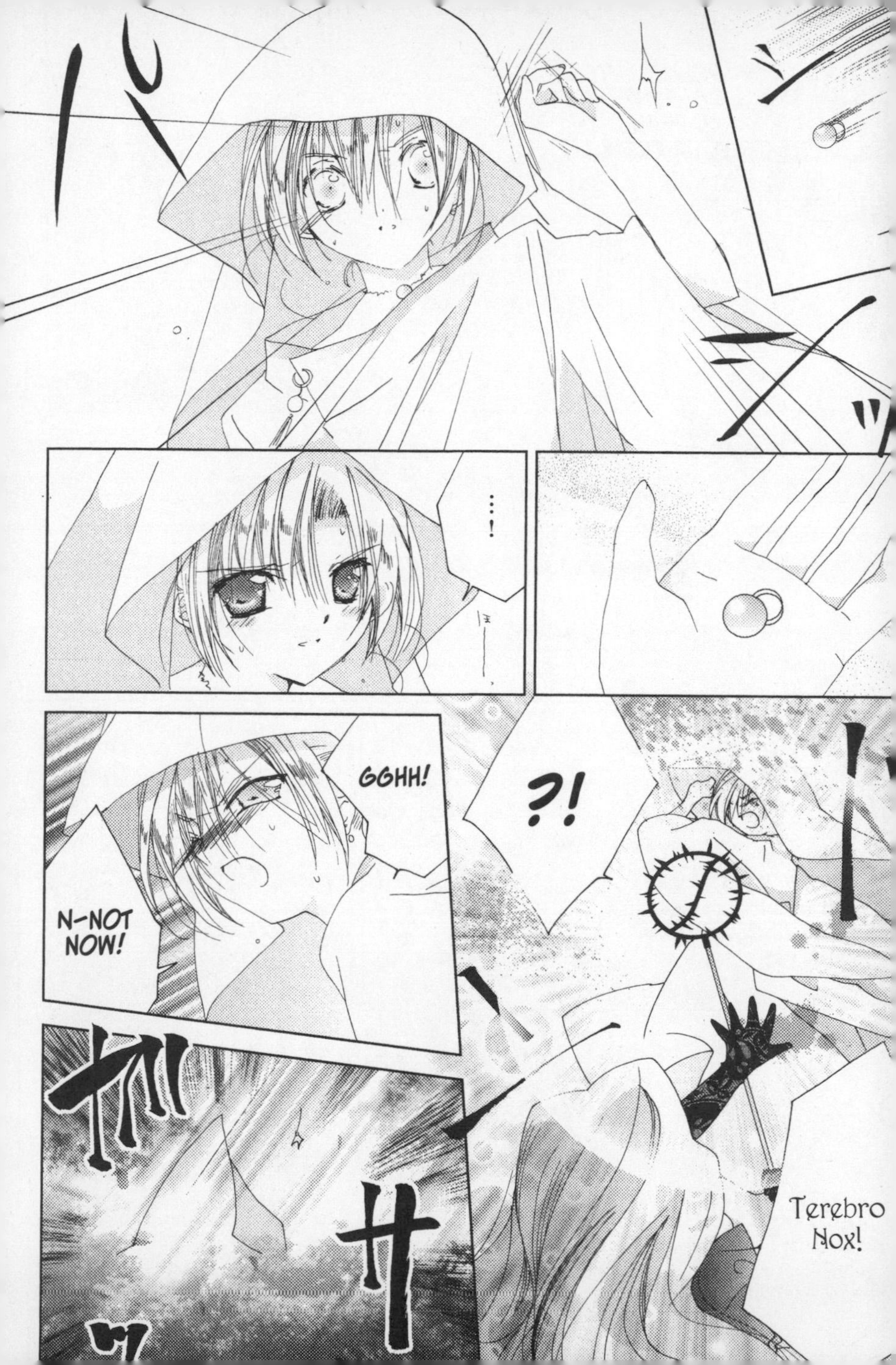
...!
?!
GGHH!
N-NOT NOW!
Terebro Nox!

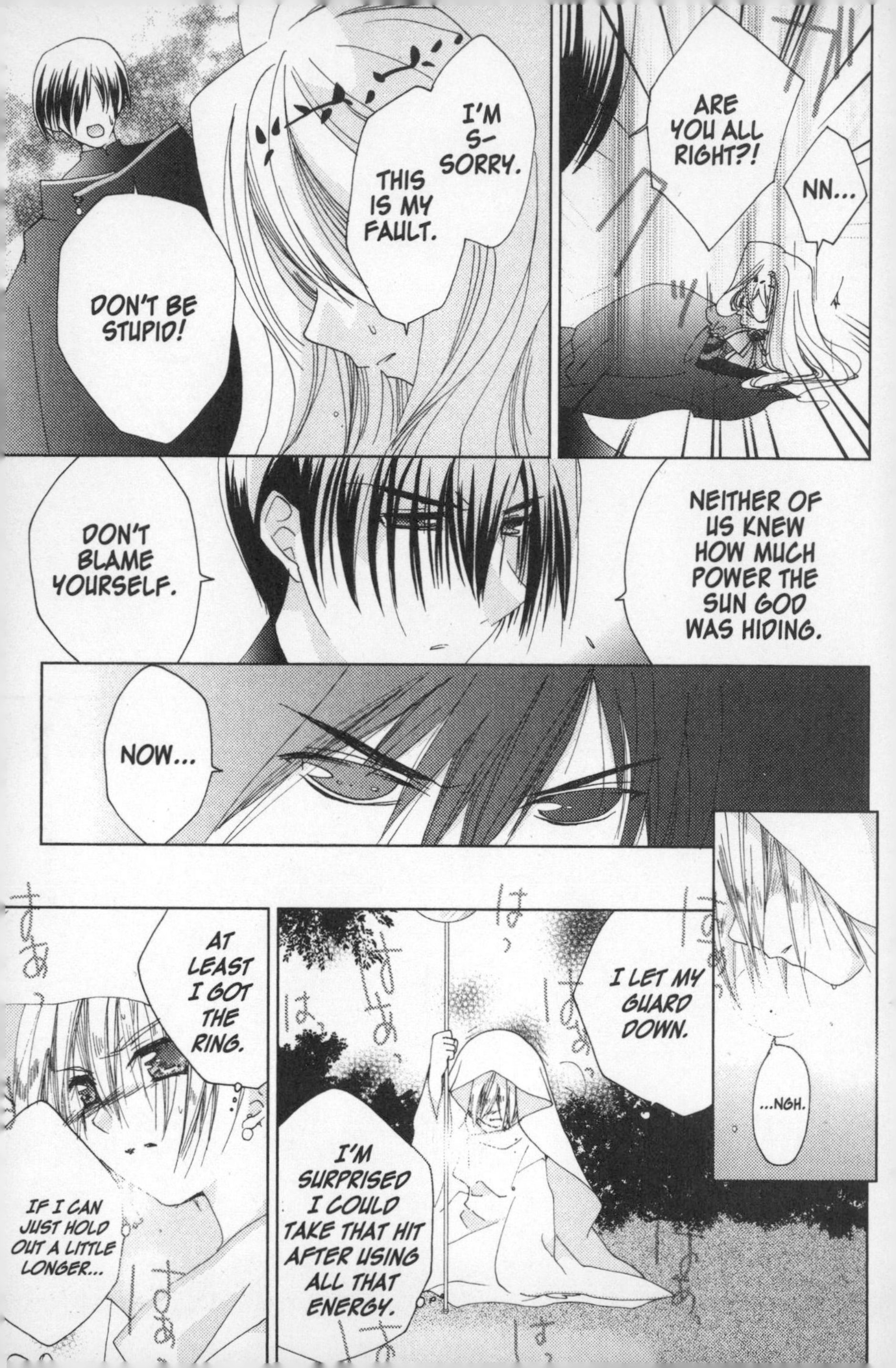
ARE YOU ALL RIGHT?!
NN...
I'M S-SORRY.
THIS IS MY FAULT.
DON'T BE STUPID!
NEITHER OF US KNEW HOW MUCH POWER THE SUN GOD WAS HIDING.
DON'T BLAME YOURSELF.
NOW...
...NGH.
I LET MY GUARD DOWN.
I'M SURPRISED I COULD TAKE THAT HIT AFTER USING ALL THAT ENERGY.
AT LEAST I GOT THE RING.
IF I CAN JUST HOLD OUT A LITTLE LONGER...

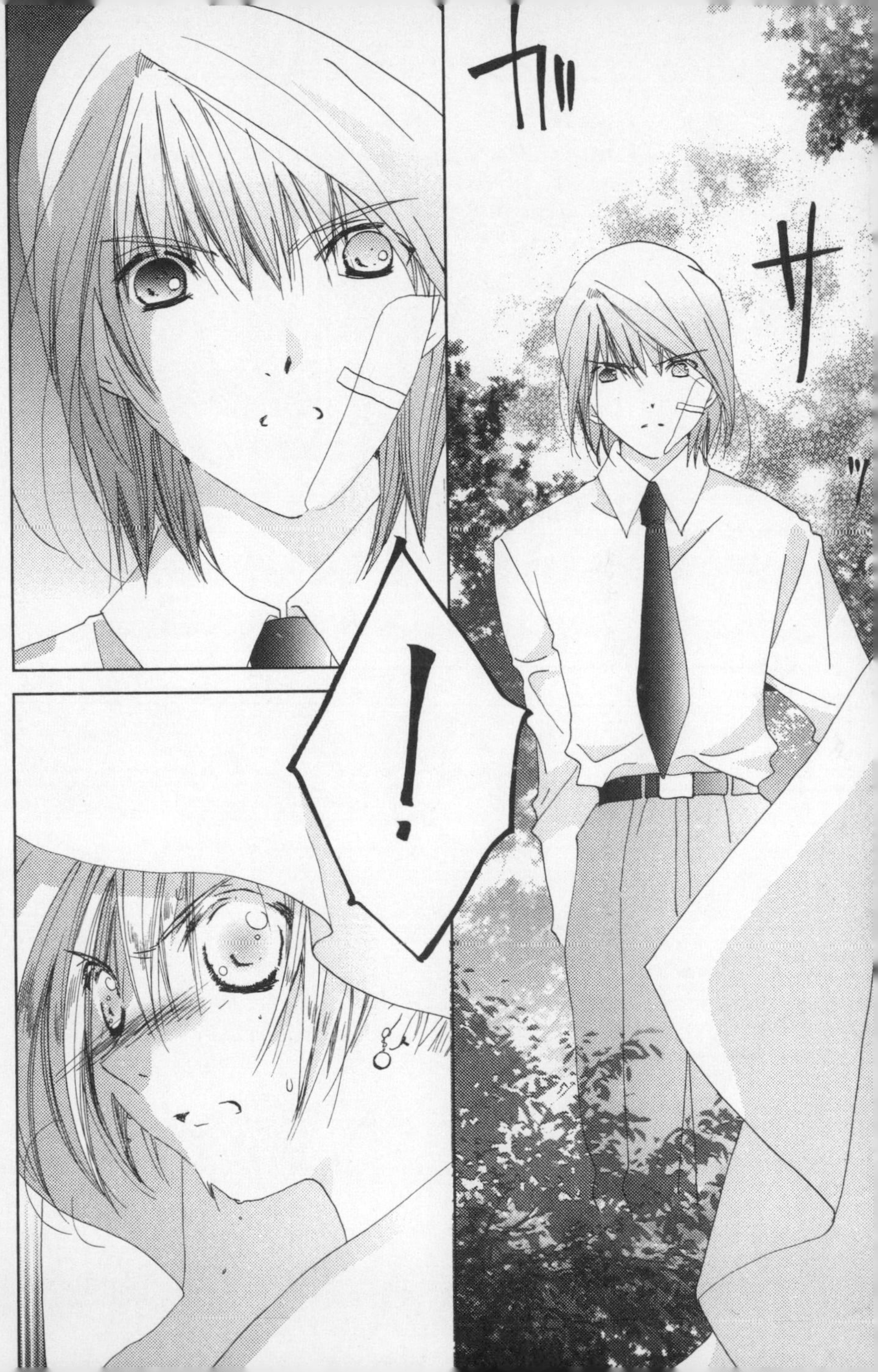
ガ
サッ
!

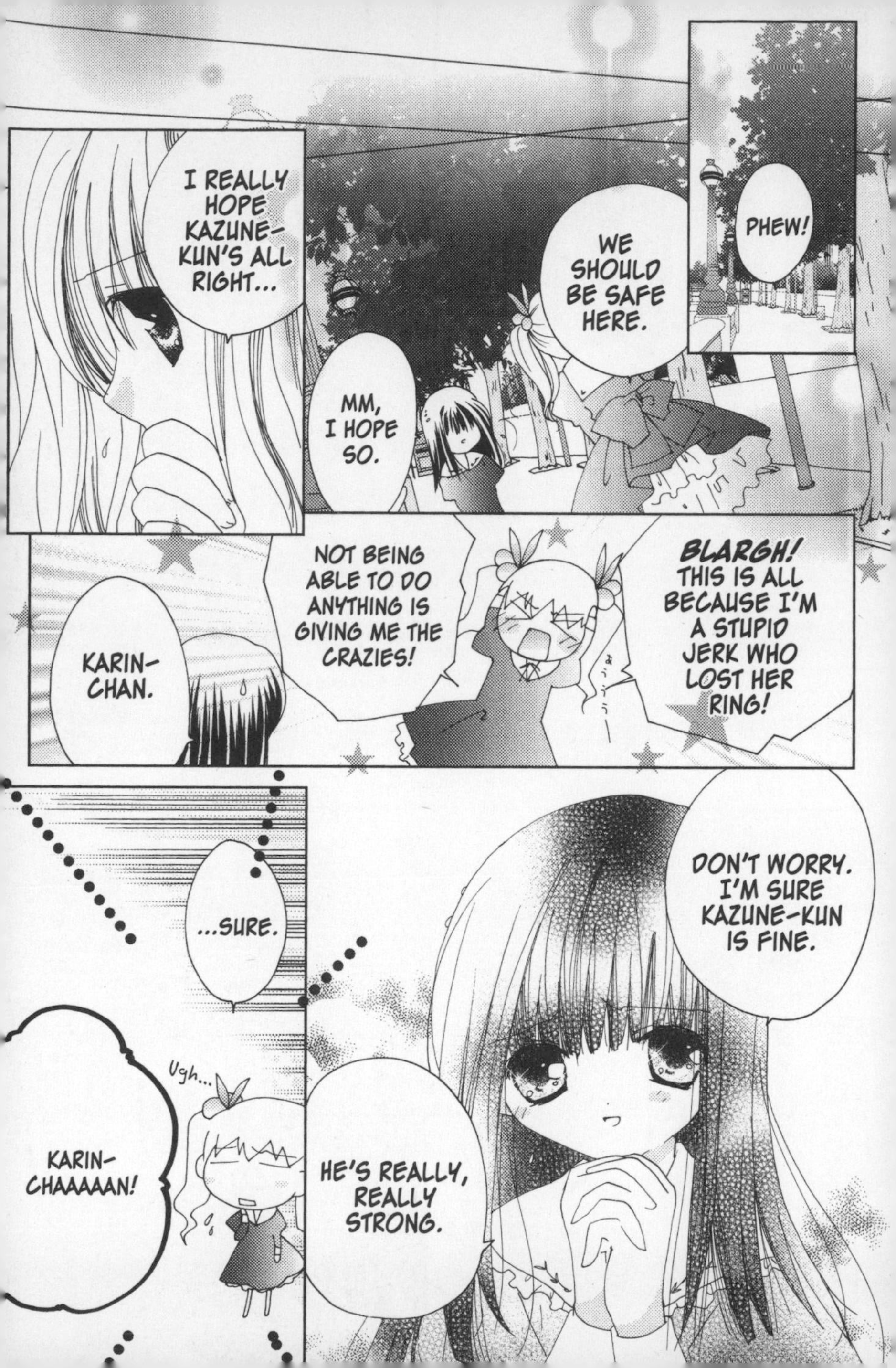
PHEW!
WE SHOULD BE SAFE HERE.
MM, I HOPE SO.
I REALLY HOPE KAZUNE-KUN'S ALL RIGHT...
BLARGH! THIS IS ALL BECAUSE I'M A STUPID JERK WHO LOST HER RING!
NOT BEING ABLE TO DO ANYTHING IS GIVING ME THE CRAZIES!
KARIN-CHAN.
DON'T WORRY. I'M SURE KAZUNE-KUN IS FINE.
HE'S REALLY, REALLY STRONG.
...SURE.
Ugh...
KARIN-CHAAAAAN!

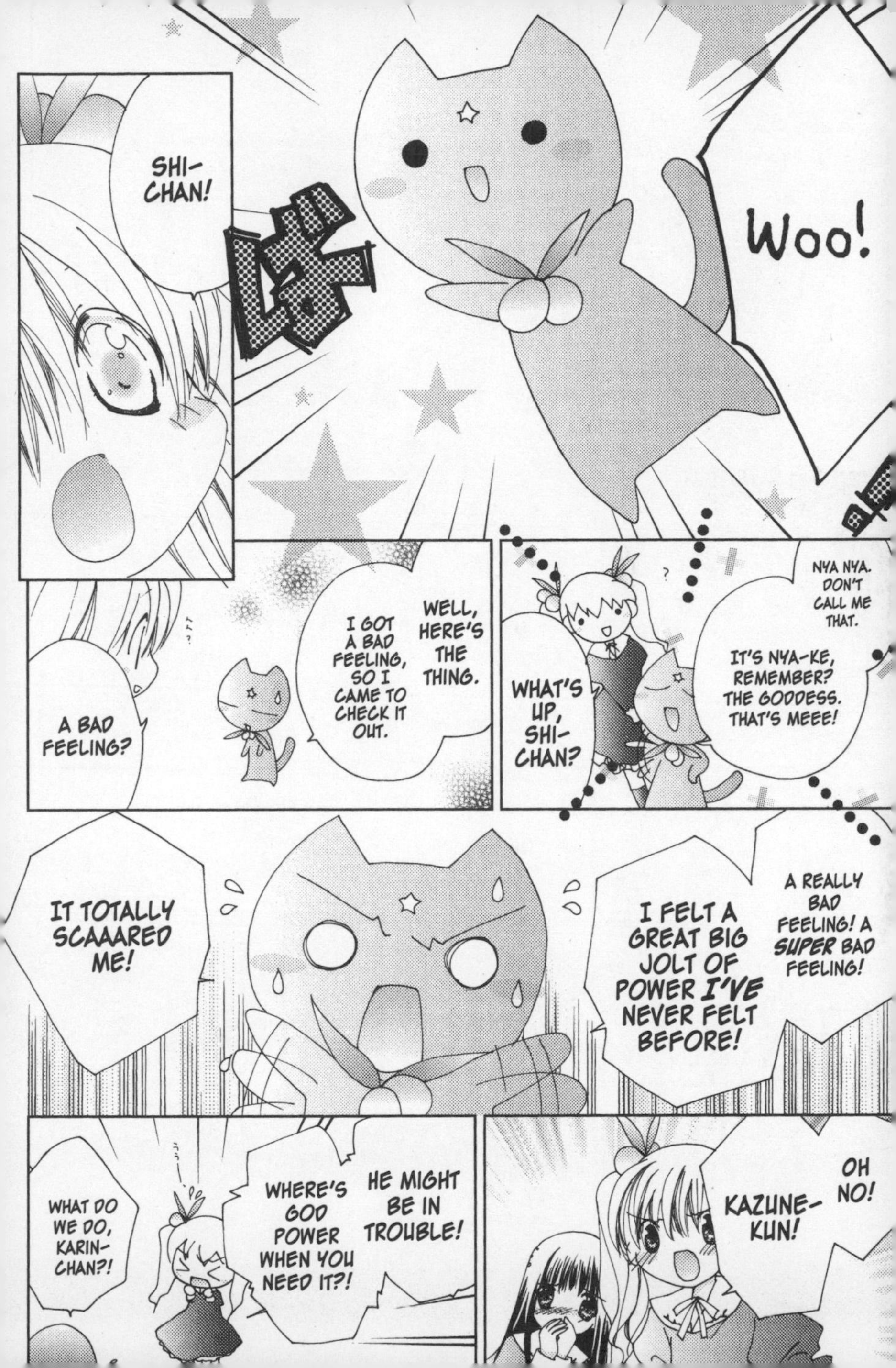

Woo!
SHI-CHAN!
NYA NYA. DON'T CALL ME THAT.
IT'S NYA-KE, REMEMBER? THE GODDESS. THAT'S MEEE!
WHAT'S UP, SHI-CHAN?
WELL, HERE'S THE THING.
I GOT A BAD FEELING, SO I CAME TO CHECK IT OUT.
A BAD FEELING?
A REALLY BAD FEELING! A SUPER BAD FEELING!
I FELT A GREAT BIG JOLT OF POWER I'VE NEVER FELT BEFORE!
IT TOTALLY SCAAARED ME!
OH NO!
KAZUNE-KUN!
HE MIGHT BE IN TROUBLE!
WHERE'S GOD POWER WHEN YOU NEED IT?!
WHAT DO WE DO, KARIN-CHAN?!

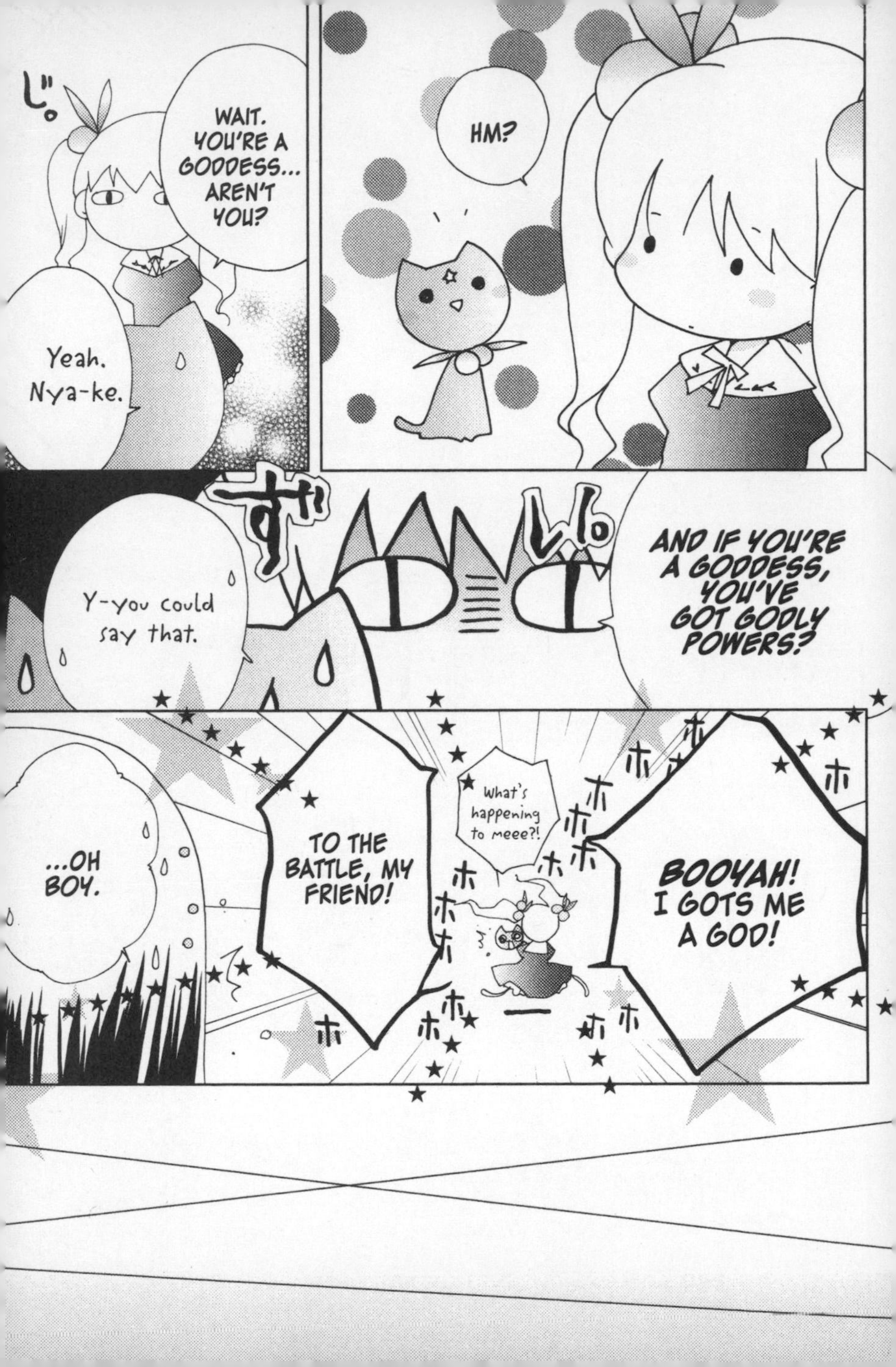
HM?
じ。
WAIT. YOU'RE A GODDESS... AREN'T YOU?
Yeah. Nya-ke.
AND IF YOU'RE A GODDESS, YOU'VE GOT GODLY POWERS?
ずい。
Y-you could say that.
BOOYAH! I GOTS ME A GOD!
What's happening to meee?!
TO THE BATTLE, MY FRIEND!
...OH BOY.

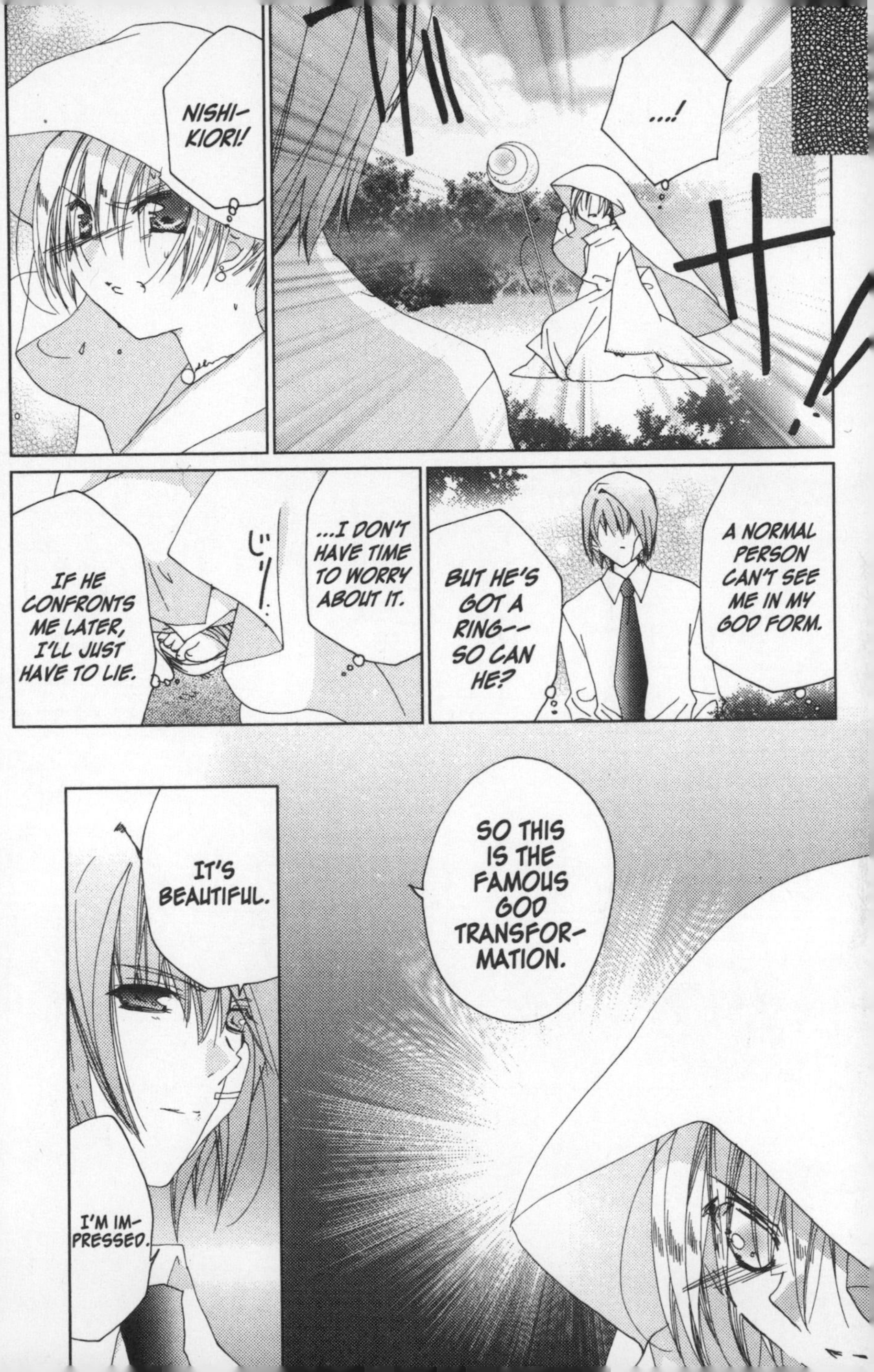
...!
NISHI-KIORI!
A NORMAL PERSON CAN'T SEE ME IN MY GOD FORM.
BUT HE'S GOT A RING-- SO CAN HE?
...I DON'T HAVE TIME TO WORRY ABOUT IT.
IF HE CONFRONTS ME LATER, I'LL JUST HAVE TO LIE.
SO THIS IS THE FAMOUS GOD TRANSFORMATION.
IT'S BEAUTIFUL.
I'M IM-PRESSED.

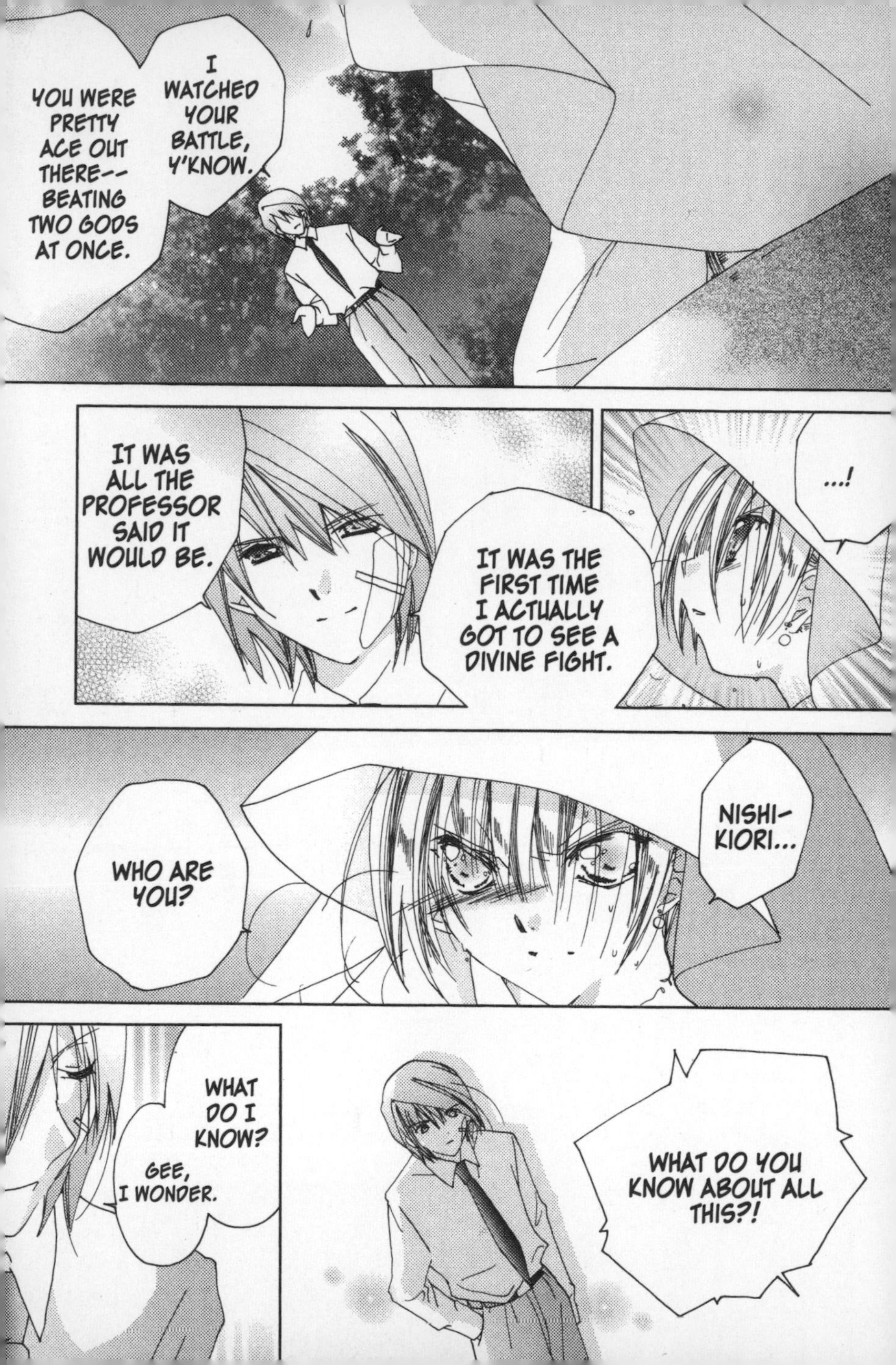
I WATCHED YOUR BATTLE, Y'KNOW.
YOU WERE PRETTY ACE OUT THERE-- BEATING TWO GODS AT ONCE.
...!
IT WAS ALL THE PROFESSOR SAID IT WOULD BE.
IT WAS THE FIRST TIME I ACTUALLY GOT TO SEE A DIVINE FIGHT.
NISHI-KIORI...
WHO ARE YOU?
WHAT DO YOU KNOW ABOUT ALL THIS?!
WHAT DO I KNOW?
GEE, I WONDER.

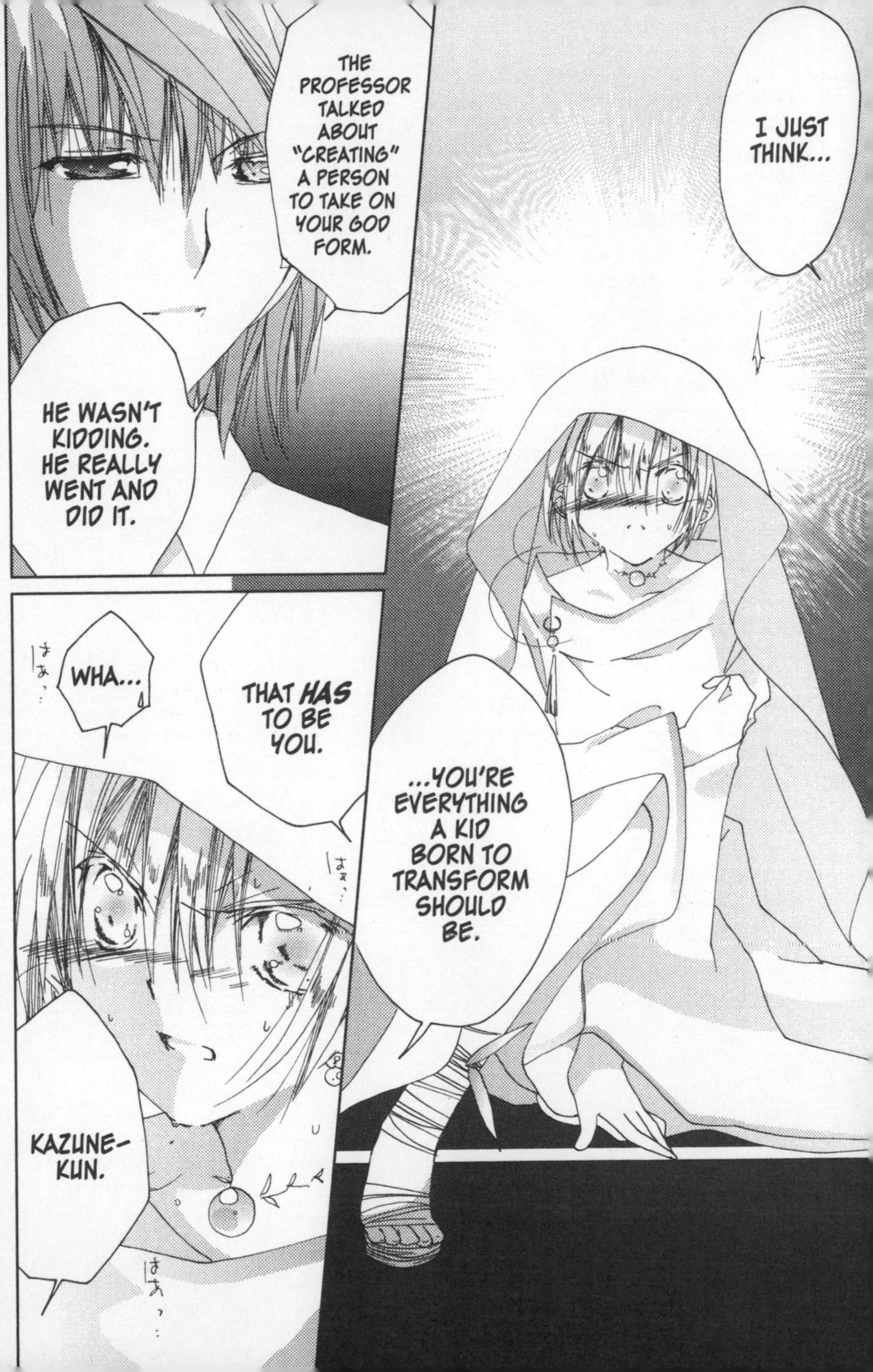
I JUST THINK...
...YOU'RE EVERYTHING A KID BORN TO TRANSFORM SHOULD BE.
THE PROFESSOR TALKED ABOUT "CREATING" A PERSON TO TAKE ON YOUR GOD FORM.
HE WASN'T KIDDING. HE REALLY WENT AND DID IT.
THAT HAS TO BE YOU.
WHA...
KAZUNE-KUN.

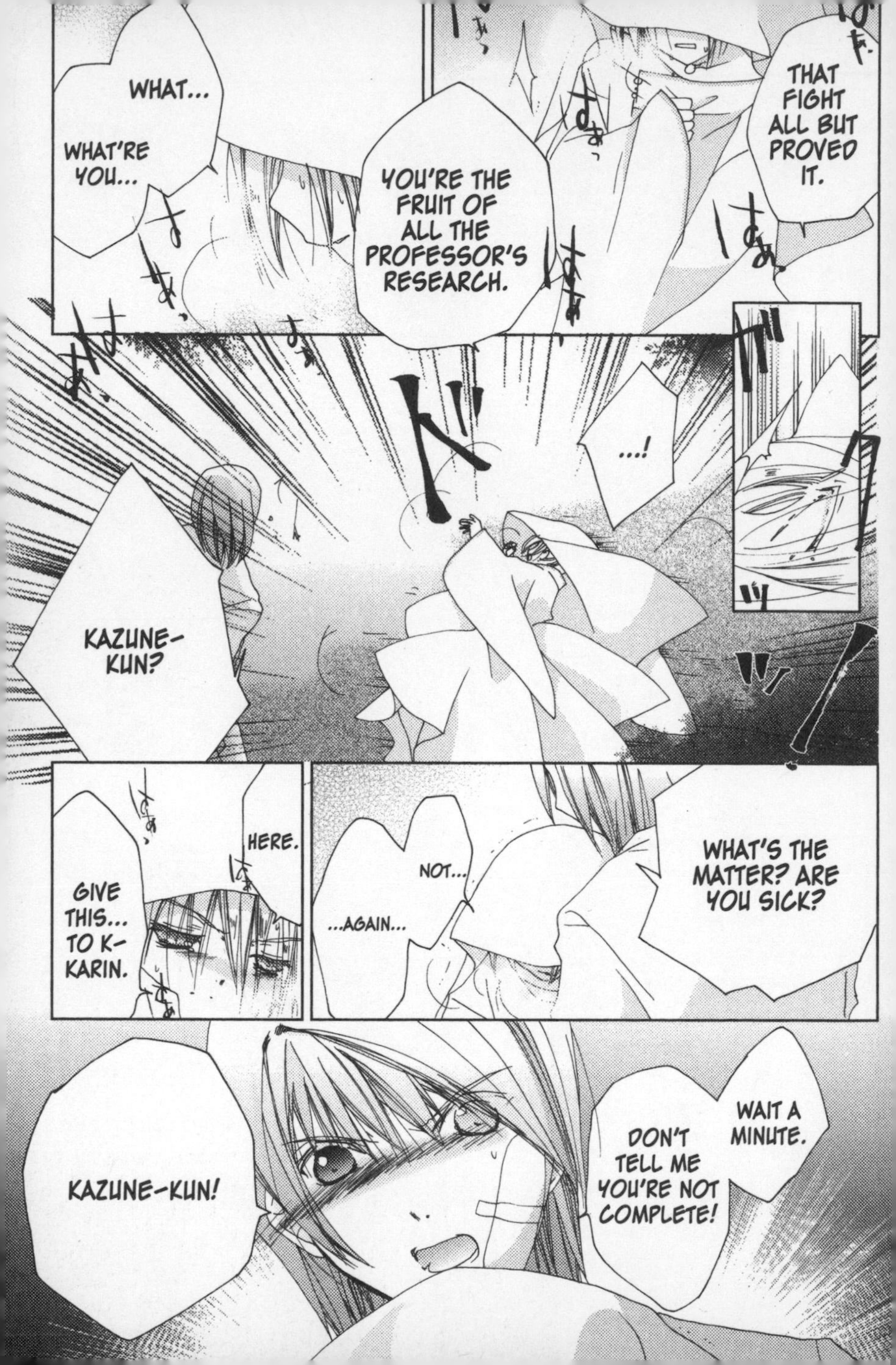

THAT FIGHT ALL BUT PROVED IT.
YOU'RE THE FRUIT OF ALL THE PROFESSOR'S RESEARCH.
WHAT...
WHAT'RE YOU...
...!
KAZUNE-KUN?
WHAT'S THE MATTER? ARE YOU SICK?
NOT...
...AGAIN...
HERE.
GIVE THIS... TO K-KARIN.
WAIT A MINUTE.
DON'T TELL ME YOU'RE NOT COMPLETE!
KAZUNE-KUN!

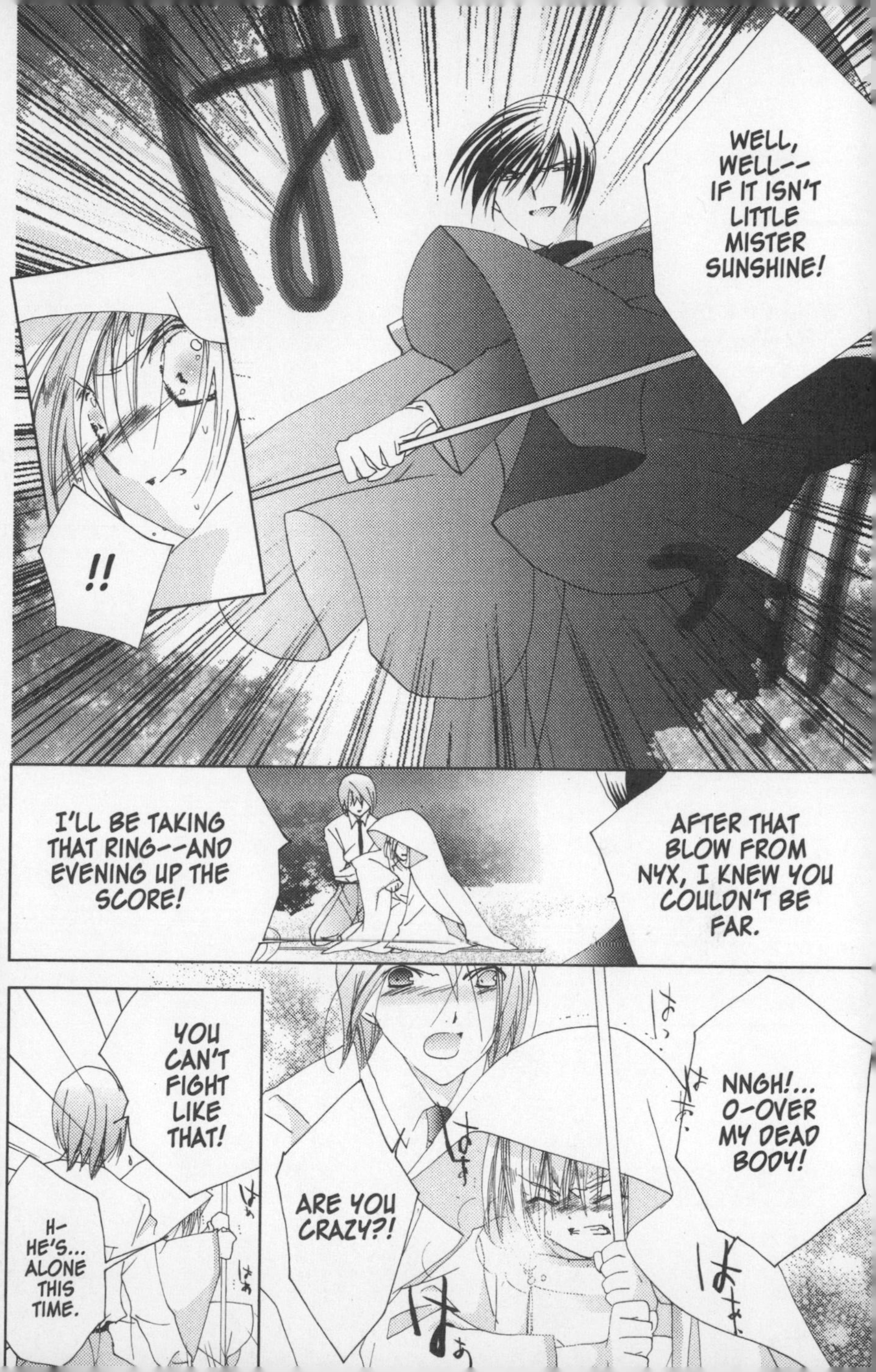

WELL, WELL--IF IT ISN'T LITTLE MISTER SUNSHINE!
!!
AFTER THAT BLOW FROM NYX, I KNEW YOU COULDN'T BE FAR.
I'LL BE TAKING THAT RING--AND EVENING UP THE SCORE!
NNGH!... O-OVER MY DEAD BODY!
ARE YOU CRAZY?!
YOU CAN'T FIGHT LIKE THAT!
H-HE'S... ALONE THIS TIME.

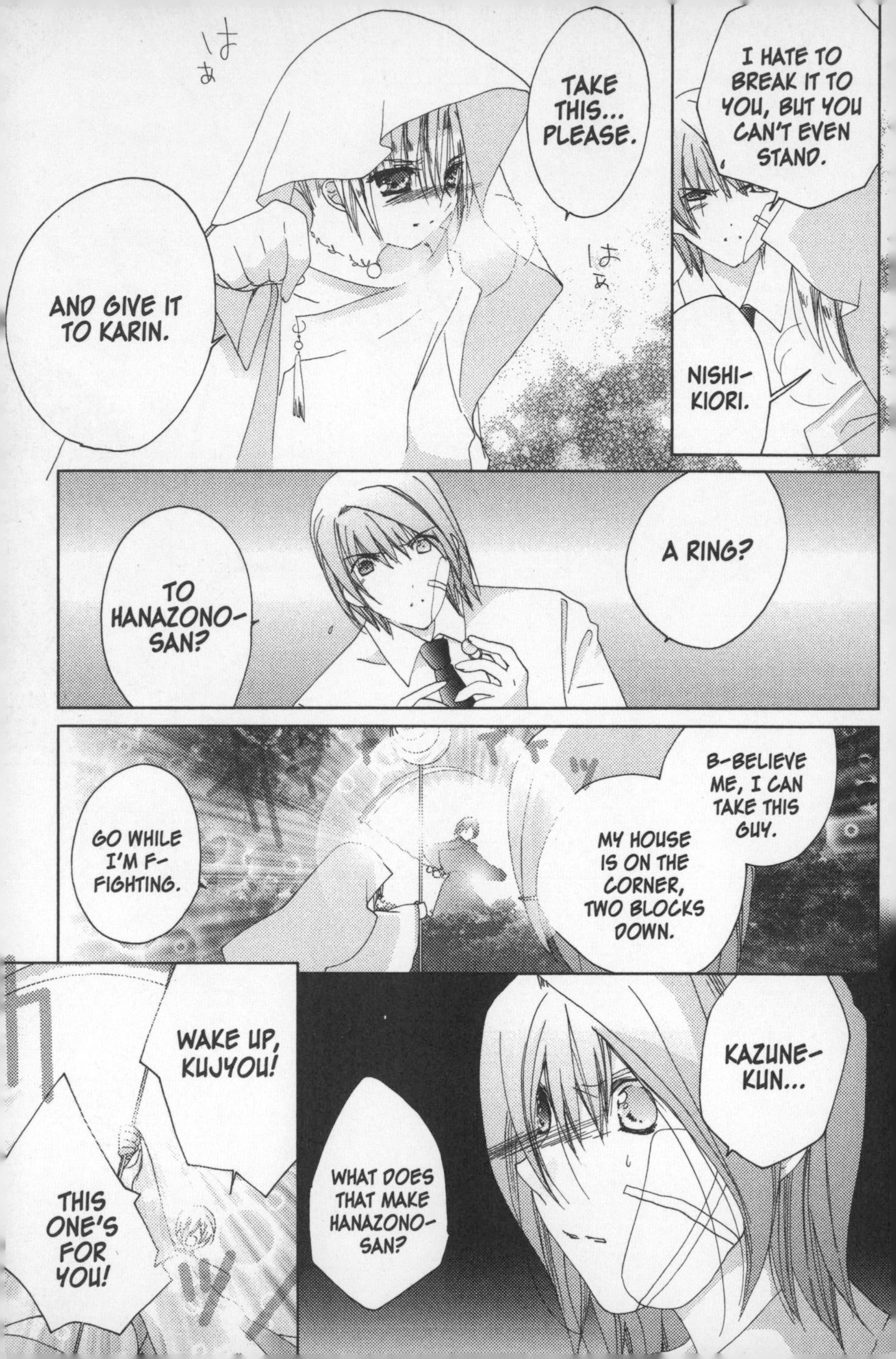
I HATE TO BREAK IT TO YOU, BUT YOU CAN'T EVEN STAND.
NISHIKIORI.
TAKE THIS... PLEASE.
はぁ
はぁ
AND GIVE IT TO KARIN.
A RING?
TO HANAZONO-SAN?
B-BELIEVE ME, I CAN TAKE THIS GUY.
MY HOUSE IS ON THE CORNER, TWO BLOCKS DOWN.
GO WHILE I'M F-FIGHTING.
KAZUNE-KUN...
WHAT DOES THAT MAKE HANAZONO-SAN?
WAKE UP, KUJYOU!
THIS ONE'S FOR YOU!

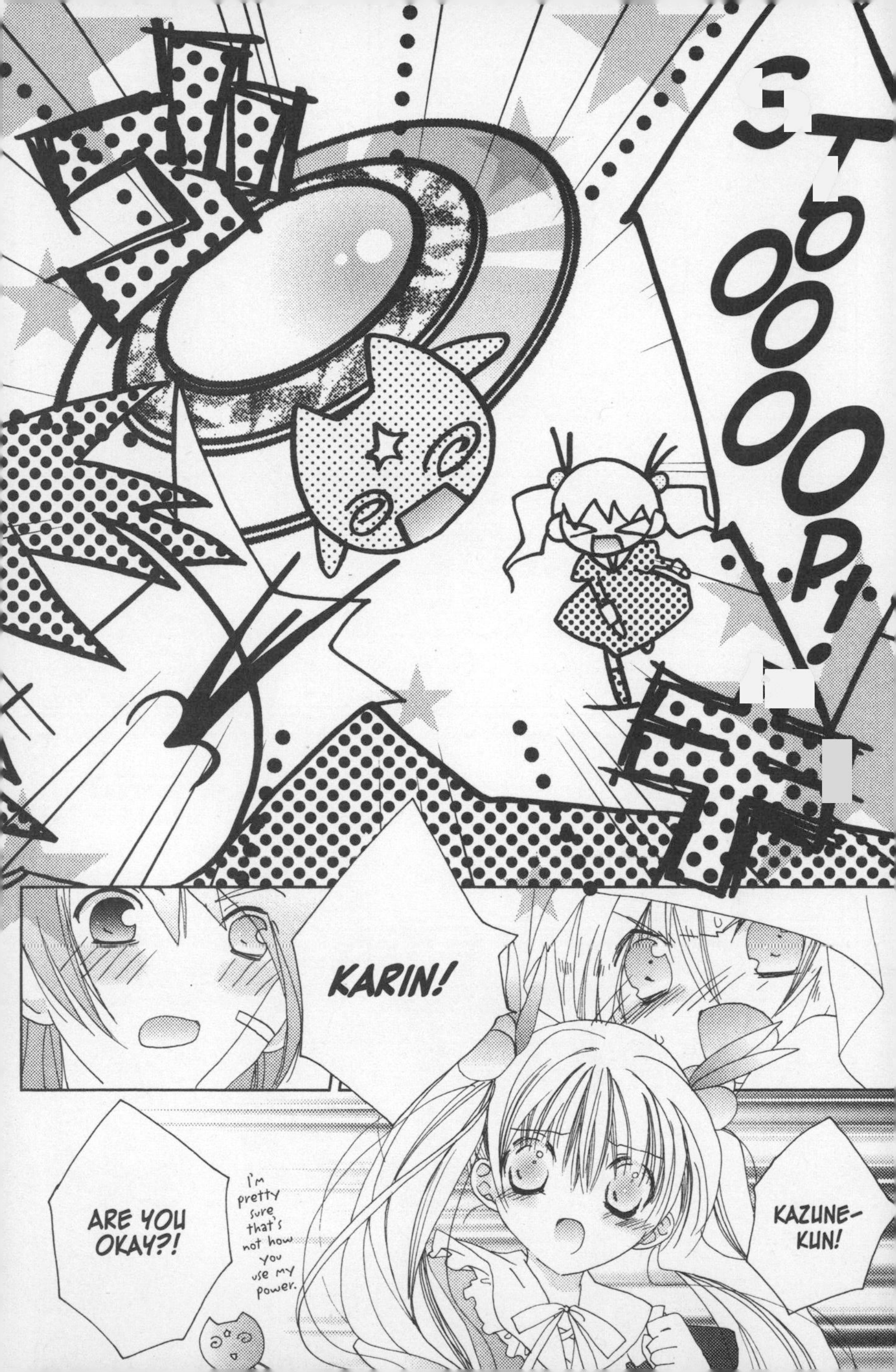
STOOOOOP!!
KARIN!
KAZUNE-KUN!
I'm pretty sure that's not how you use my power.
ARE YOU OKAY?!

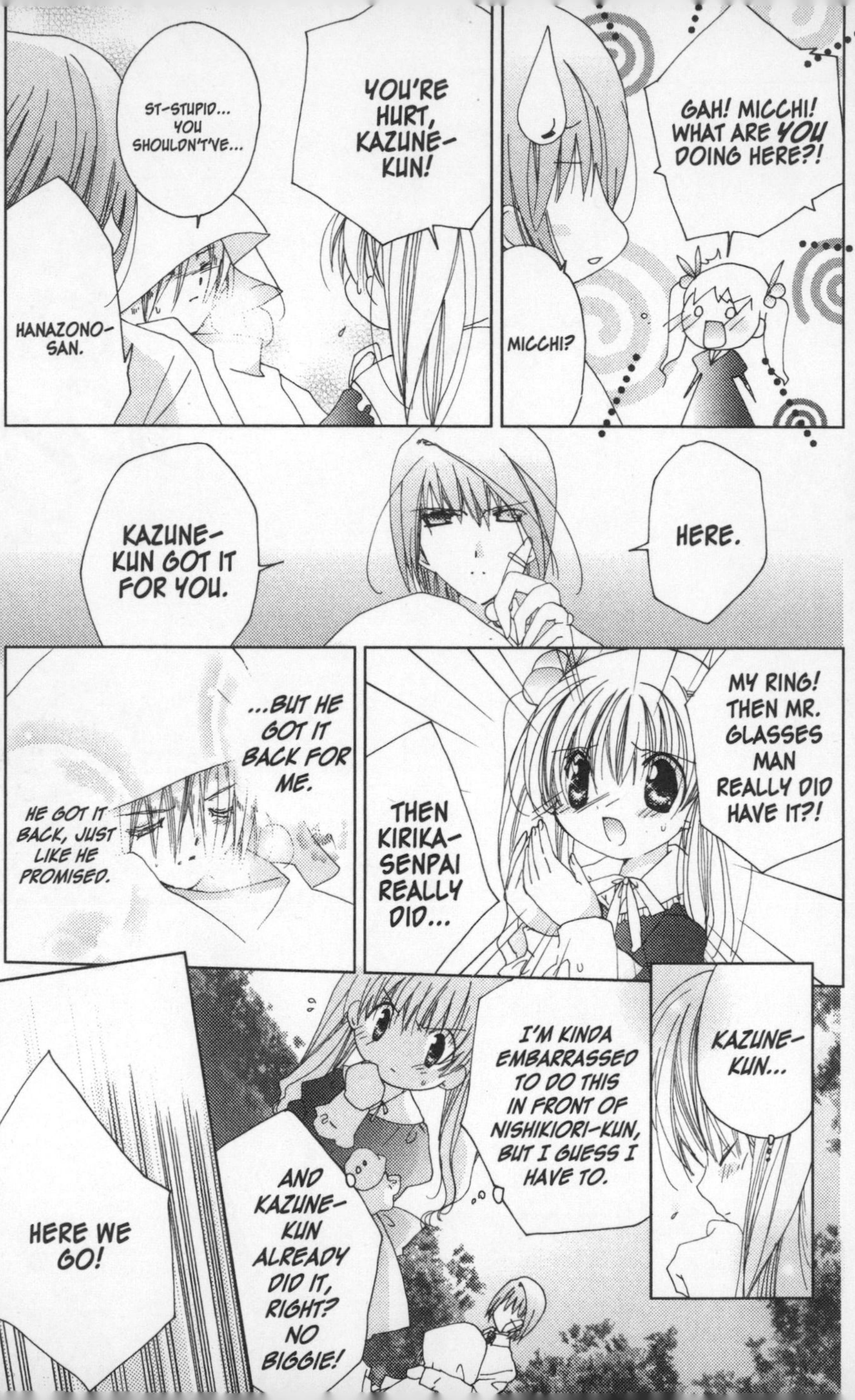
GAH! MICCHI! WHAT ARE YOU DOING HERE?!
MICCHI?
YOU'RE HURT, KAZUNE-KUN!
ST-STUPID... YOU SHOULDN'T'VE...
HANAZONO-SAN.
HERE.
KAZUNE-KUN GOT IT FOR YOU.
MY RING! THEN MR. GLASSES MAN REALLY DID HAVE IT?!
THEN KIRIKA-SENPAI REALLY DID...
...BUT HE GOT IT BACK FOR ME.
HE GOT IT BACK, JUST LIKE HE PROMISED.
KAZUNE-KUN...
I'M KINDA EMBARRASSED TO DO THIS IN FRONT OF NISHIKIORI-KUN, BUT I GUESS I HAVE TO.
AND KAZUNE-KUN ALREADY DID IT, RIGHT? NO BIGGIE!
HERE WE GO!

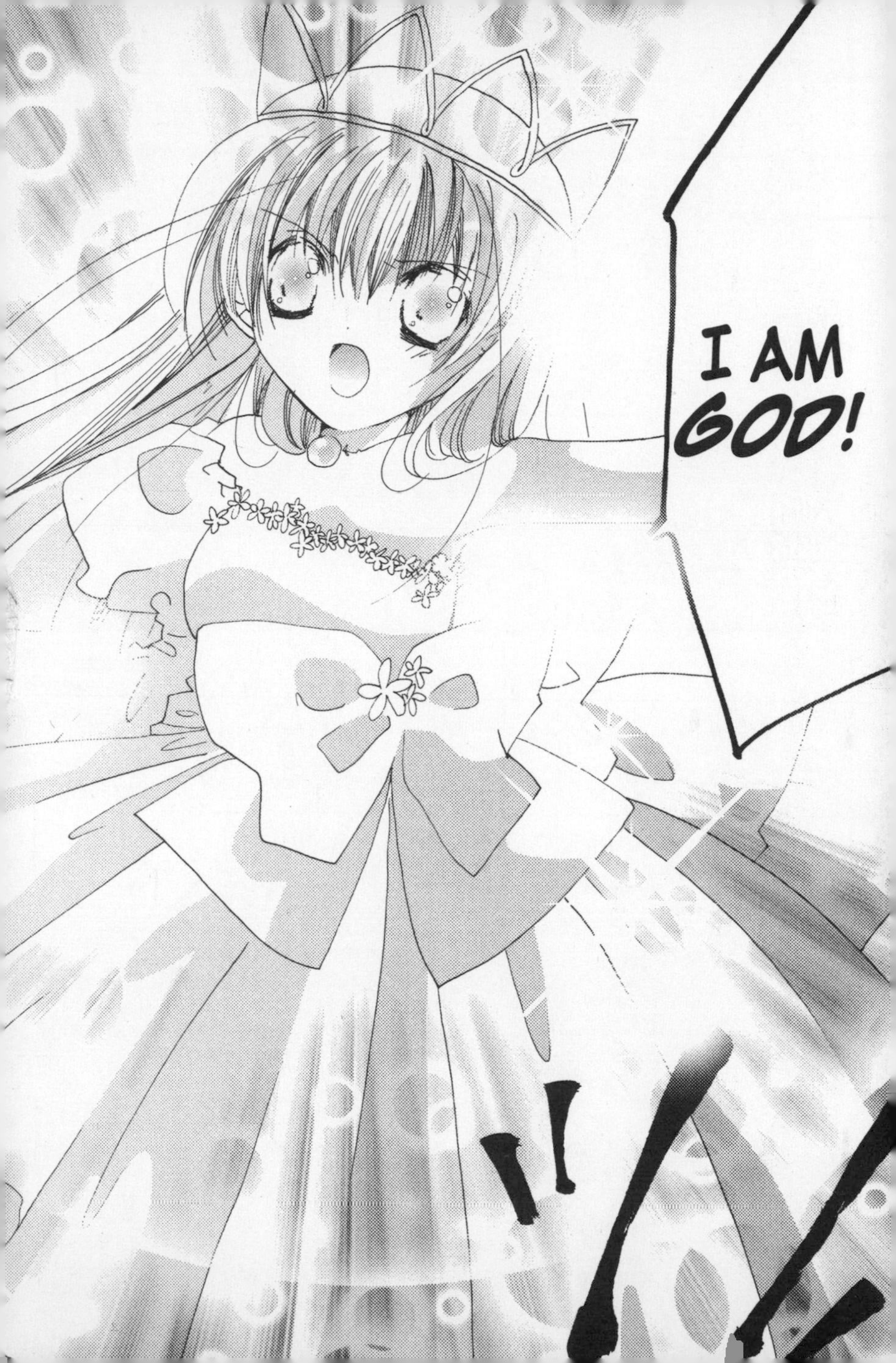
I AM GOD!
!!

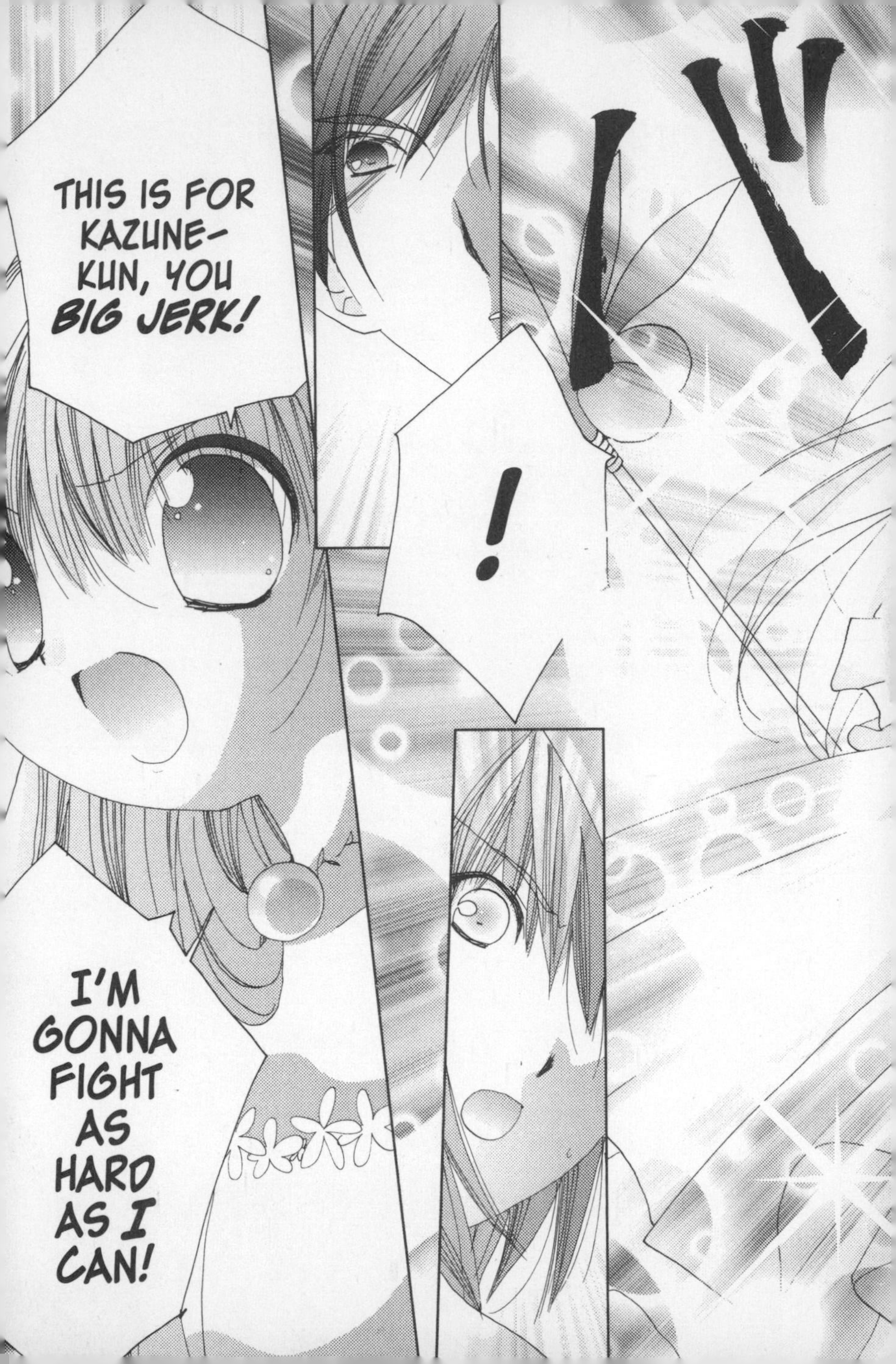
!
THIS IS FOR KAZUNE-KUN, YOU *BIG JERK!*
I'M GONNA FIGHT AS HARD AS I CAN!

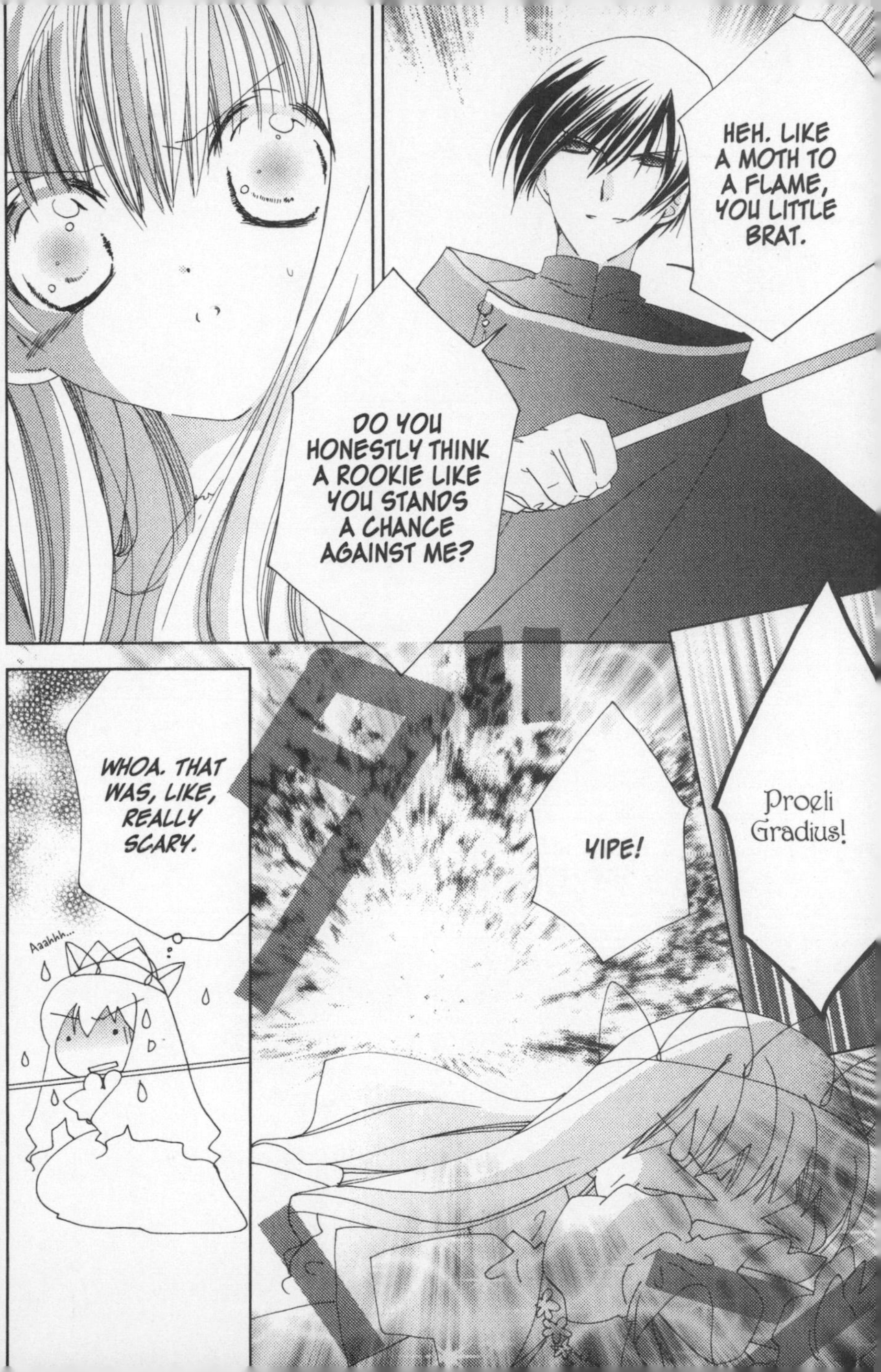
HEH. LIKE A MOTH TO A FLAME, YOU LITTLE BRAT.
DO YOU HONESTLY THINK A ROOKIE LIKE YOU STANDS A CHANCE AGAINST ME?
Proeli Gradius!
YIPE!
WHOA. THAT WAS, LIKE, REALLY SCARY.
Aaahhh...

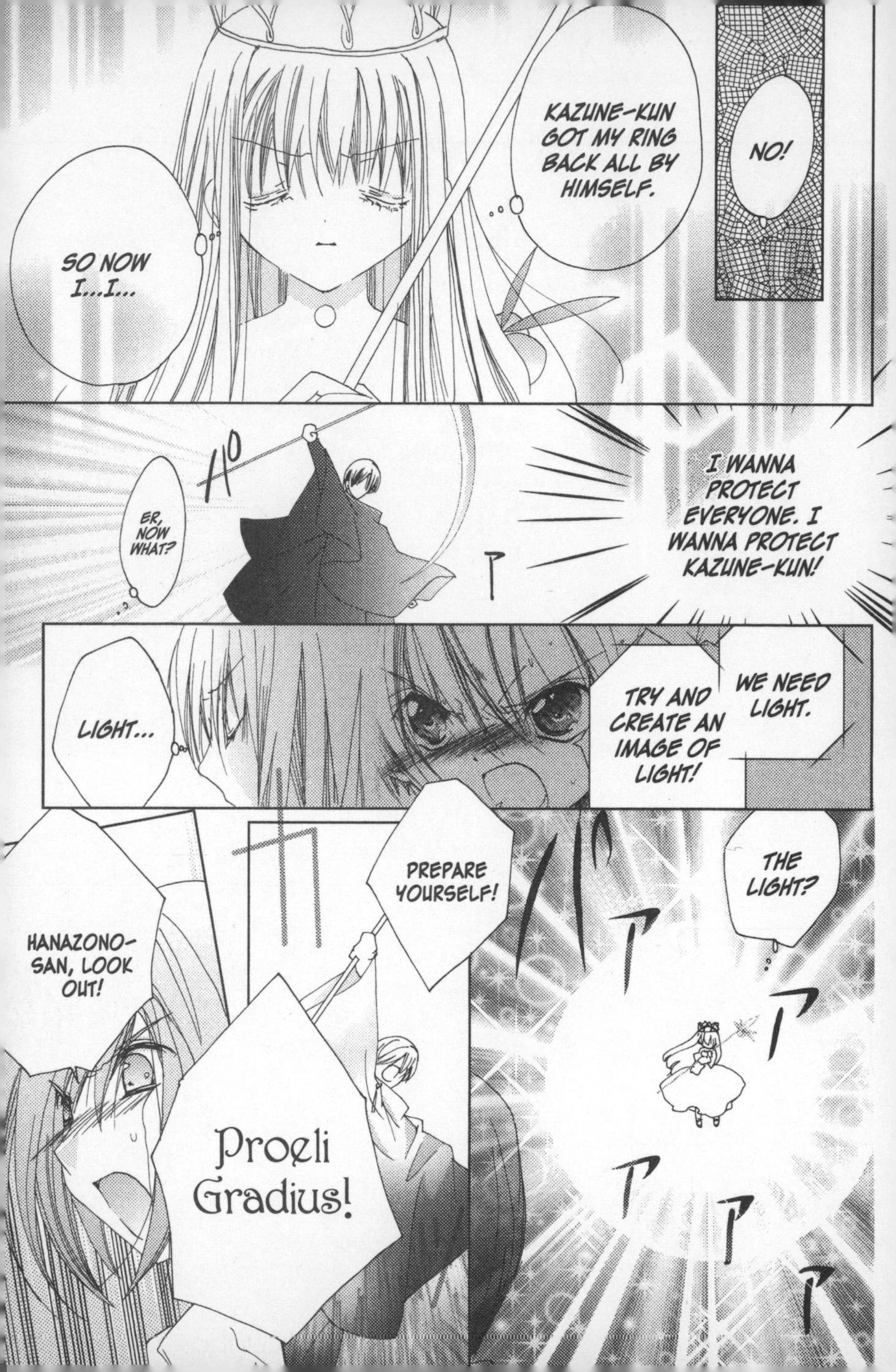
NO!
KAZUNE-KUN GOT MY RING BACK ALL BY HIMSELF.
SO NOW I...I...
I WANNA PROTECT EVERYONE. I WANNA PROTECT KAZUNE-KUN!
ER, NOW WHAT?
WE NEED LIGHT.
TRY AND CREATE AN IMAGE OF LIGHT!
LIGHT...
THE LIGHT?
PREPARE YOURSELF!
HANAZONO-SAN, LOOK OUT!
Proeli Gradius!

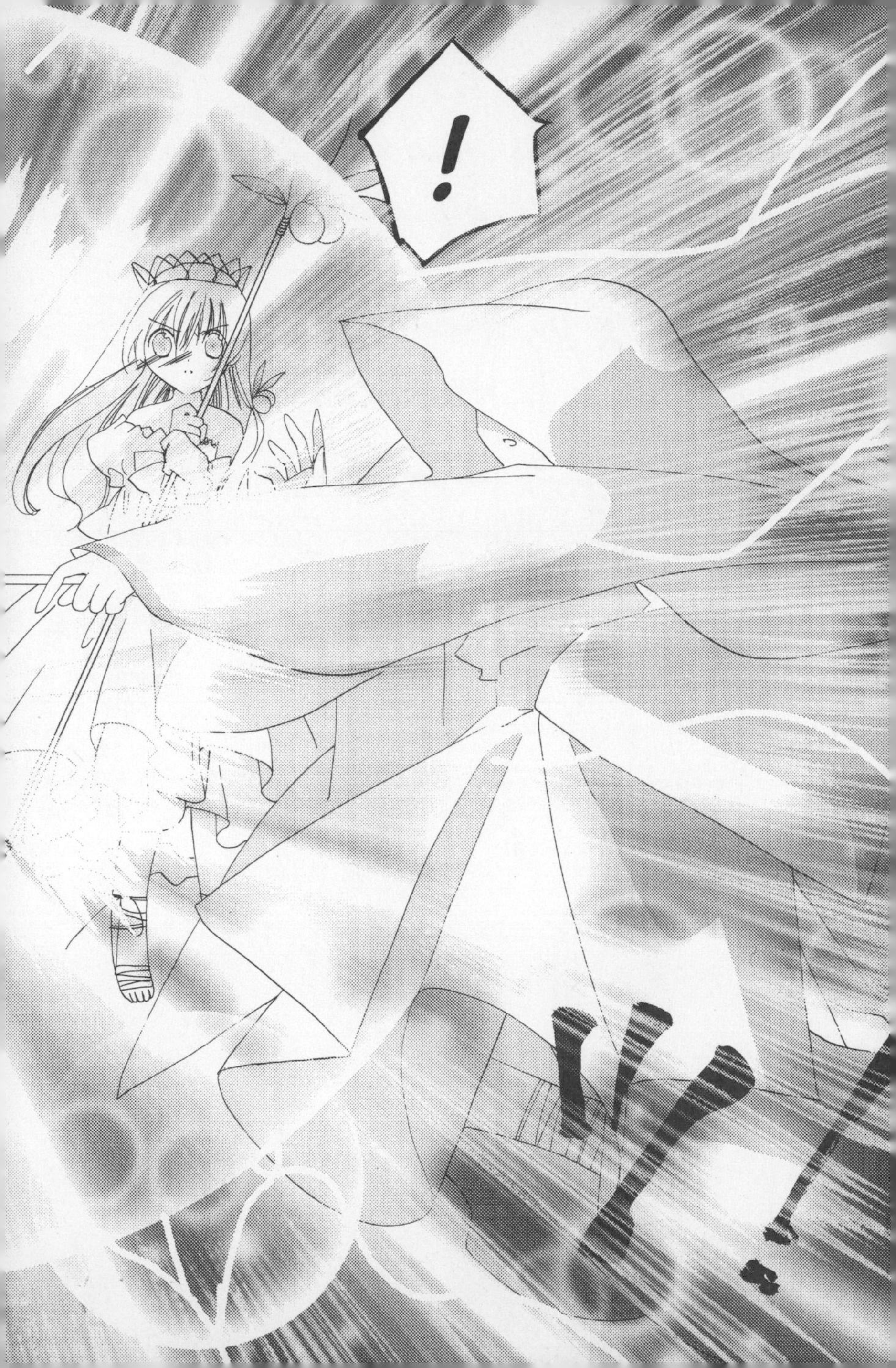
!

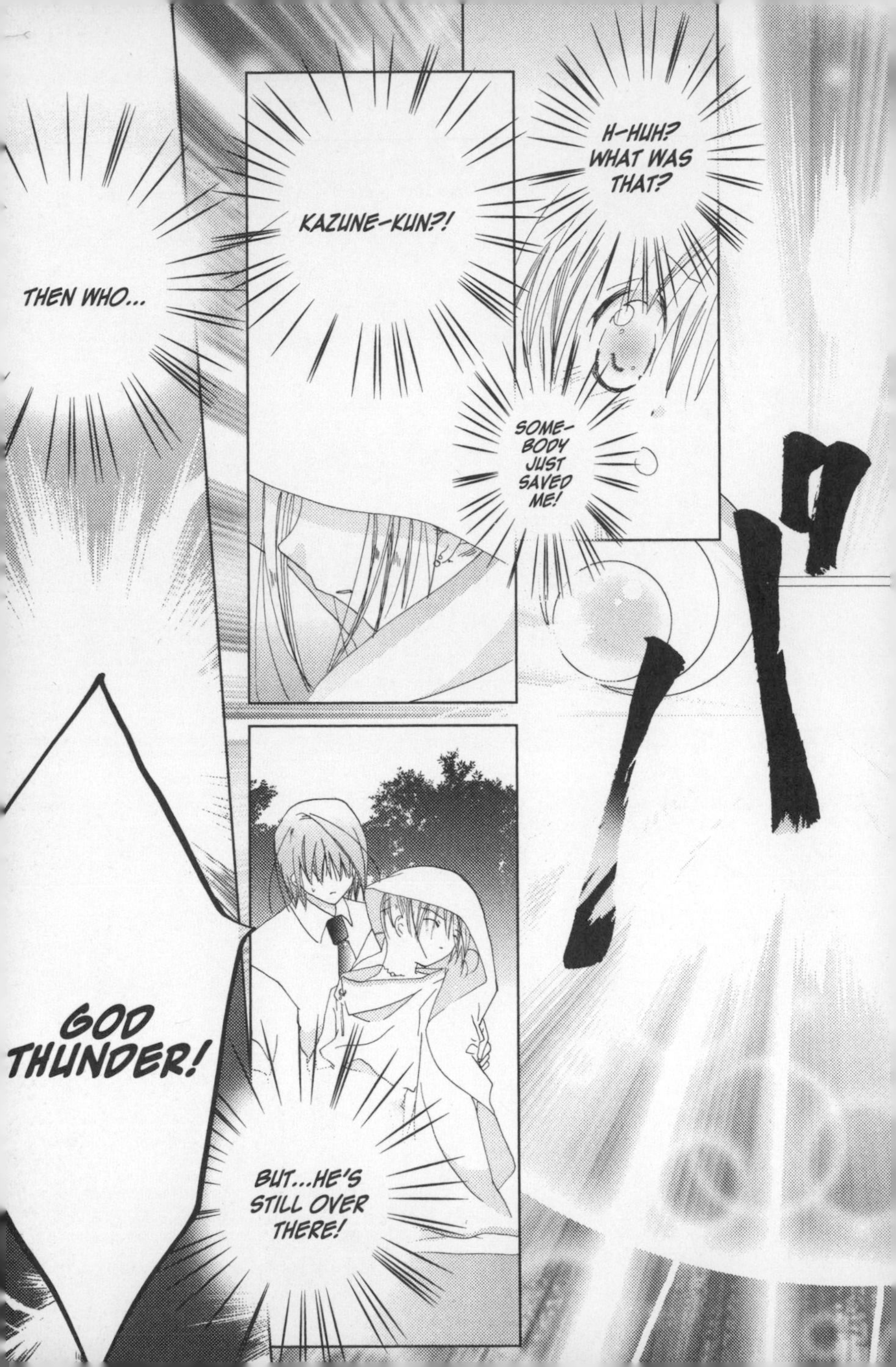

H-HUH? WHAT WAS THAT?
SOME-BODY JUST SAVED ME!
KAZUNE-KUN?!
BUT...HE'S STILL OVER THERE!
THEN WHO...
GOD THUNDER!

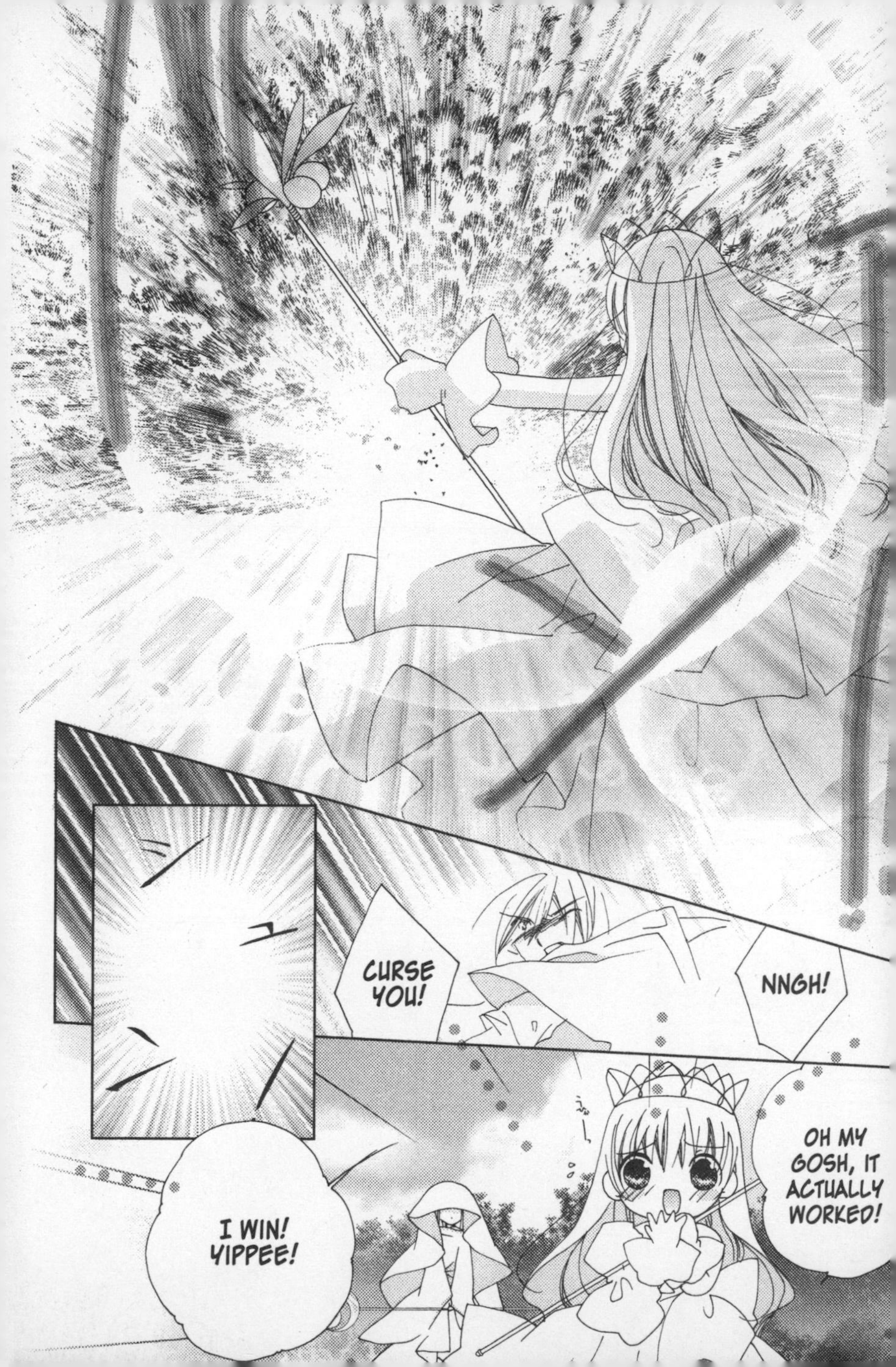
NNGH!
CURSE YOU!
OH MY GOSH, IT ACTUALLY WORKED!
I WIN! YIPPEE!

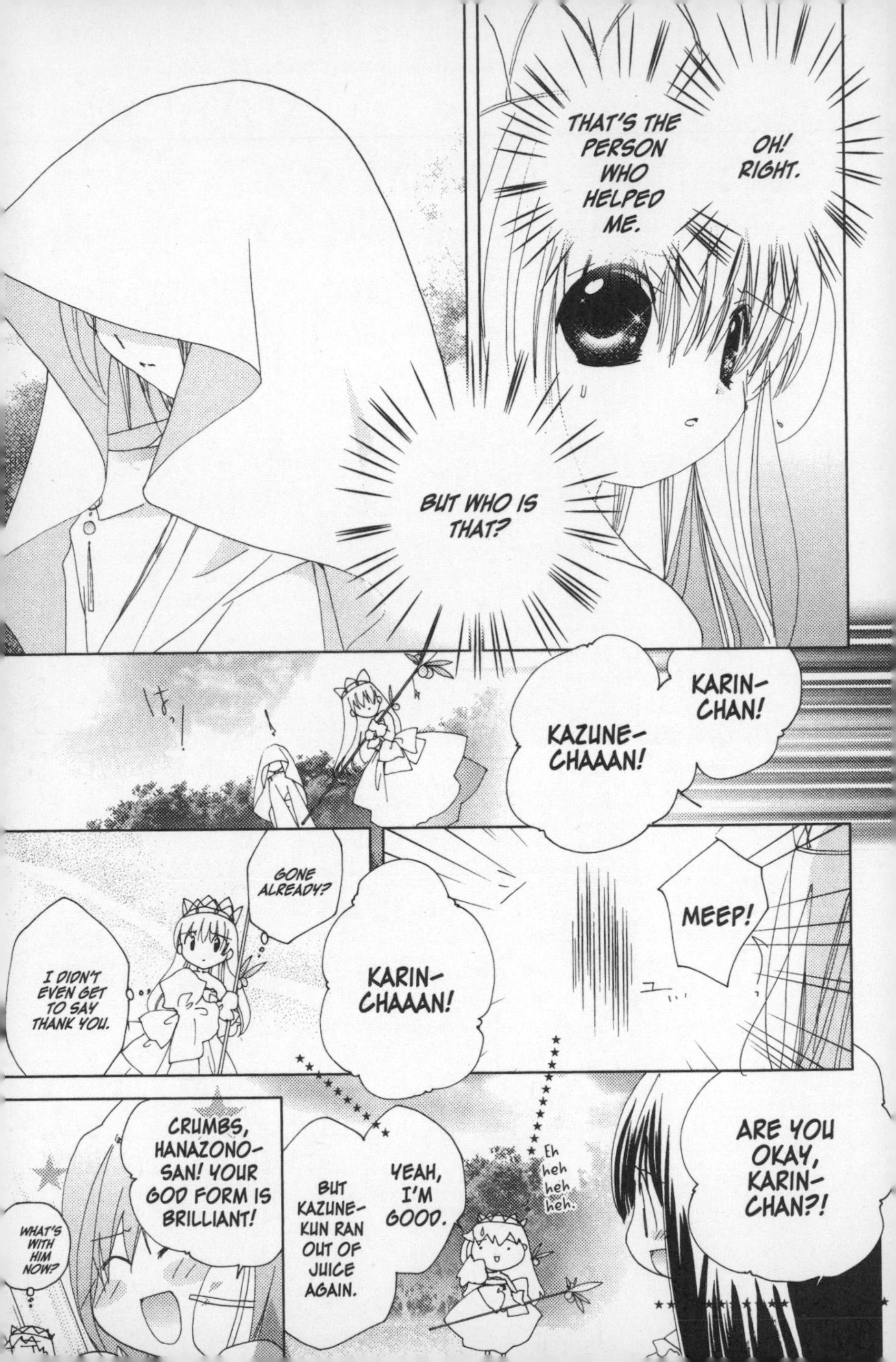
OH! RIGHT.
THAT'S THE PERSON WHO HELPED ME.
BUT WHO IS THAT?
KARIN-CHAN!
KAZUNE-CHAAAN!
MEEP!
KARIN-CHAAAN!
GONE ALREADY?
I DIDN'T EVEN GET TO SAY THANK YOU.
ARE YOU OKAY, KARIN-CHAN?!
YEAH, I'M GOOD.
Eh heh heh heh.
BUT KAZUNE-KUN RAN OUT OF JUICE AGAIN.
CRUMBS, HANAZONO-SAN! YOUR GOD FORM IS BRILLIANT!
WHAT'S WITH HIM NOW?

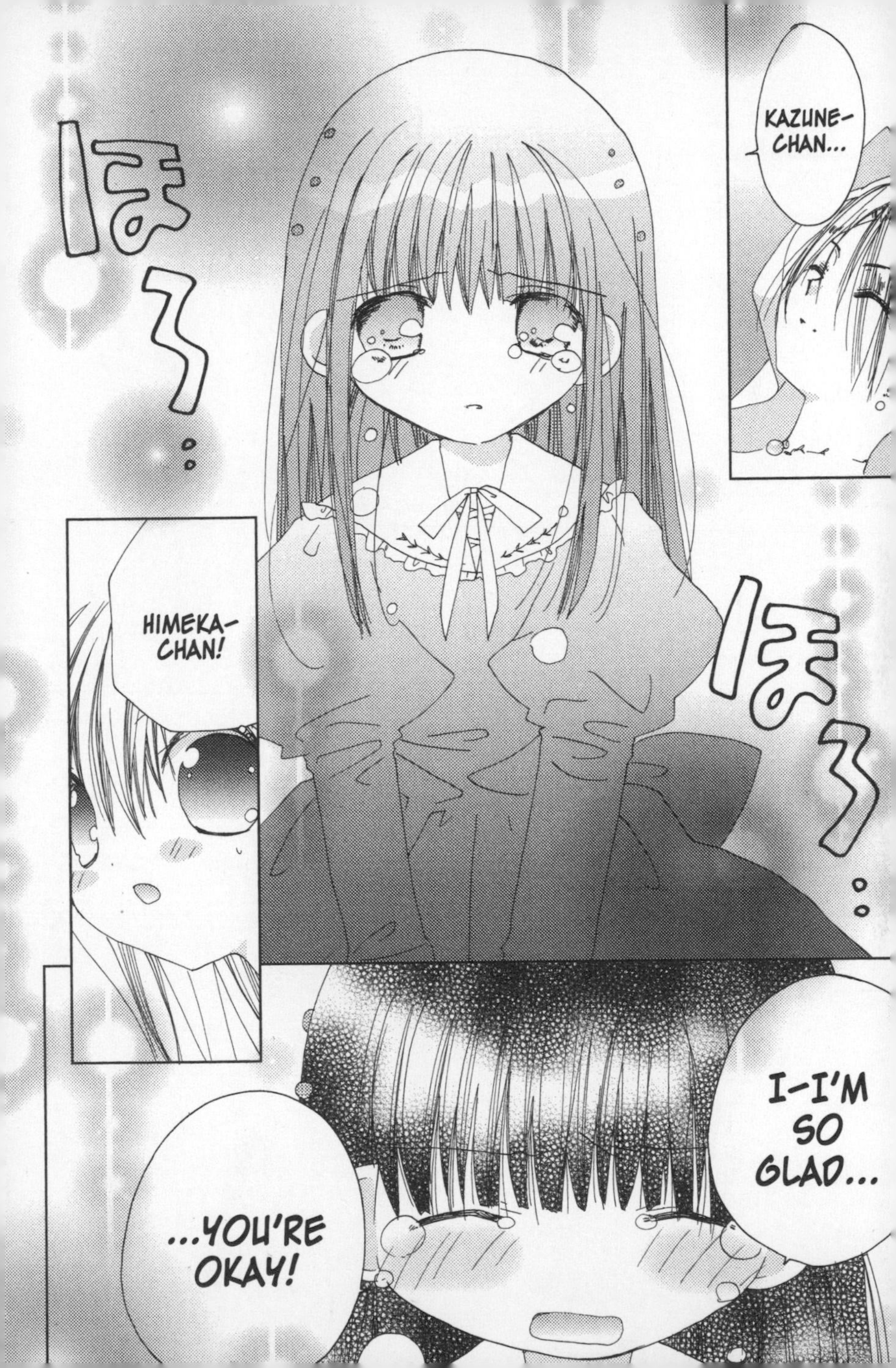
KAZUNE-CHAN...
ほろ..
ほろ..
HIMEKA-CHAN!
I-I'M SO GLAD...
...YOU'RE OKAY!

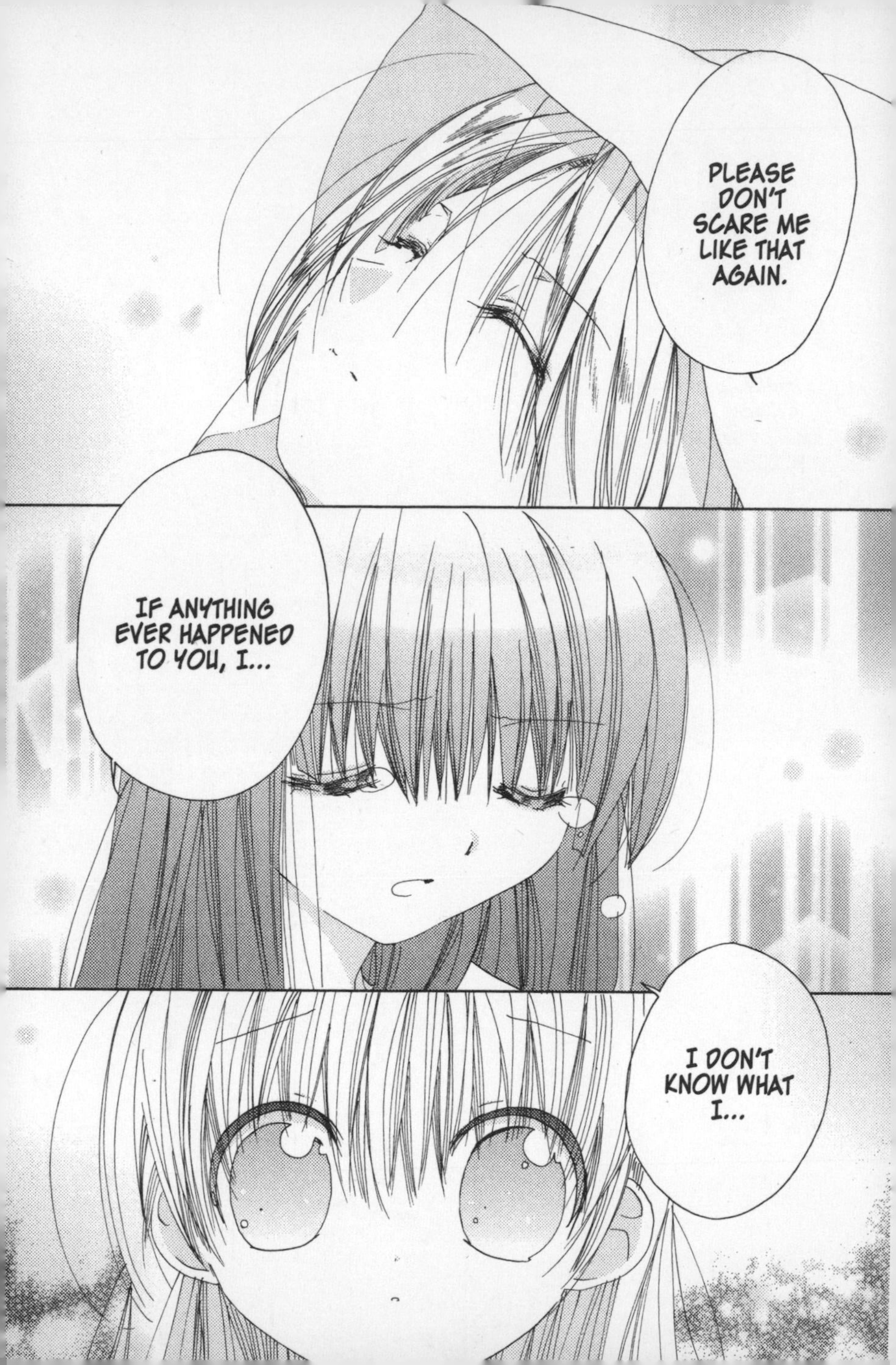
PLEASE DON'T SCARE ME LIKE THAT AGAIN.
IF ANYTHING EVER HAPPENED TO YOU, I...
I DON'T KNOW WHAT I...

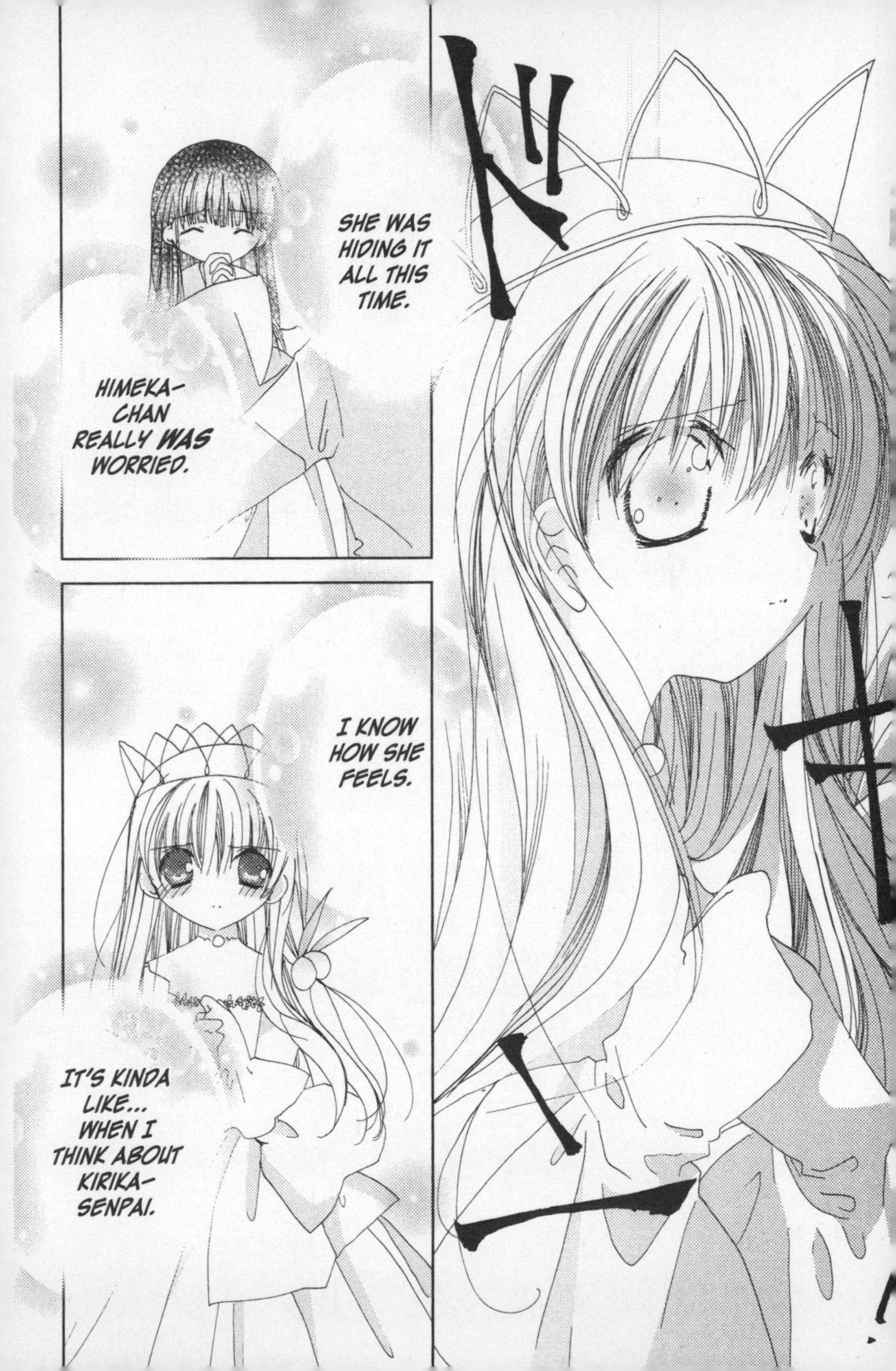
SHE WAS HIDING IT ALL THIS TIME.
HIMEKA-CHAN REALLY **WAS** WORRIED.
I KNOW HOW SHE FEELS.
IT'S KINDA LIKE... WHEN I THINK ABOUT KIRIKA-SENPAI.

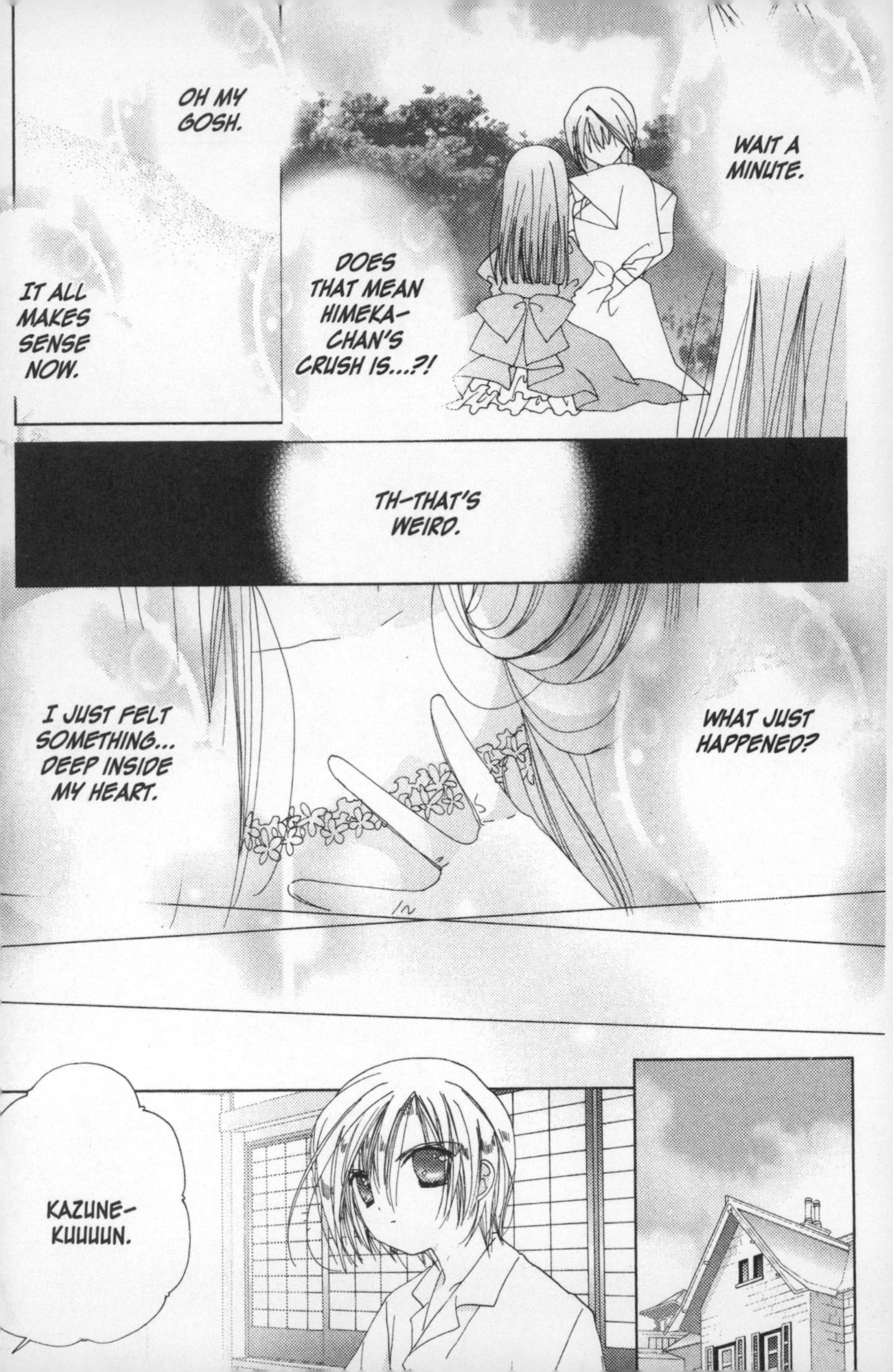
WAIT A MINUTE.
DOES THAT MEAN HIMEKA-CHAN'S CRUSH IS...?!
OH MY GOSH.
IT ALL MAKES SENSE NOW.
TH-THAT'S WEIRD.
WHAT JUST HAPPENED?
I JUST FELT SOMETHING... DEEP INSIDE MY HEART.
KAZUNE-KUUUUN.

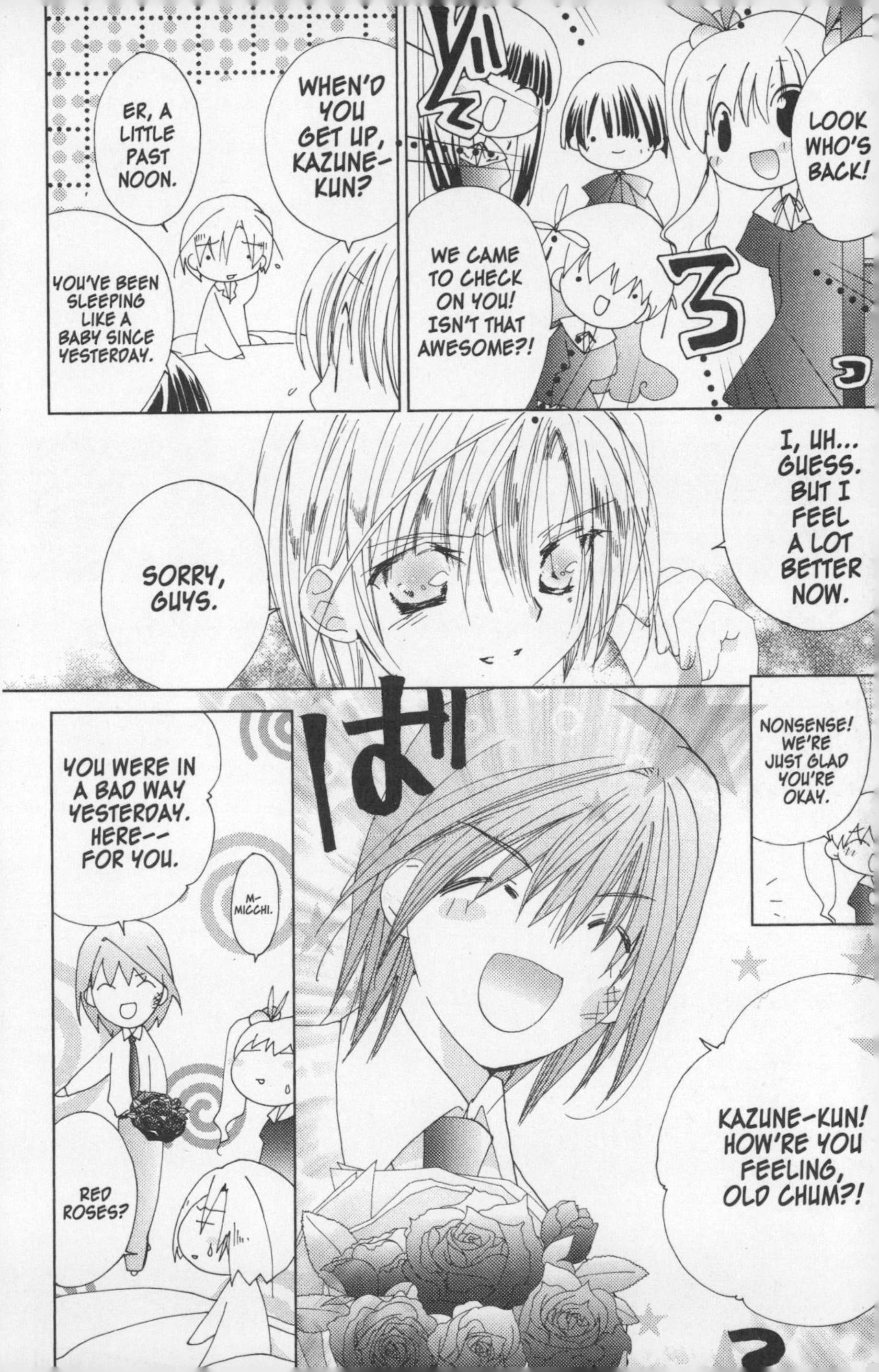
LOOK WHO'S BACK!
WE CAME TO CHECK ON YOU! ISN'T THAT AWESOME?!
WHEN'D YOU GET UP, KAZUNE-KUN?
ER, A LITTLE PAST NOON.
YOU'VE BEEN SLEEPING LIKE A BABY SINCE YESTERDAY.
I, UH... GUESS. BUT I FEEL A LOT BETTER NOW.
SORRY, GUYS.
NONSENSE! WE'RE JUST GLAD YOU'RE OKAY.
KAZUNE-KUN! HOW'RE YOU FEELING, OLD CHUM?!
YOU WERE IN A BAD WAY YESTERDAY. HERE-- FOR YOU.
M-MICCHI.
RED ROSES?

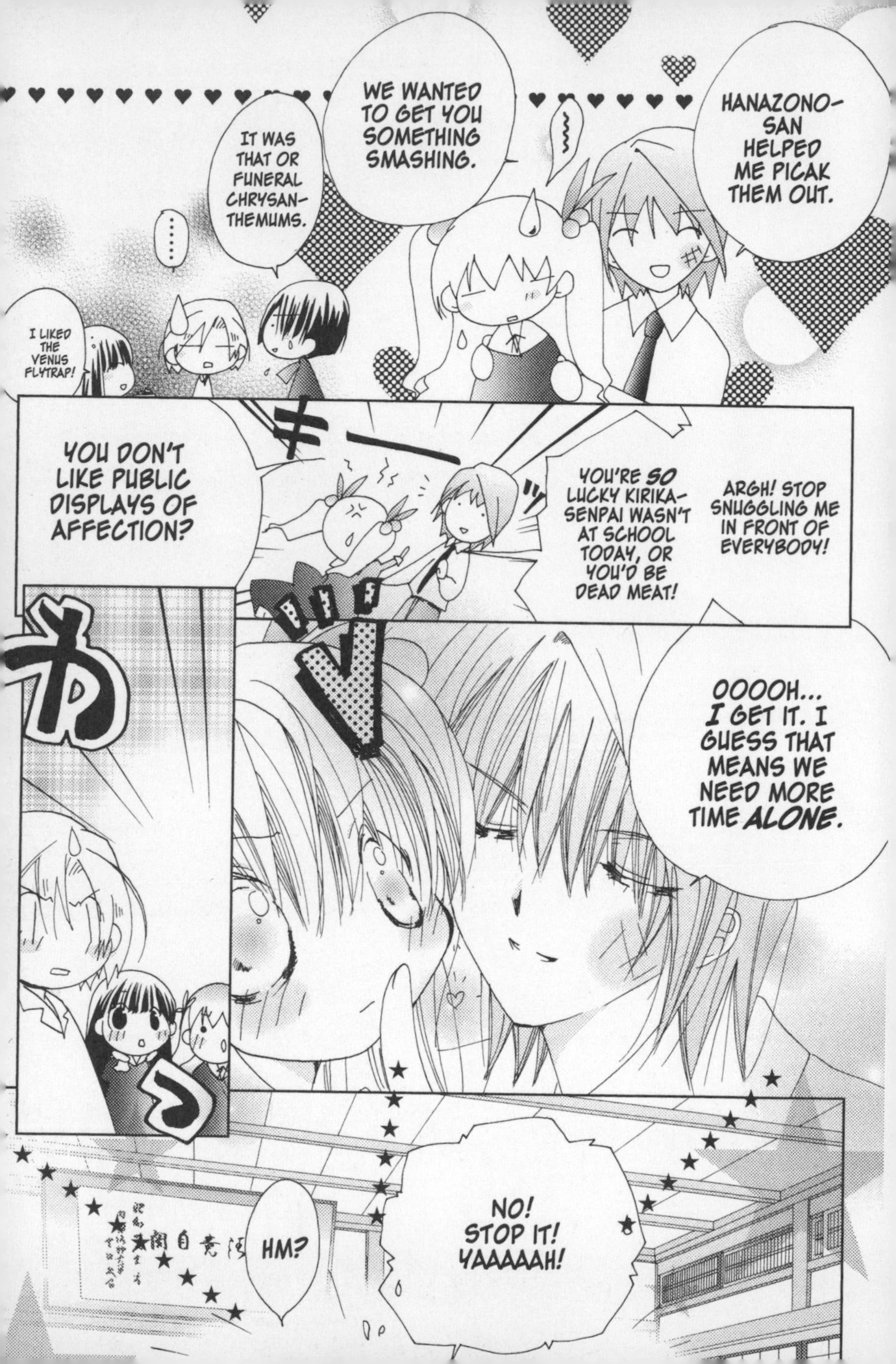
HANAZONO-SAN HELPED ME PICAK THEM OUT.
WE WANTED TO GET YOU SOMETHING SMASHING.
IT WAS THAT OR FUNERAL CHRYSAN-THEMUMS.
......
I LIKED THE VENUS FLYTRAP!
ARGH! STOP SNUGGLING ME IN FRONT OF EVERYBODY!
YOU'RE *SO* LUCKY KIRIKA-SENPAI WASN'T AT SCHOOL TODAY, OR YOU'D BE DEAD MEAT!
キー
YOU DON'T LIKE PUBLIC DISPLAYS OF AFFECTION?
OOOOH... *I* GET IT. I GUESS THAT MEANS WE NEED MORE TIME ***ALONE***.
わっ
NO! STOP IT! YAAAAAH!
HM?

Meh.

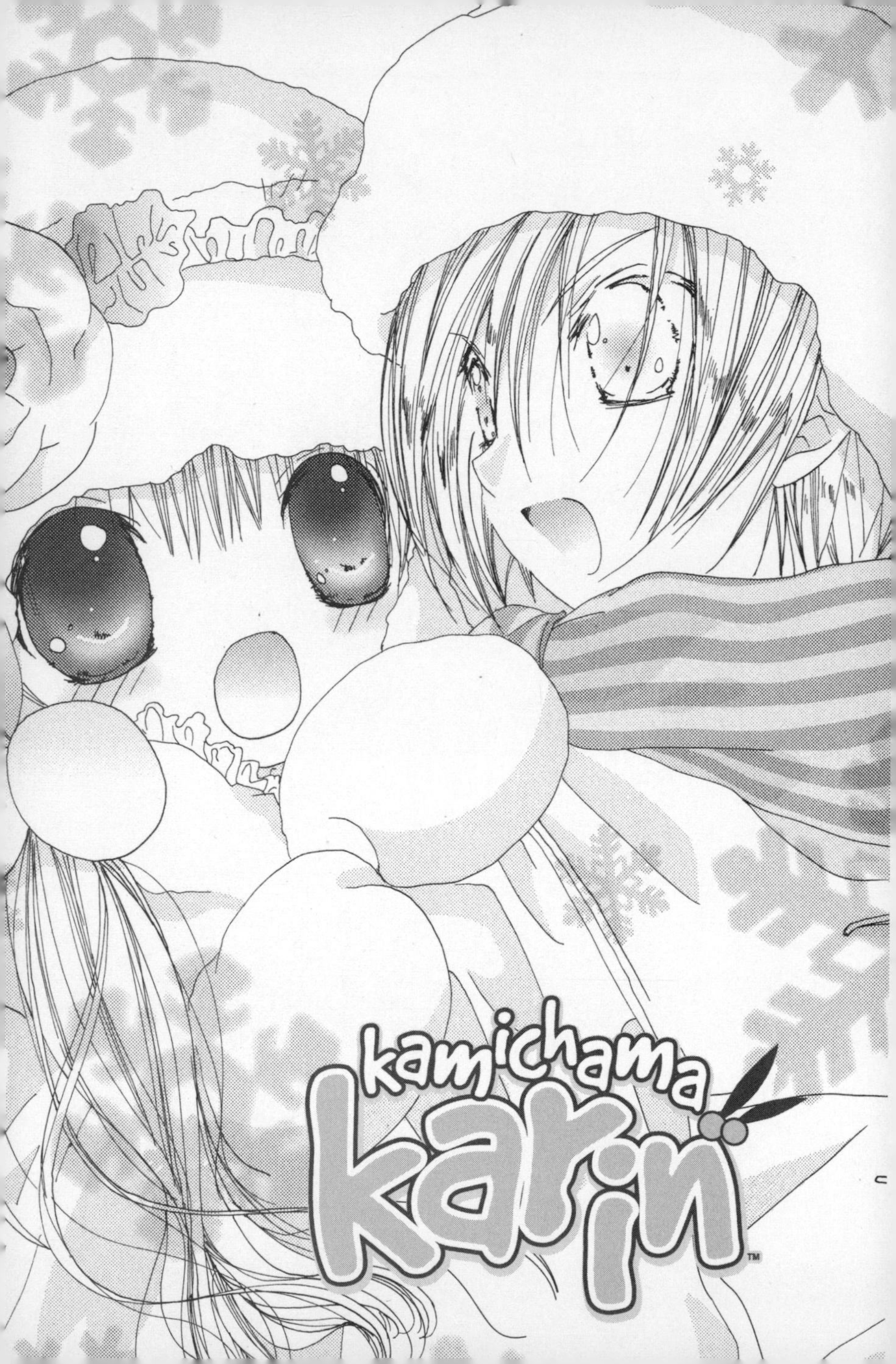

kamichama karin™

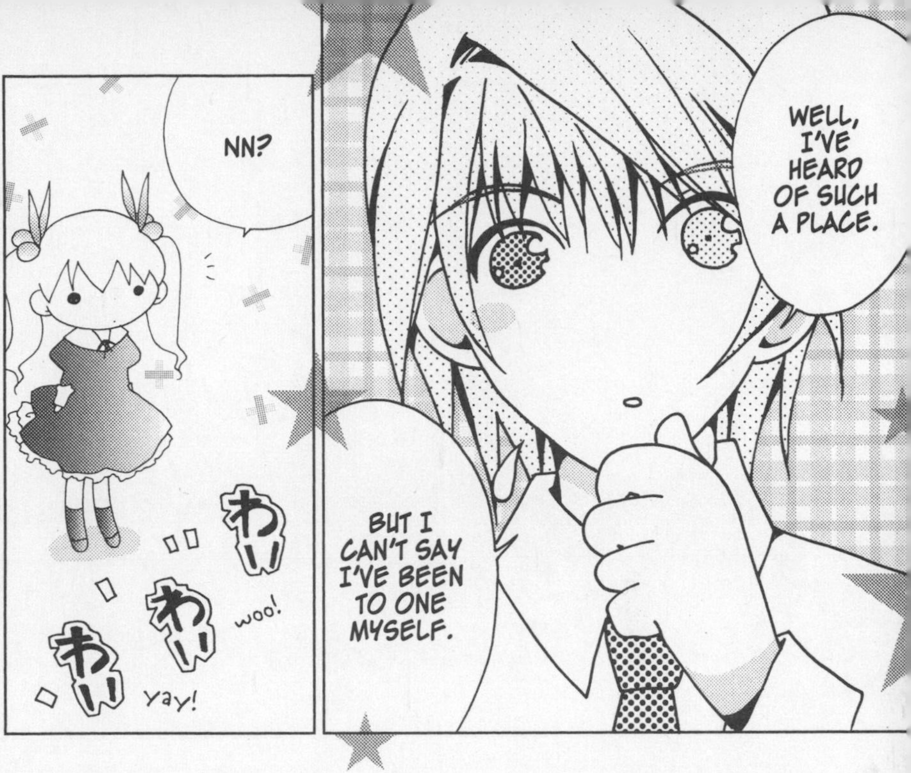
WELL, I'VE HEARD OF SUCH A PLACE.
BUT I CAN'T SAY I'VE BEEN TO ONE MYSELF.
NN?
わい
わい
わい
woo!
yay!

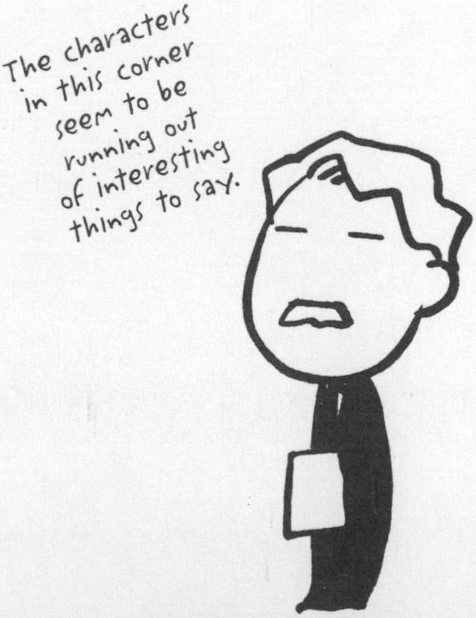
The characters in this corner seem to be running out of interesting things to say.

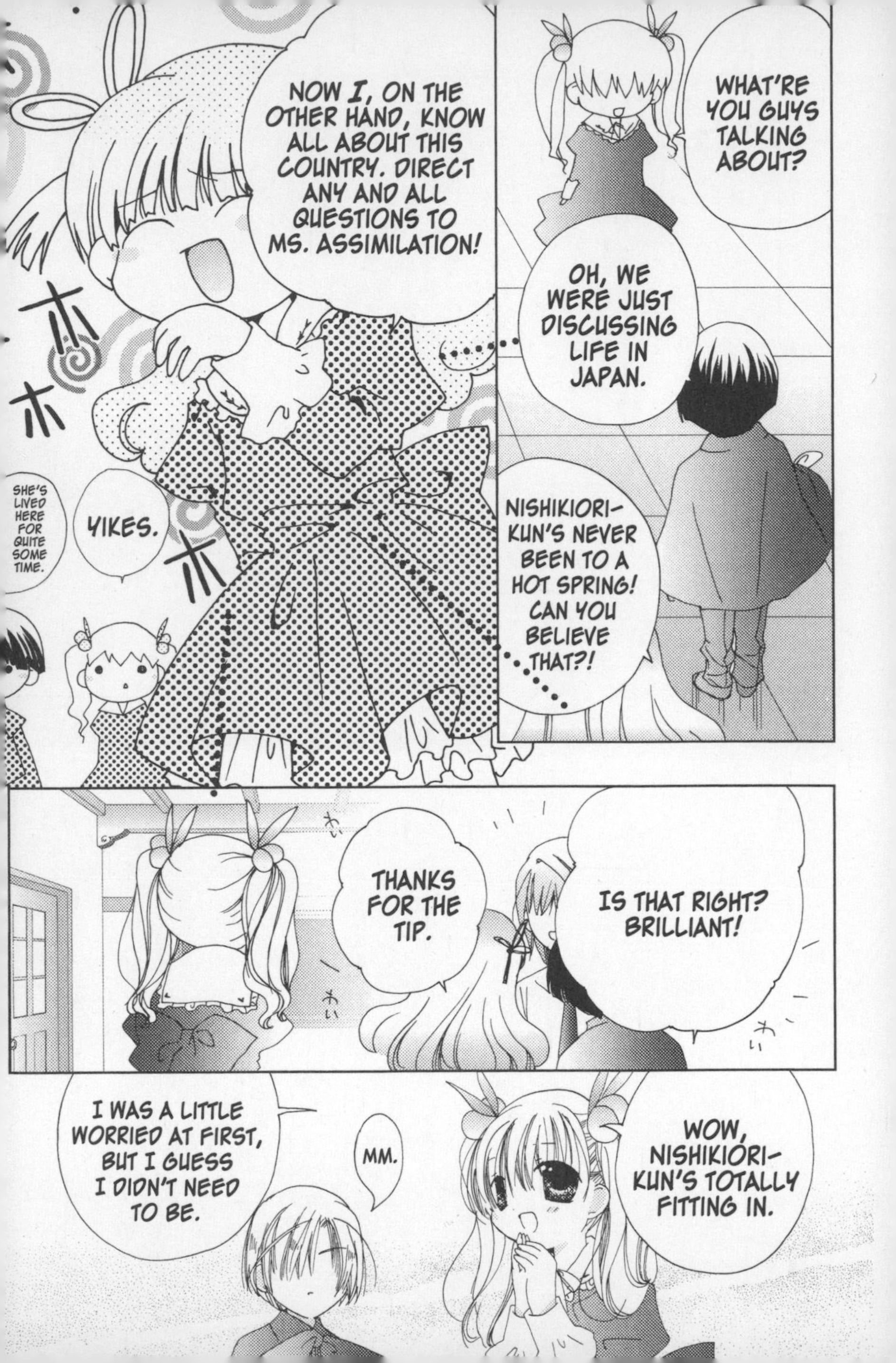
WHAT'RE YOU GUYS TALKING ABOUT?
OH, WE WERE JUST DISCUSSING LIFE IN JAPAN.
NISHIKIORI-KUN'S NEVER BEEN TO A HOT SPRING! CAN YOU BELIEVE THAT?!
NOW *I*, ON THE OTHER HAND, KNOW ALL ABOUT THIS COUNTRY. DIRECT ANY AND ALL QUESTIONS TO MS. ASSIMILATION!
ホホホ
YIKES.
SHE'S LIVED HERE FOR QUITE SOME TIME.
IS THAT RIGHT? BRILLIANT!
THANKS FOR THE TIP.
WOW, NISHIKIORI-KUN'S TOTALLY FITTING IN.
MM.
I WAS A LITTLE WORRIED AT FIRST, BUT I GUESS I DIDN'T NEED TO BE.

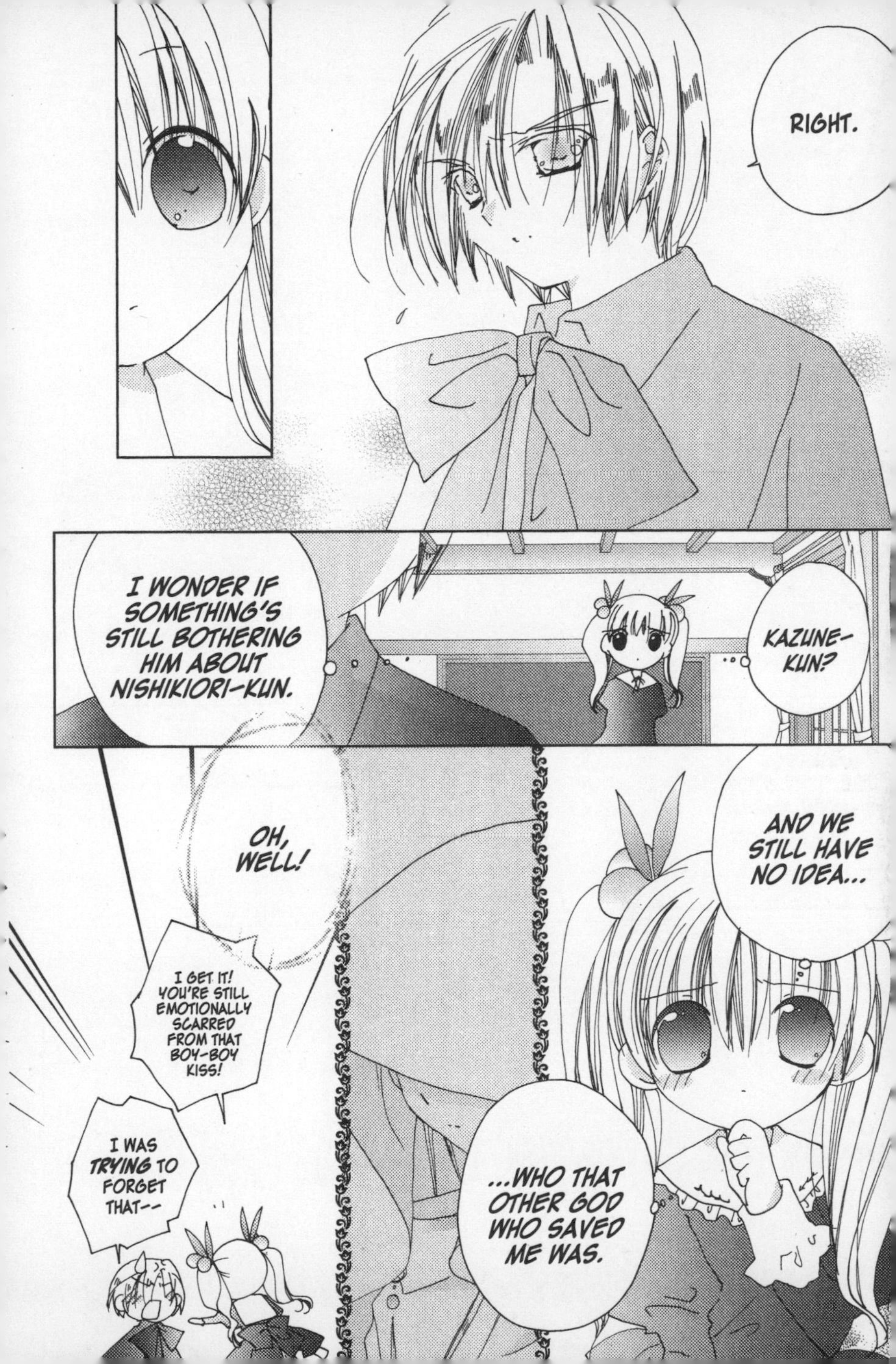
RIGHT.
KAZUNE-KUN?
I WONDER IF SOMETHING'S STILL BOTHERING HIM ABOUT NISHIKIORI-KUN.
AND WE STILL HAVE NO IDEA...
...WHO THAT OTHER GOD WHO SAVED ME WAS.
OH, WELL!
I GET IT! YOU'RE STILL EMOTIONALLY SCARRED FROM THAT BOY-BOY KISS!
I WAS *TRYING* TO FORGET THAT--

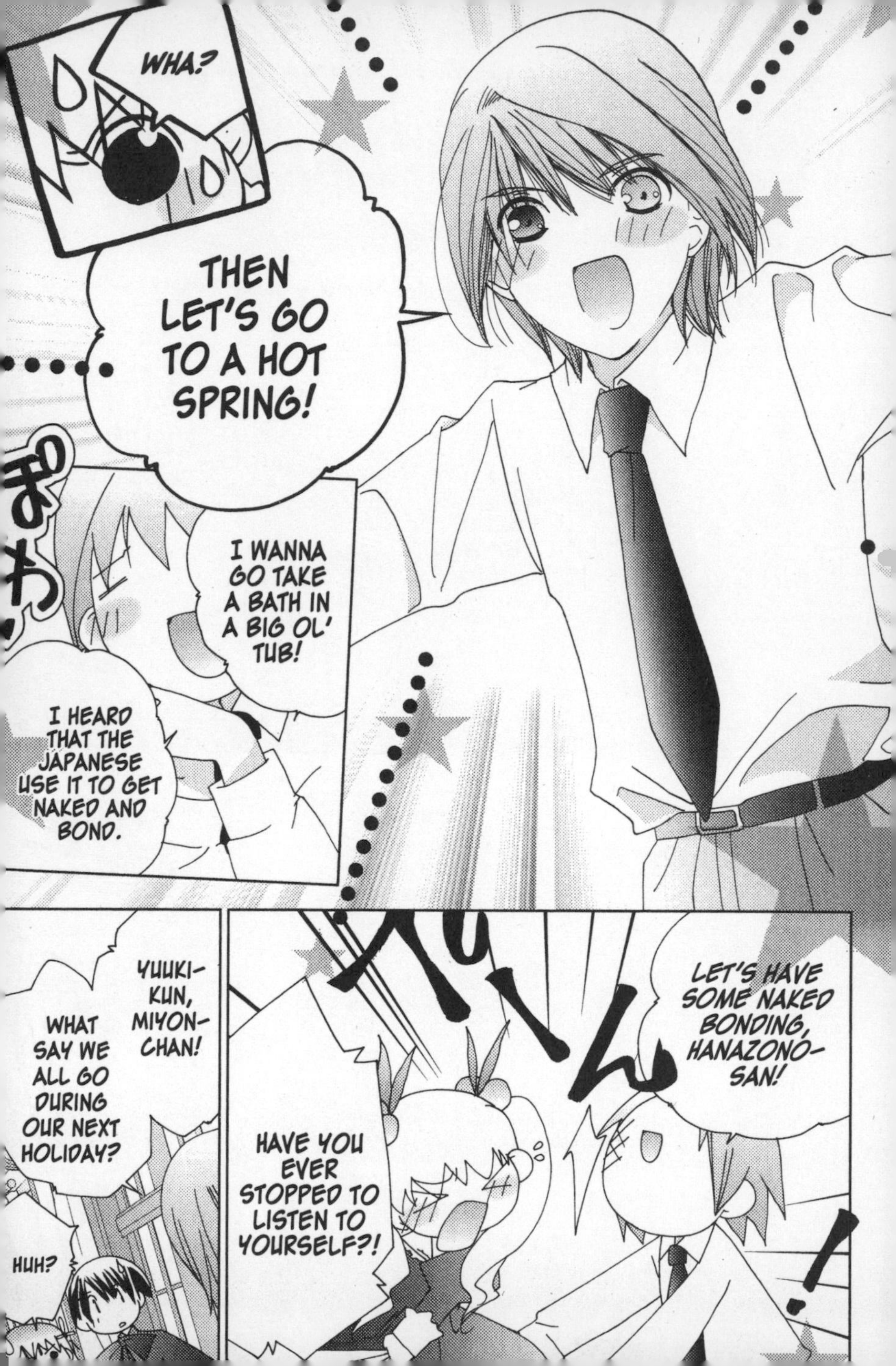
THEN LET'S GO TO A HOT SPRING!
WHA?
I WANNA GO TAKE A BATH IN A BIG OL' TUB!
I HEARD THAT THE JAPANESE USE IT TO GET NAKED AND BOND.
LET'S HAVE SOME NAKED BONDING, HANAZONO-SAN!
HAVE YOU EVER STOPPED TO LISTEN TO YOURSELF?!
YUUKI-KUN, MIYON-CHAN!
WHAT SAY WE ALL GO DURING OUR NEXT HOLIDAY?
HUH?

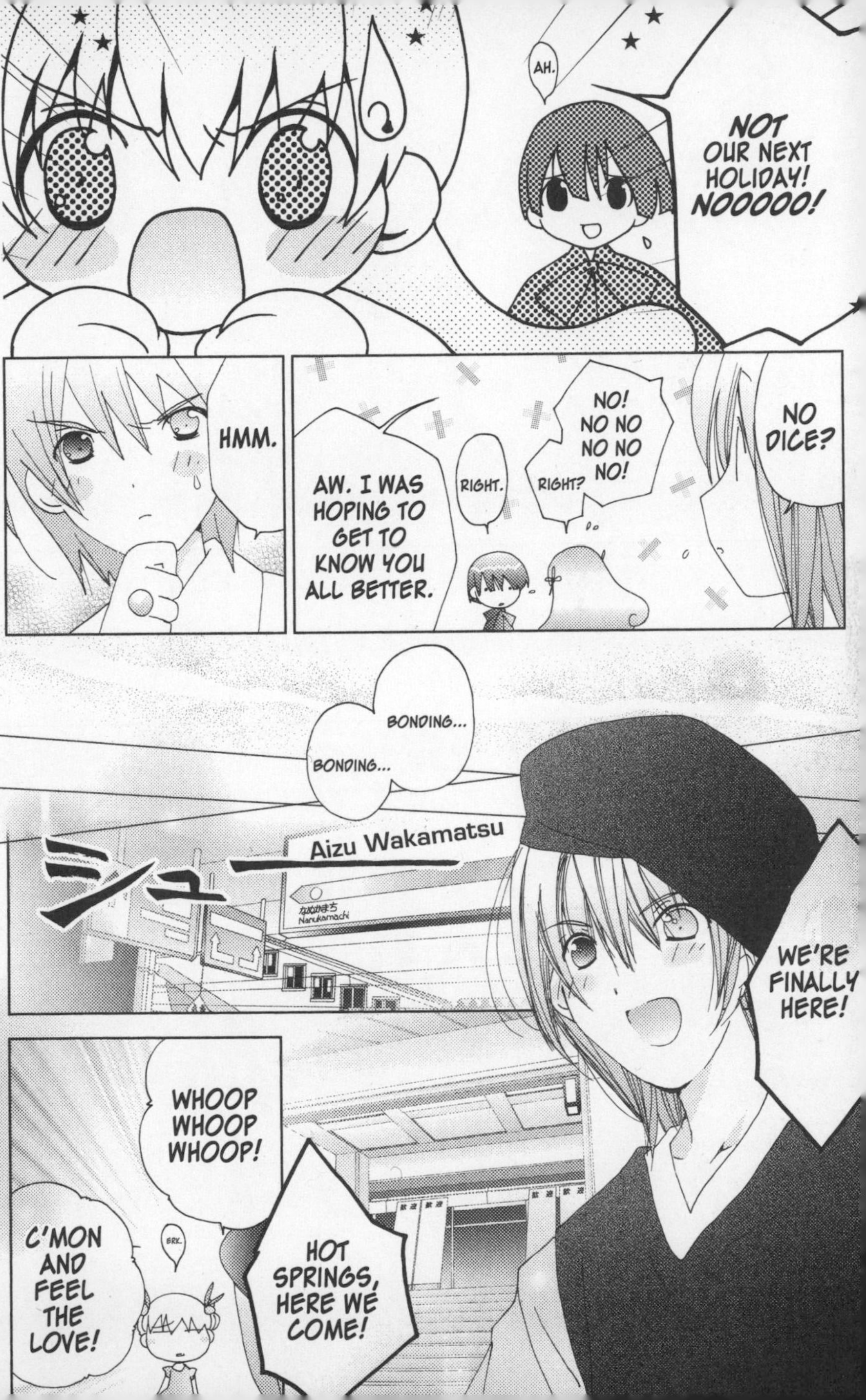
NOT OUR NEXT HOLIDAY! NOOOOO!
AH.
NO DICE?
NO! NO NO NO NO NO!
RIGHT?
RIGHT.
AW. I WAS HOPING TO GET TO KNOW YOU ALL BETTER.
HMM.
WE'RE FINALLY HERE!
BONDING...
BONDING...
Aizu Wakamatsu
Nanukamachi
シュー
HOT SPRINGS, HERE WE COME!
WHOOP WHOOP WHOOP!
ERK.
C'MON AND FEEL THE LOVE!

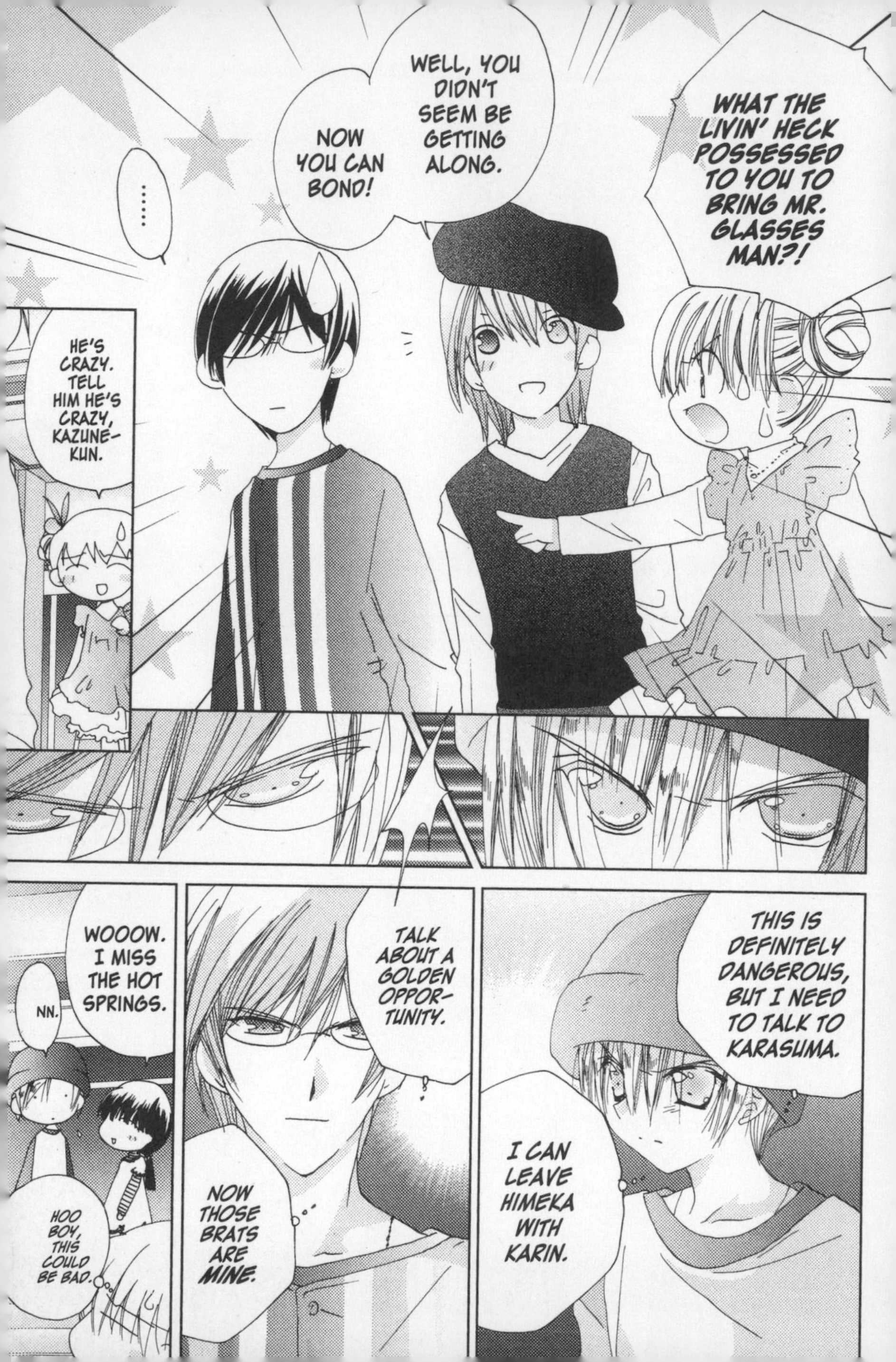
WHAT THE LIVIN' HECK POSSESSED TO YOU TO BRING MR. GLASSES MAN?!
WELL, YOU DIDN'T SEEM BE GETTING ALONG.
NOW YOU CAN BOND!
......
HE'S CRAZY. TELL HIM HE'S CRAZY, KAZUNE-KUN.
THIS IS DEFINITELY DANGEROUS, BUT I NEED TO TALK TO KARASUMA.
I CAN LEAVE HIMEKA WITH KARIN.
TALK ABOUT A GOLDEN OPPOR-TUNITY.
NOW THOSE BRATS ARE MINE.
WOOOW. I MISS THE HOT SPRINGS.
NN.
HOO BOY, THIS COULD BE BAD.

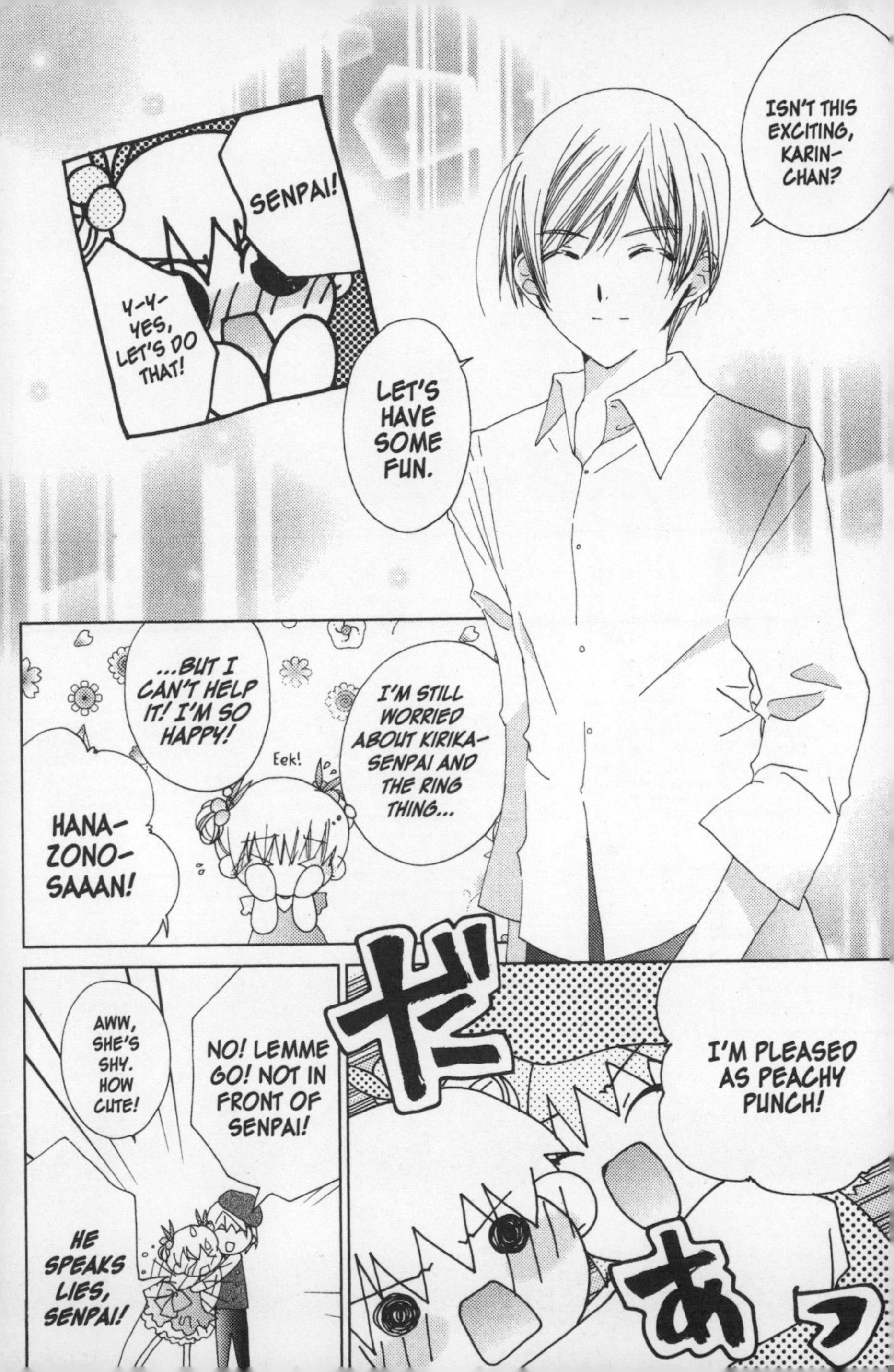
ISN'T THIS EXCITING, KARIN-CHAN?
LET'S HAVE SOME FUN.
SENPAI!
Y-Y-YES, LET'S DO THAT!
I'M STILL WORRIED ABOUT KIRIKA-SENPAI AND THE RING THING...
...BUT I CAN'T HELP IT! I'M SO HAPPY!
Eek!
HANA-ZONO-SAAAN!
だ
I'M PLEASED AS PEACHY PUNCH!
あっ
NO! LEMME GO! NOT IN FRONT OF SENPAI!
AWW, SHE'S SHY. HOW CUTE!
HE SPEAKS LIES, SENPAI!

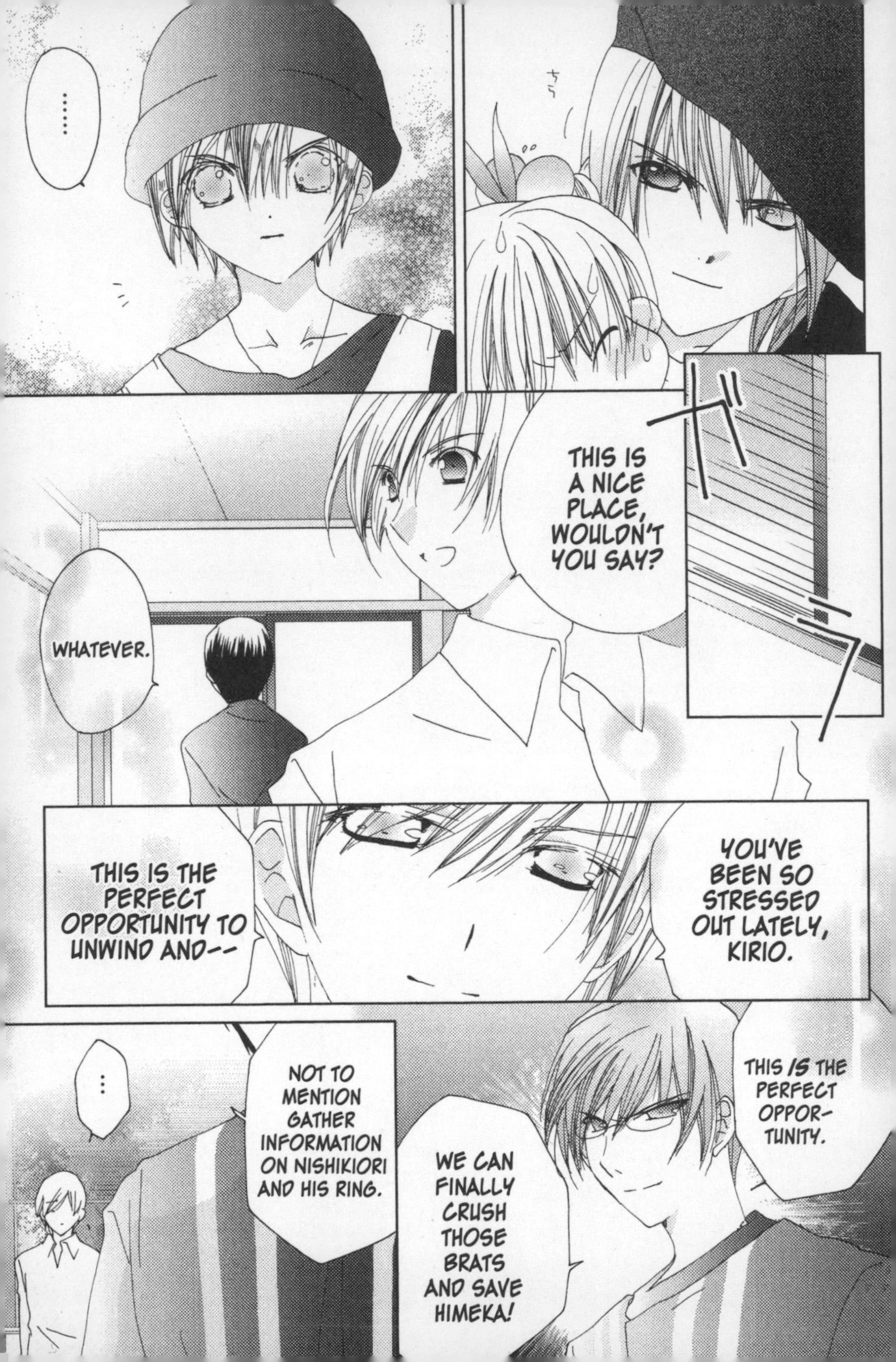
......
THIS IS A NICE PLACE, WOULDN'T YOU SAY?
WHATEVER.
YOU'VE BEEN SO STRESSED OUT LATELY, KIRIO.
THIS IS THE PERFECT OPPORTUNITY TO UNWIND AND--
THIS *IS* THE PERFECT OPPOR-TUNITY.
WE CAN FINALLY CRUSH THOSE BRATS AND SAVE HIMEKA!
NOT TO MENTION GATHER INFORMATION ON NISHIKIORI AND HIS RING.
...

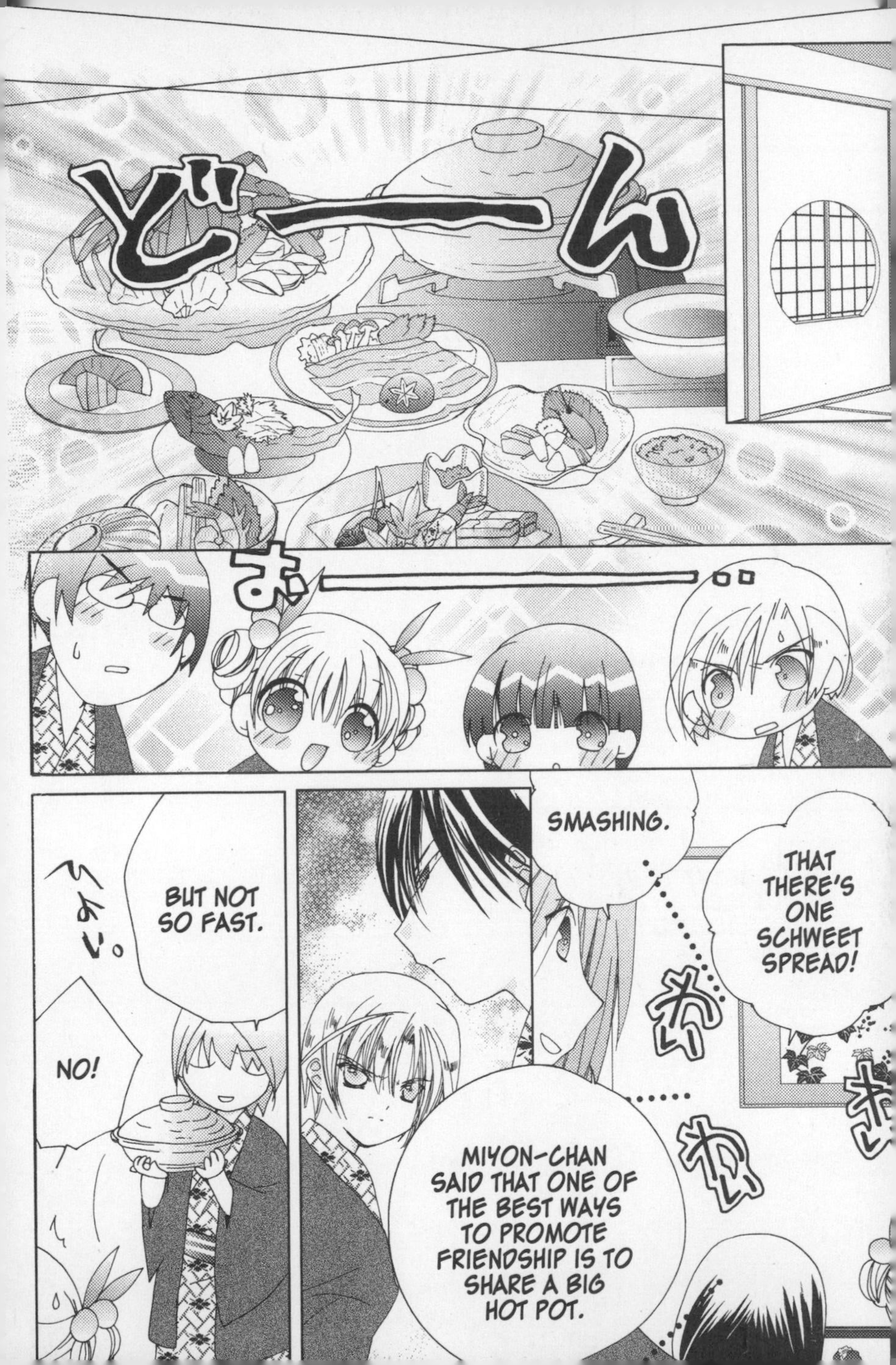
どーーん
お——。。
THAT THERE'S ONE SCHWEET SPREAD!
SMASHING.
......
MIYON-CHAN SAID THAT ONE OF THE BEST WAYS TO PROMOTE FRIENDSHIP IS TO SHARE A BIG HOT POT.
BUT NOT SO FAST.
ひょい。
NO!

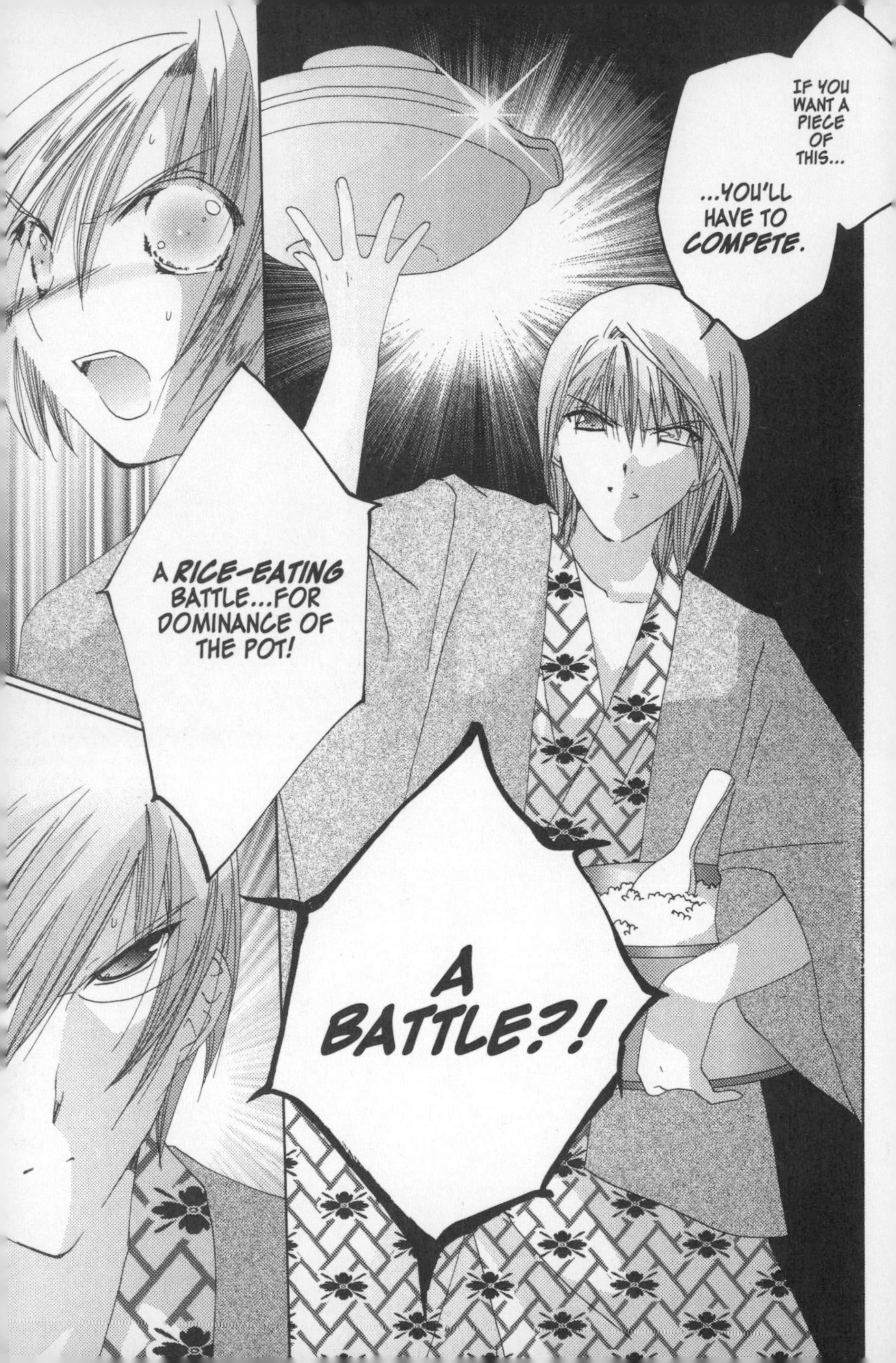
IF YOU WANT A PIECE OF THIS...
...YOU'LL HAVE TO COMPETE.
A RICE-EATING BATTLE...FOR DOMINANCE OF THE POT!
A BATTLE?!

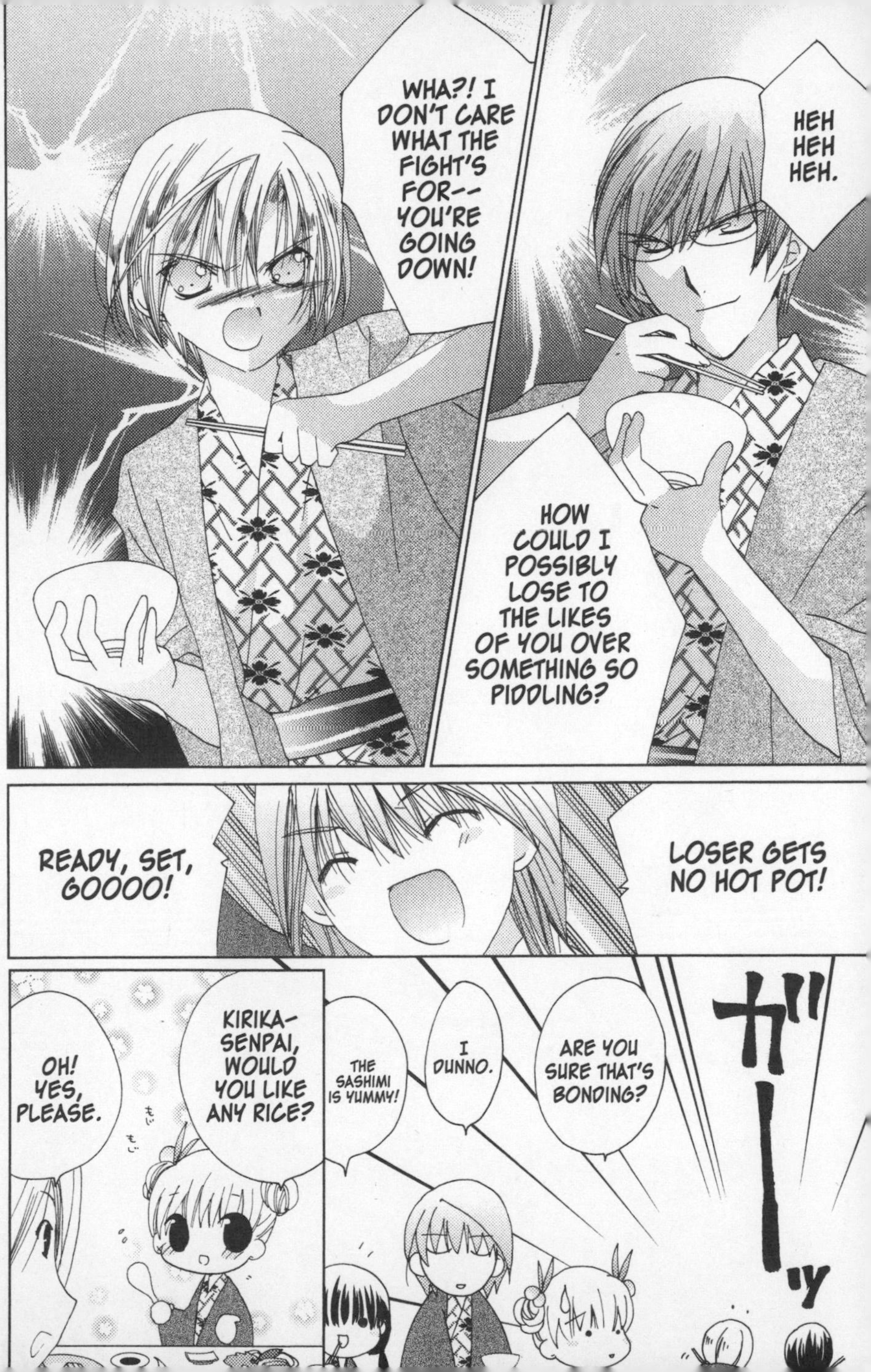
HEH HEH HEH.
HOW COULD I POSSIBLY LOSE TO THE LIKES OF YOU OVER SOMETHING SO PIDDLING?
WHA?! I DON'T CARE WHAT THE FIGHT'S FOR-- YOU'RE GOING DOWN!
LOSER GETS NO HOT POT!
READY, SET, GOOOO!
ガーッ
ARE YOU SURE THAT'S BONDING?
I DUNNO.
THE SASHIMI IS YUMMY!
KIRIKA-SENPAI, WOULD YOU LIKE ANY RICE?
OH! YES, PLEASE.
もじもじ

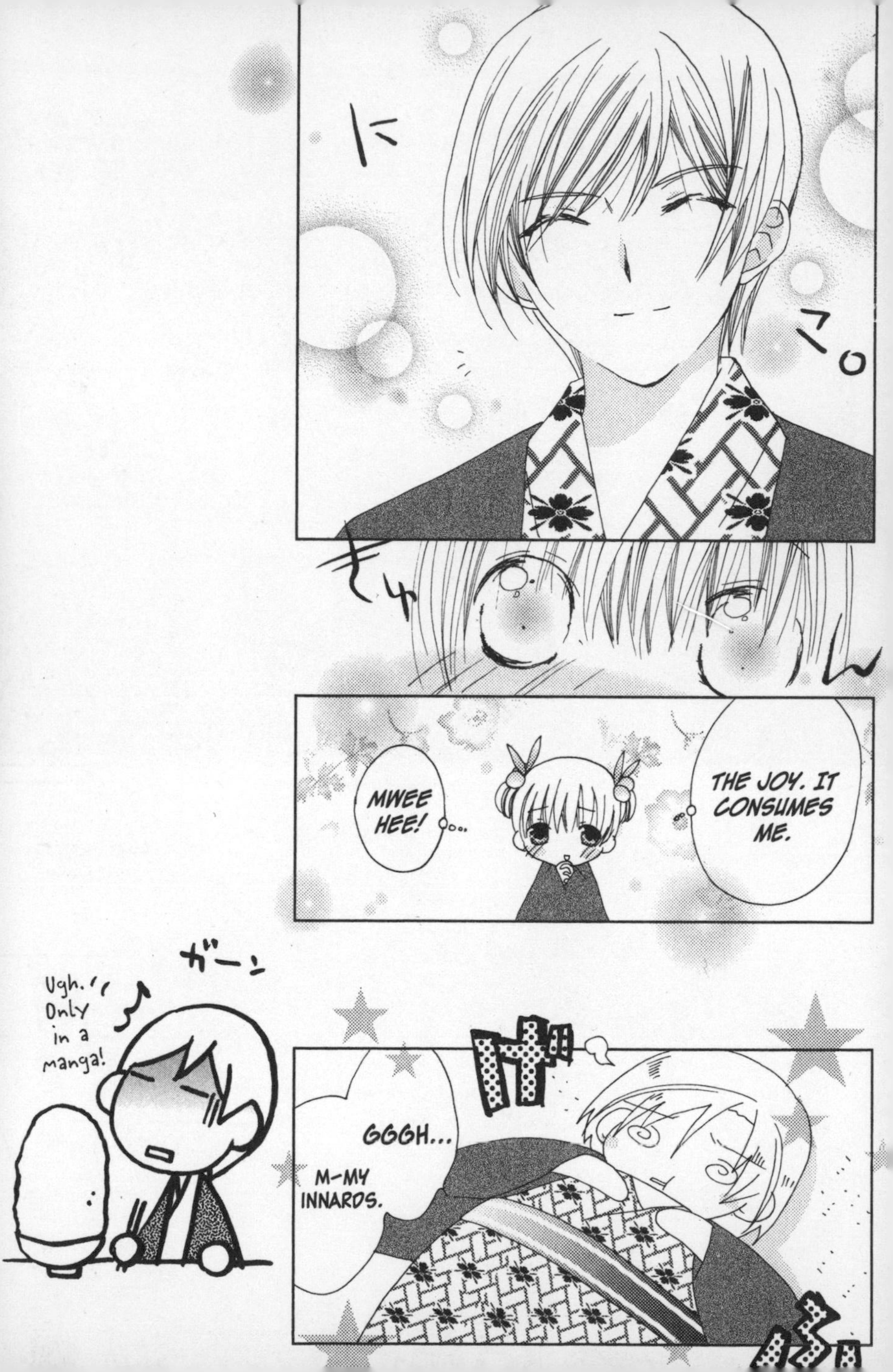

THE JOY. IT CONSUMES ME.
MWEE HEE!
GGGH...
M-MY INNARDS.
Ugh. Only in a manga!

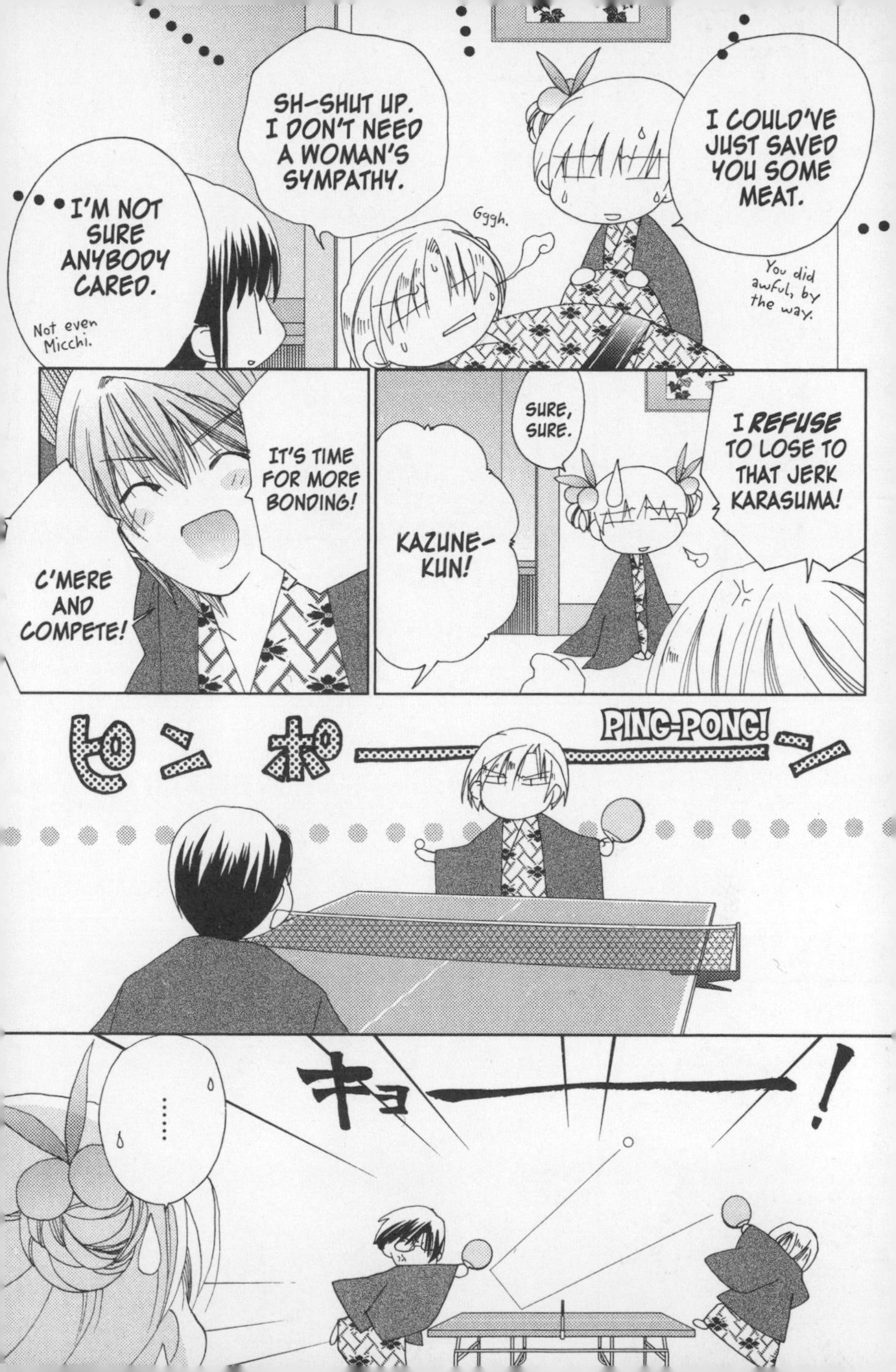
I COULD'VE JUST SAVED YOU SOME MEAT.
You did awful, by the way.
Gggh.
SH-SHUT UP. I DON'T NEED A WOMAN'S SYMPATHY.
I'M NOT SURE ANYBODY CARED.
Not even Micchi.
I REFUSE TO LOSE TO THAT JERK KARASUMA!
SURE, SURE.
KAZUNE-KUN!
IT'S TIME FOR MORE BONDING!
C'MERE AND COMPETE!
ピンポーン
PING-PONG!
キョーー!
......

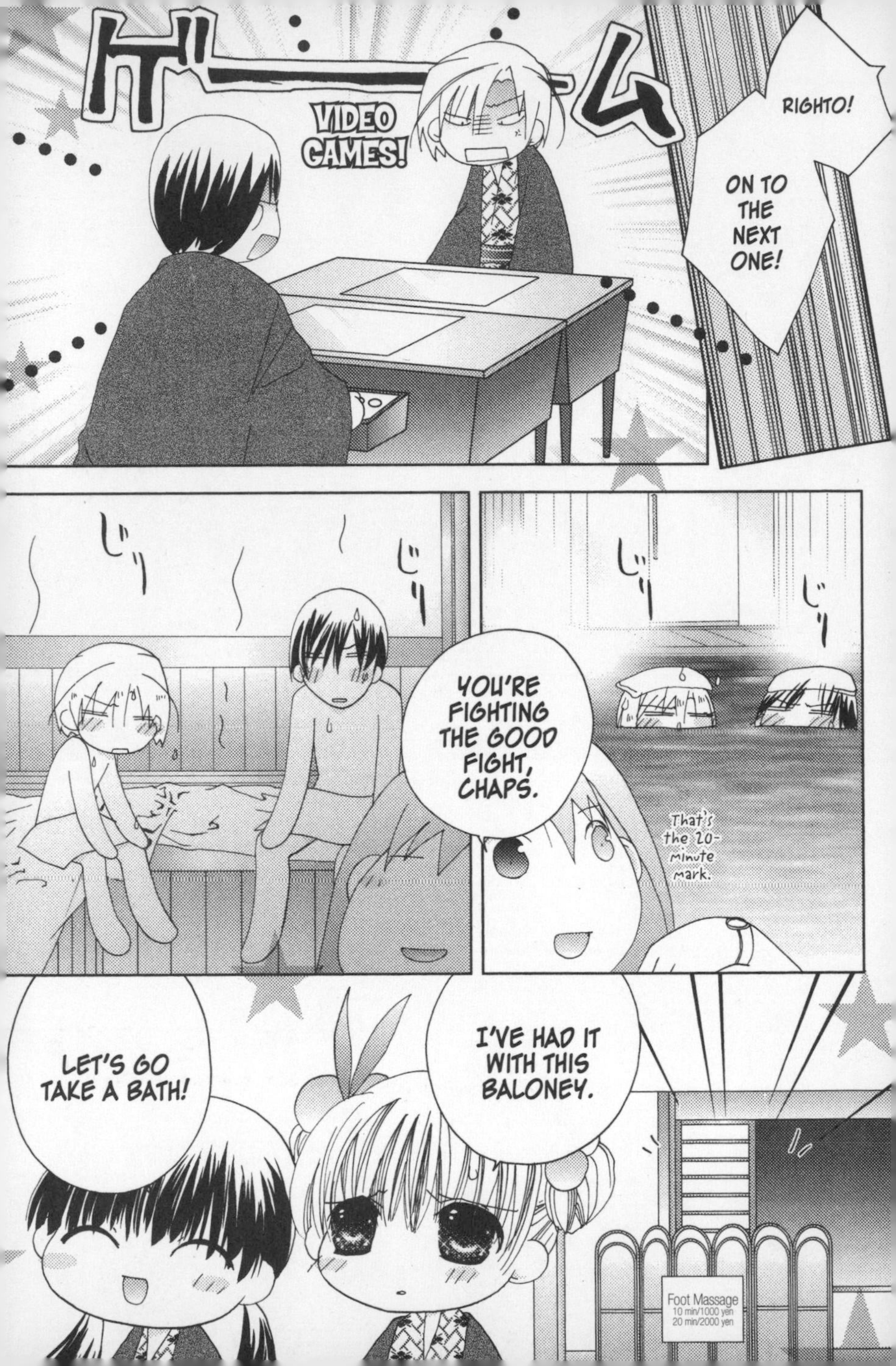

RIGHTO!
ON TO THE NEXT ONE!
ゲーーム
VIDEO GAMES!
じり
じり
YOU'RE FIGHTING THE GOOD FIGHT, CHAPS.
That's the 20-minute mark.
じり
じり
I'VE HAD IT WITH THIS BALONEY.
LET'S GO TAKE A BATH!
Foot Massage
10 min/1000 yen
20 min/2000 yen

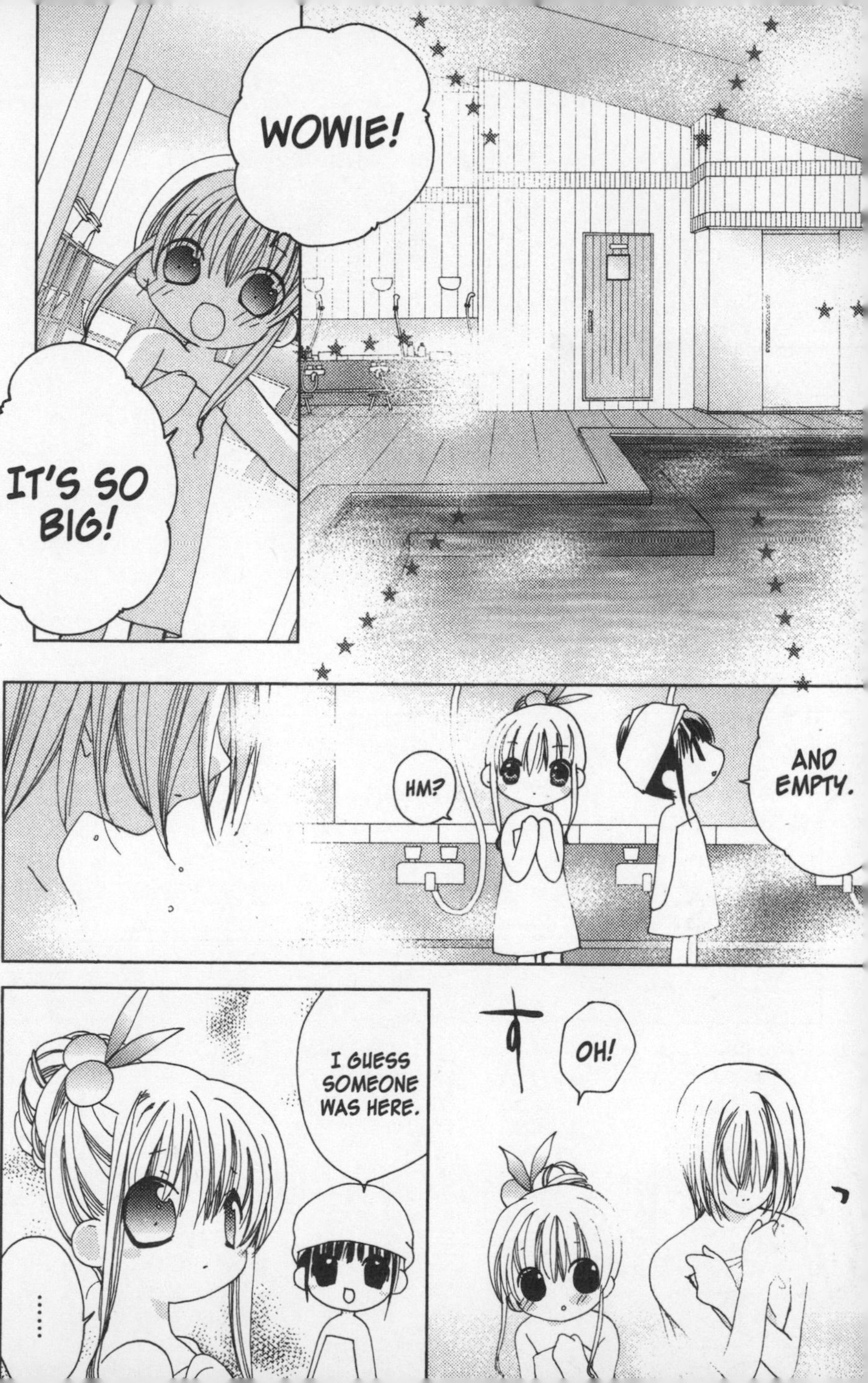
WOWIE!
IT'S SO BIG!
AND EMPTY.
HM?
OH!
I GUESS SOMEONE WAS HERE.
......

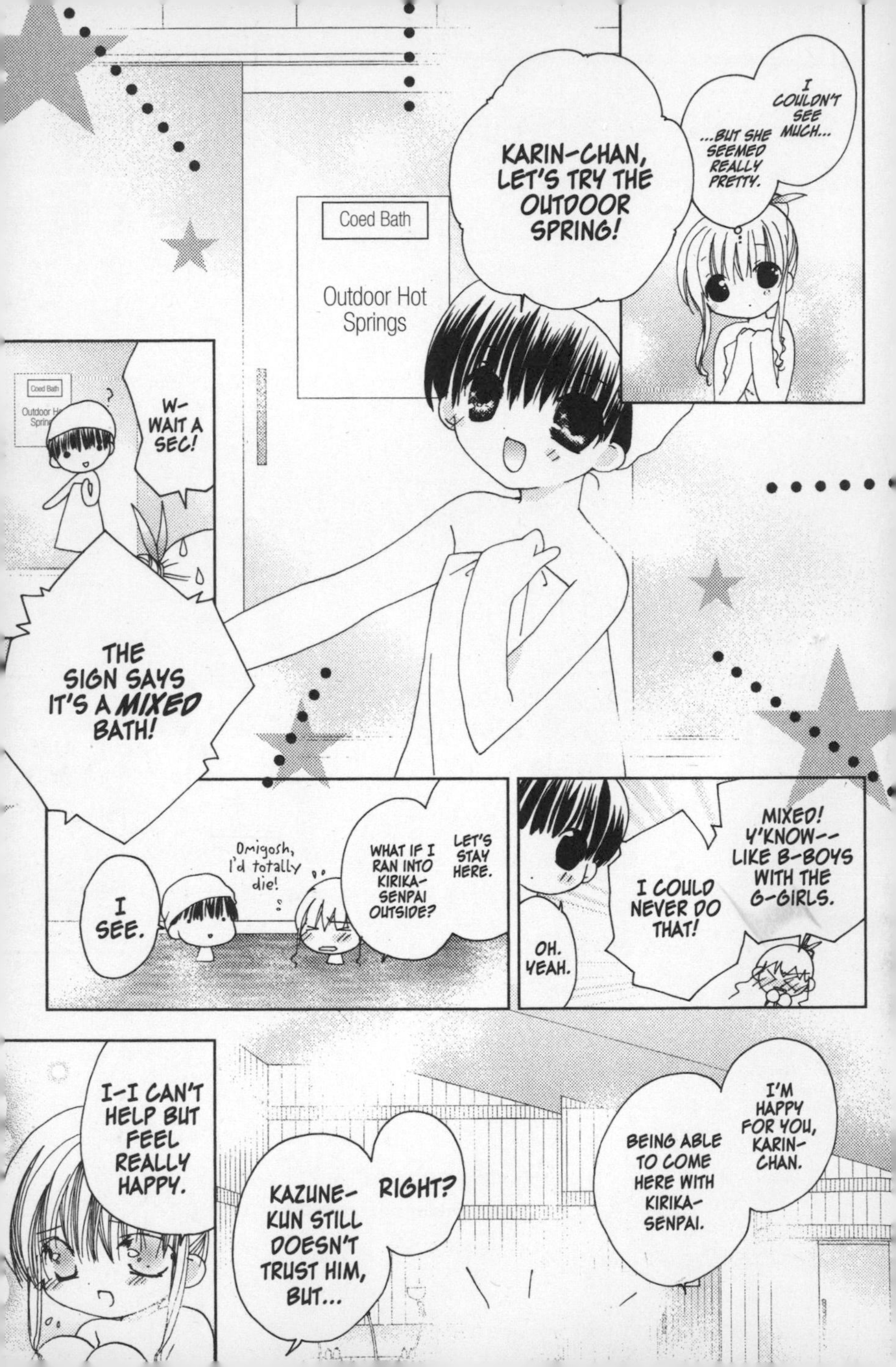
I COULDN'T SEE MUCH...
...BUT SHE SEEMED REALLY PRETTY.
KARIN-CHAN, LET'S TRY THE OUTDOOR SPRING!
Coed Bath
Outdoor Hot Springs
W-WAIT A SEC!
THE SIGN SAYS IT'S A MIXED BATH!
MIXED! Y'KNOW--LIKE B-BOYS WITH THE G-GIRLS.
I COULD NEVER DO THAT!
OH. YEAH.
LET'S STAY HERE.
WHAT IF I RAN INTO KIRIKA-SENPAI OUTSIDE?
Omigosh, I'd totally die!
I SEE.
I'M HAPPY FOR YOU, KARIN-CHAN.
BEING ABLE TO COME HERE WITH KIRIKA-SENPAI.
RIGHT?
KAZUNE-KUN STILL DOESN'T TRUST HIM, BUT...
I-I CAN'T HELP BUT FEEL REALLY HAPPY.

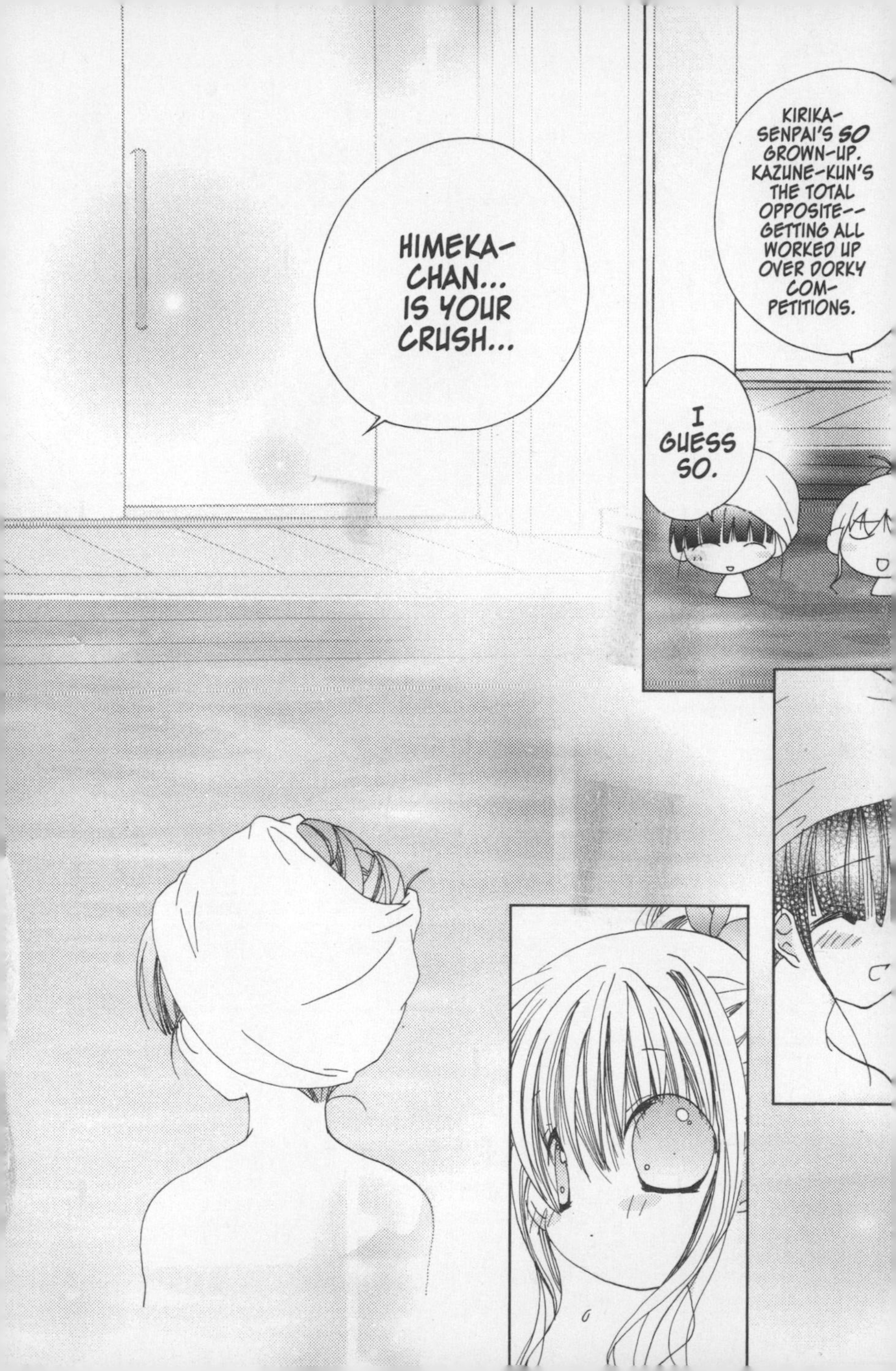
KIRIKA-SENPAI'S *SO* GROWN-UP. KAZUNE-KUN'S THE TOTAL OPPOSITE-- GETTING ALL WORKED UP OVER DORKY COM-PETITIONS.
I GUESS SO.
HIMEKA-CHAN... IS YOUR CRUSH...

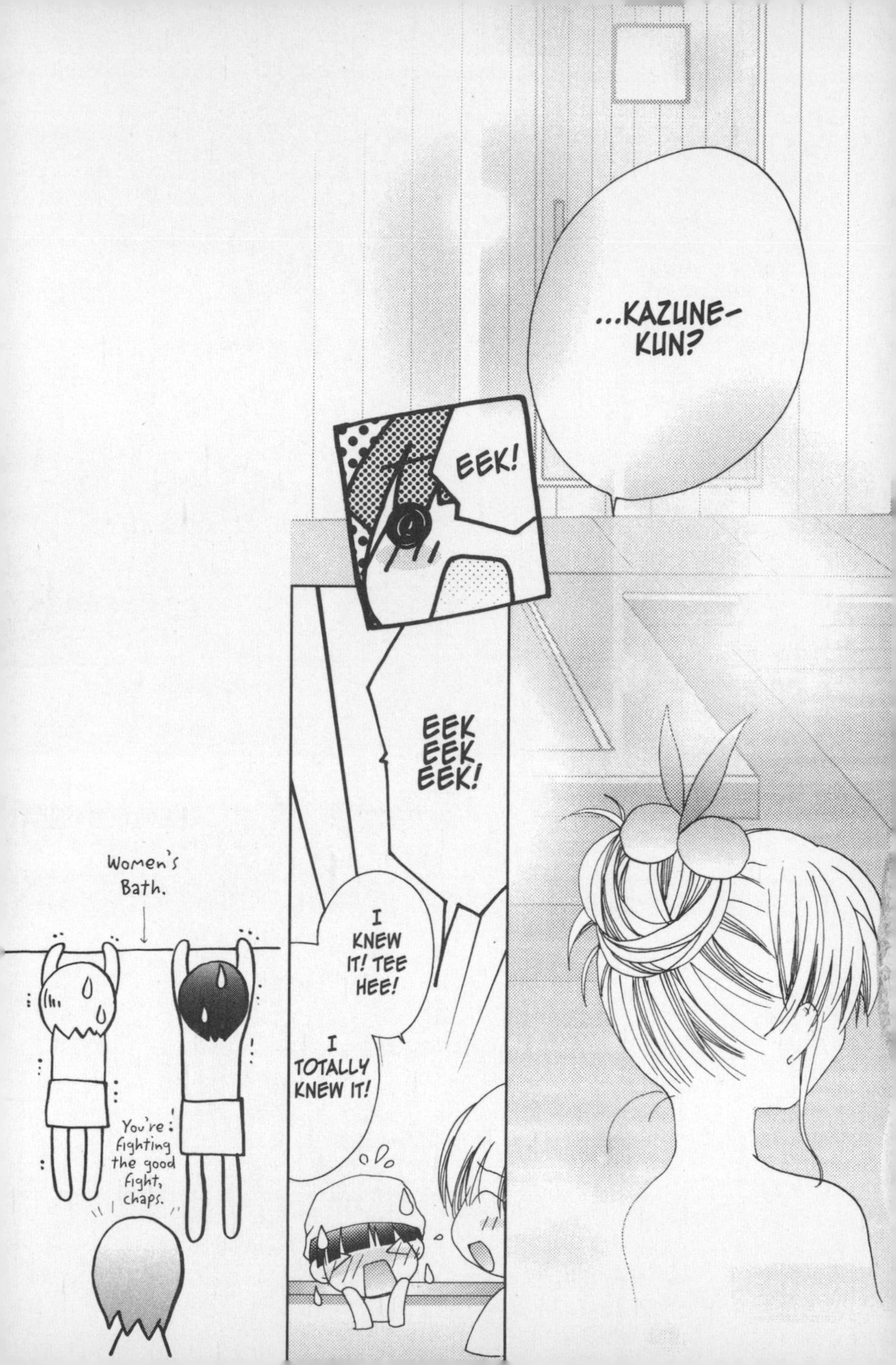
...KAZUNE-KUN?
EEK!
EEK EEK EEK!
I KNEW IT! TEE HEE!
I TOTALLY KNEW IT!
Women's Bath.
You're fighting the good fight, chaps.

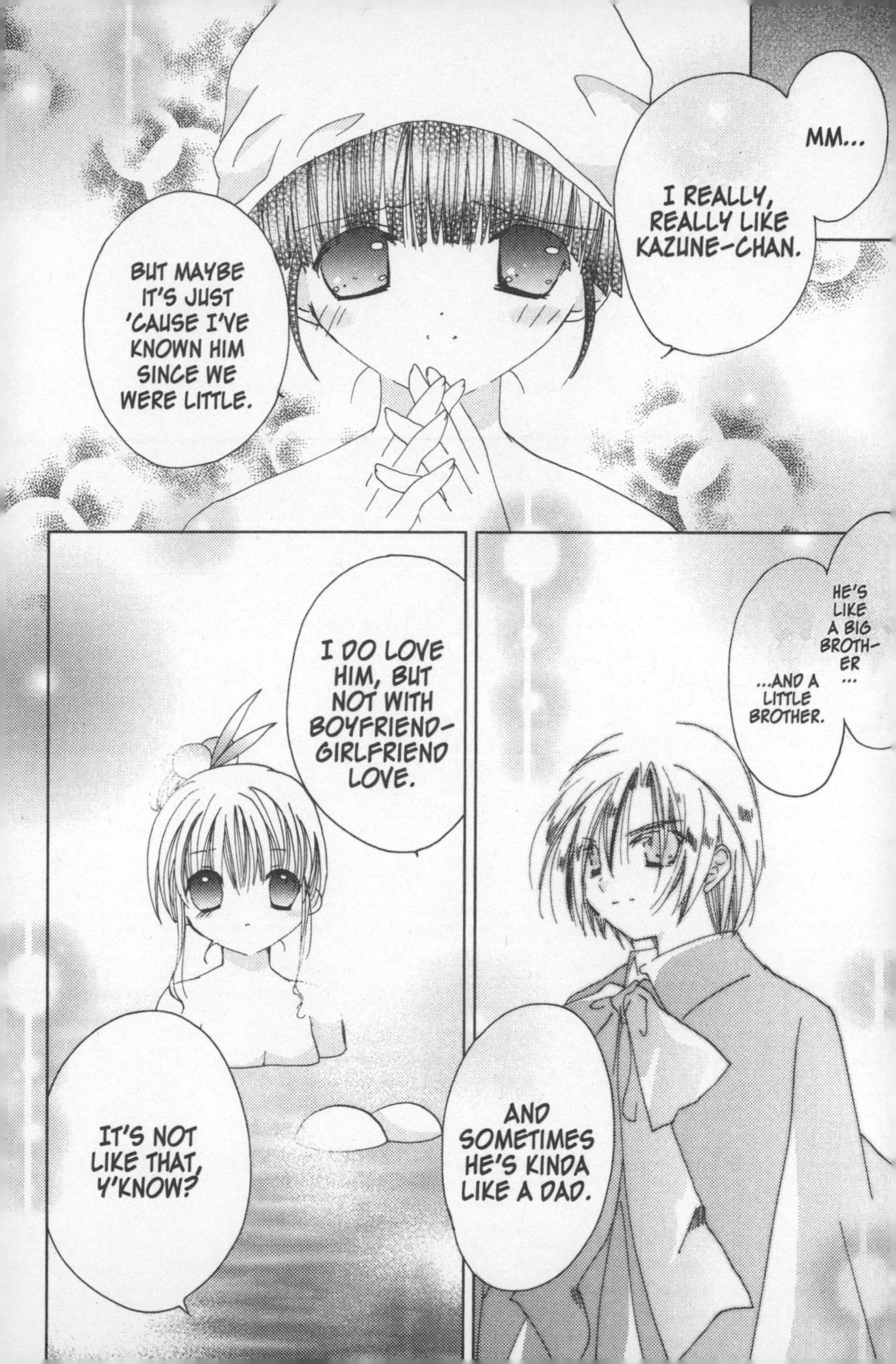
MM... I REALLY, REALLY LIKE KAZUNE-CHAN.
BUT MAYBE IT'S JUST 'CAUSE I'VE KNOWN HIM SINCE WE WERE LITTLE.
HE'S LIKE A BIG BROTH-ER... ...AND A LITTLE BROTHER.
AND SOMETIMES HE'S KINDA LIKE A DAD.
I DO LOVE HIM, BUT NOT WITH BOYFRIEND-GIRLFRIEND LOVE.
IT'S NOT LIKE THAT, Y'KNOW?

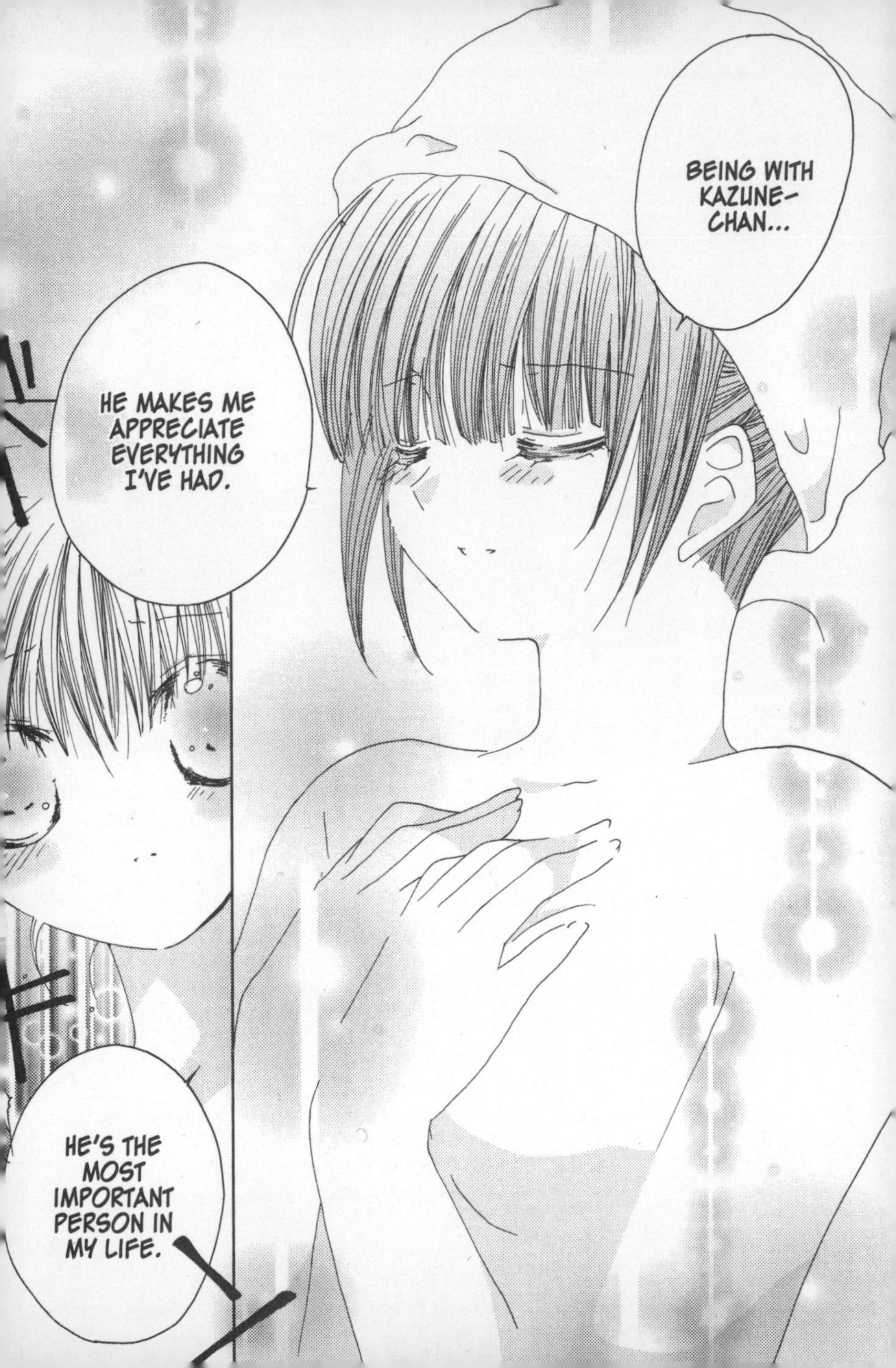
BEING WITH KAZUNE-CHAN...
HE MAKES ME APPRECIATE EVERYTHING I'VE HAD.
HE'S THE MOST IMPORTANT PERSON IN MY LIFE.

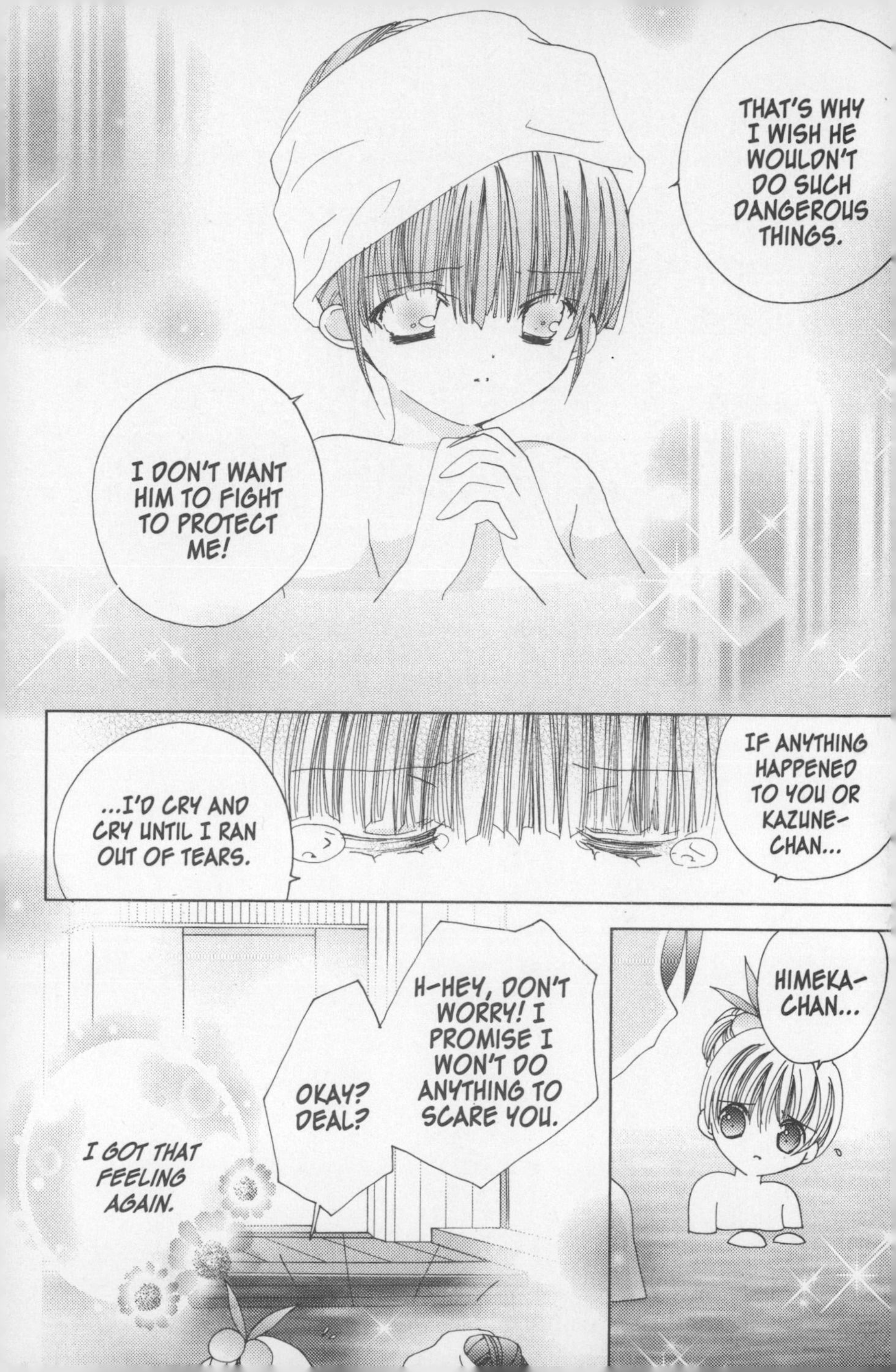
THAT'S WHY I WISH HE WOULDN'T DO SUCH DANGEROUS THINGS.
I DON'T WANT HIM TO FIGHT TO PROTECT ME!
IF ANYTHING HAPPENED TO YOU OR KAZUNE-CHAN...
...I'D CRY AND CRY UNTIL I RAN OUT OF TEARS.
HIMEKA-CHAN...
H-HEY, DON'T WORRY! I PROMISE I WON'T DO ANYTHING TO SCARE YOU.
OKAY? DEAL?
I GOT THAT FEELING AGAIN.

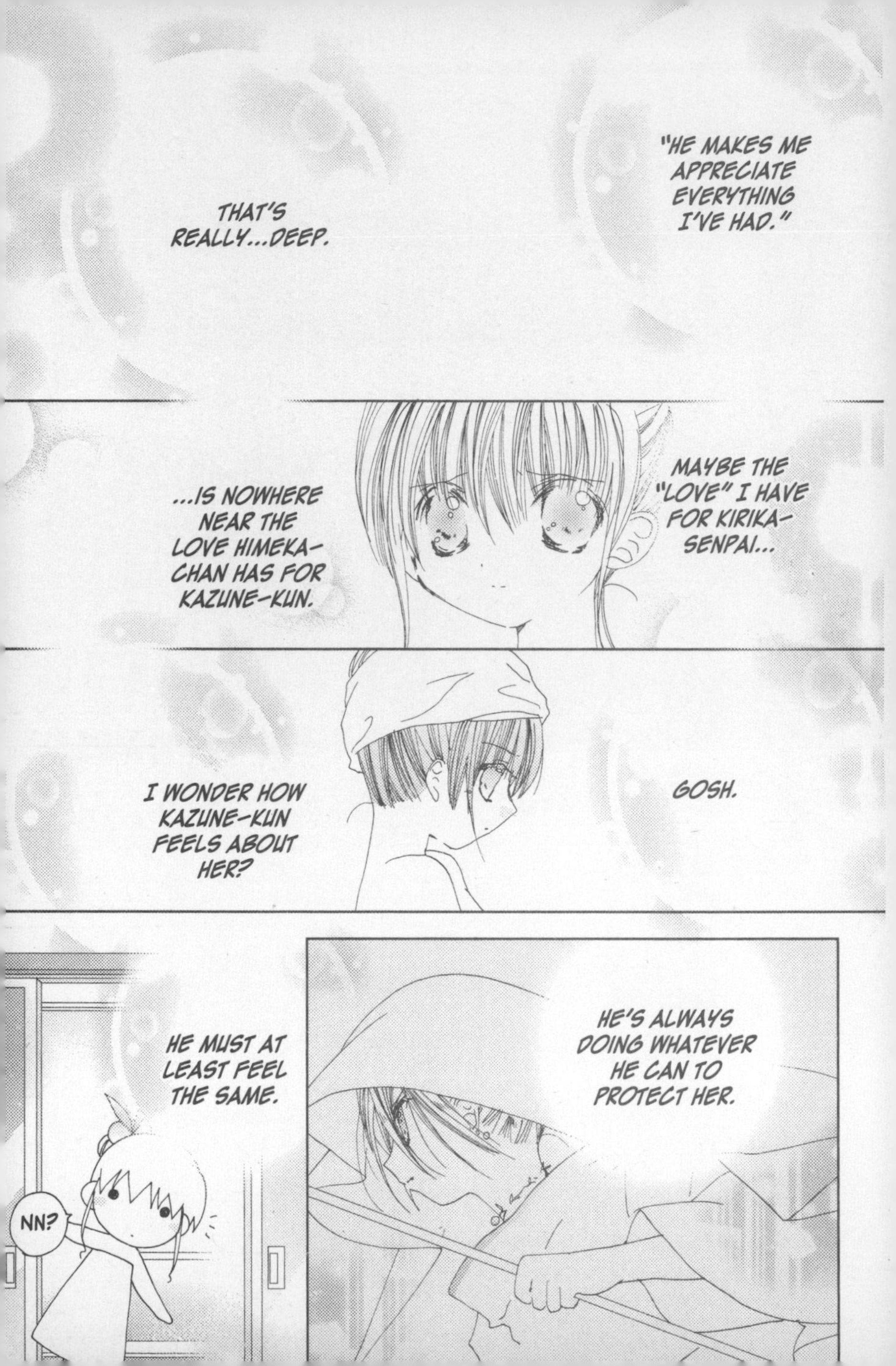
"HE MAKES ME APPRECIATE EVERYTHING I'VE HAD."
THAT'S REALLY...DEEP.
MAYBE THE "LOVE" I HAVE FOR KIRIKA-SENPAI...
...IS NOWHERE NEAR THE LOVE HIMEKA-CHAN HAS FOR KAZUNE-KUN.
GOSH.
I WONDER HOW KAZUNE-KUN FEELS ABOUT HER?
HE'S ALWAYS DOING WHATEVER HE CAN TO PROTECT HER.
HE MUST AT LEAST FEEL THE SAME.
NN?

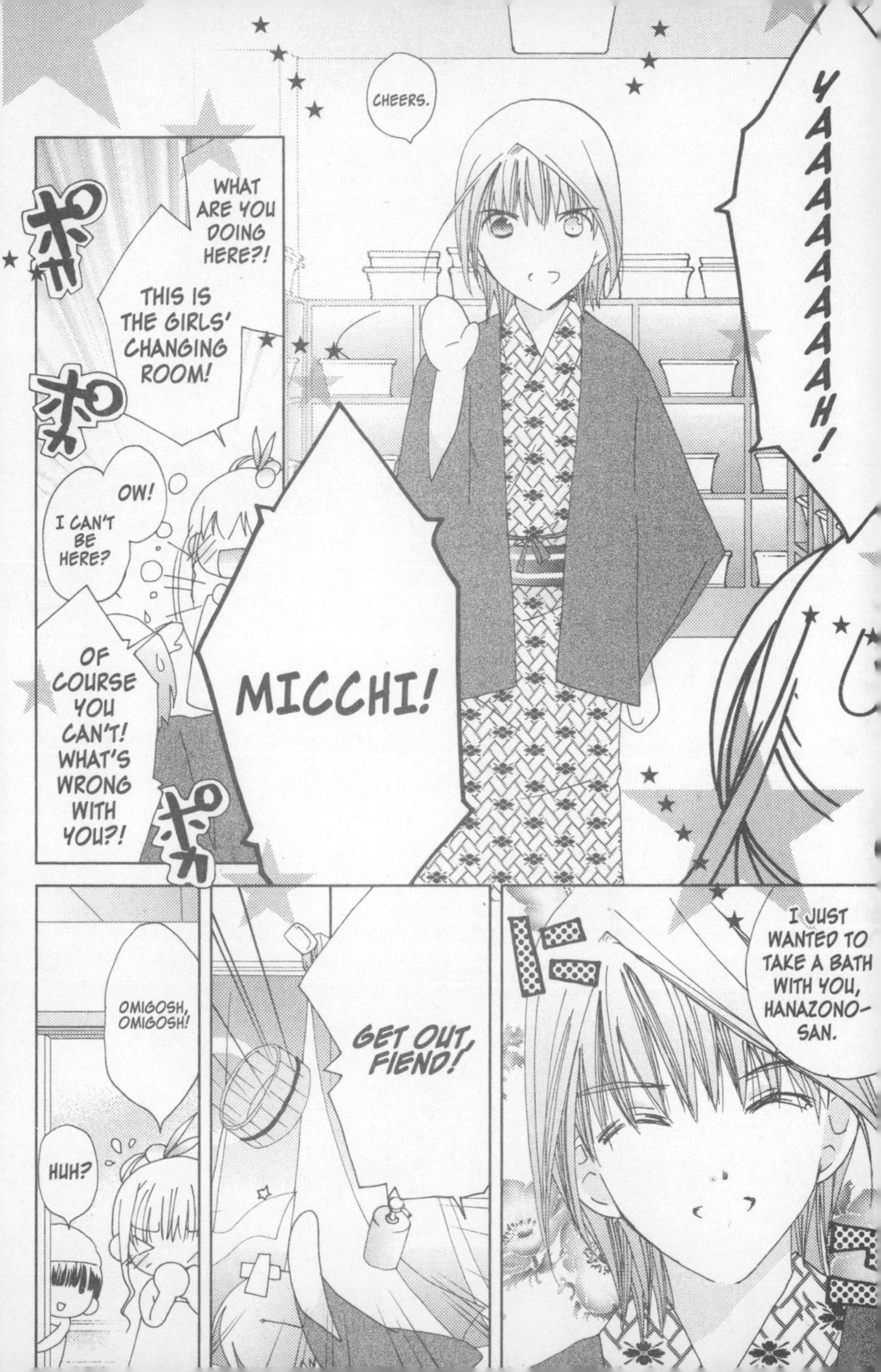
YAAAAAAAAAAH!
CHEERS.
MICCHI!
WHAT ARE YOU DOING HERE?!
THIS IS THE GIRLS' CHANGING ROOM!
OW!
I CAN'T BE HERE?
OF COURSE YOU CAN'T! WHAT'S WRONG WITH YOU?!
I JUST WANTED TO TAKE A BATH WITH YOU, HANAZONO-SAN.
GET OUT, FIEND!
OMIGOSH, OMIGOSH!
HUH?

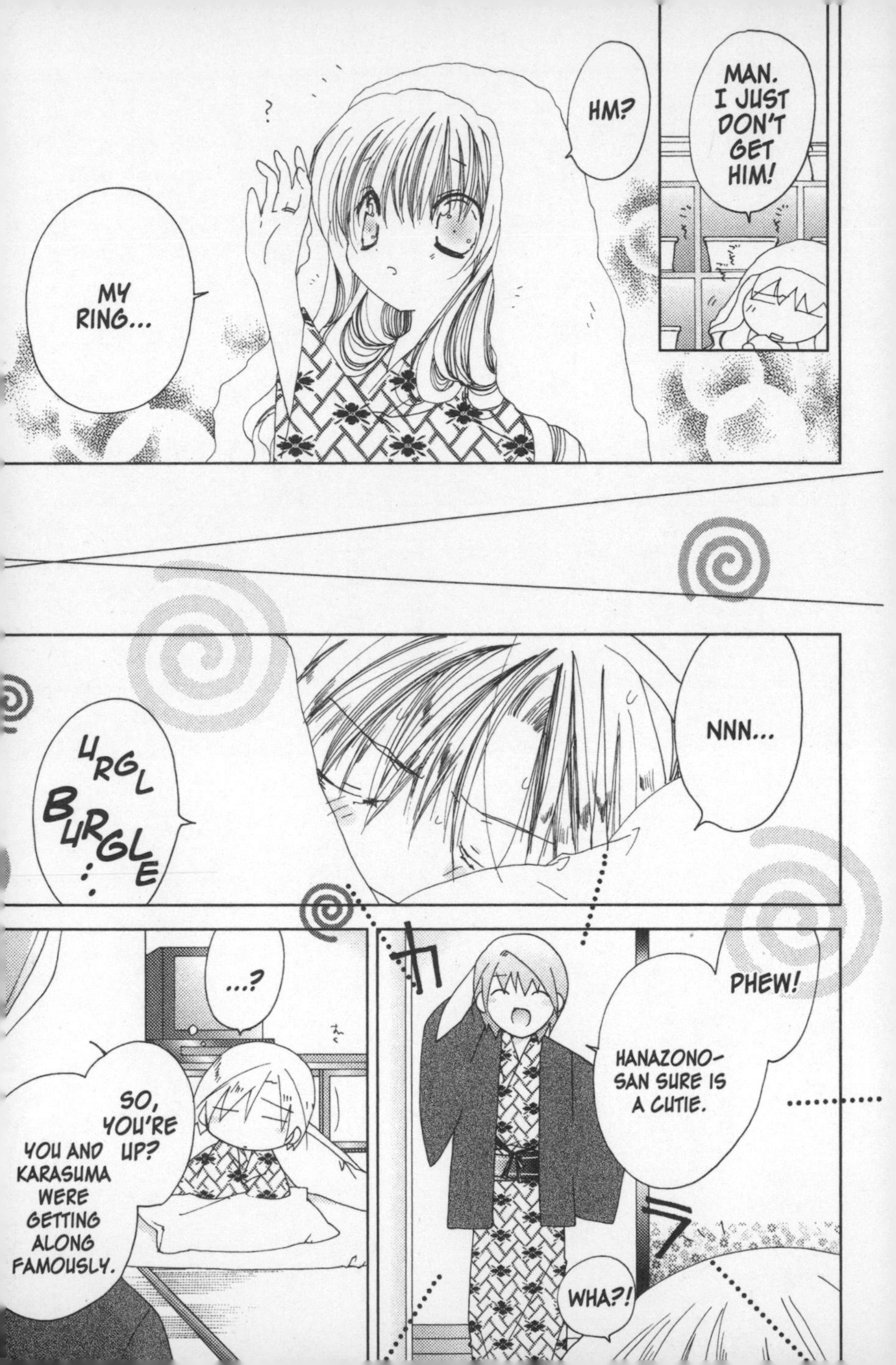
MAN. I JUST DON'T GET HIM!
HM?
MY RING...
NNN...
URGL BURGLE...
PHEW!
HANAZONO-SAN SURE IS A CUTIE.
....
WHA?!
...?
SO, YOU'RE UP?
YOU AND KARASUMA WERE GETTING ALONG FAMOUSLY.

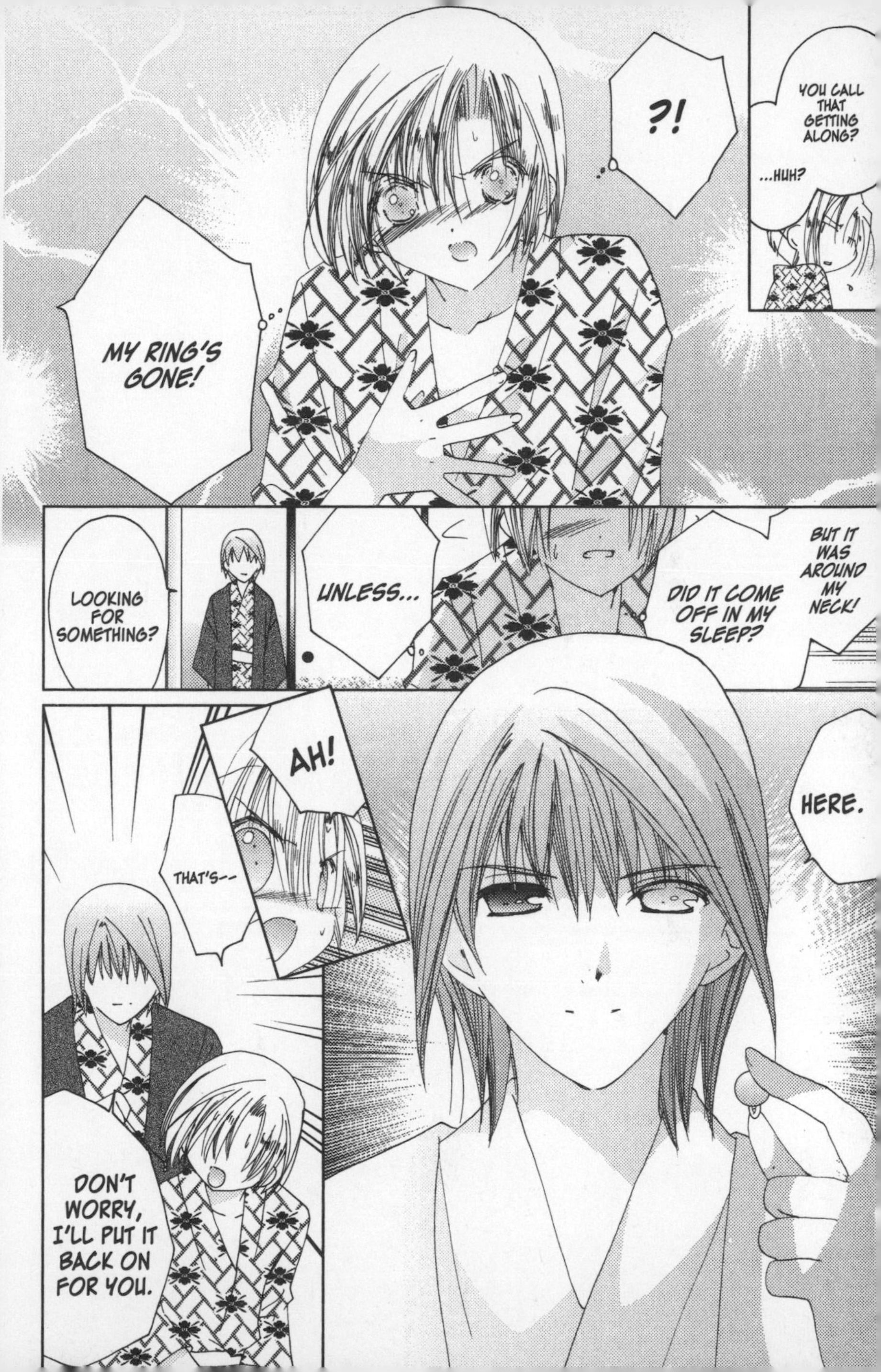
YOU CALL THAT GETTING ALONG?
...HUH?
?!
MY RING'S GONE!
BUT IT WAS AROUND MY NECK!
DID IT COME OFF IN MY SLEEP?
UNLESS...
LOOKING FOR SOMETHING?
HERE.
AH!
THAT'S--
DON'T WORRY, I'LL PUT IT BACK ON FOR YOU.

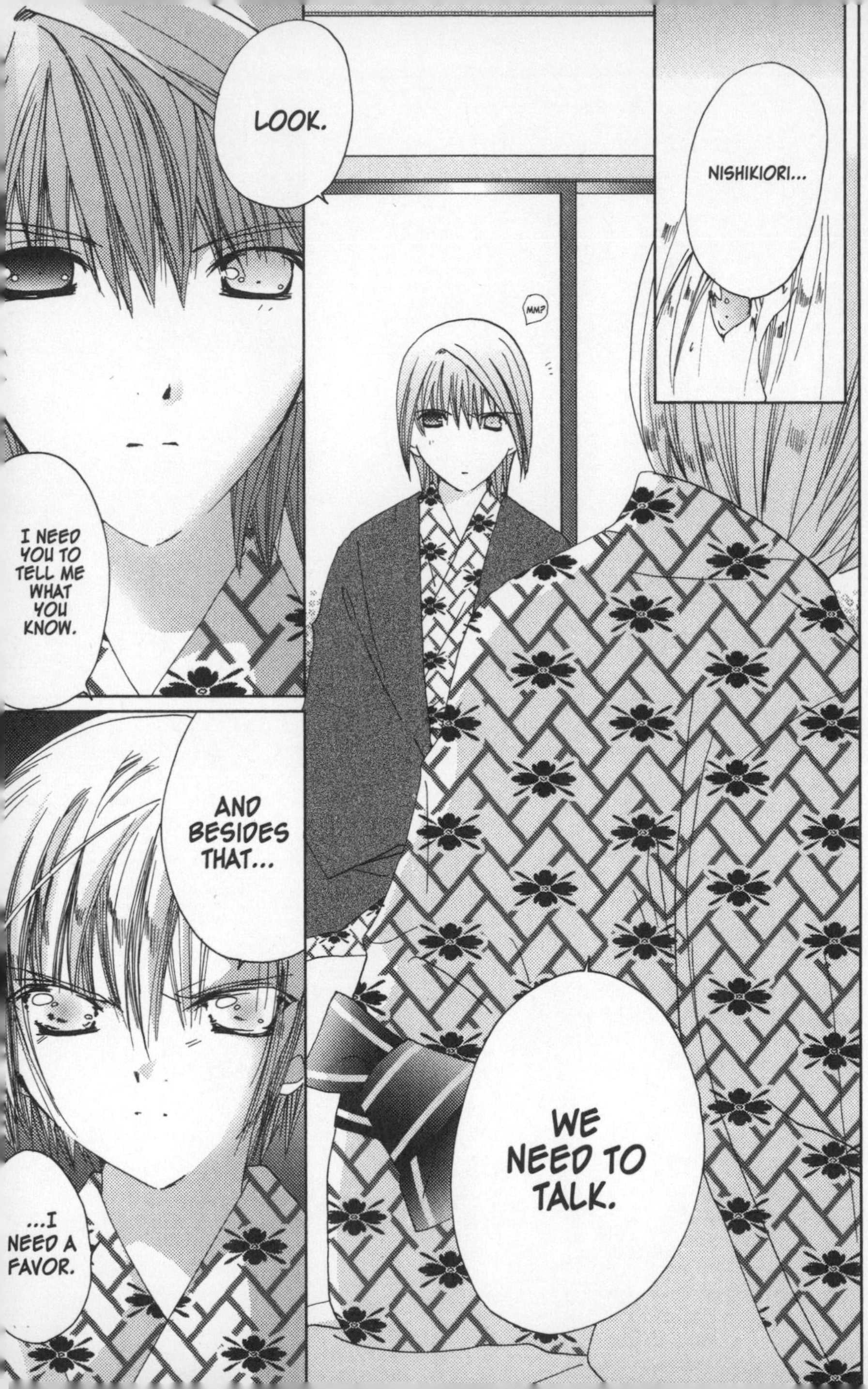
NISHIKIORI...
MM?
WE NEED TO TALK.
LOOK.
I NEED YOU TO TELL ME WHAT YOU KNOW.
AND BESIDES THAT...
...I NEED A FAVOR.

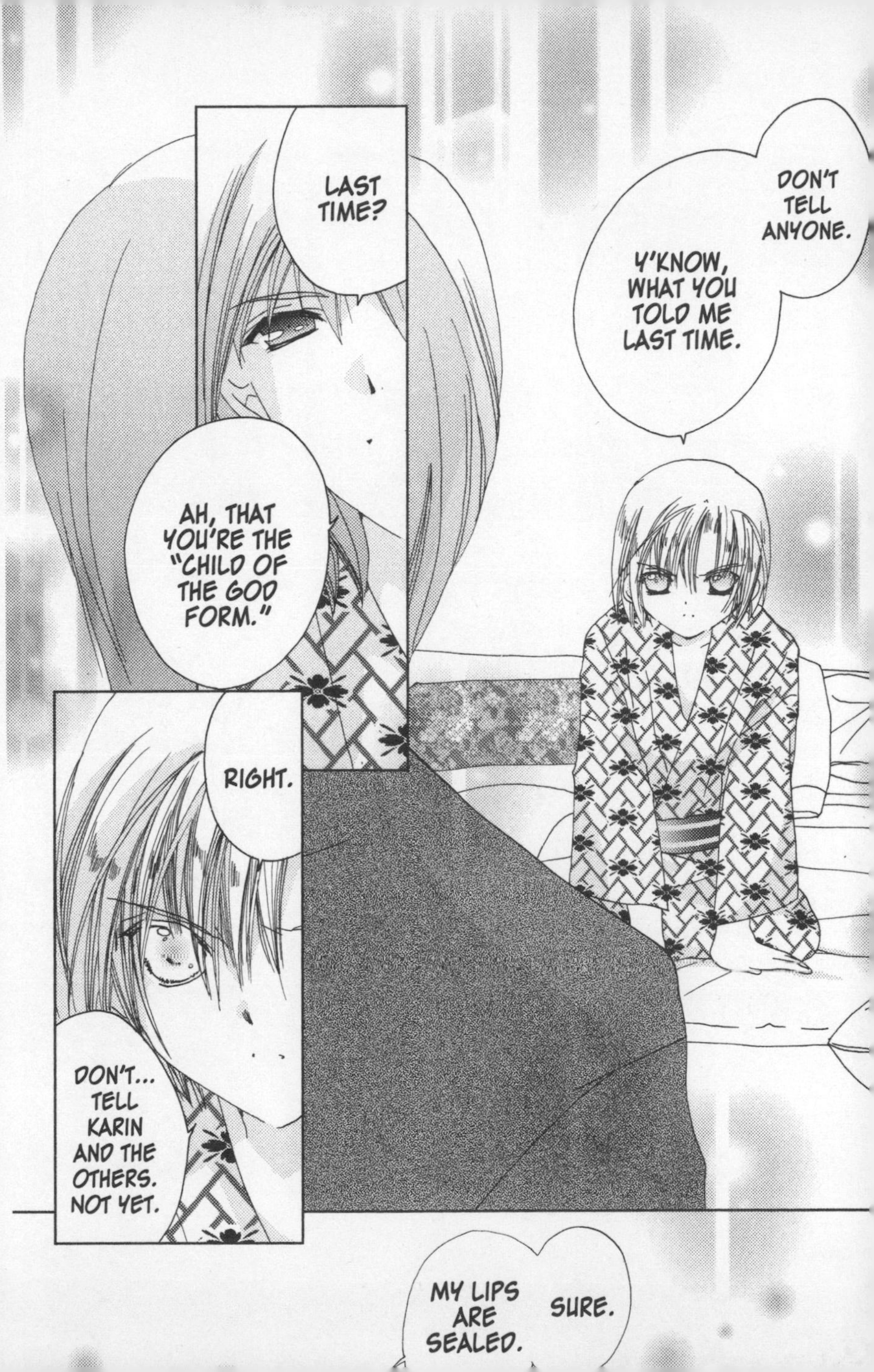
DON'T TELL ANYONE.
Y'KNOW, WHAT YOU TOLD ME LAST TIME.
LAST TIME?
AH, THAT YOU'RE THE "CHILD OF THE GOD FORM."
RIGHT.
DON'T... TELL KARIN AND THE OTHERS. NOT YET.
SURE.
MY LIPS ARE SEALED.

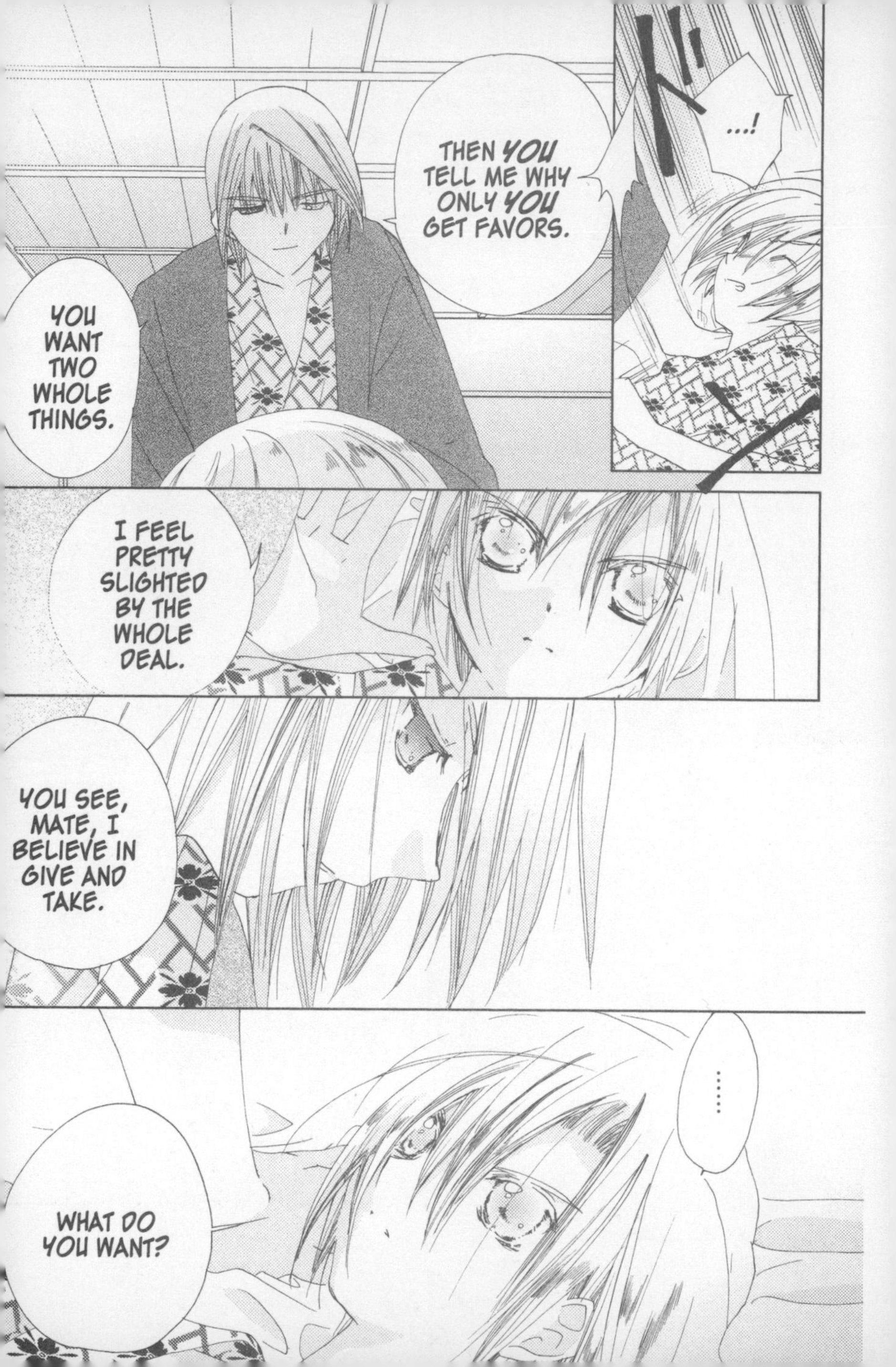
...!
THEN *YOU* TELL ME WHY ONLY *YOU* GET FAVORS.
YOU WANT TWO WHOLE THINGS.
I FEEL PRETTY SLIGHTED BY THE WHOLE DEAL.
YOU SEE, MATE, I BELIEVE IN GIVE AND TAKE.
......
WHAT DO YOU WANT?

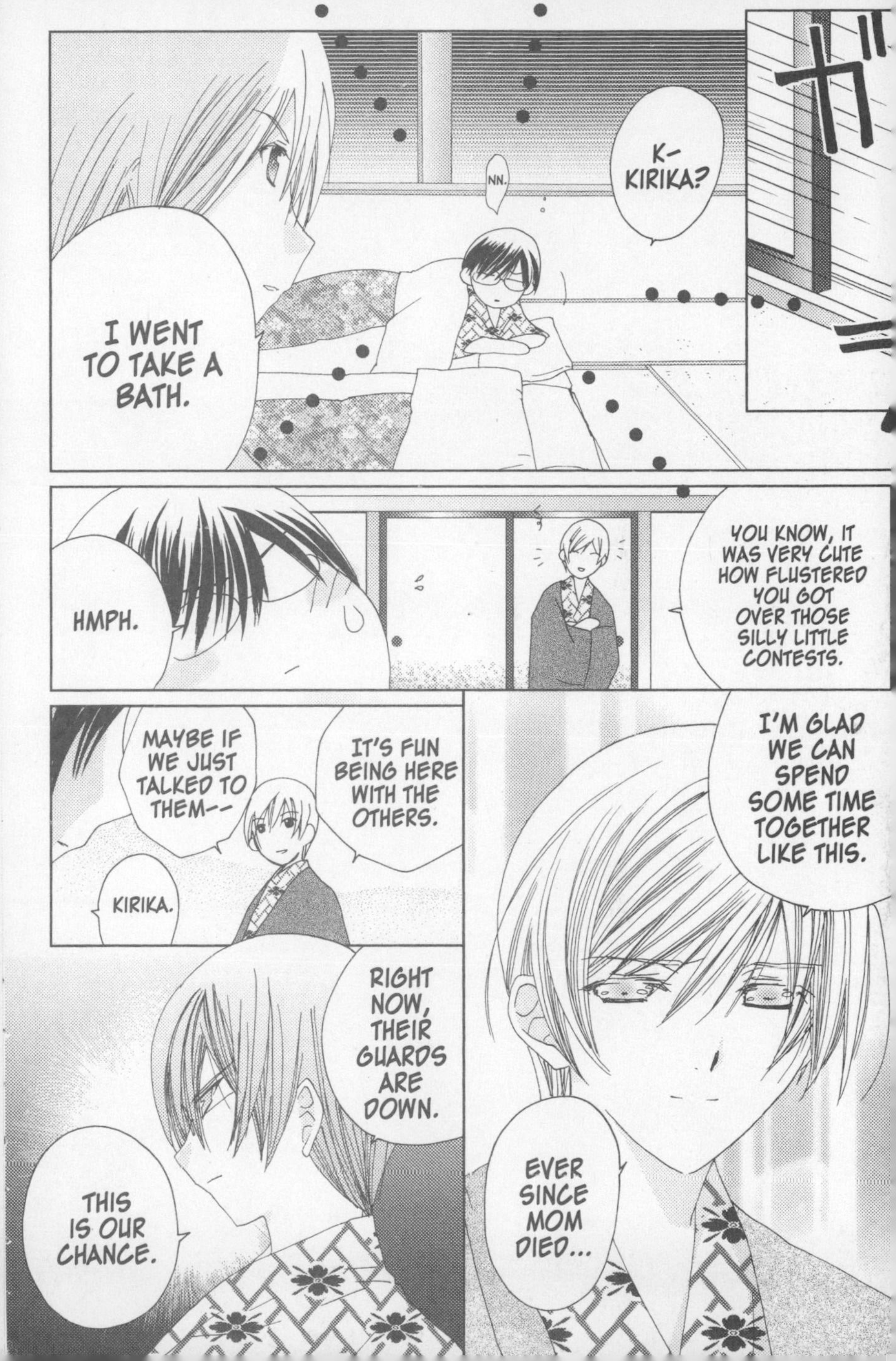

K-KIRIKA?
NN.
I WENT TO TAKE A BATH.
YOU KNOW, IT WAS VERY CUTE HOW FLUSTERED YOU GOT OVER THOSE SILLY LITTLE CONTESTS.
HMPH.
I'M GLAD WE CAN SPEND SOME TIME TOGETHER LIKE THIS.
EVER SINCE MOM DIED...
IT'S FUN BEING HERE WITH THE OTHERS.
MAYBE IF WE JUST TALKED TO THEM--
KIRIKA.
RIGHT NOW, THEIR GUARDS ARE DOWN.
THIS IS OUR CHANCE.

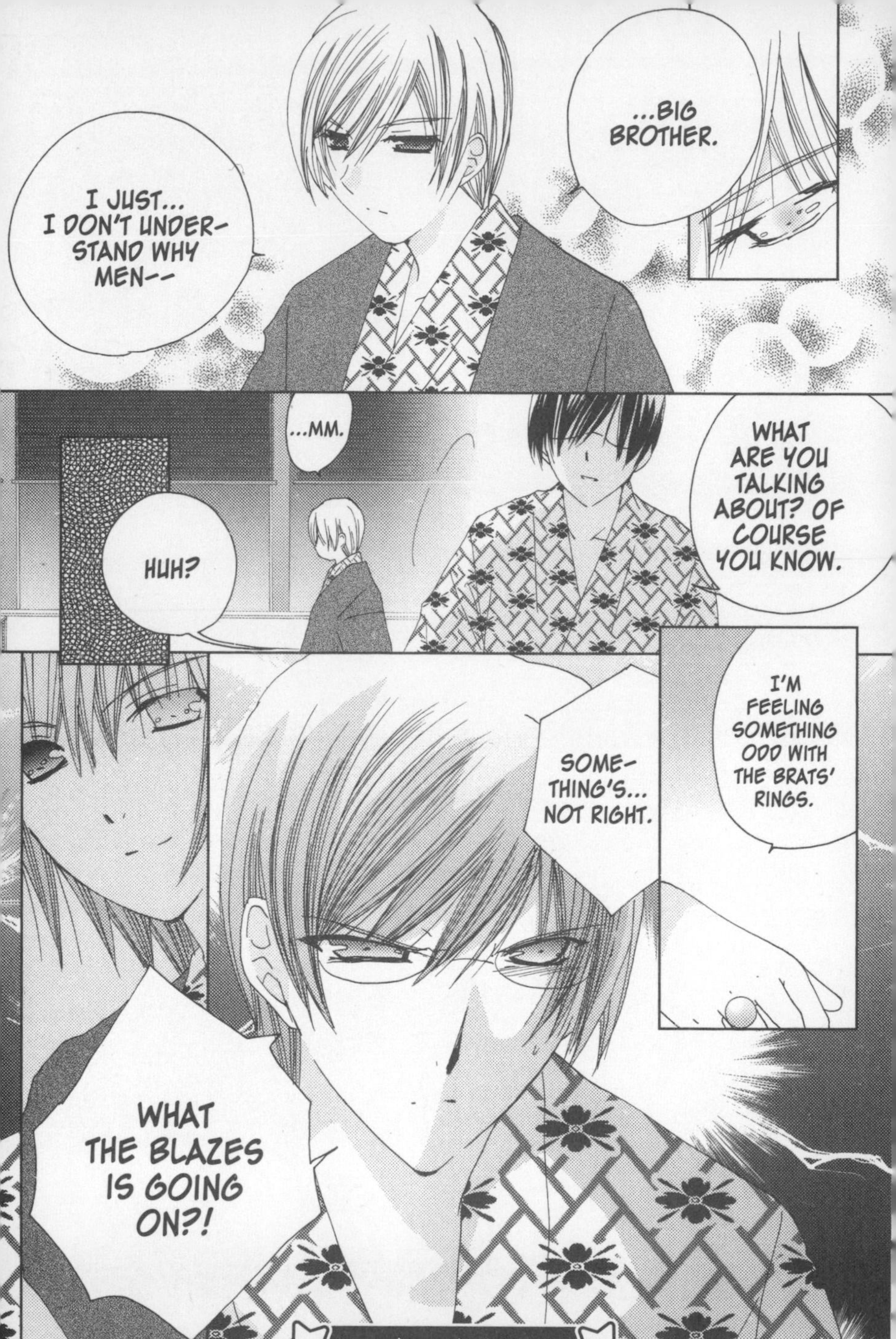
...BIG BROTHER.
I JUST... I DON'T UNDER-STAND WHY MEN--
WHAT ARE YOU TALKING ABOUT? OF COURSE YOU KNOW.
...MM.
HUH?
I'M FEELING SOMETHING ODD WITH THE BRATS' RINGS.
SOME-THING'S... NOT RIGHT.
WHAT THE BLAZES IS GOING ON?!

Continued in Book 4!

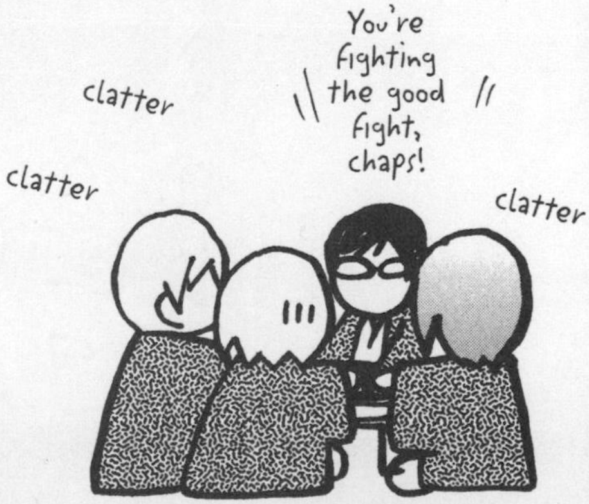
clatter
clatter
You're fighting the good fight, chaps!
clatter

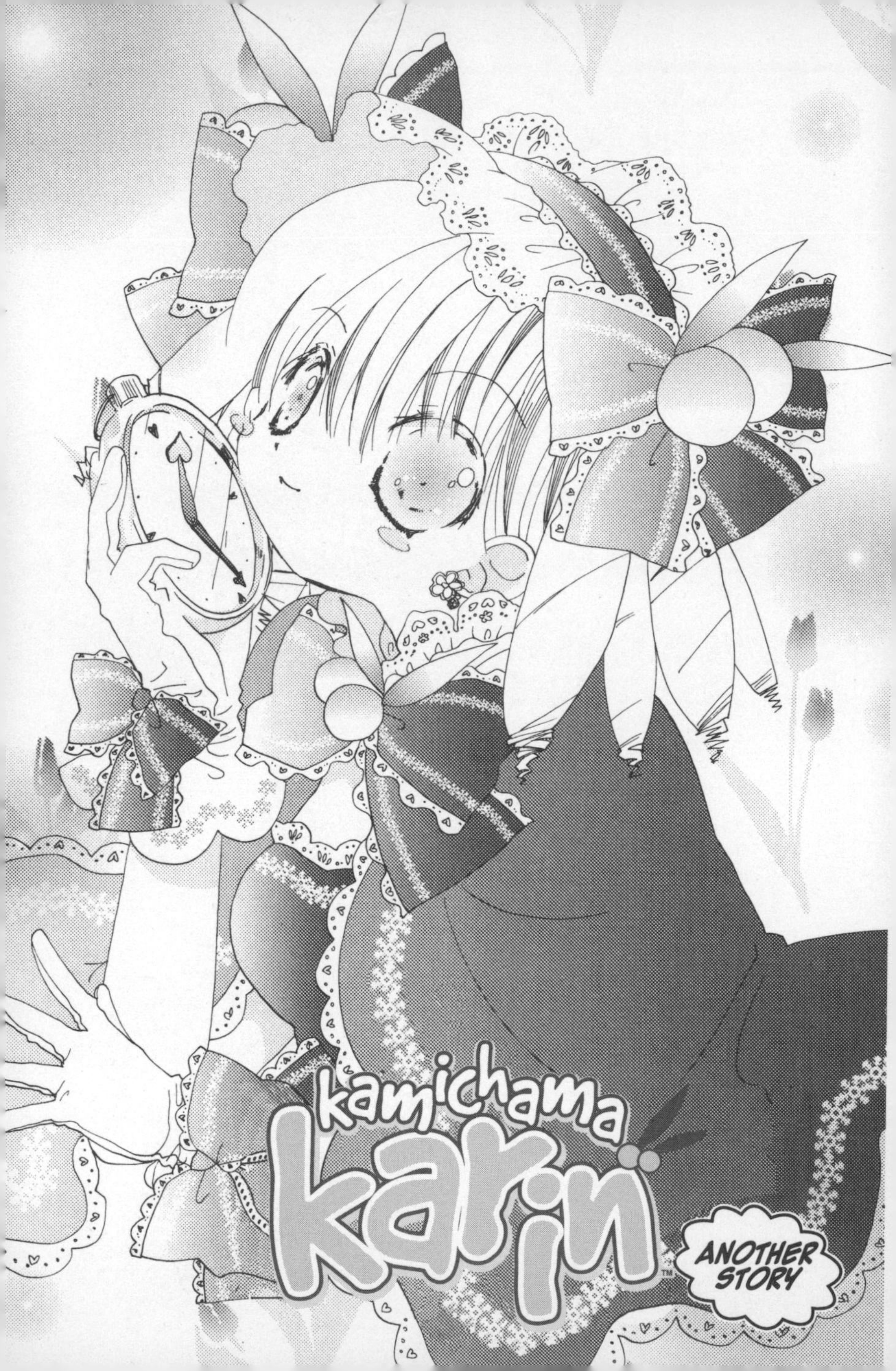
kamichama karin™
ANOTHER STORY

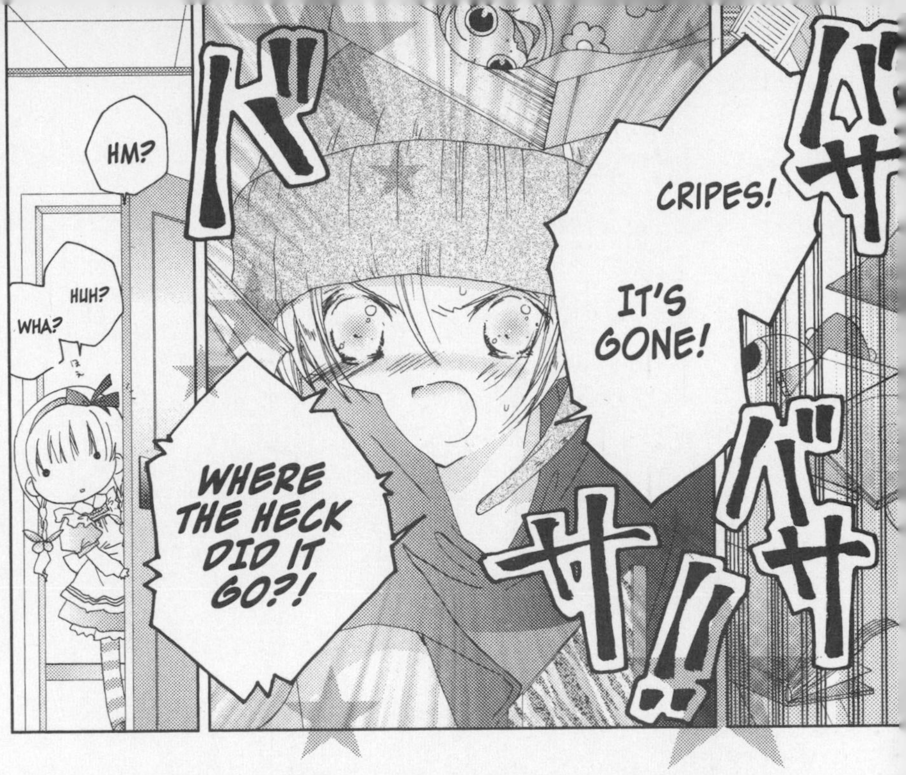

バサ
CRIPES!
IT'S GONE!
バサ
サ!!
ド
WHERE THE HECK DID IT GO?!
HM?
HUH?
WHA?

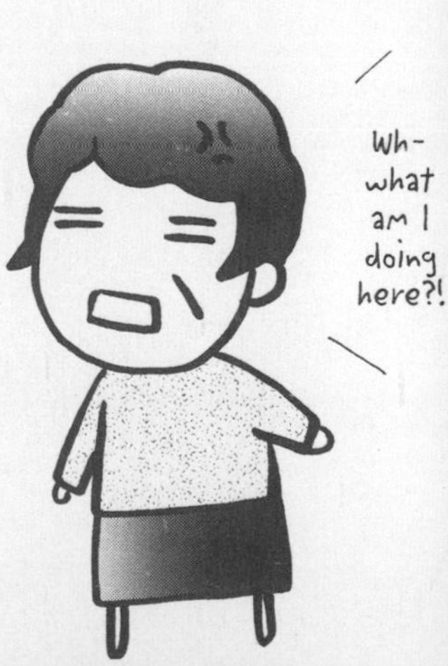

Wh-what am I doing here?!

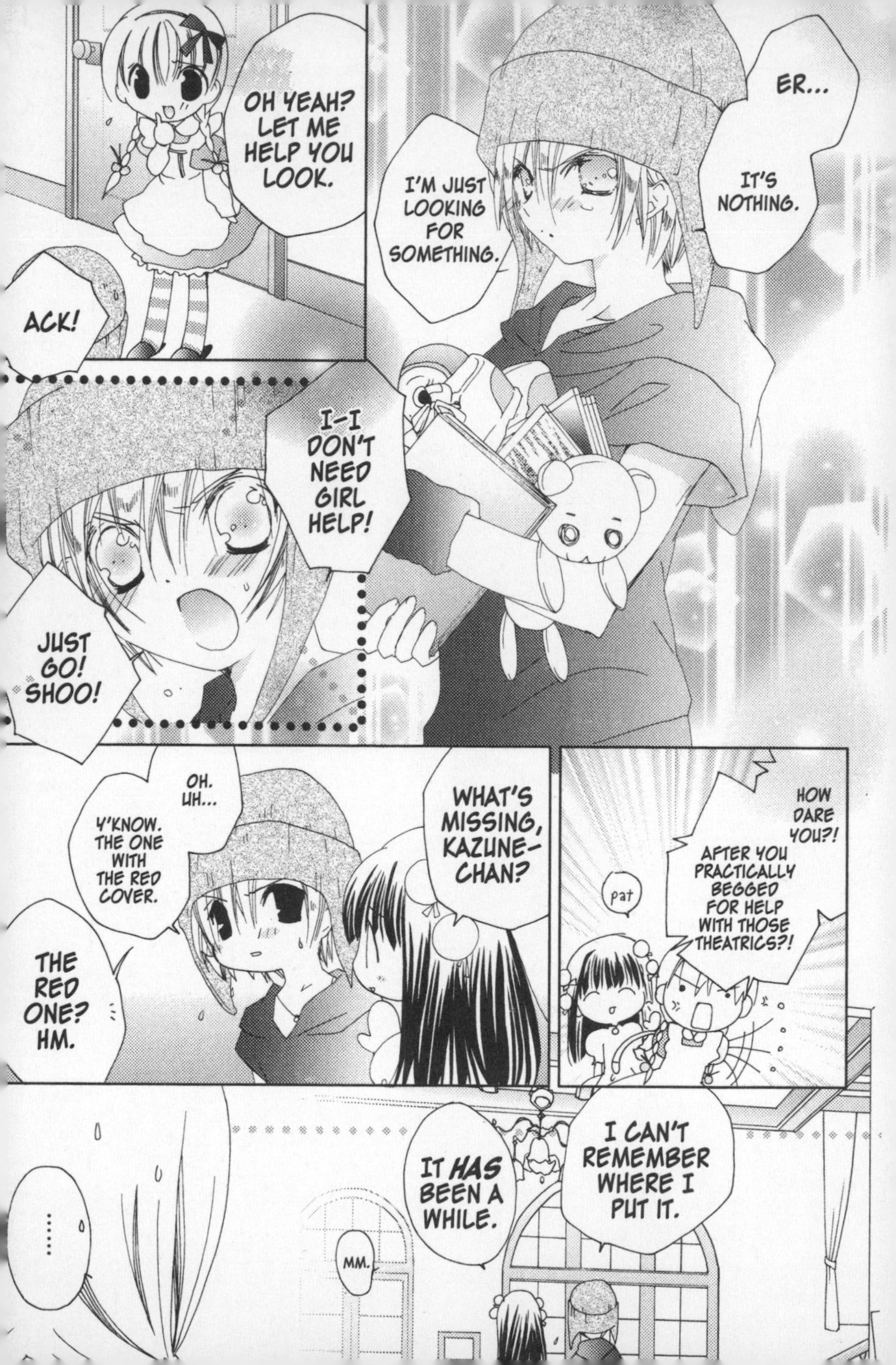
ER...
IT'S NOTHING.
I'M JUST LOOKING FOR SOMETHING.
OH YEAH? LET ME HELP YOU LOOK.
ACK!
I-I DON'T NEED GIRL HELP!
JUST GO! SHOO!
HOW DARE YOU?!
AFTER YOU PRACTICALLY BEGGED FOR HELP WITH THOSE THEATRICS?!
pat
WHAT'S MISSING, KAZUNE-CHAN?
OH. UH...
Y'KNOW. THE ONE WITH THE RED COVER.
THE RED ONE? HM.
I CAN'T REMEMBER WHERE I PUT IT.
IT *HAS* BEEN A WHILE.
MM.
......

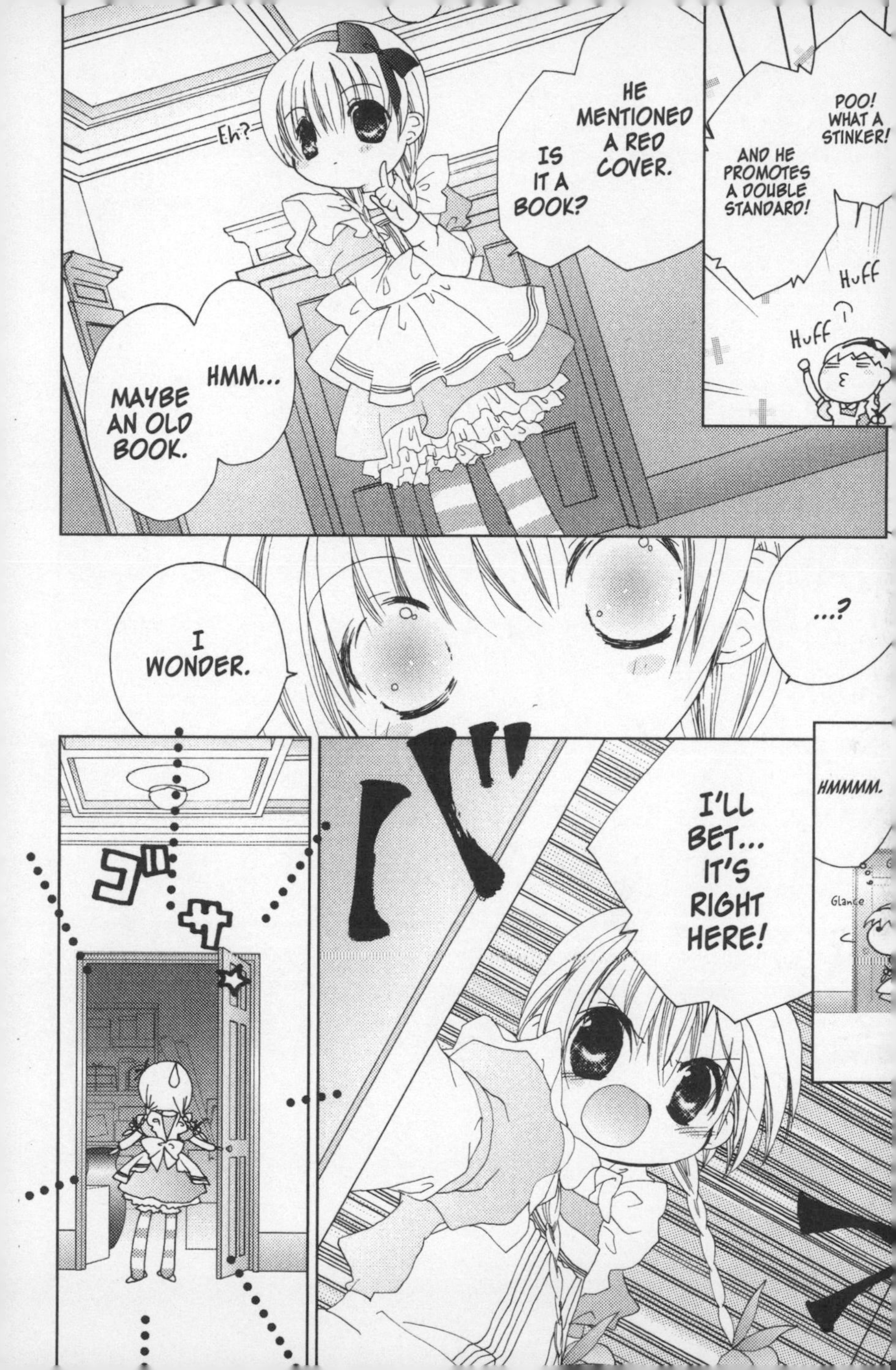
POO! WHAT A STINKER!
AND HE PROMOTES A DOUBLE STANDARD!
Huff
Huff
HE MENTIONED A RED COVER.
IS IT A BOOK?
Eh?
HMM...
MAYBE AN OLD BOOK.
...?
I WONDER.
HMMMM.
Glance
I'LL BET... IT'S RIGHT HERE!

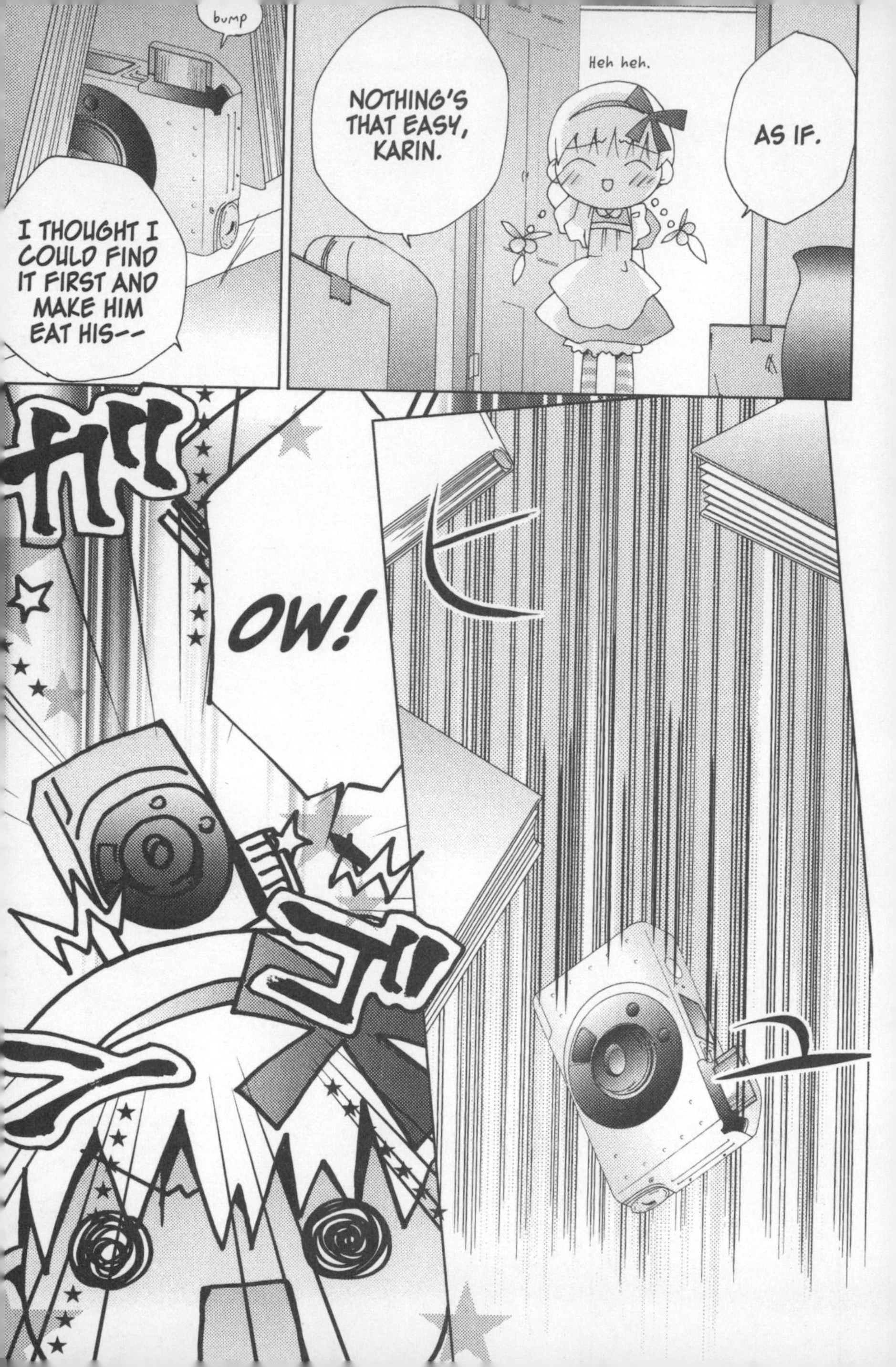
Heh heh.
AS IF.
NOTHING'S THAT EASY, KARIN.
bump
I THOUGHT I COULD FIND IT FIRST AND MAKE HIM EAT HIS--
OW!

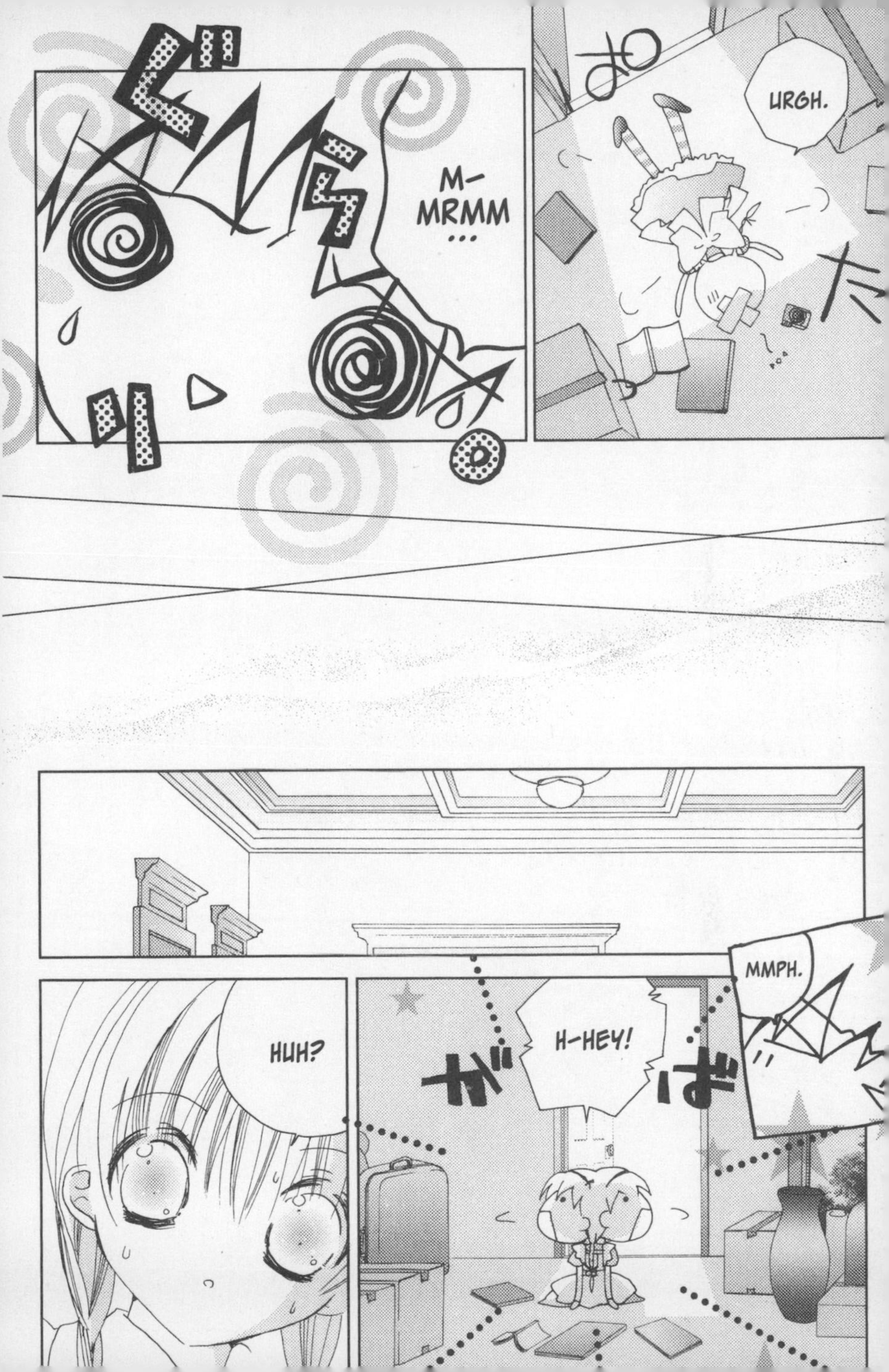
URGH.
M-MRMM...
MMPH.
H-HEY!
HUH?

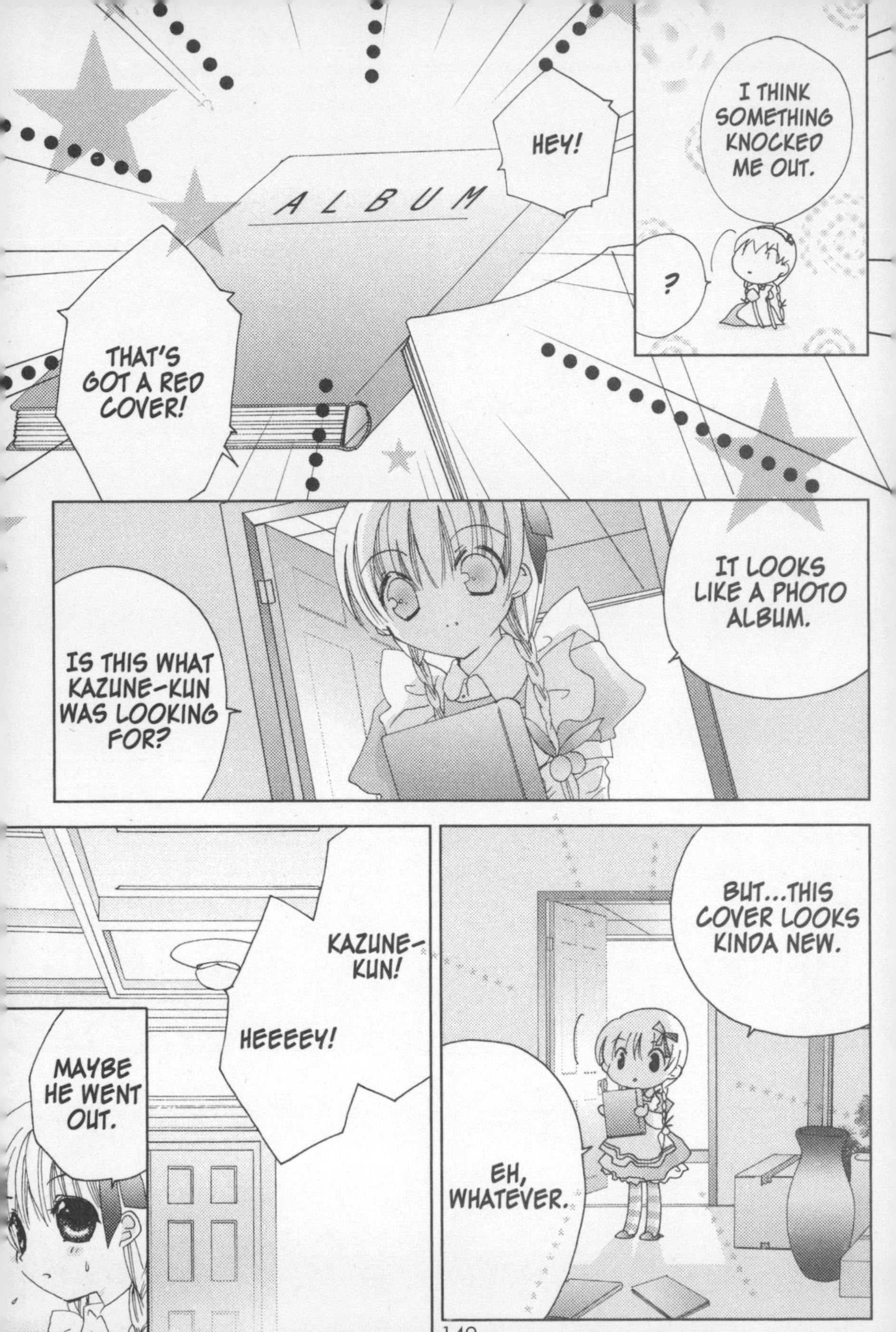
I THINK SOMETHING KNOCKED ME OUT.
?
HEY!
ALBUM
THAT'S GOT A RED COVER!
IT LOOKS LIKE A PHOTO ALBUM.
IS THIS WHAT KAZUNE-KUN WAS LOOKING FOR?
BUT...THIS COVER LOOKS KINDA NEW.
EH, WHATEVER.
KAZUNE-KUN!
HEEEEY!
MAYBE HE WENT OUT.

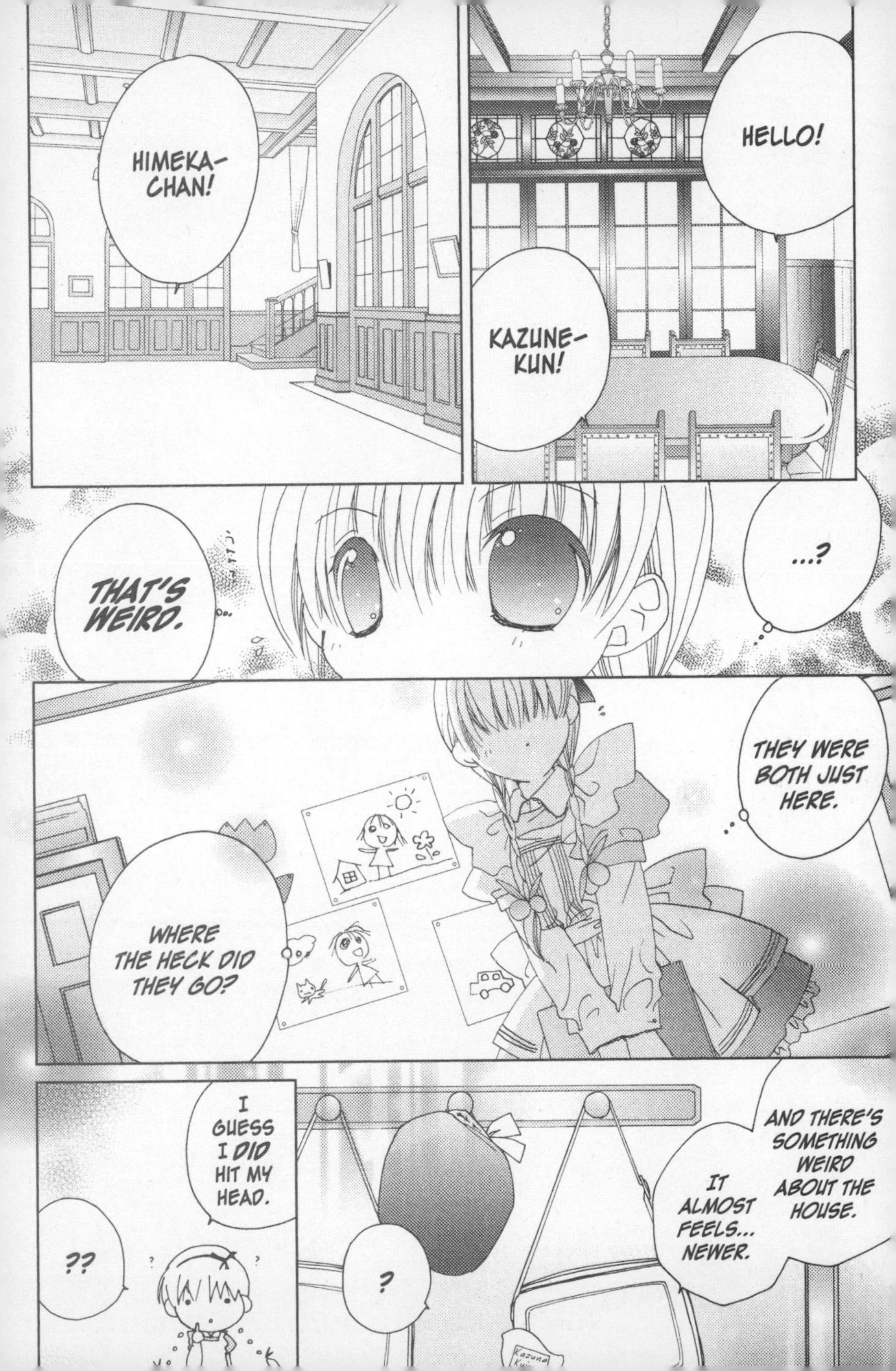

HELLO!
KAZUNE-KUN!
HIMEKA-CHAN!
...?
THAT'S WEIRD.
THEY WERE BOTH JUST HERE.
WHERE THE HECK DID THEY GO?
AND THERE'S SOMETHING WEIRD ABOUT THE HOUSE.
IT ALMOST FEELS... NEWER.
?
I GUESS I DID HIT MY HEAD.
??

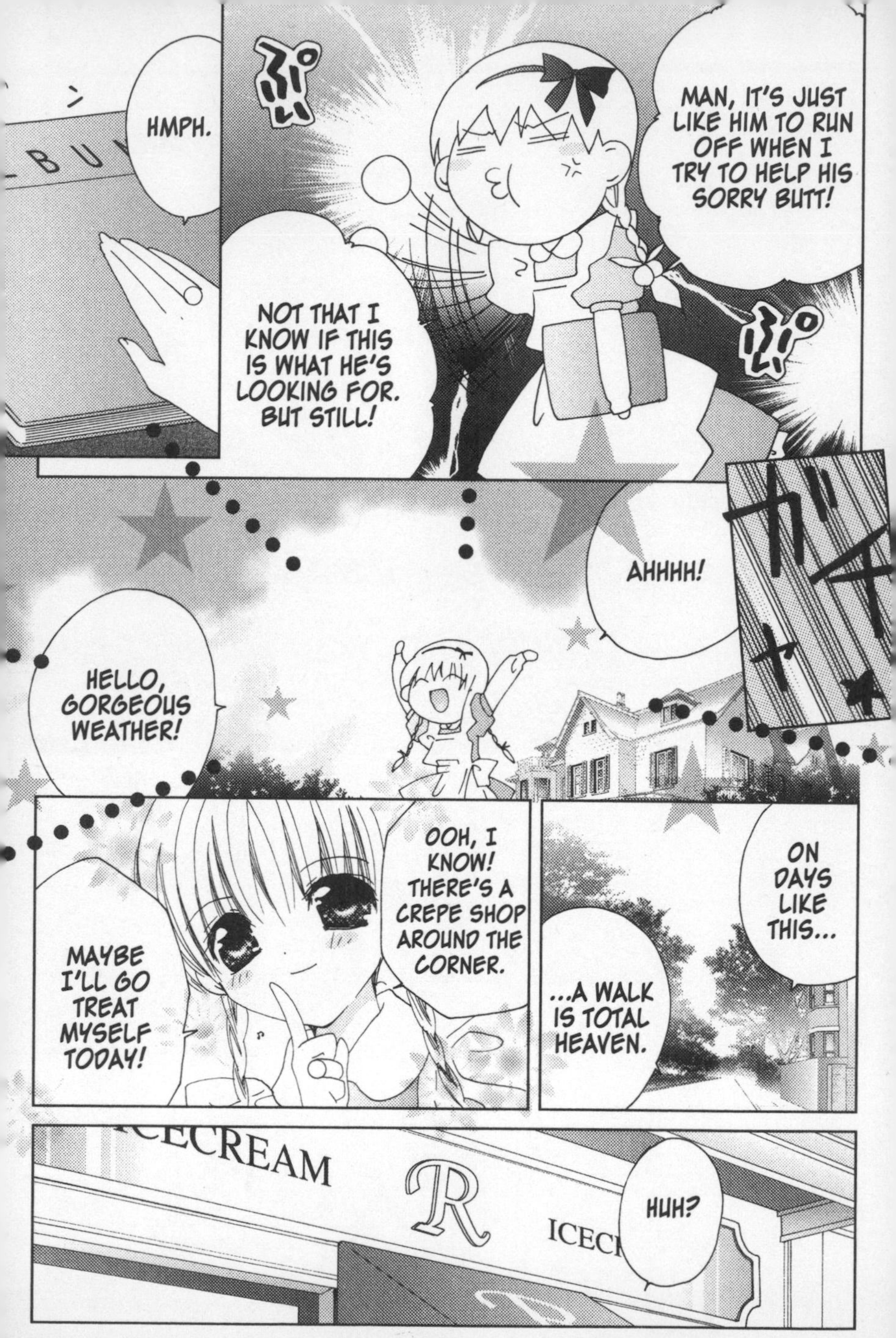
ぷい
MAN, IT'S JUST LIKE HIM TO RUN OFF WHEN I TRY TO HELP HIS SORRY BUTT!
ぷい
NOT THAT I KNOW IF THIS IS WHAT HE'S LOOKING FOR. BUT STILL!
HMPH.
ガチャ
AHHHH!
HELLO, GORGEOUS WEATHER!
ON DAYS LIKE THIS...
...A WALK IS TOTAL HEAVEN.
OOH, I KNOW! THERE'S A CREPE SHOP AROUND THE CORNER.
MAYBE I'LL GO TREAT MYSELF TODAY!
ICECREAM
R
HUH?

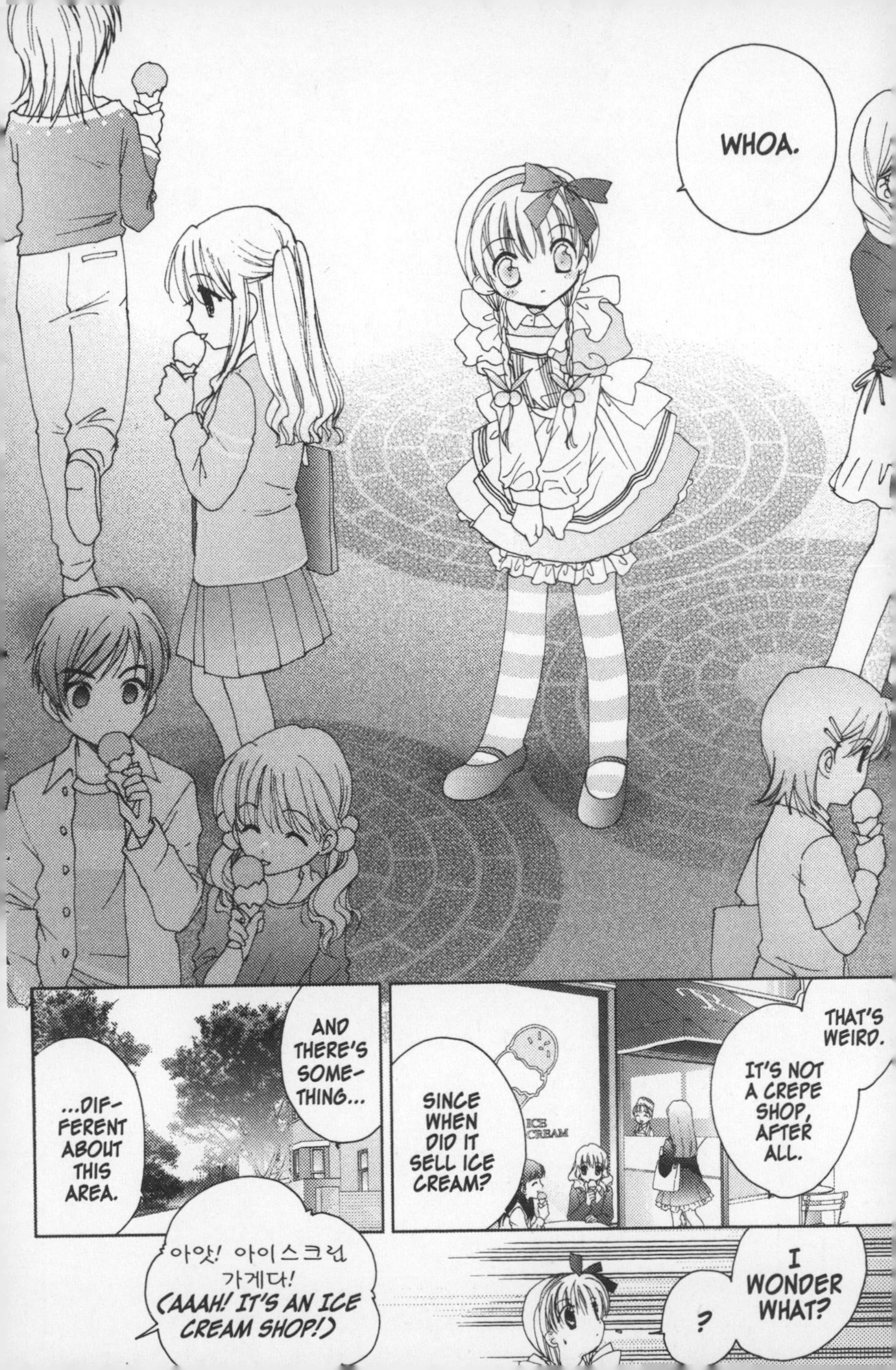
WHOA.
THAT'S WEIRD.
IT'S NOT A CREPE SHOP, AFTER ALL.
SINCE WHEN DID IT SELL ICE CREAM?
ICE CREAM
AND THERE'S SOME-THING...
...DIF-FERENT ABOUT THIS AREA.
I WONDER WHAT?
?
아앗! 아이스크림 가게다!
(AAAH! IT'S AN ICE CREAM SHOP!)

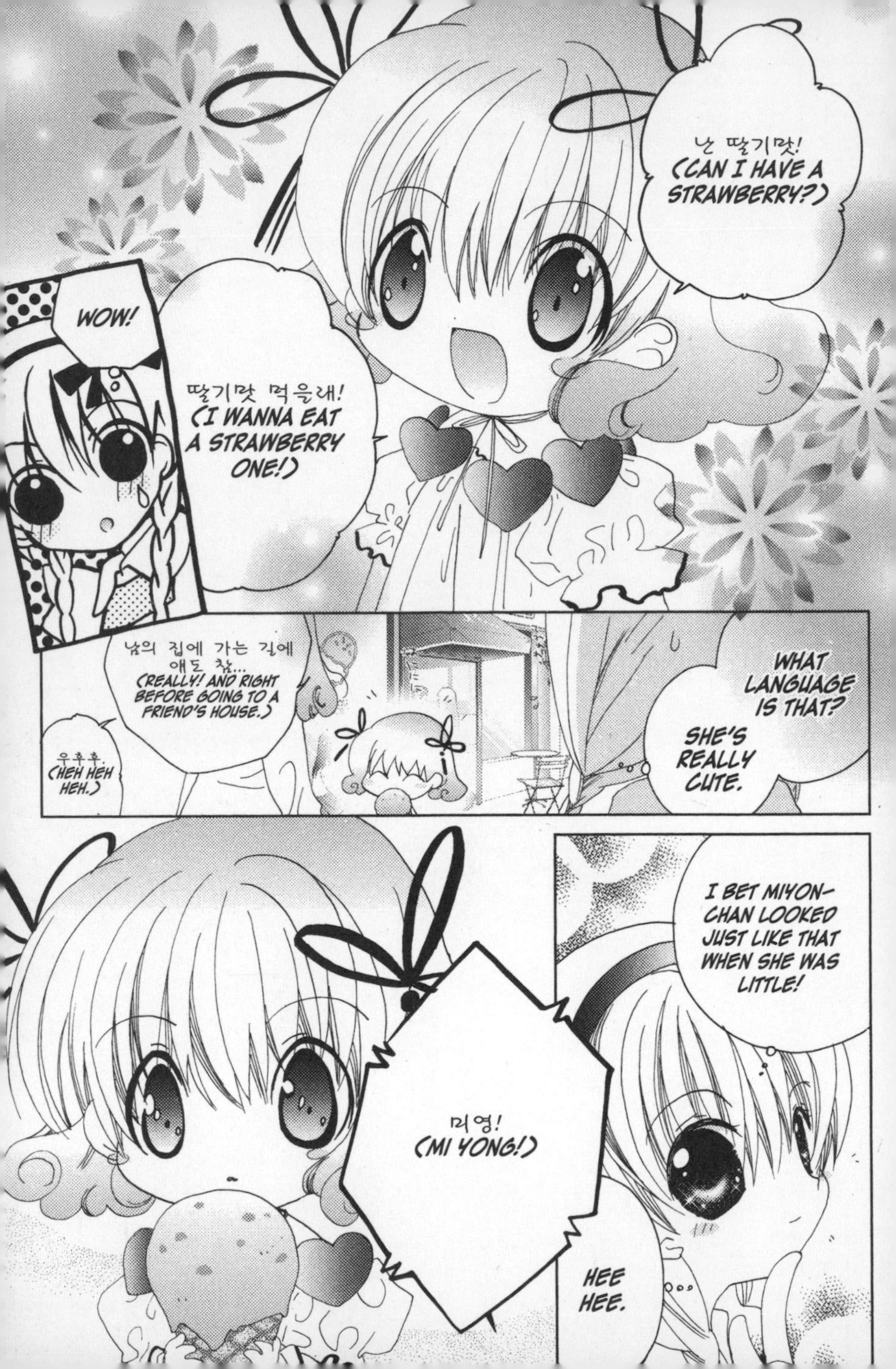
난 딸기맛! (CAN I HAVE A STRAWBERRY?)
딸기맛 먹을래! (I WANNA EAT A STRAWBERRY ONE!)
WOW!
WHAT LANGUAGE IS THAT?
SHE'S REALLY CUTE.
남의 집에 가는 길에 애도 참... (REALLY! AND RIGHT BEFORE GOING TO A FRIEND'S HOUSE.)
우후후. (HEH HEH HEH.)
I BET MIYON-CHAN LOOKED JUST LIKE THAT WHEN SHE WAS LITTLE!
HEE HEE.
미영! (MI YONG!)

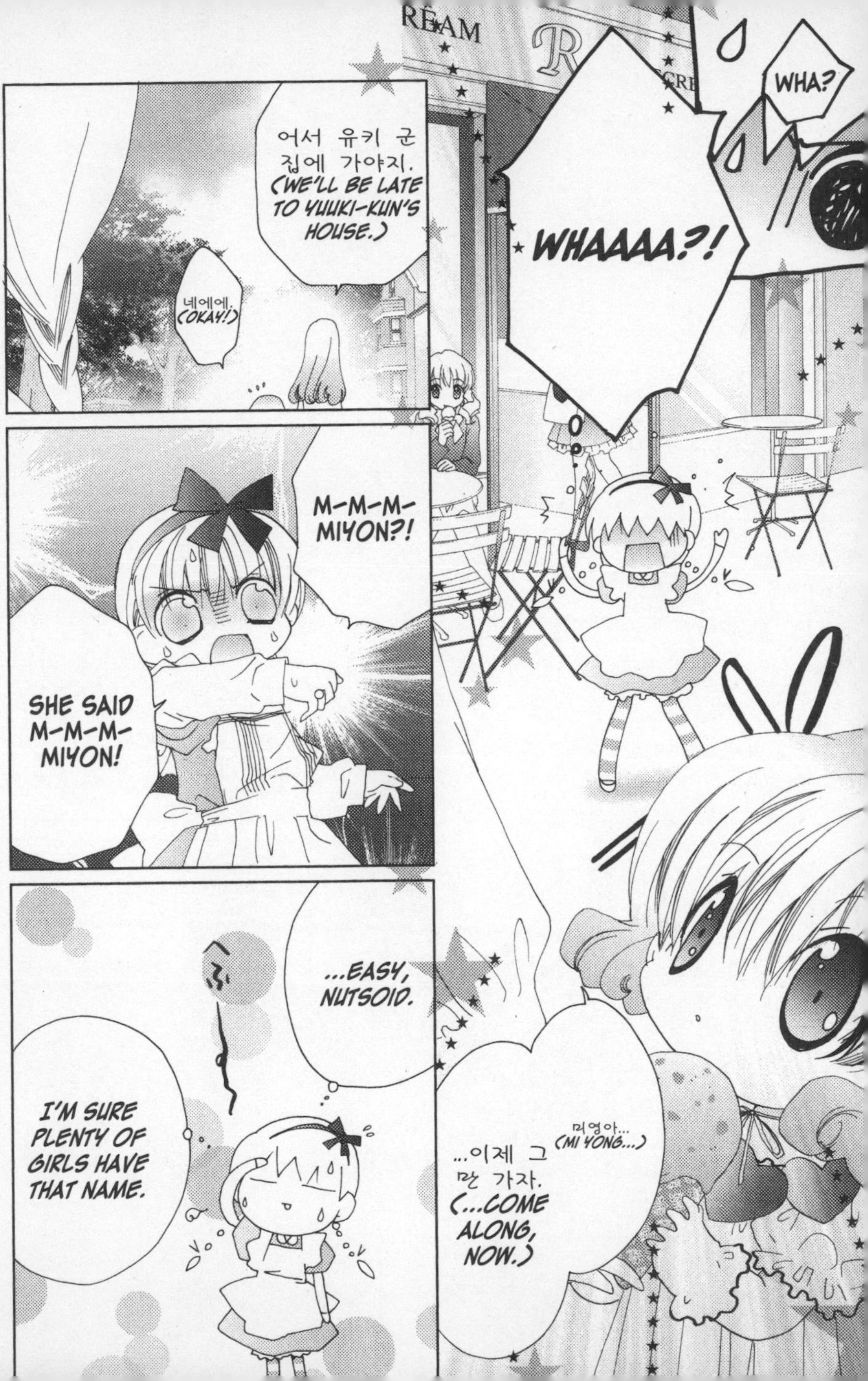
WHA?
WHAAAA?!
미영아... (MI YONG...)
...이제 그만 가자. (...COME ALONG, NOW.)
어서 유키 군 집에 가야지. (WE'LL BE LATE TO YUUKI-KUN'S HOUSE.)
네에에. (OKAY!)
M-M-M-MIYON?!
SHE SAID M-M-M-MIYON!
...EASY, NUTSOID.
I'M SURE PLENTY OF GIRLS HAVE THAT NAME.

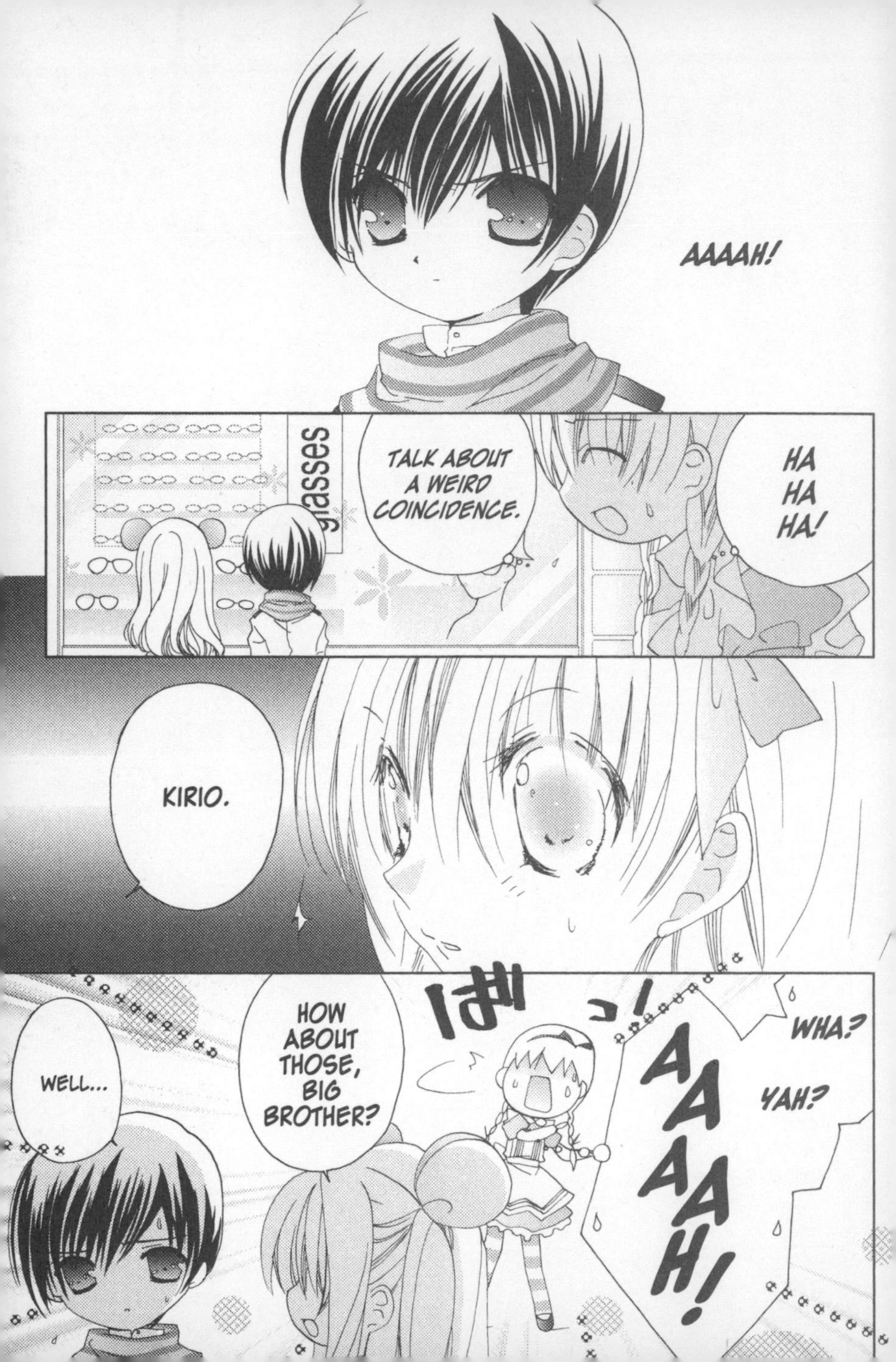
AAAAH!
HA HA HA!
TALK ABOUT A WEIRD COINCIDENCE.
glasses
KIRIO.
WHA? YAH?
AAAAH!
ぱっ!
HOW ABOUT THOSE, BIG BROTHER?
WELL...

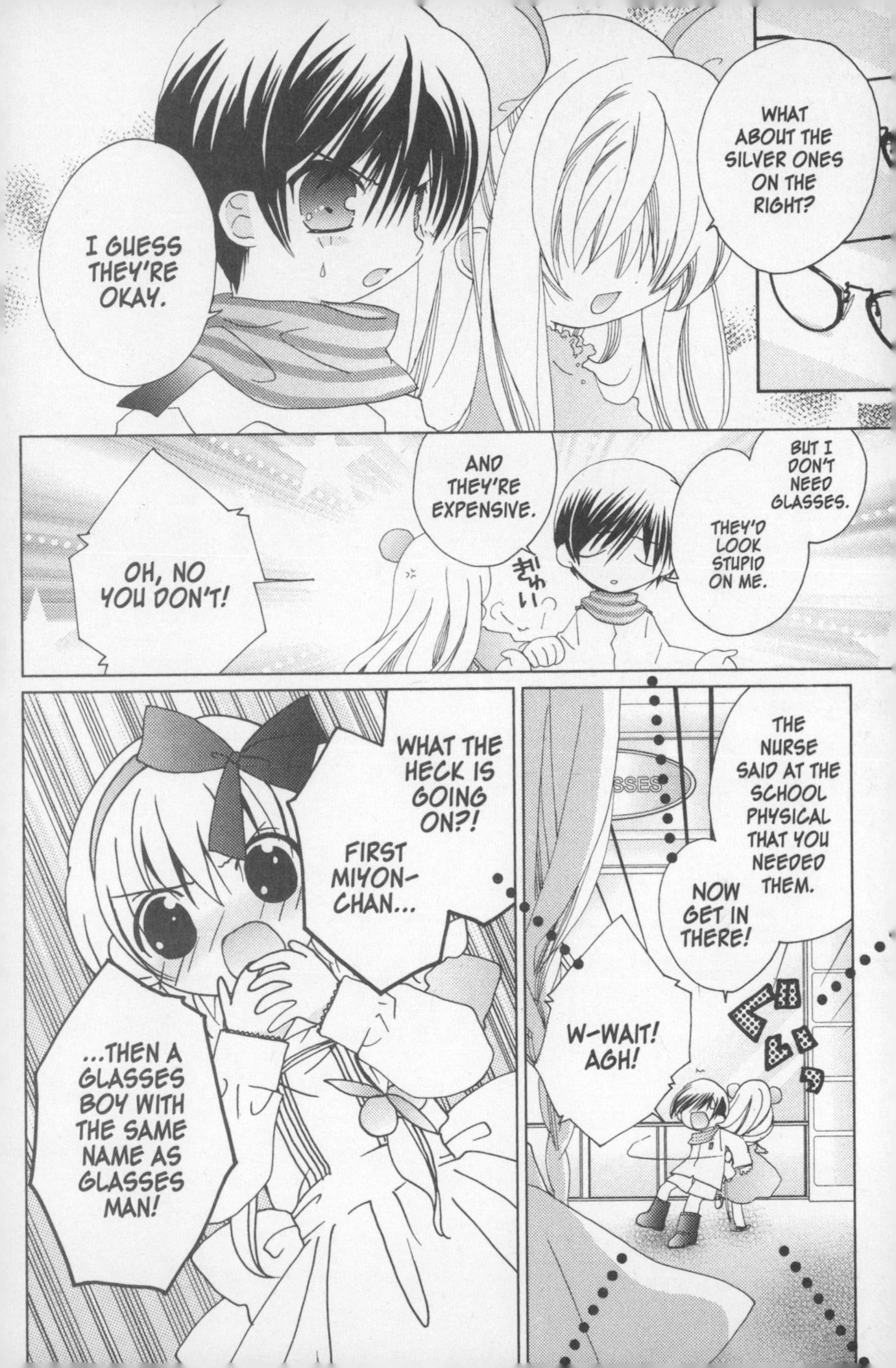
WHAT ABOUT THE SILVER ONES ON THE RIGHT?
I GUESS THEY'RE OKAY.
BUT I DON'T NEED GLASSES.
THEY'D LOOK STUPID ON ME.
AND THEY'RE EXPENSIVE.
OH, NO YOU DON'T!
THE NURSE SAID AT THE SCHOOL PHYSICAL THAT YOU NEEDED THEM.
NOW GET IN THERE!
W-WAIT! AGH!
WHAT THE HECK IS GOING ON?!
FIRST MIYON-CHAN...
...THEN A GLASSES BOY WITH THE SAME NAME AS GLASSES MAN!

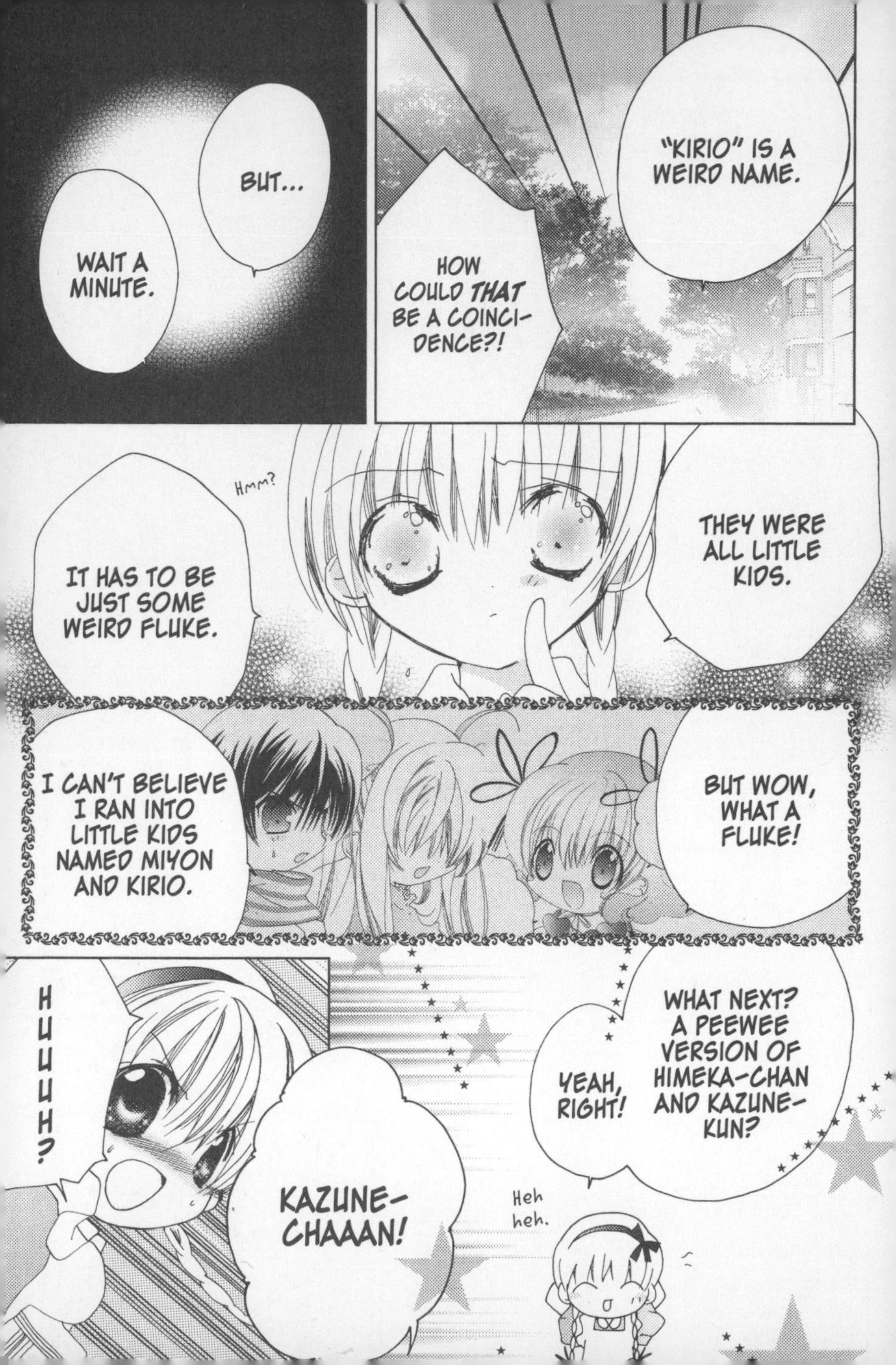
"KIRIO" IS A WEIRD NAME.
HOW COULD *THAT* BE A COINCIDENCE?!
BUT...
WAIT A MINUTE.
THEY WERE ALL LITTLE KIDS.
Hmm?
IT HAS TO BE JUST SOME WEIRD FLUKE.
BUT WOW, WHAT A FLUKE!
I CAN'T BELIEVE I RAN INTO LITTLE KIDS NAMED MIYON AND KIRIO.
WHAT NEXT? A PEEWEE VERSION OF HIMEKA-CHAN AND KAZUNE-KUN?
YEAH, RIGHT!
Heh heh.
HUUUH?
KAZUNE-CHAAAN!

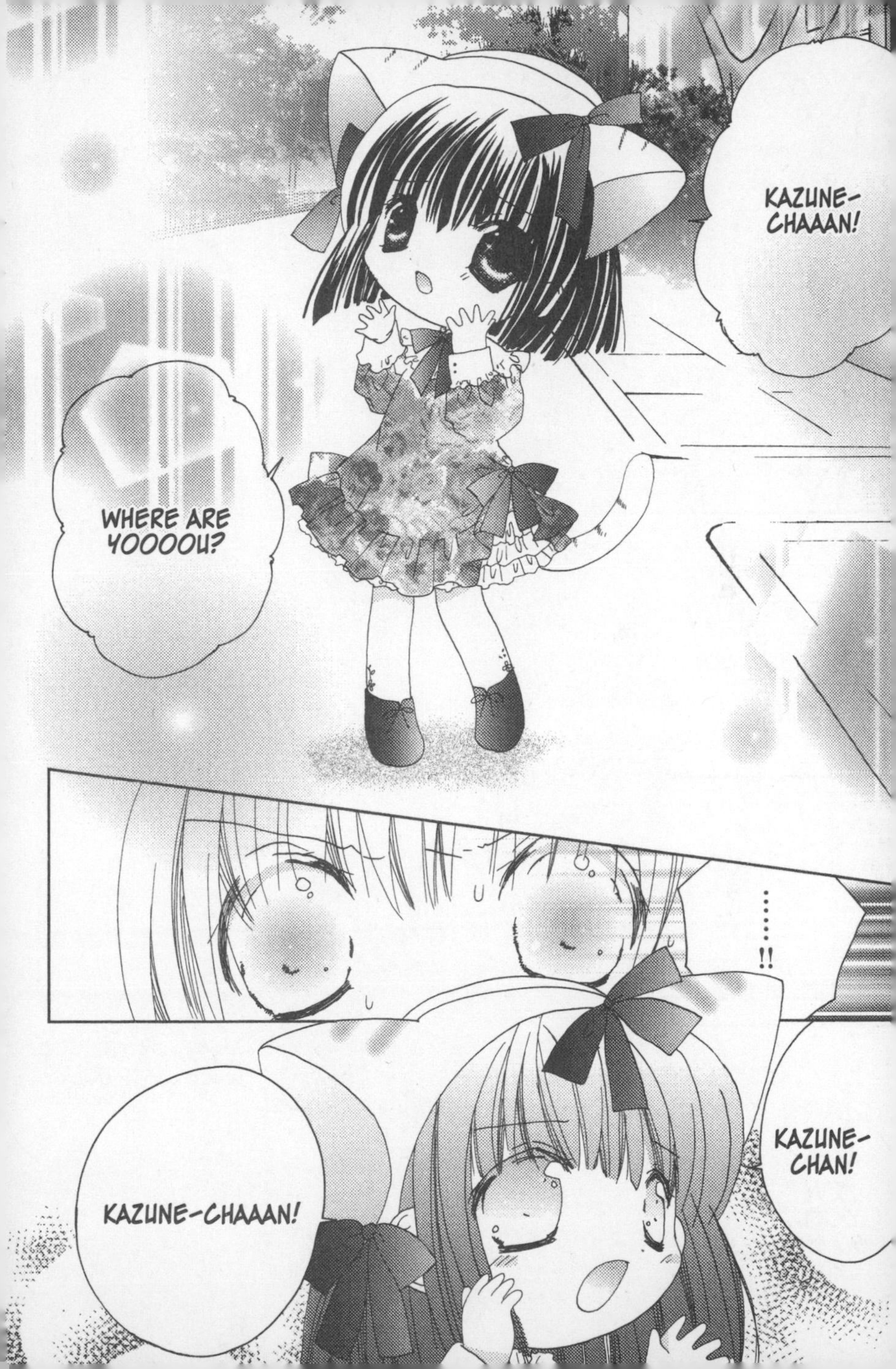
KAZUNE-
CHAAAN!
WHERE ARE
YOOOOU?
......!!
KAZUNE-
CHAN!
KAZUNE-CHAAAN!

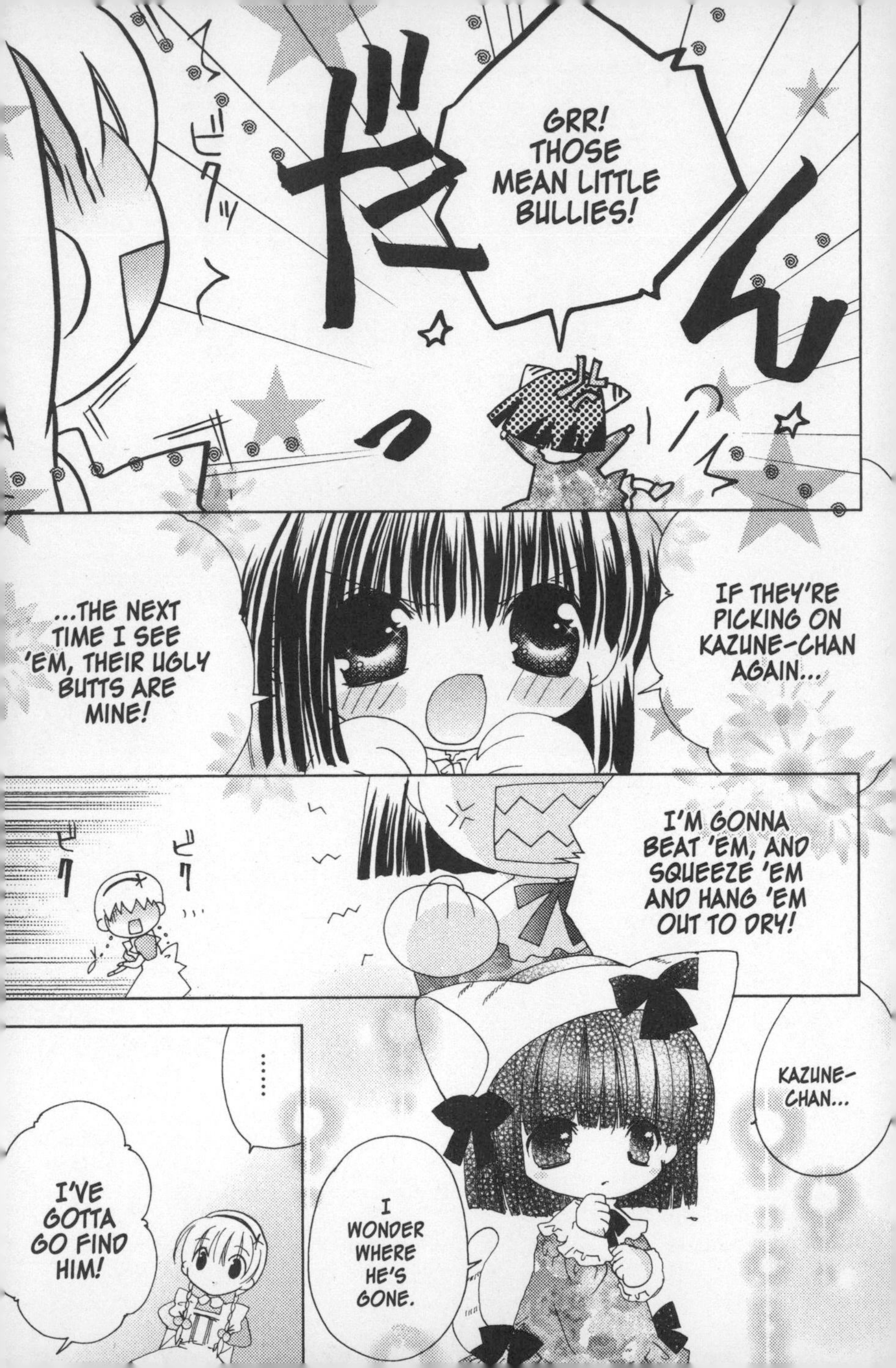
GRR! THOSE MEAN LITTLE BULLIES!
IF THEY'RE PICKING ON KAZUNE-CHAN AGAIN...
...THE NEXT TIME I SEE 'EM, THEIR UGLY BUTTS ARE MINE!
I'M GONNA BEAT 'EM, AND SQUEEZE 'EM AND HANG 'EM OUT TO DRY!
KAZUNE-CHAN...
I WONDER WHERE HE'S GONE.
......
I'VE GOTTA GO FIND HIM!

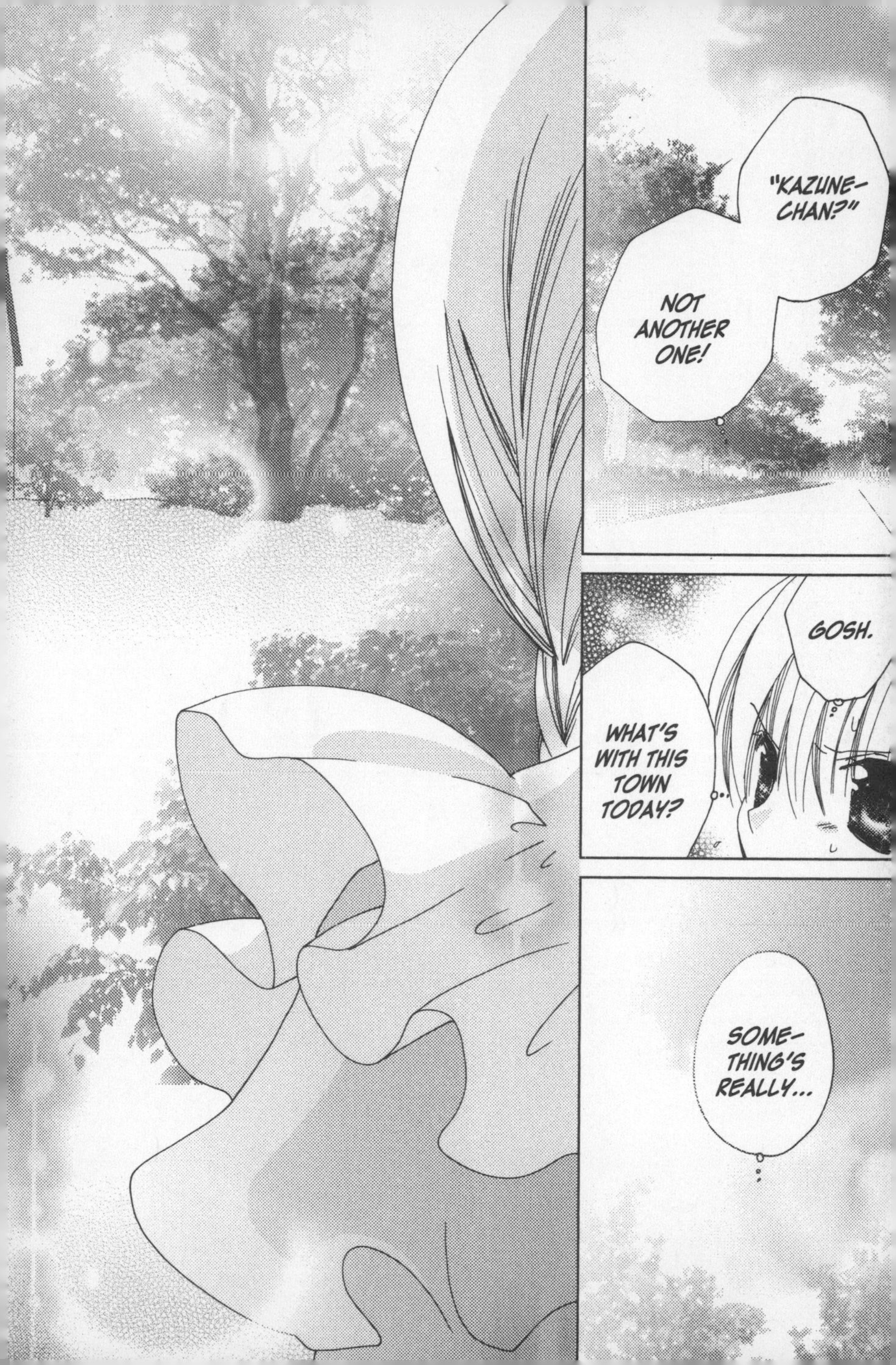
"KAZUNE-CHAN?"
NOT ANOTHER ONE!
GOSH.
WHAT'S WITH THIS TOWN TODAY?
SOME-THING'S REALLY...

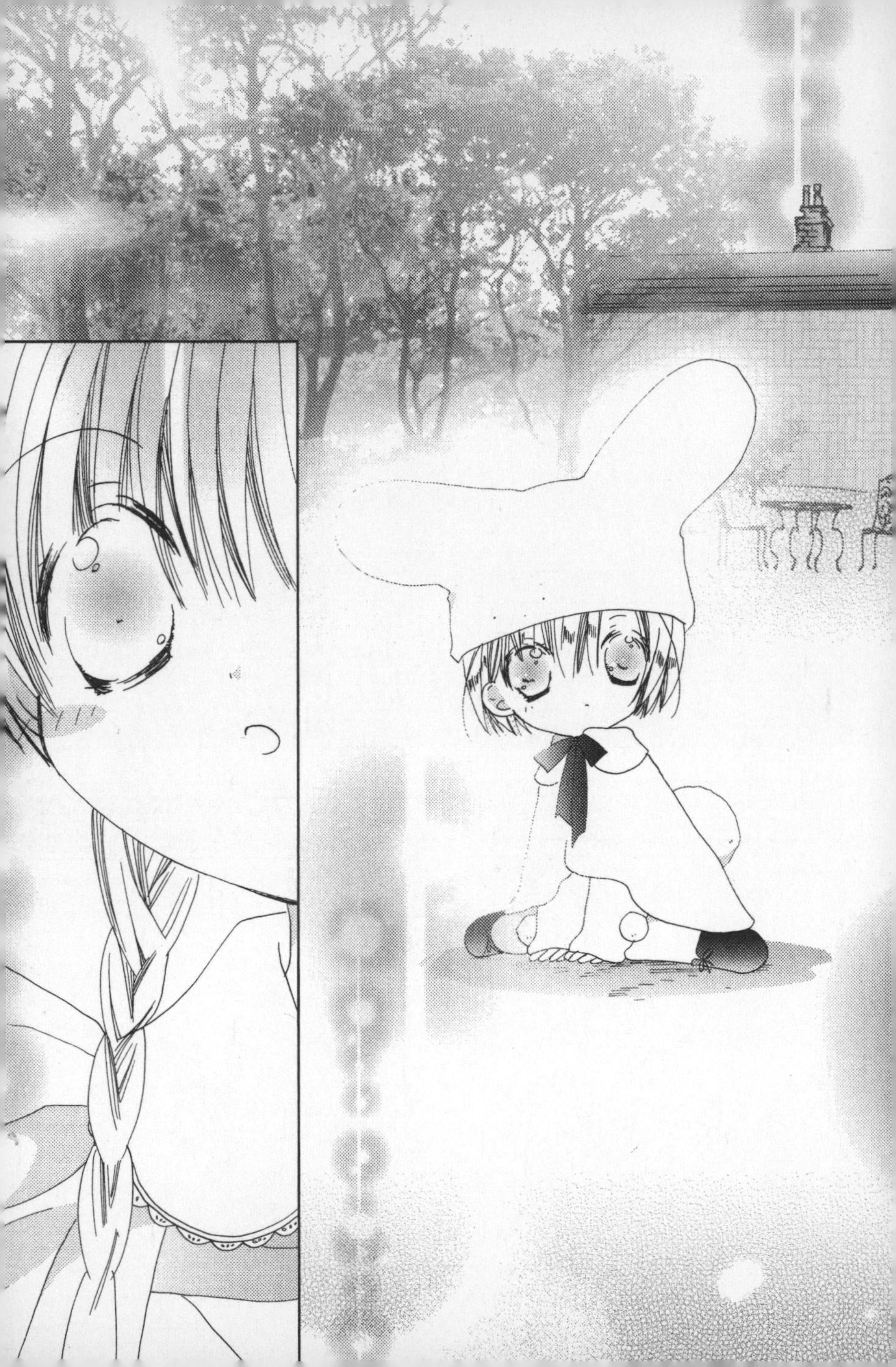

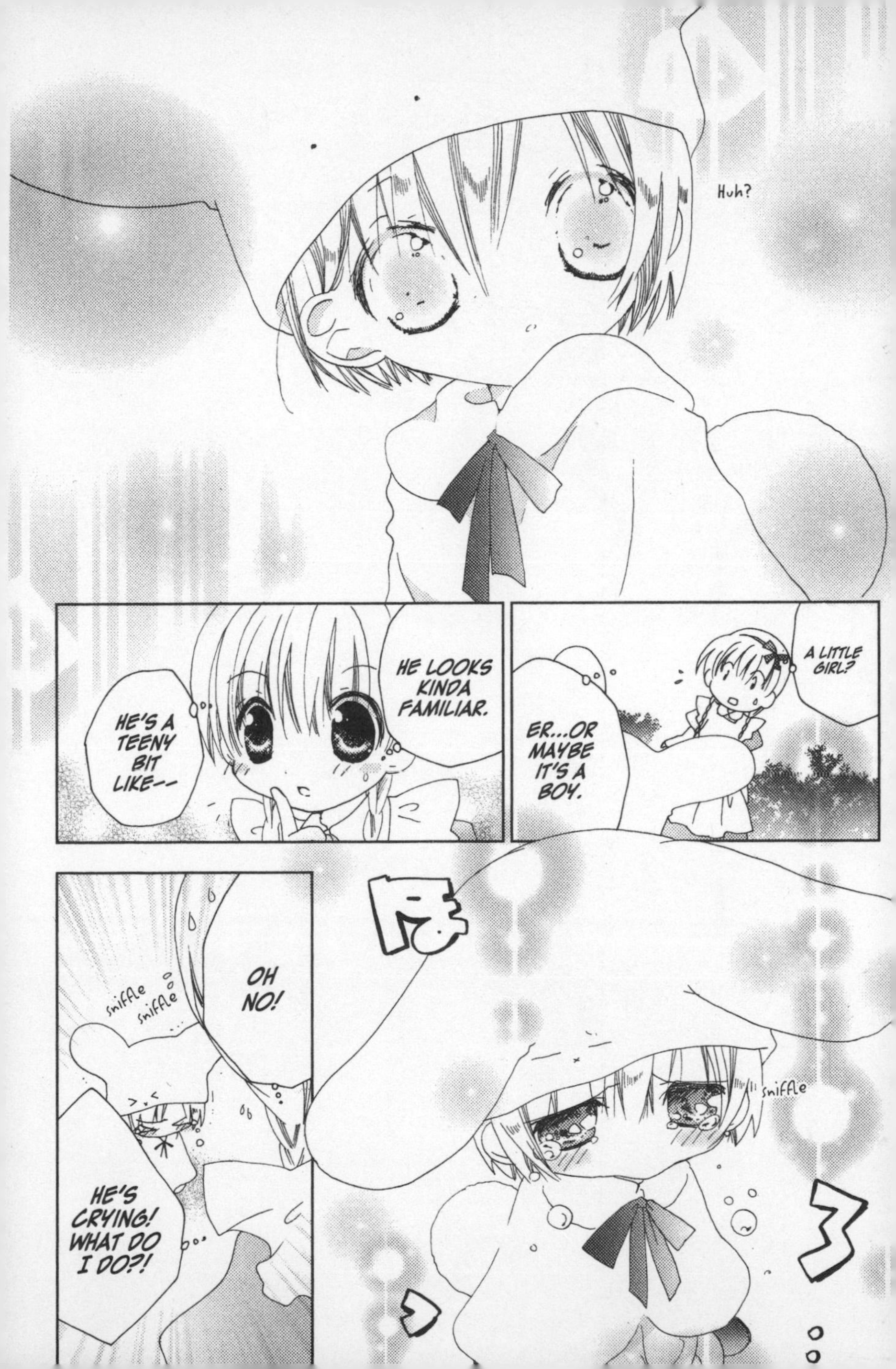

Huh?
A LITTLE GIRL?
ER...OR MAYBE IT'S A BOY.
HE LOOKS KINDA FAMILIAR.
HE'S A TEENY BIT LIKE--
sniffle
OH NO!
sniffle sniffle
HE'S CRYING! WHAT DO I DO?!

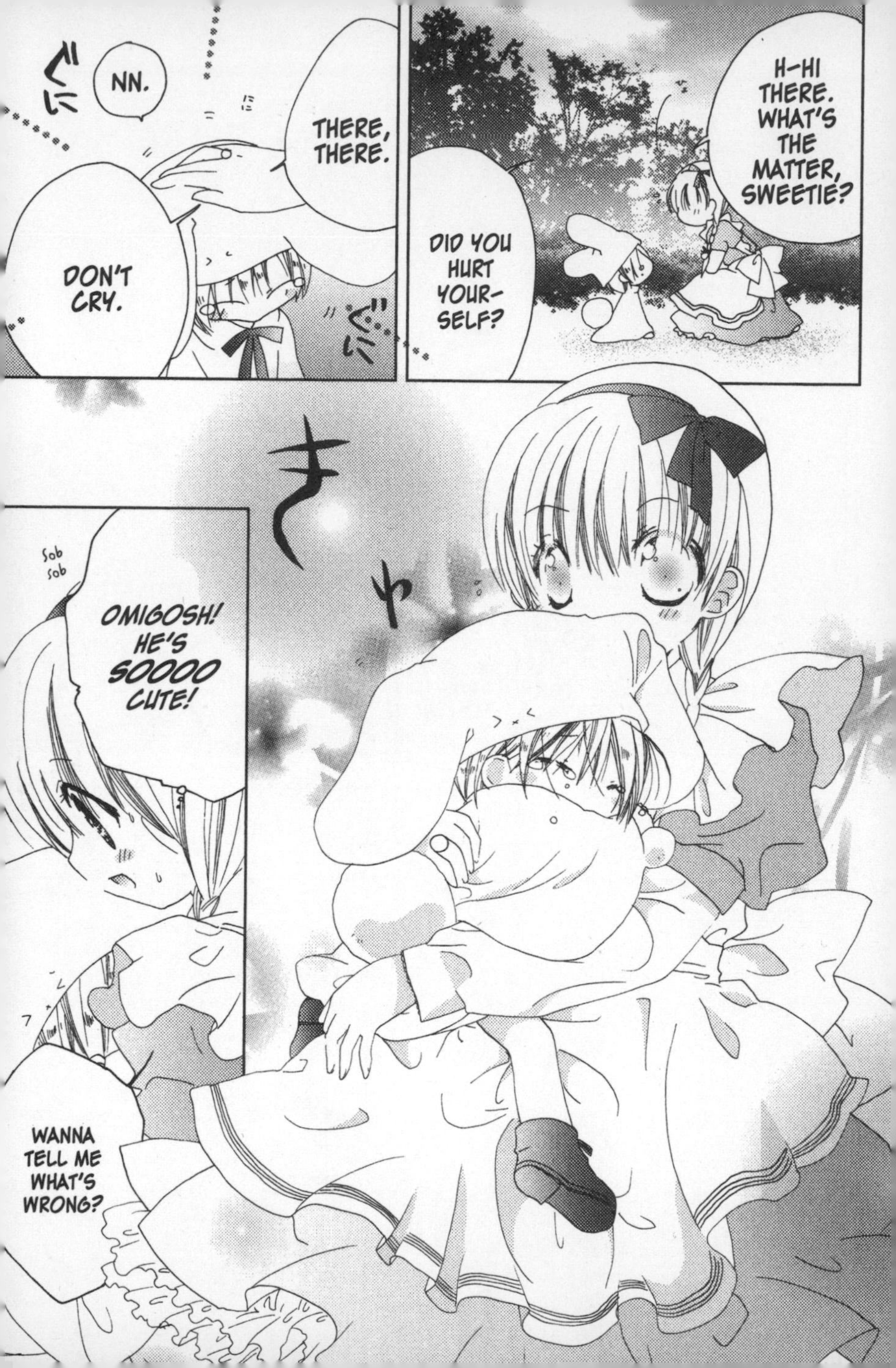

H-HI THERE. WHAT'S THE MATTER, SWEETIE?
DID YOU HURT YOUR-SELF?
THERE, THERE.
NN.
ぐに
DON'T CRY.
ぐに
Sob sob
OMIGOSH! HE'S SOOOO CUTE!
WANNA TELL ME WHAT'S WRONG?

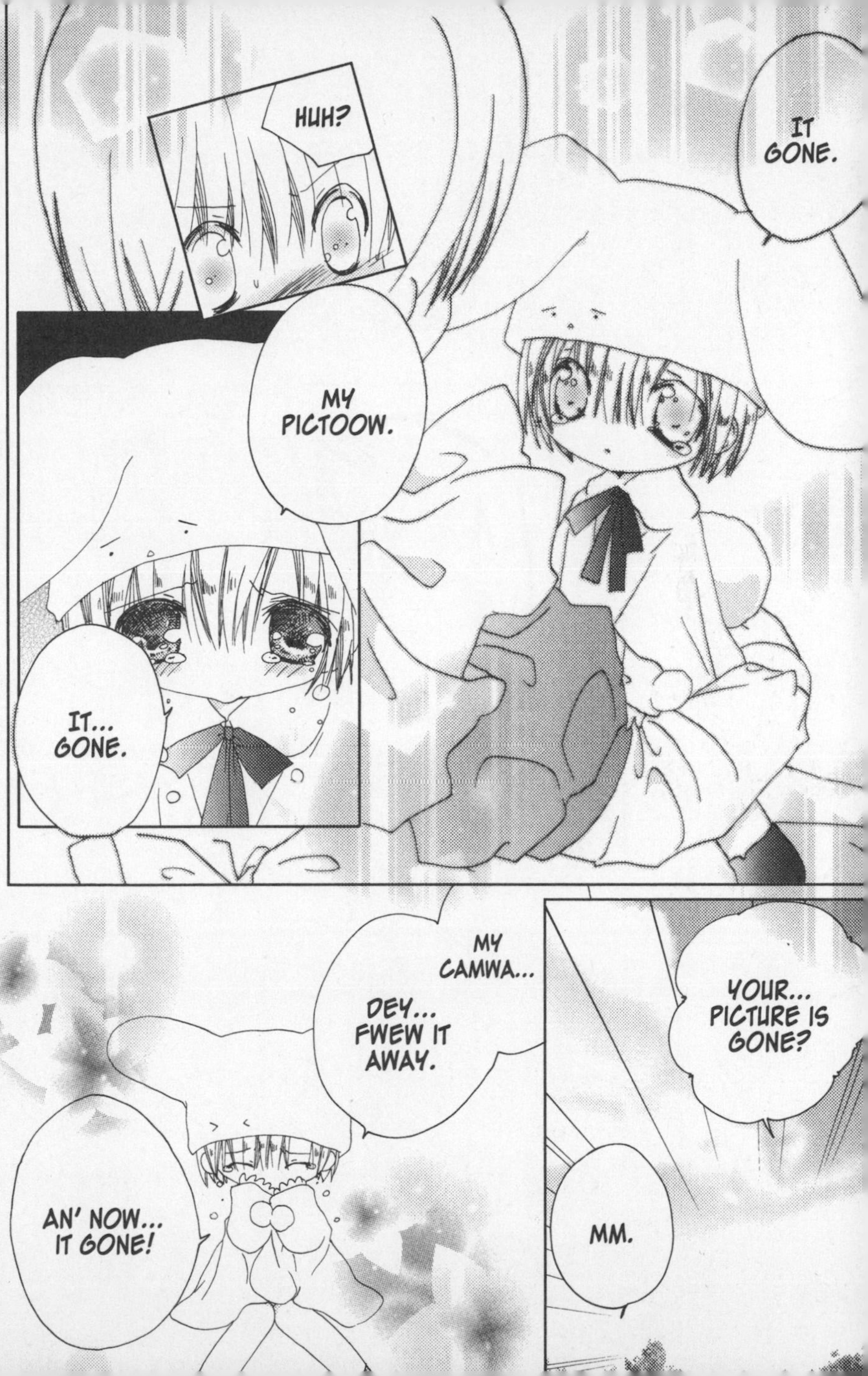
IT GONE.
HUH?
MY PICTOOW.
IT... GONE.
YOUR... PICTURE IS GONE?
MM.
MY CAMWA...
DEY... FWEW IT AWAY.
AN' NOW... IT GONE!

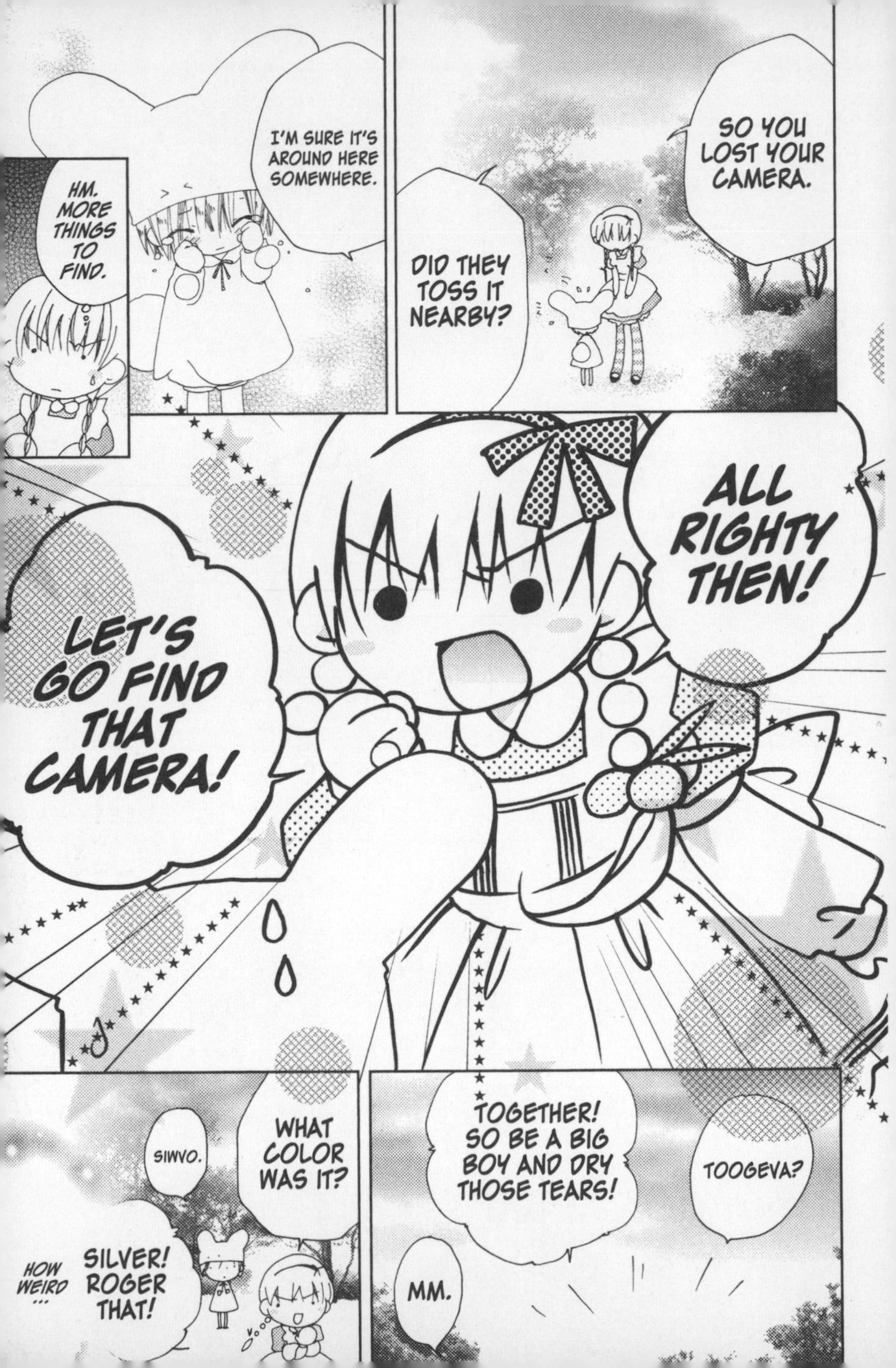
SO YOU LOST YOUR CAMERA.
DID THEY TOSS IT NEARBY?
I'M SURE IT'S AROUND HERE SOMEWHERE.
HM. MORE THINGS TO FIND.
ALL RIGHTY THEN!
LET'S GO FIND THAT CAMERA!
TOGETHER! SO BE A BIG BOY AND DRY THOSE TEARS!
TOOGEVA?
MM.
WHAT COLOR WAS IT?
SIWVO.
SILVER! ROGER THAT!
HOW WEIRD...

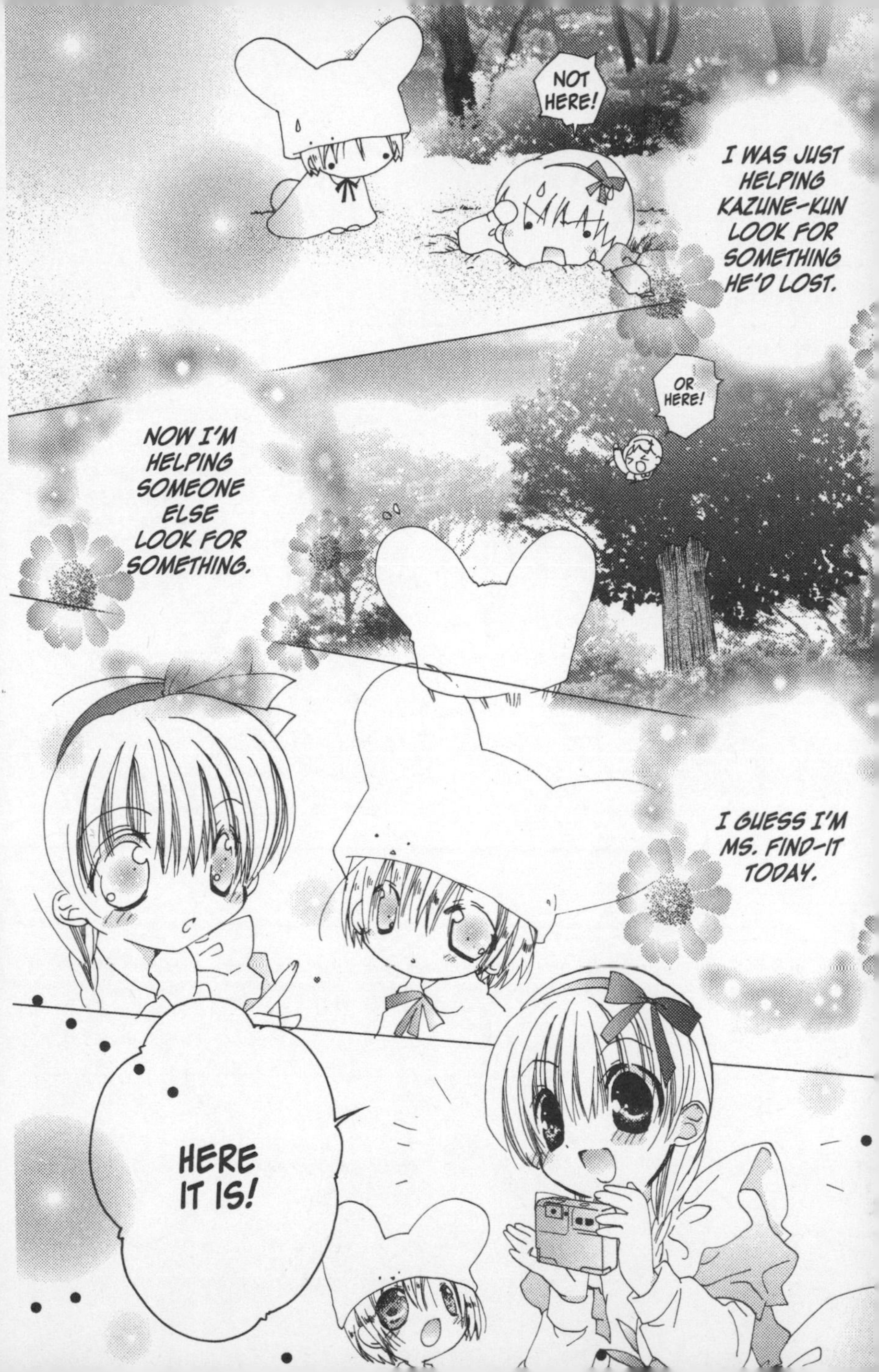
I WAS JUST HELPING KAZUNE-KUN LOOK FOR SOMETHING HE'D LOST.
NOT HERE!
OR HERE!
NOW I'M HELPING SOMEONE ELSE LOOK FOR SOMETHING.
I GUESS I'M MS. FIND-IT TODAY.
HERE IT IS!

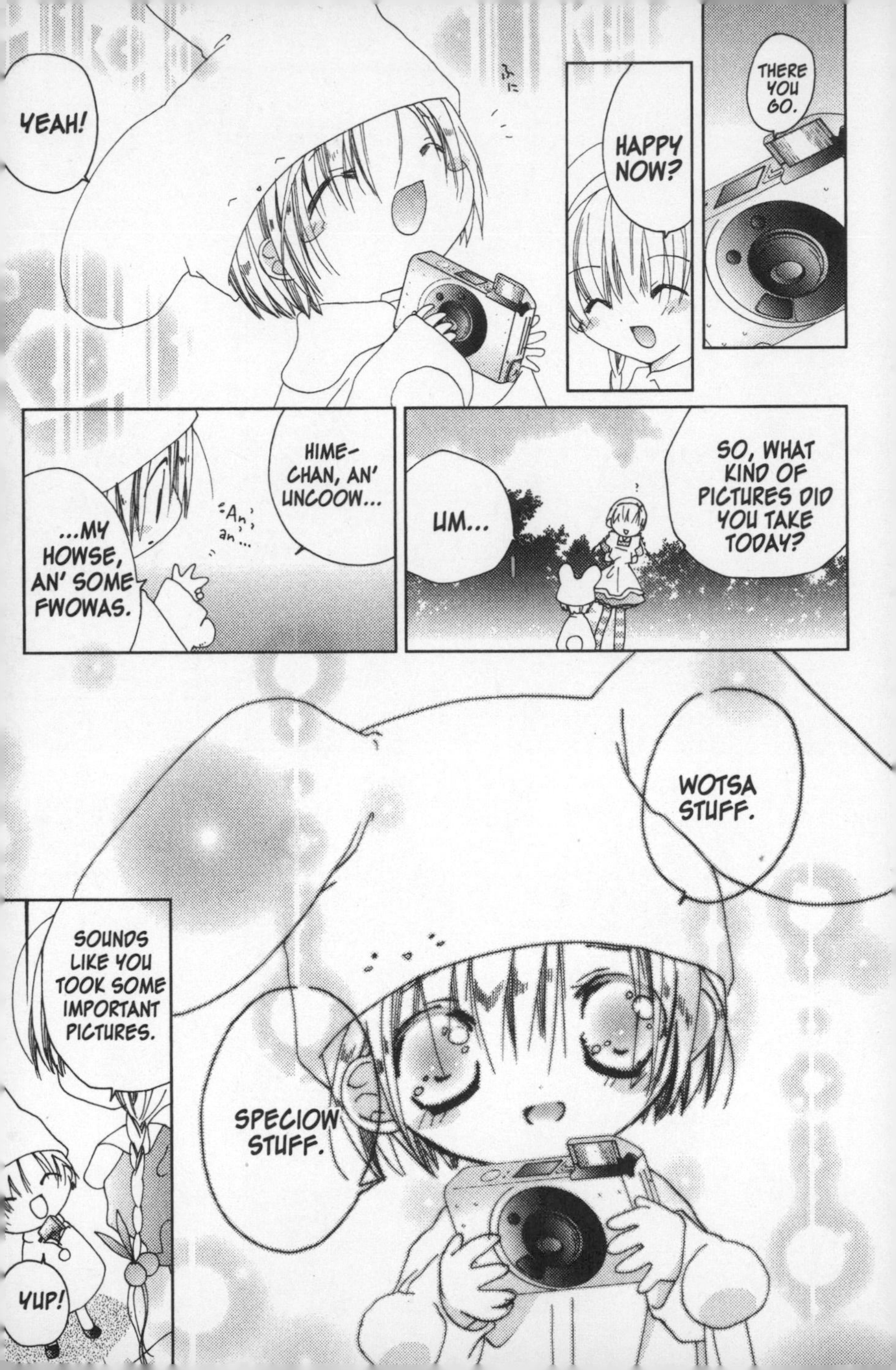
THERE YOU GO.
HAPPY NOW?
YEAH!
SO, WHAT KIND OF PICTURES DID YOU TAKE TODAY?
UM...
HIME-CHAN, AN' UNCOOW...
An' an'...
...MY HOWSE, AN' SOME FWOWAS.
WOTSA STUFF.
SPECIOW STUFF.
SOUNDS LIKE YOU TOOK SOME IMPORTANT PICTURES.
YUP!

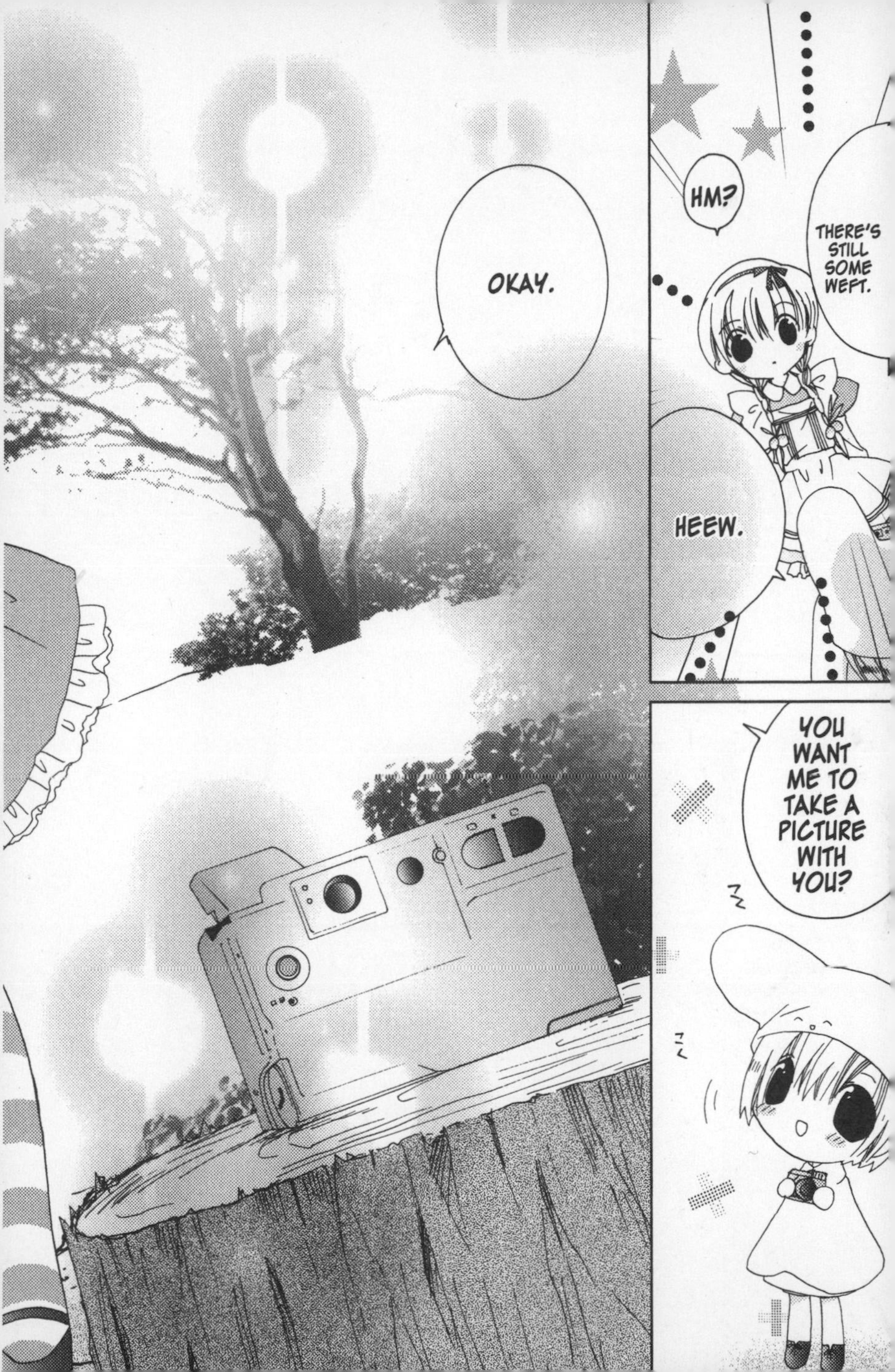
HM?
THERE'S STILL SOME WEFT.
HEEW.
YOU WANT ME TO TAKE A PICTURE WITH YOU?
OKAY.

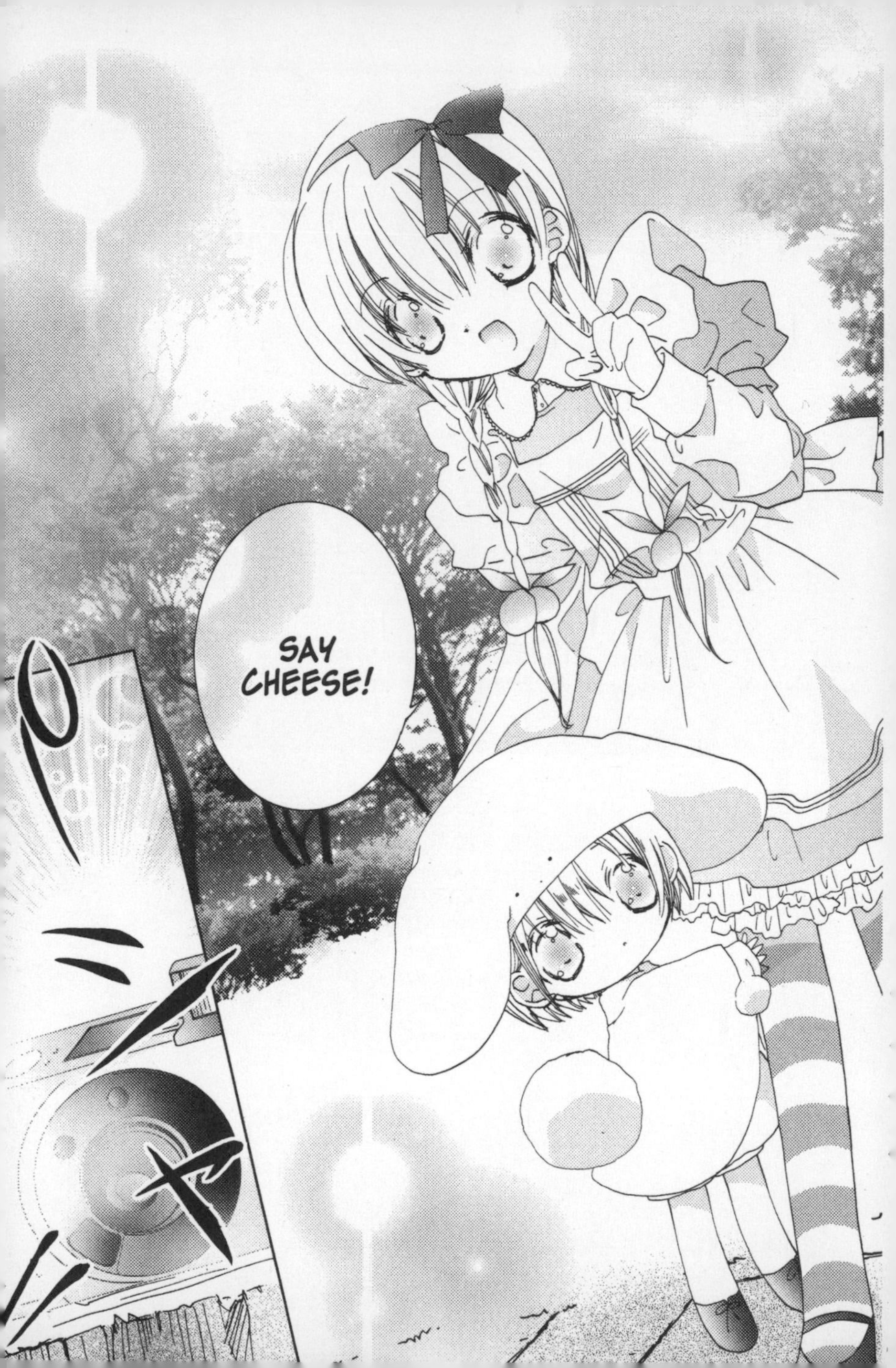
SAY CHEESE!

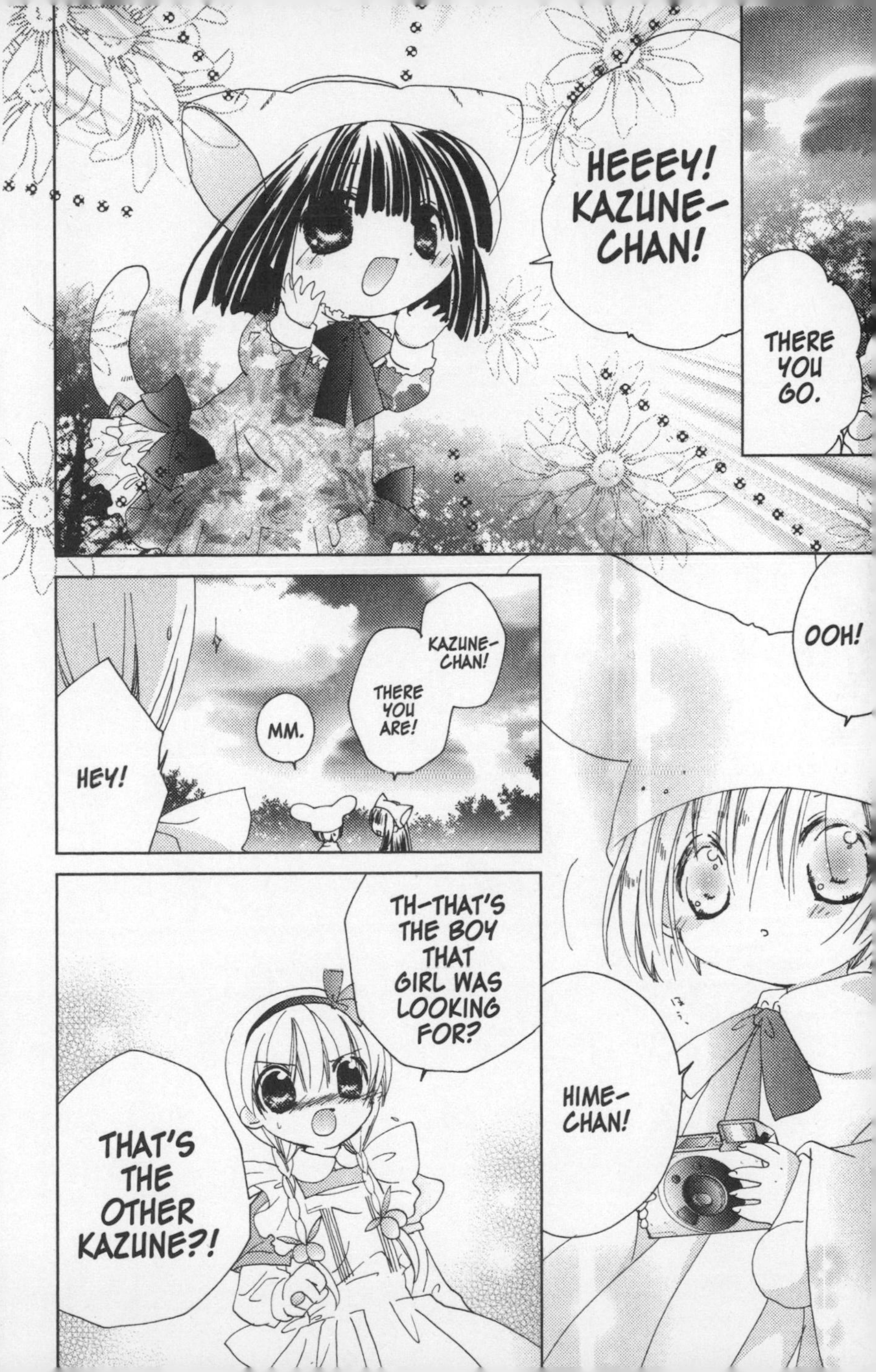
THERE YOU GO.
HEEEY! KAZUNE-CHAN!
OOH!
HIME-CHAN!
KAZUNE-CHAN!
THERE YOU ARE!
MM.
HEY!
TH-THAT'S THE BOY THAT GIRL WAS LOOKING FOR?
THAT'S THE OTHER KAZUNE?!

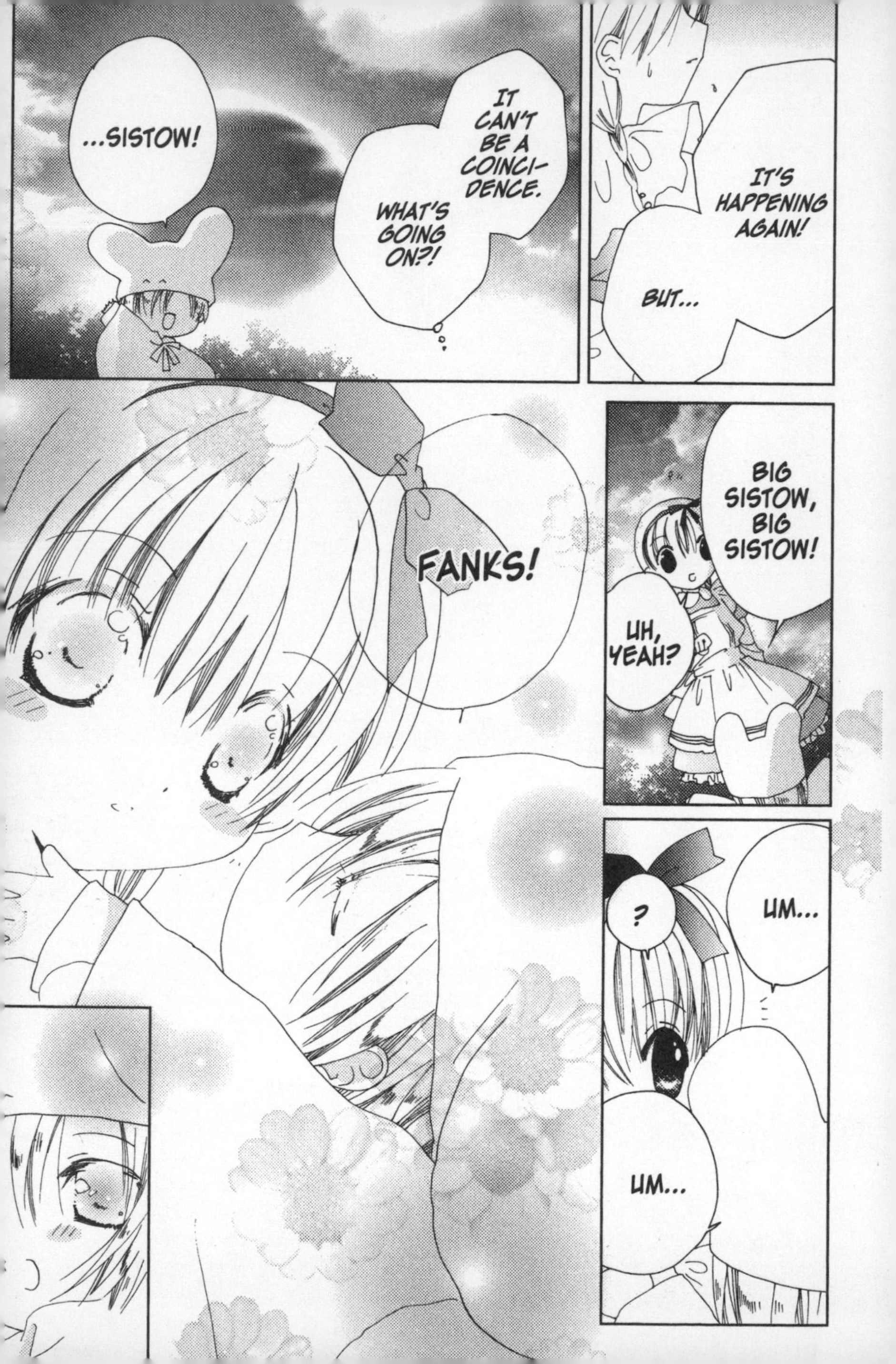
IT'S HAPPENING AGAIN!
BUT...
IT CAN'T BE A COINCI-DENCE.
WHAT'S GOING ON?!
...SISTOW!
BIG SISTOW, BIG SISTOW!
UH, YEAH?
UM...
?
UM...
FANKS!

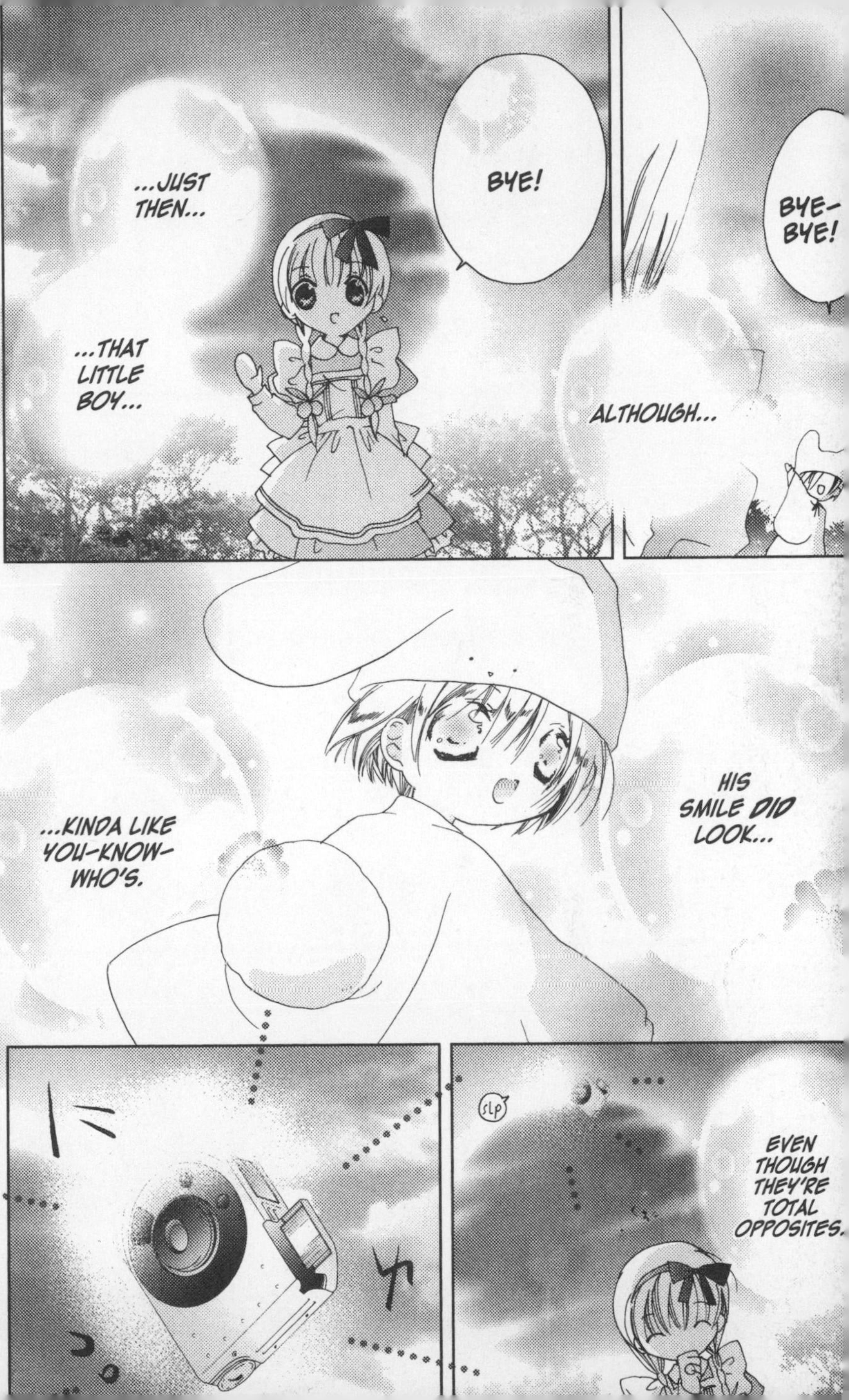
BYE-BYE!
ALTHOUGH...
BYE!
...JUST THEN...
...THAT LITTLE BOY...
HIS SMILE DID LOOK...
...KINDA LIKE YOU-KNOW-WHO'S.
slp
EVEN THOUGH THEY'RE TOTAL OPPOSITES.

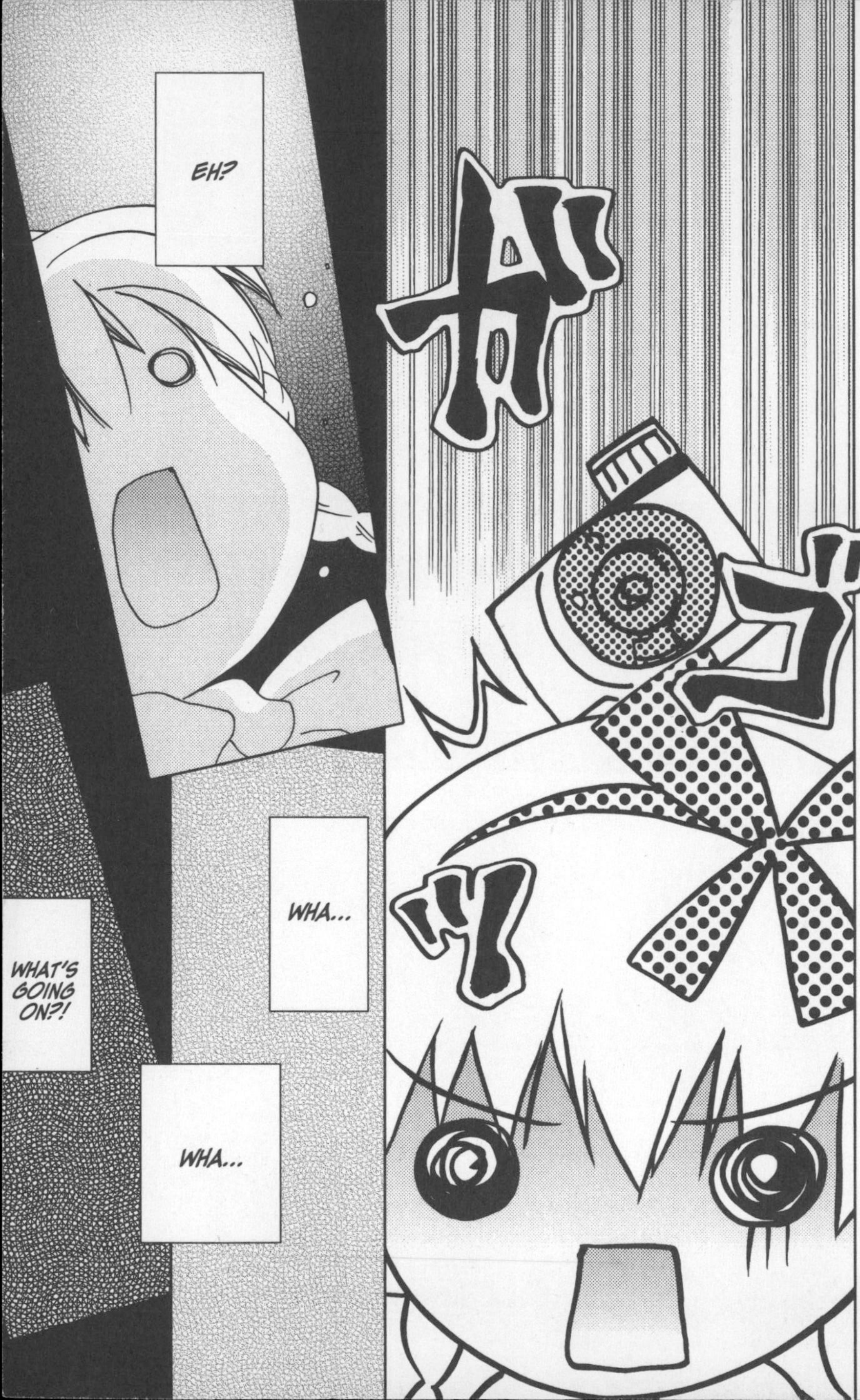
EH?
WHA...
WHAT'S GOING ON?!
WHA...

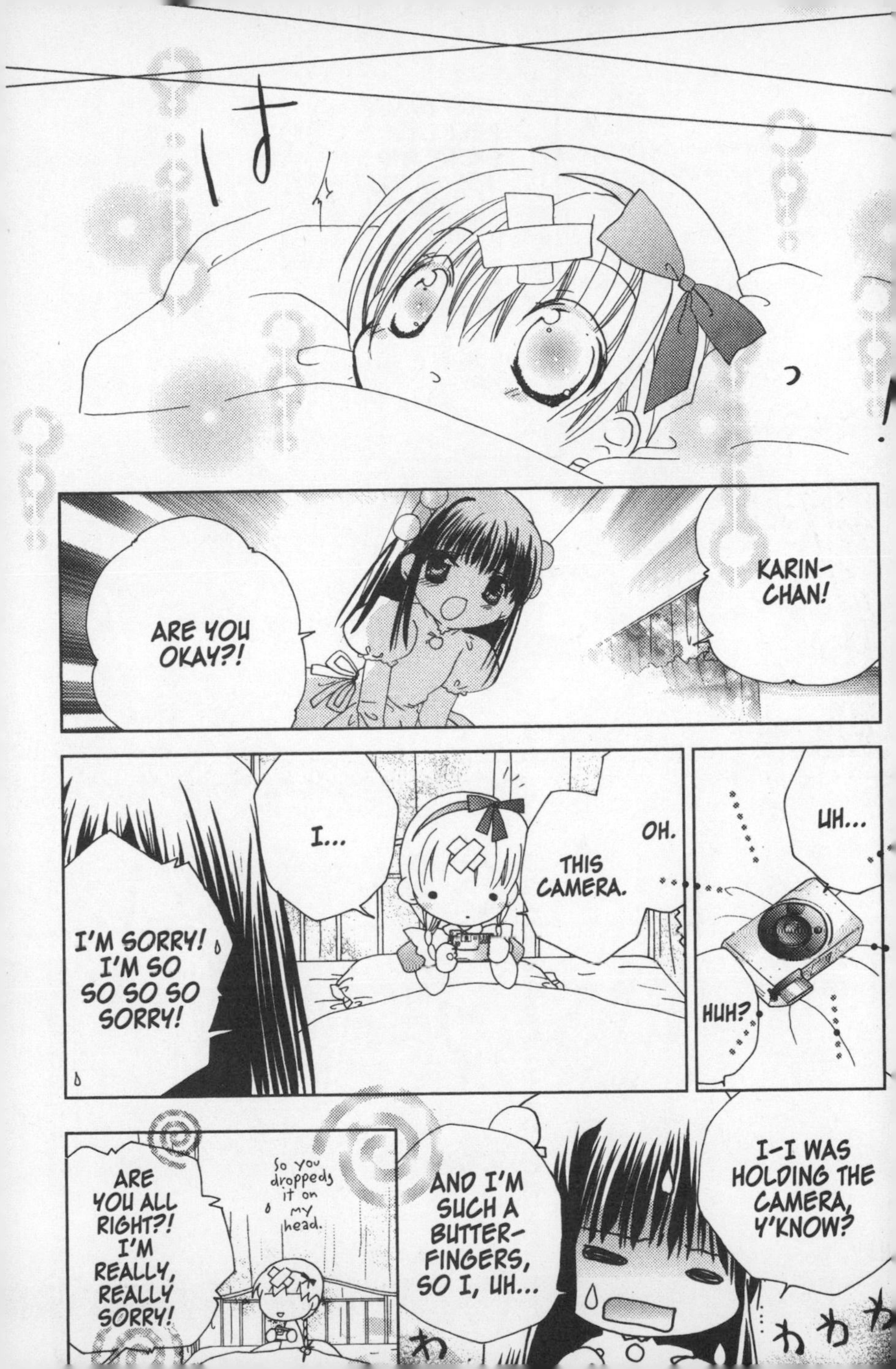
はっ
KARIN-CHAN!
ARE YOU OKAY?!
UH...
HUH?
OH.
THIS CAMERA.
I...
I'M SORRY! I'M SO SO SO SO SORRY!
I-I WAS HOLDING THE CAMERA, Y'KNOW?
AND I'M SUCH A BUTTER-FINGERS, SO I, UH...
わわわ
So you droppeds it on my head.
ARE YOU ALL RIGHT?! I'M REALLY, REALLY SORRY!

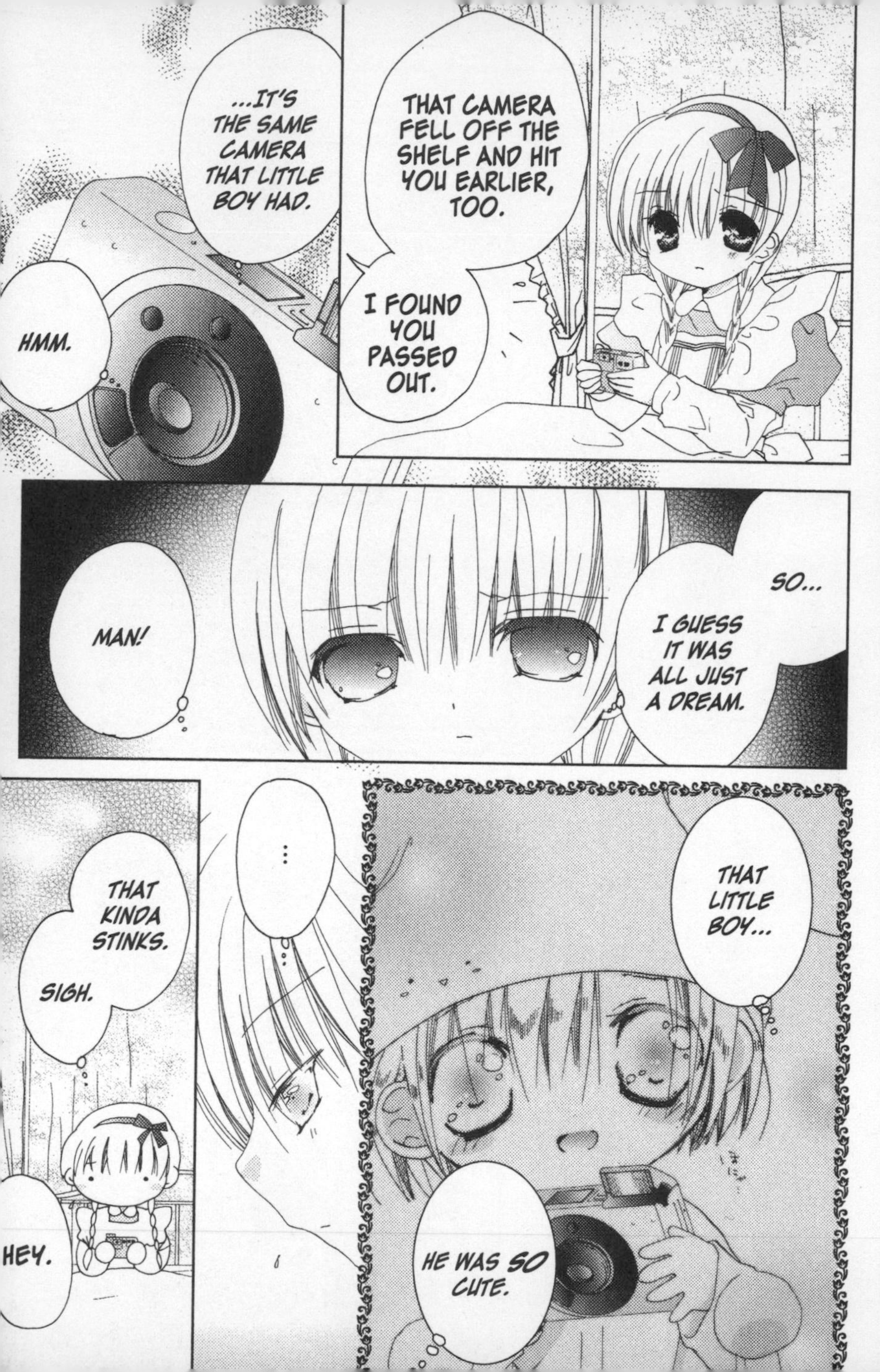
THAT CAMERA FELL OFF THE SHELF AND HIT YOU EARLIER, TOO.
I FOUND YOU PASSED OUT.
...IT'S THE SAME CAMERA THAT LITTLE BOY HAD.
HMM.
SO...
I GUESS IT WAS ALL JUST A DREAM.
MAN!
THAT LITTLE BOY...
HE WAS SO CUTE.
...
THAT KINDA STINKS.
SIGH.
HEY.

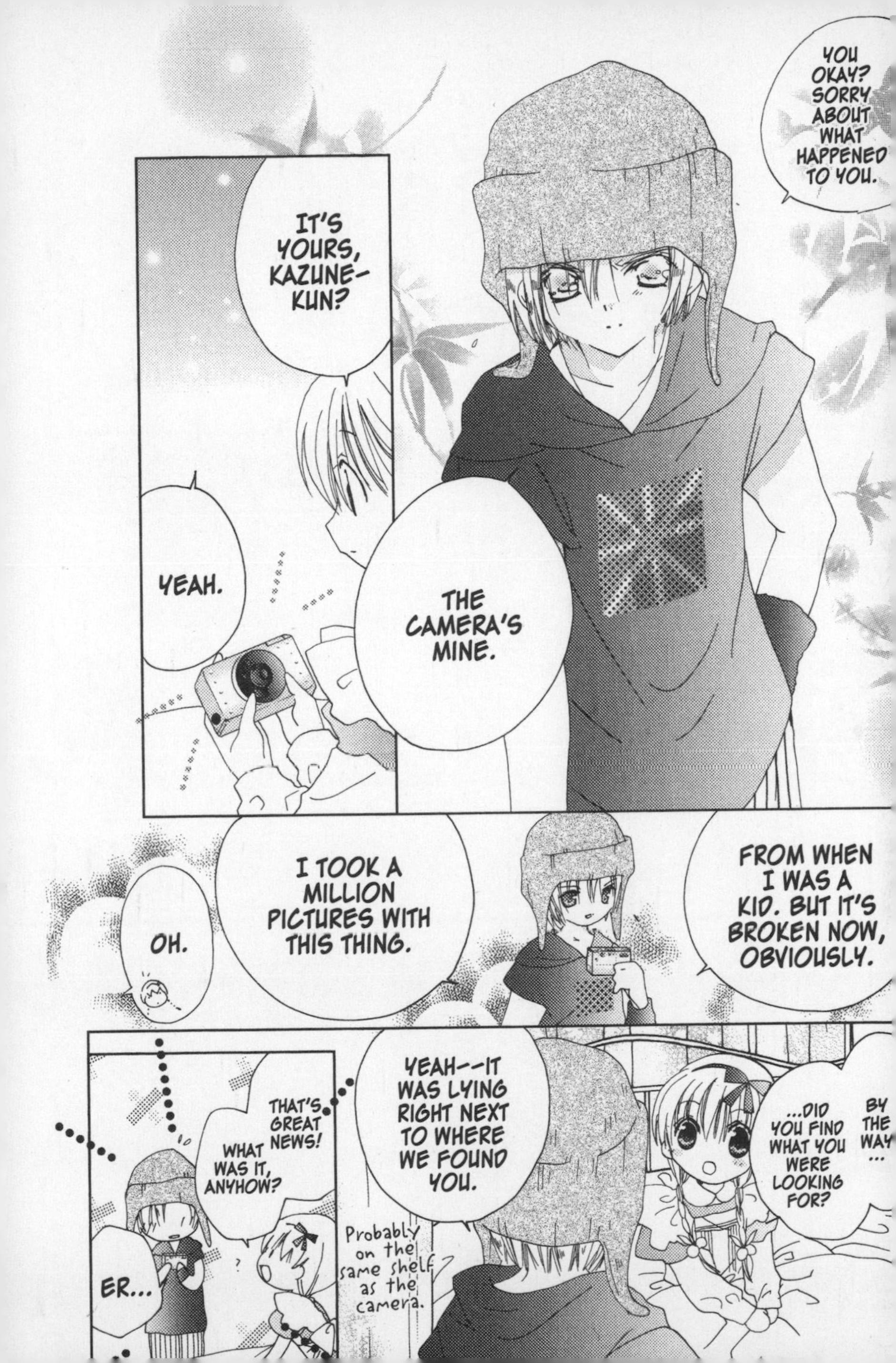
YOU OKAY? SORRY ABOUT WHAT HAPPENED TO YOU.
THE CAMERA'S MINE.
IT'S YOURS, KAZUNE-KUN?
YEAH.
FROM WHEN I WAS A KID. BUT IT'S BROKEN NOW, OBVIOUSLY.
I TOOK A MILLION PICTURES WITH THIS THING.
OH.
BY THE WAY...
...DID YOU FIND WHAT YOU WERE LOOKING FOR?
YEAH--IT WAS LYING RIGHT NEXT TO WHERE WE FOUND YOU.
Probably on the same shelf as the camera.
THAT'S GREAT NEWS!
WHAT WAS IT, ANYHOW?
ER...

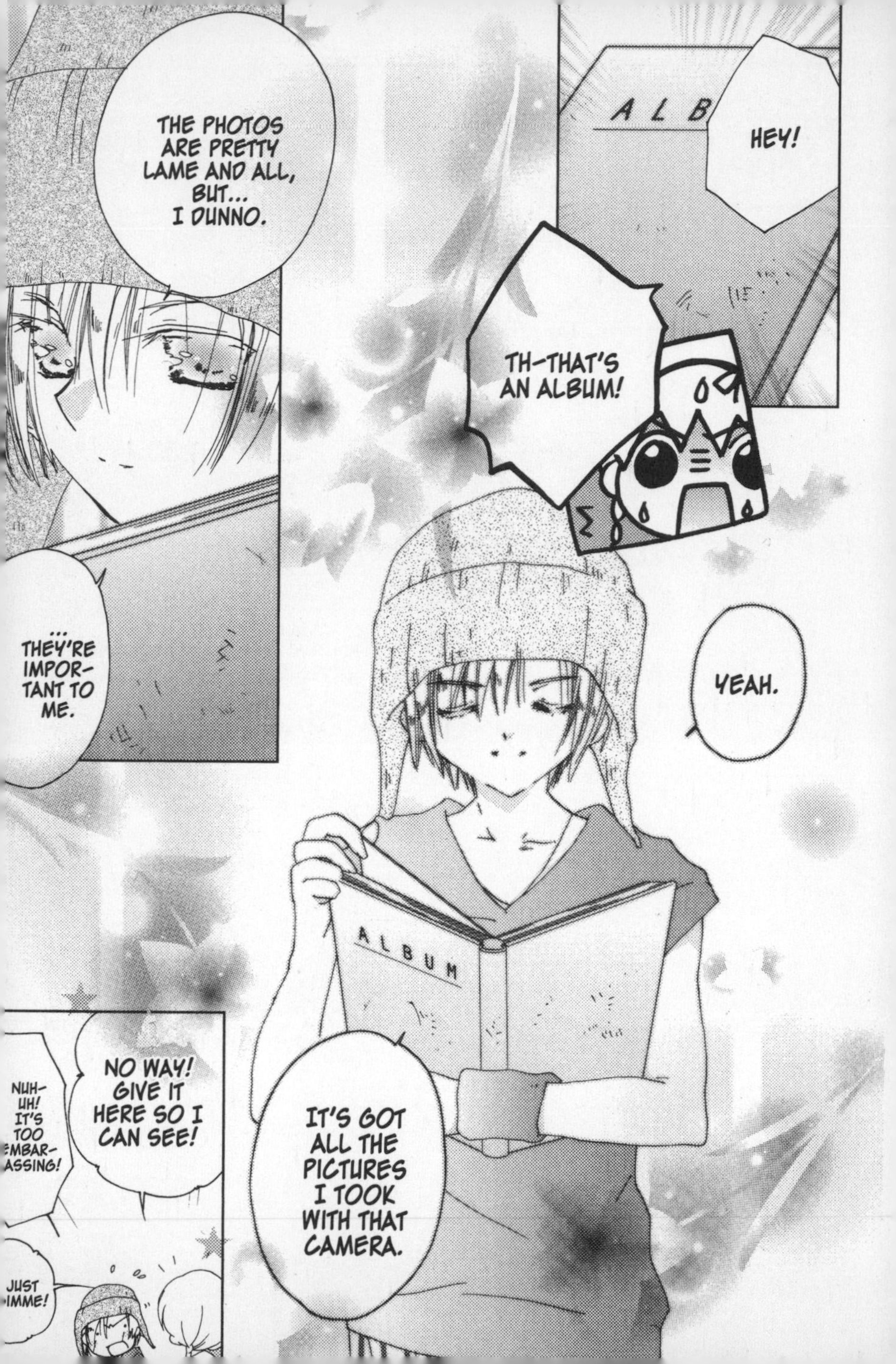

HEY!
ALB
THE PHOTOS ARE PRETTY LAME AND ALL, BUT... I DUNNO.
TH-THAT'S AN ALBUM!
... THEY'RE IMPORTANT TO ME.
YEAH.
ALBUM
IT'S GOT ALL THE PICTURES I TOOK WITH THAT CAMERA.
NO WAY! GIVE IT HERE SO I CAN SEE!
NUH-UH! IT'S TOO EMBAR-ASSING!
JUST IMME!

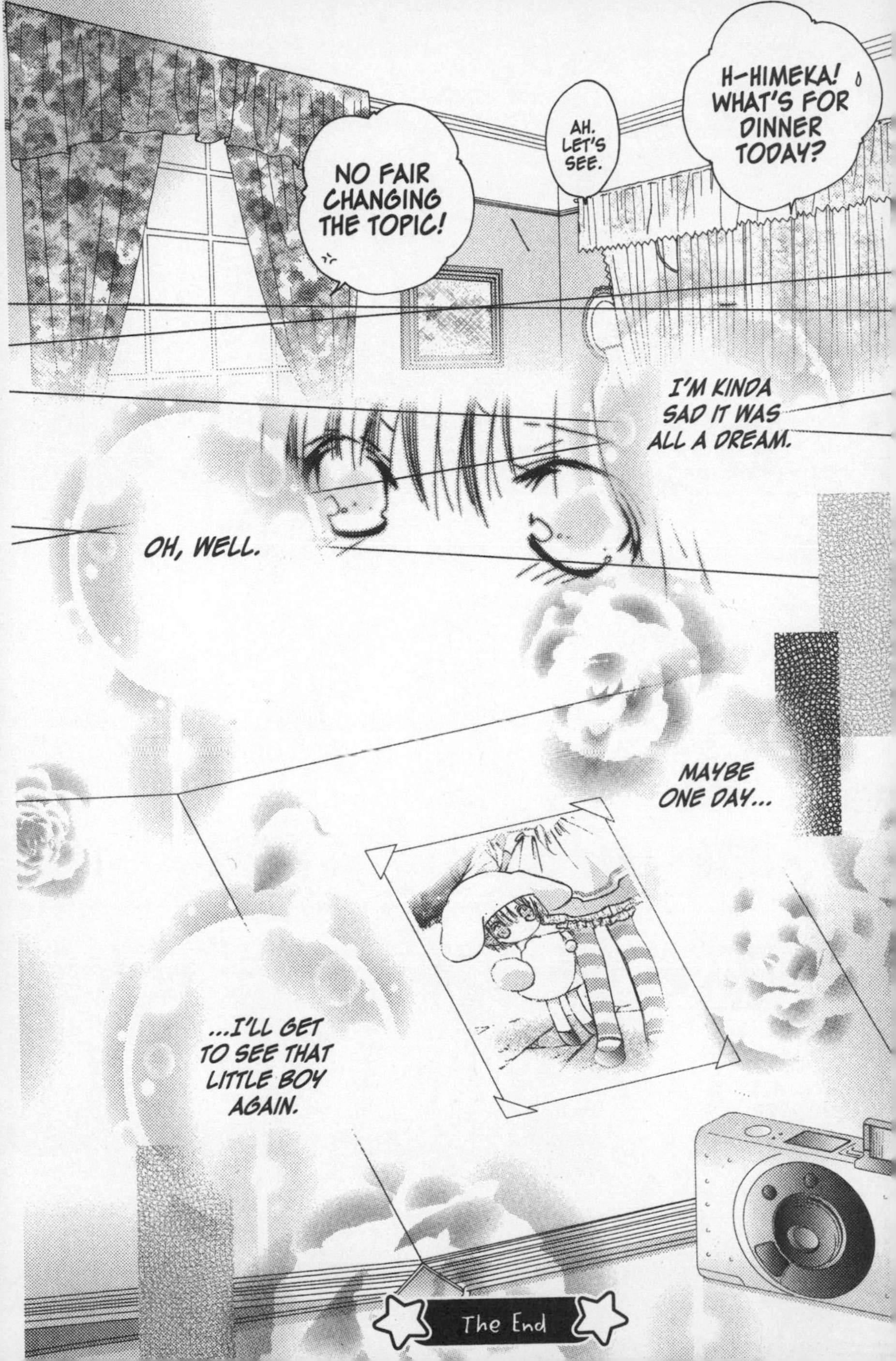
H-HIMEKA! WHAT'S FOR DINNER TODAY?
AH. LET'S SEE.
NO FAIR CHANGING THE TOPIC!
I'M KINDA SAD IT WAS ALL A DREAM.
OH, WELL.
MAYBE ONE DAY...
...I'LL GET TO SEE THAT LITTLE BOY AGAIN.
The End

● Hey there! Thanks so much for picking up and reading through *Kamichama Karin* Volume 3. I managed to save an entire page for the afterword this time.

● Time sure does fly! We're already into the third volume, but I'm pleased to announce that even this early in the game, I've already managed to completely bomb one of my goals from Volume 1. Specifically, my goal for backgrounds from Western settings.

● When I first began this series, I did extensive research on the West and gathered tons of books and resources...but as you can tell from the hot springs episode, that didn't go over too well. The manga's become pretty familiar, which in a sense isn't bad, but it still kinda reeks of being very shoddy and homemade. But whatever--what can you do? I've decided to scrap those high hopes once and for all. I even kinda forgot I had them to begin with. Ah, c'est la vie.

● Onward to Volume 4! Please also take a look at that when it arrives. Of course, if you were really that curious to see what happens next, you could always pick up the monthly magazine *Nakayoshi*. It's weird, but with the pace I've kept in putting out these comic compilations, I've actually managed to catch up with the monthly run of the story. Ha ha! Maybe you could try the two formats together for a fuller effect.

● In the next pages you'll find the story of Prince Kazune. And below, you'll find a picture of His Royal Highness as well.

February 3rd, 2004. Koge-Donbo
Thanks...Kaie Midorino.

AFTERWORD

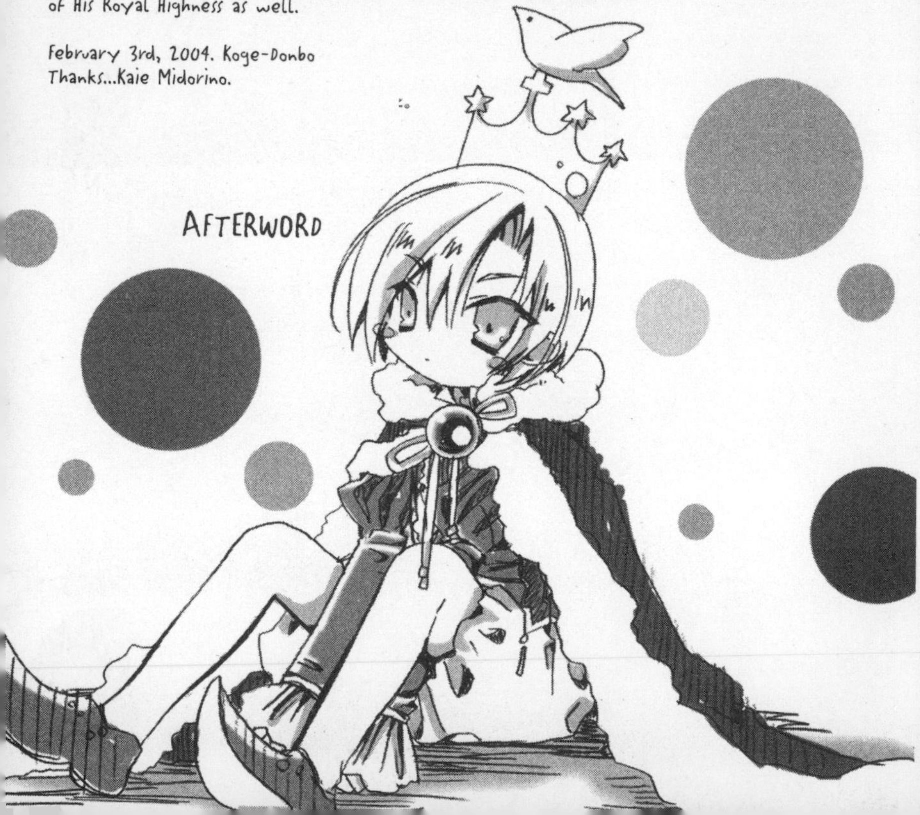

Go Go Prince Kazune!

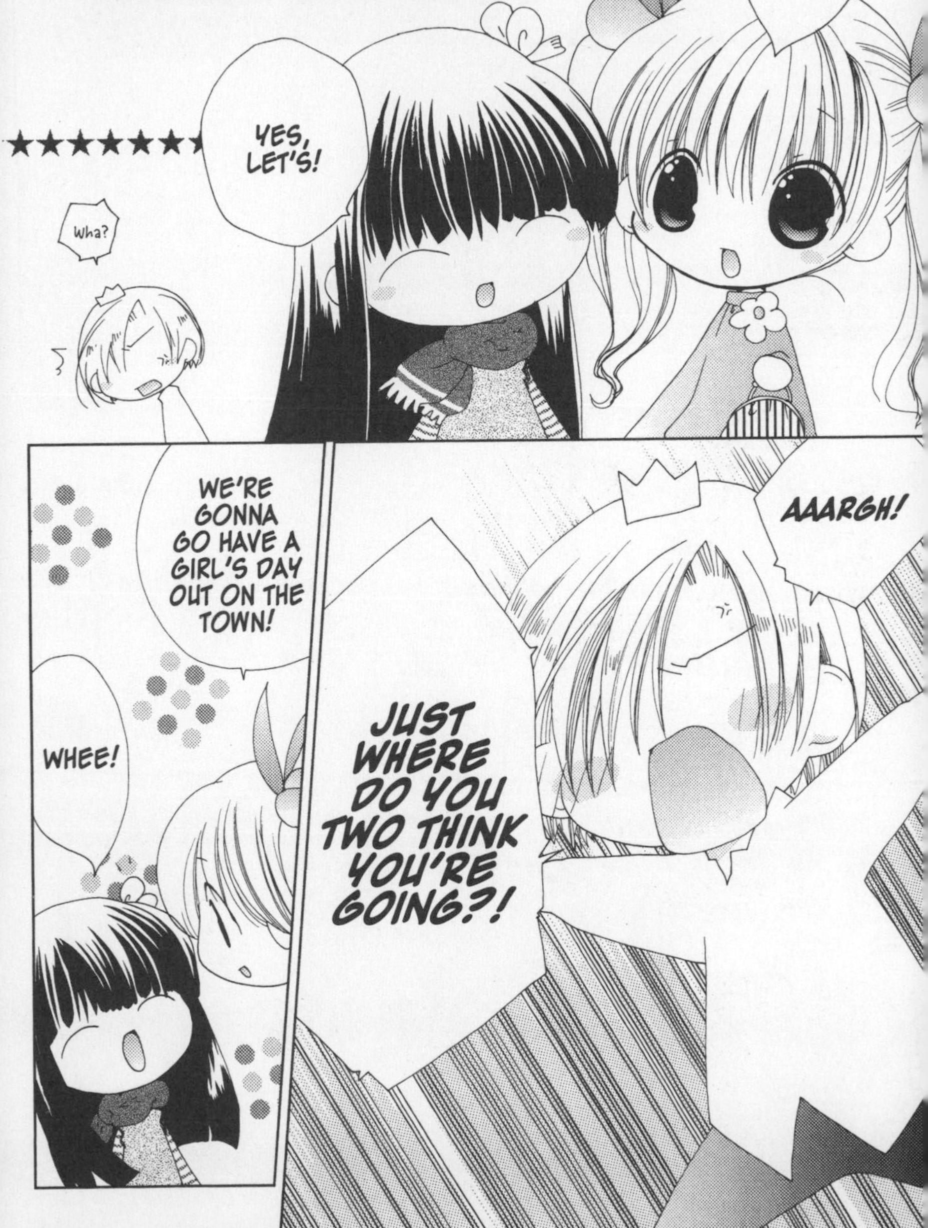
LET'S GO.
YES, LET'S!
Wha?
AAARGH!
JUST WHERE DO YOU TWO THINK YOU'RE GOING?!
WE'RE GONNA GO HAVE A GIRL'S DAY OUT ON THE TOWN!
WHEE!

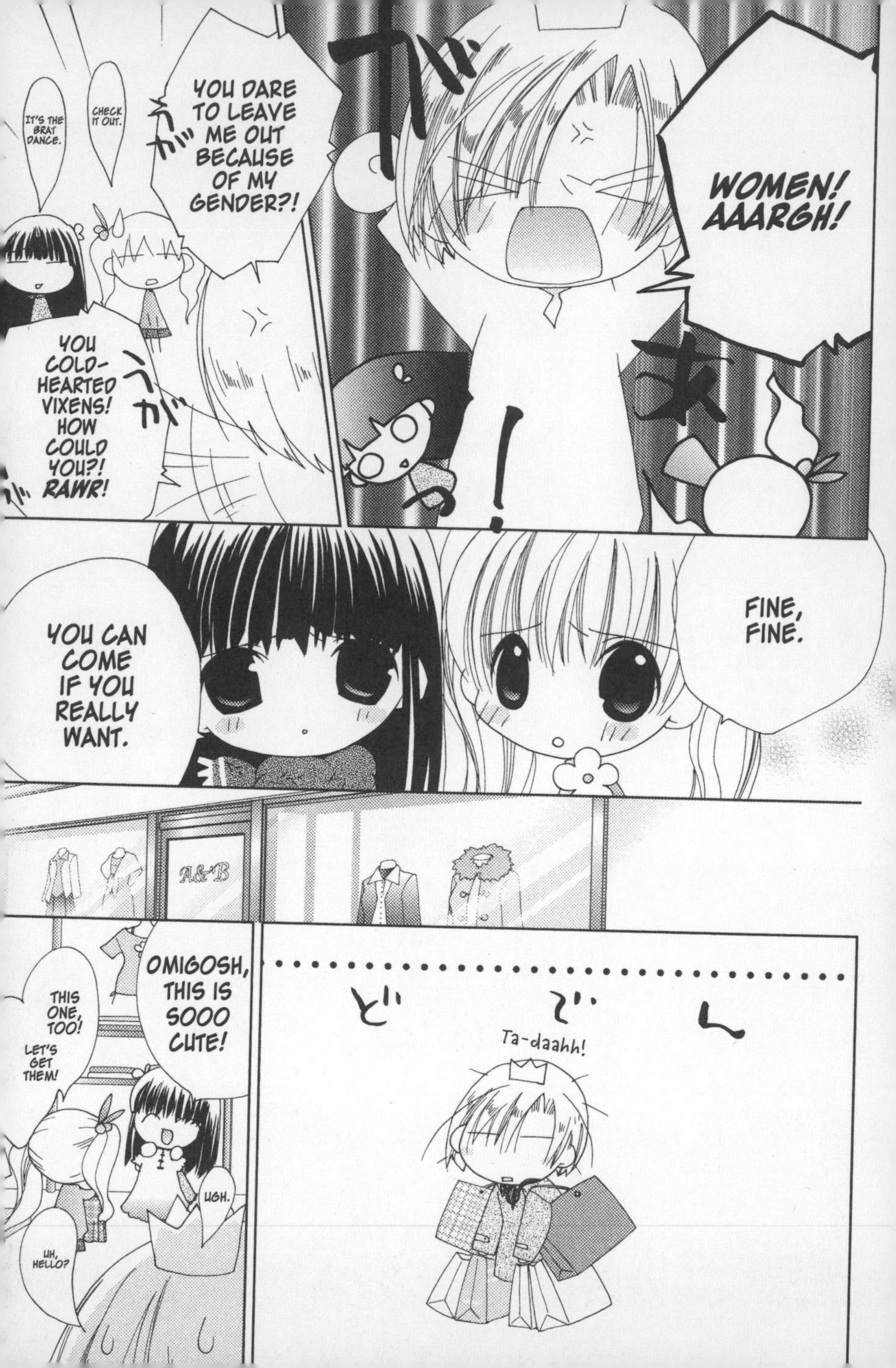
WOMEN! AAARGH!
YOU DARE TO LEAVE ME OUT BECAUSE OF MY GENDER?!
CHECK IT OUT.
IT'S THE BRAT DANCE.
YOU COLD-HEARTED VIXENS! HOW COULD YOU?! RAWR!
FINE, FINE.
YOU CAN COME IF YOU REALLY WANT.
A&B
....
どでん
Ta-daahh!
OMIGOSH, THIS IS SOOO CUTE!
THIS ONE, TOO!
LET'S GET THEM!
UGH.
UH, HELLO?

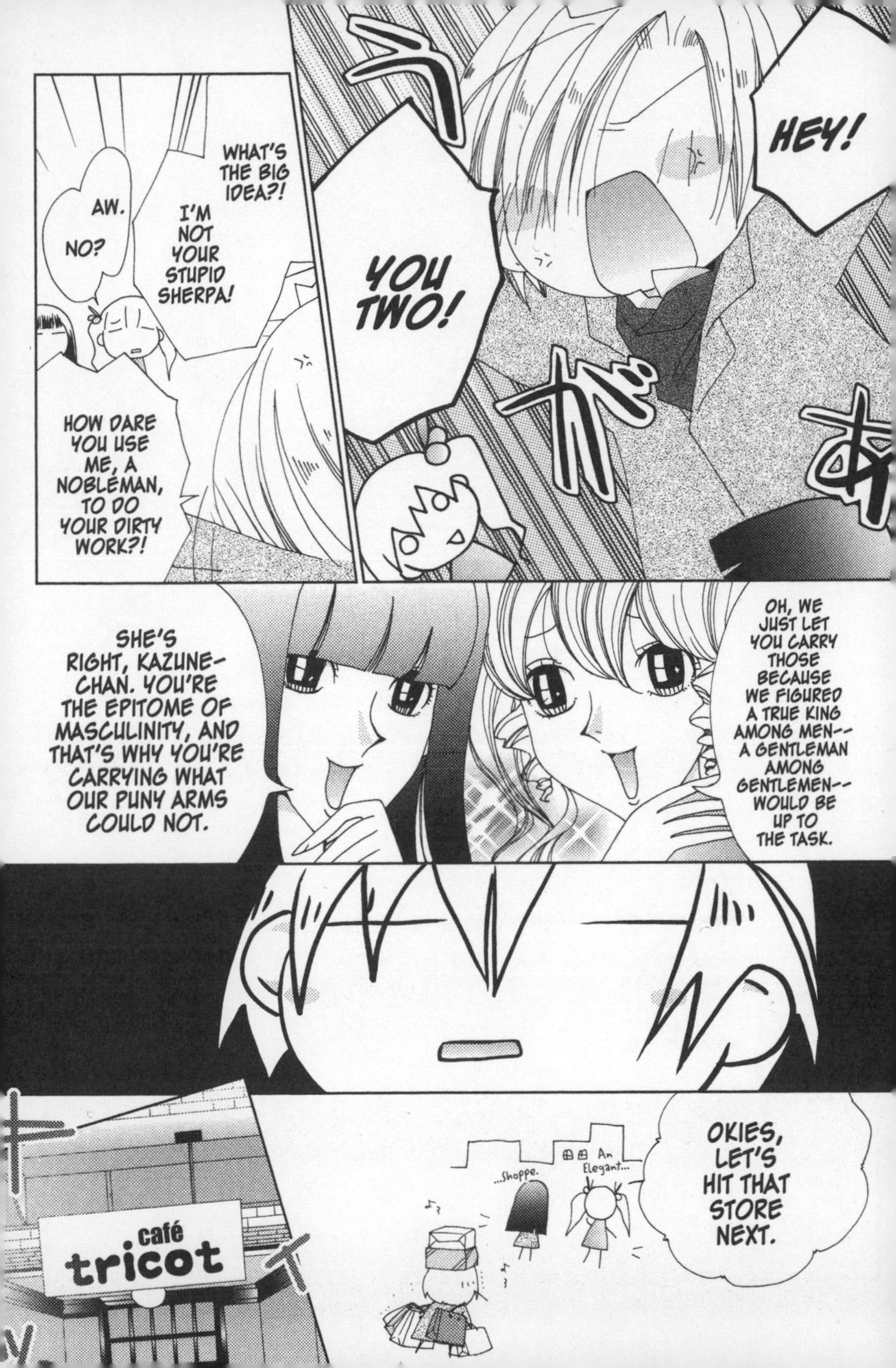
HEY!
YOU TWO!
WHAT'S THE BIG IDEA?!
I'M NOT YOUR STUPID SHERPA!
AW.
NO?
HOW DARE YOU USE ME, A NOBLEMAN, TO DO YOUR DIRTY WORK?!
OH, WE JUST LET YOU CARRY THOSE BECAUSE WE FIGURED A TRUE KING AMONG MEN-- A GENTLEMAN AMONG GENTLEMEN-- WOULD BE UP TO THE TASK.
SHE'S RIGHT, KAZUNE-CHAN. YOU'RE THE EPITOME OF MASCULINITY, AND THAT'S WHY YOU'RE CARRYING WHAT OUR PUNY ARMS COULD NOT.
OKIES, LET'S HIT THAT STORE NEXT.
An Elegant...
...Shoppe.
café tricot

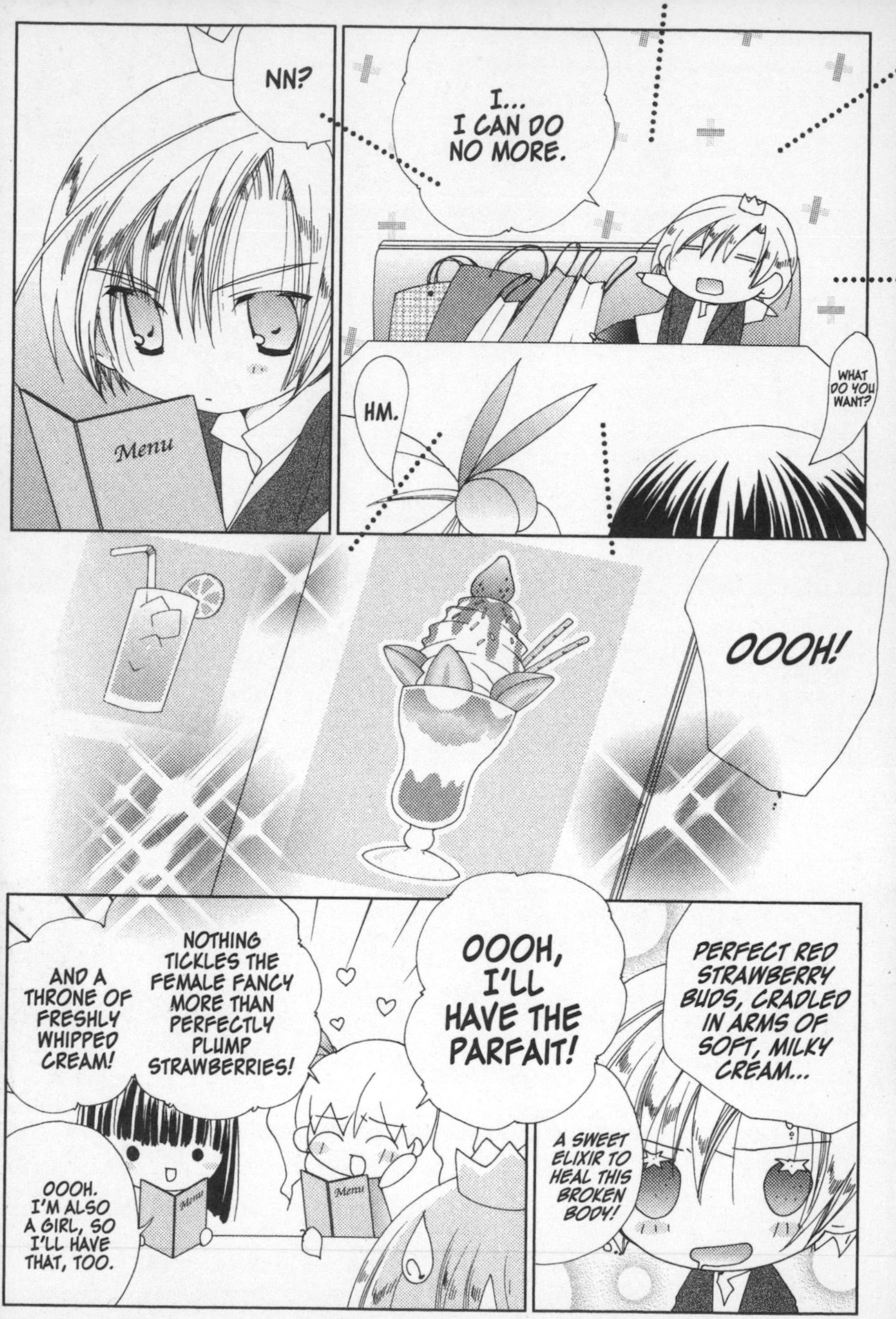
I... I CAN DO NO MORE.
WHAT DO YOU WANT?
HM.
NN?
Menu
OOOH!
PERFECT RED STRAWBERRY BUDS, CRADLED IN ARMS OF SOFT, MILKY CREAM...
A SWEET ELIXIR TO HEAL THIS BROKEN BODY!
OOOH, I'LL HAVE THE PARFAIT!
NOTHING TICKLES THE FEMALE FANCY MORE THAN PERFECTLY PLUMP STRAWBERRIES!
AND A THRONE OF FRESHLY WHIPPED CREAM!
OOOH. I'M ALSO A GIRL, SO I'LL HAVE THAT, TOO.

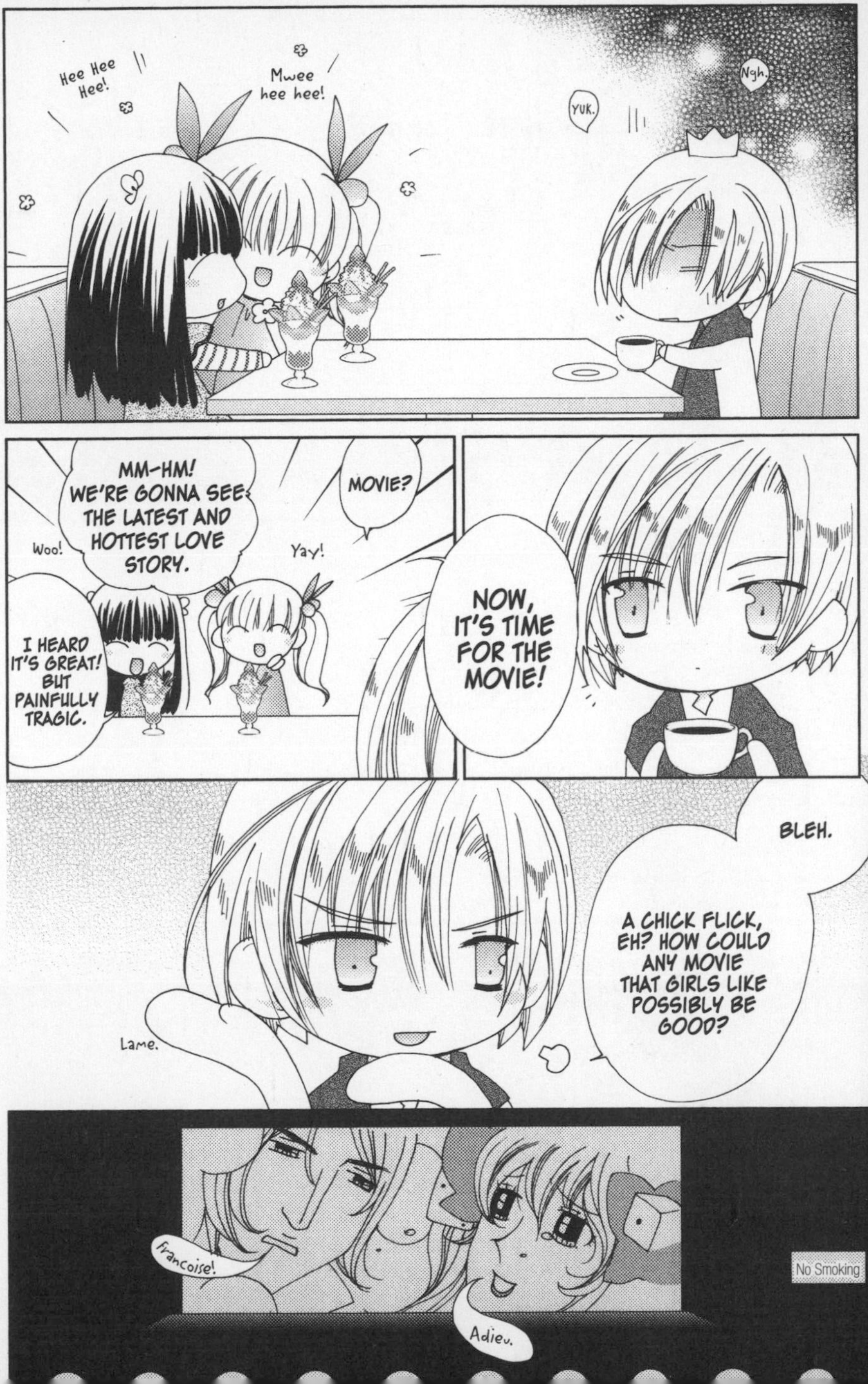
Ngh.
YUK.
Mwee hee hee!
Hee Hee Hee!
NOW, IT'S TIME FOR THE MOVIE!
MOVIE?
MM-HM! WE'RE GONNA SEE THE LATEST AND HOTTEST LOVE STORY.
Yay!
Woo!
I HEARD IT'S GREAT! BUT PAINFULLY TRAGIC.
BLEH.
A CHICK FLICK, EH? HOW COULD ANY MOVIE THAT GIRLS LIKE POSSIBLY BE GOOD?
Lame.
No Smoking
Francoise!
Adieu.

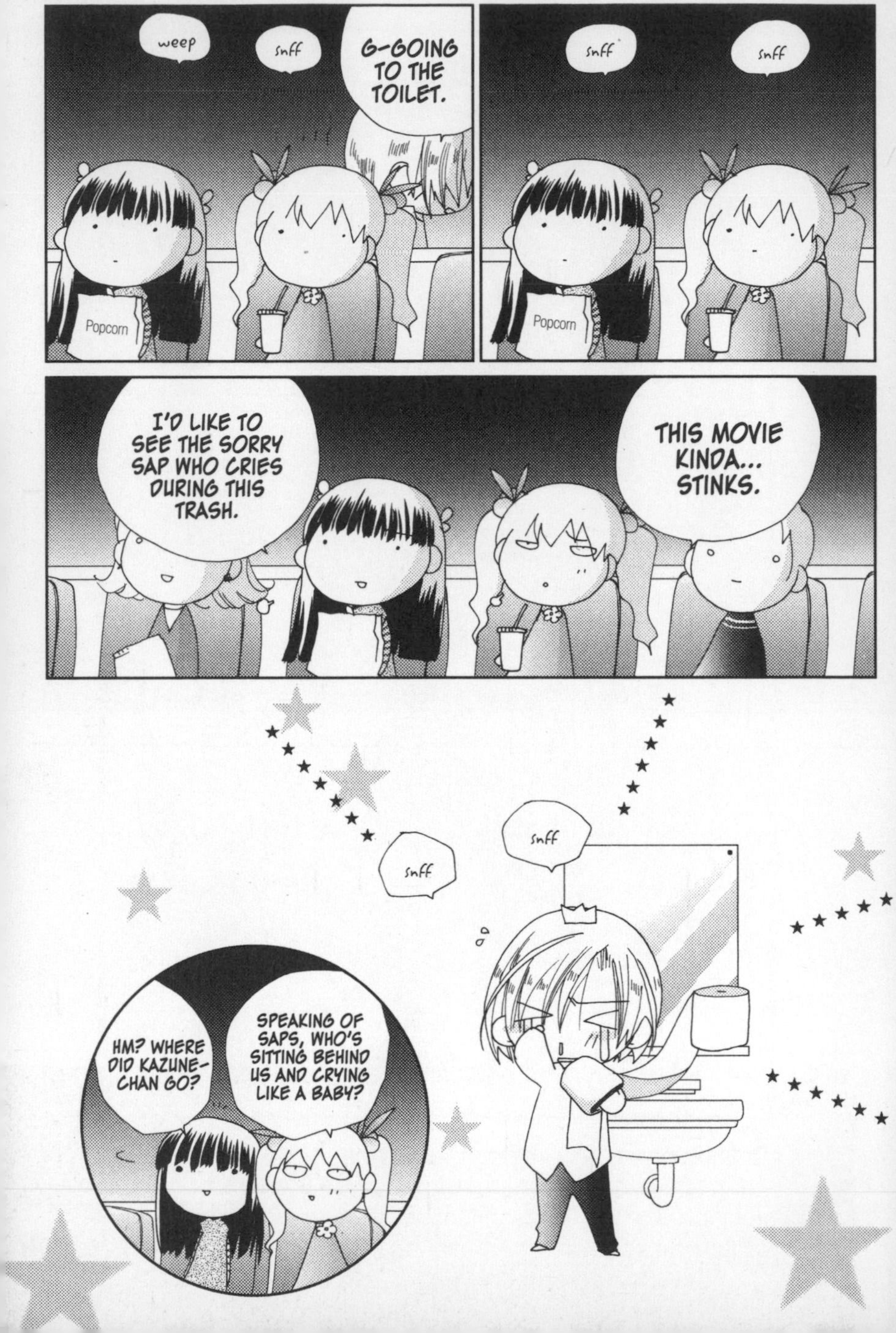
snff
snff
G-GOING TO THE TOILET.
snff
weep
THIS MOVIE KINDA... STINKS.
I'D LIKE TO SEE THE SORRY SAP WHO CRIES DURING THIS TRASH.
Popcorn
snff
snff
SPEAKING OF SAPS, WHO'S SITTING BEHIND US AND CRYING LIKE A BABY?
HM? WHERE DID KAZUNE-CHAN GO?

Next time in...

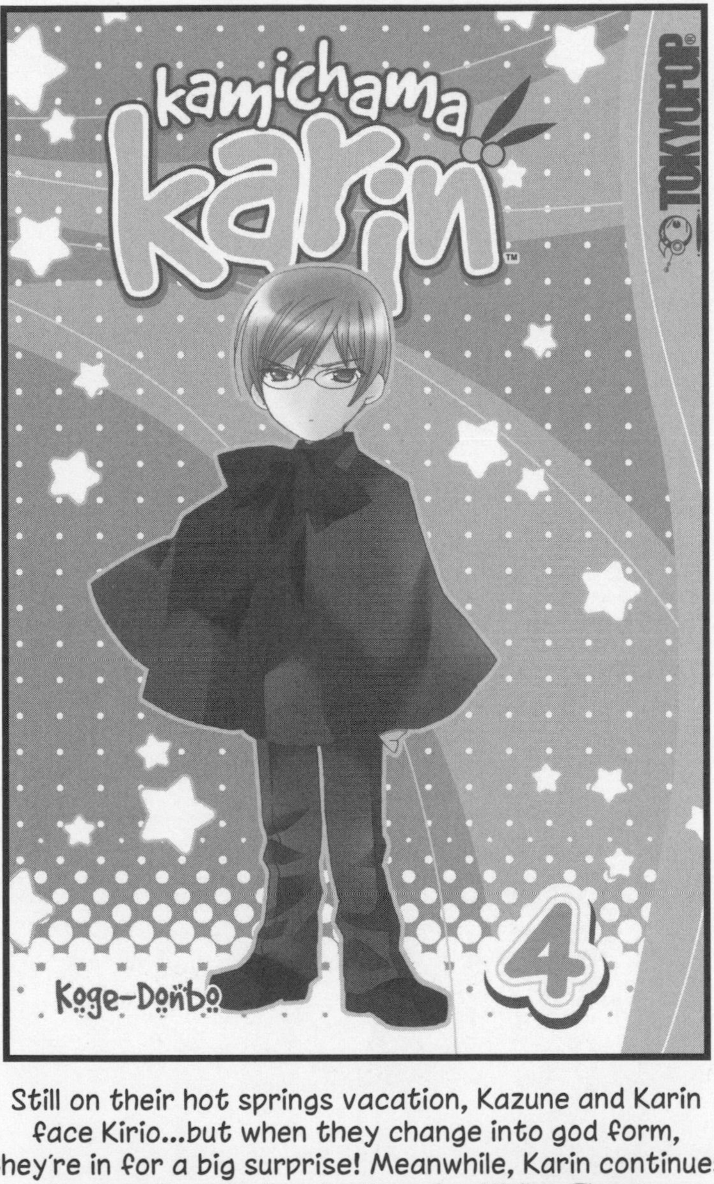
TOKYOPOP
kamichama karin™
Koge-Donbo
4

Still on their hot springs vacation, Kazune and Karin face Kirio...but when they change into god form, they're in for a big surprise! Meanwhile, Karin continues to wrestle with her feelings for Kirika. There's definitely something *different* about him...

Calling all fan artists!

Crazy for Kazune? Head over heels for Himeka? Mad about Miyon? Now's your chance to show it! Draw your favorite character from Kamichama Karin, get your parent's signature if you're under 18, and send your masterpiece to:

Kamichama Karin Fan Art
ATTN: Carol Fox, Editor
TOKYOPOP
5900 Wilshire Blvd.,
Ste. 2000
Los Angeles, CA 90036

You may just see your work in the next volume of Kamichama Karin!

Oh--and while you're at it, please let us know what you think of the book.

Thanks for reading!

TOKYOPOP SHOP

WWW.TOKYOPOP.COM/SHOP

Check out all the sizzling hot merchandise and your favorite manga at the shop!

HOT NEWS!
Check out the TOKYOPOP SHOP! The world's best collection of manga in English is now available online in one place!

BIZENGHAST POSTER

PRINCESS AI POSTCARDS

WWW.TOKYOPOP.COM/SHOP

I Luv Halloween Glow-in-the-Dark STICKERS!

I LUV HALLOWEEN BUTTONS & STICKERS

- LOOK FOR SPECIAL OFFERS
- PRE-ORDER UPCOMING RELEASES
- COMPLETE YOUR COLLECTIONS

I LUV HALLOWEEN © Keith Giffen and Benjamin Roman. Princess Ai © & ™ TOKYOPOP Inc. Bizenghast © M. Alice LeGrow and TOKYOPOP Inc.

SPOTLIGHT   TOKYOPOP MANGA SUPPLEMENT

FRUITS BASKET
BY NATSUKI TAKAYA

Tohru Honda was an orphan with no place to go...until the mysterious Sohma family offers her a place to call home. Tohru's ordinary high school life is turned upside down when she's introduced to the Sohmas' world of magical curses and family intrigue. Discover for yourself the Secret of the Zodiac, and find out why *Fruits Basket* has won the hearts of readers the world over!

THE BESTSELLING MANGA IN THE U.S.!

T TEEN AGE 13+

© Natsuki Takaya

FOR MORE INFORMATION VISIT WWW.TOKYOPOP.COM

THIS FALL, TOKYOPOP CREATES A FRESH, NEW CHAPTER IN TEEN NOVELS...

For Adventurers...
Witches' Forest:
The Adventures of Duan Surk

By Mishio Fukazawa
Duan Surk is a 16-year-old Level 2 fighter who embarks on the quest of a lifetime—battling mythical creatures and outwitting evil sorceresses, all in an impossible rescue mission in the spooky Witches' Forest!

BASED ON THE FAMOUS
FORTUNE QUEST WORLD

For Dreamers...
Magic Moon

By Wolfgang and Heike Hohlbein
Kim enters the enigmatic realm of Magic Moon, where he battles unthinkable monsters and fantastical creatures—in order to unravel the secret that keeps his sister locked in a coma.

THE WORLDWIDE BESTSELLING FANTASY
THRILLOGY ARRIVES IN THE U.S.!

ART SUBJECT TO CHANGE
Witches' Forest: The Adventures of Duan Surk © 2006 MISHIO FUKAZAWA
Magic Moon © 1983, 2001 by Verlag Carl Ueberreuter, Vienna.

POP FICTION

TOKYOPOP PRESENTS

For Believers...

Scrapped Princess:
A Tale of Destiny

By Ichiro Sakaki

A dark prophecy reveals that the queen will give birth to a daughter who will usher in the Apocalypse. But despite all attempts to destroy the baby, the myth of the "Scrapped Princess" lingers on...

THE INSPIRATION FOR THE HIT ANIME AND MANGA SERIES!

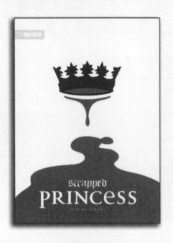

For Thinkers...

Kino no Tabi:
Book One of The Beautiful World

By Keiichi Sigsawa

Kino roams the world on the back of Hermes, her unusual motorcycle, in a journey filled with happiness and pain, decadence and violence, and magic and loss.

THE SENSATIONAL BESTSELLER IN JAPAN HAS FINALLY ARRIVED!

ART SUBJECT TO CHANGE.
Scrapped Princess: A Tale of Destiny © ICHIRO SAKAKI, GO YABUKI and YUKINOBU AZUMI.
Kino no Tabi: Book One of The Beautiful World © KEIICHI SIGSAWA.

STOP!

This is the back of the book.
You wouldn't want to spoil a great ending!

This book is printed "manga-style," in the authentic Japanese right-to-left format. Since none of the artwork has been flipped or altered, readers get to experience the story just as the creator intended. You've been asking for it, so TOKYOPOP® delivered: authentic, hot-off-the-press, and far more fun!

DIRECTIONS

If this is your first time reading manga-style, here's a quick guide to help you understand how it works.

It's easy... just start in the top right panel and follow the numbers. Have fun, and look for more 100% authentic manga from TOKYOPOP®!